india's blind spot

'It is India's moment in the global order. For India to make the most of this opportunity, it is imperative for the world and India to deliver on urbanization. This book does a brilliant job of combining economics, history and international relations to highlight the importance of well-planned, sustainable cities for India, and to illustrate how to implement sound urbanization. The book is a must-read for anyone who is interested in urbanization being the key driver of India's growth story. Insightful, evidence-backed, comprehensive, progressive and scholarly.'
– Amitabh Kant, G20 Sherpa and former CEO, NITI Aayog

'National power is a function of dynamic citizenry and innovative habitats. Cities are, indeed, symbols and drivers of influence. As India rises and takes on a new role in global affairs, our cities must reimagine their purpose and their importance. Devashish's book provides us with an insightful and comprehensive account of issues that hold our cities

Celebrating
30 Years of Publishing
in India

back, while also highlighting their potential to take the country forward. He tackles this complex subject in a manner that is highly accessible, and makes it an essential read for not just policymakers and investors, but also curious citizens.'

— Dr Samir Saran, President, Observer Research Foundation (ORF)

'Historically, growth and urban transition have moved together. Developed countries significantly benefited from urbanization with policies and actions to exploit agglomeration economies, while managing the negative consequences of density. They gained from learning, matching, sharing and networking. Well-governed cities have been remarkably entrepreneurial and resilient. They drove innovation, economic prosperity and human development. This book is concerned with the long neglect of cities in India. The author argues that we are so unfair to urbanization that it has become our "greatest, biggest, and perhaps the most fatal blind spot". He calls for systemically and efficiently making up for the lack of priority to cities. The book highlights the dimensions of urban governance deficit in India, including under-investment in infrastructure and disregard for equity and sustainability. It suggests solutions, including empowerment of local governments. The book is state-of-the-art and will be of immense value to students, teachers, scholars, administrators and policymakers.'

— Dr Prasanna K. Mohanty, former chief secretary to Government of Andhra Pradesh, author of several books on India's urban issues

'*India's Blind Spot* presents a compelling case for India to shed its reluctance and embrace its urban future willingly and confidently. Devashish's enthusiasm for India's urban destiny is palpable. I hope this book motivates urban policymakers in India to usher in reforms to city governance with the same enthusiasm. India's youth in particular would do well to have *India's Blind Spot* as an illuminating fellow traveller in their leadership journeys.'

— Srikanth Viswanathan, CEO, Janaagraha Centre for Citizenship and Democracy

india's blind spot

UNDERSTANDING AND MANAGING OUR CITIES

DEVASHISH DHAR

HarperCollins *Publishers* India

First published in hardback in India by HarperCollins *Publishers* 2023
4th Floor, Tower A, Building No. 10, Phase II, DLF Cyber City,
Gurugram, Haryana – 122002
www.harpercollins.co.in

2 4 6 8 10 9 7 5 3 1

Copyright © Devashish Dhar 2023

P-ISBN: 978-93-5489-520-3
E-ISBN: 978-93-5489-542-5

The views and opinions expressed in this book are the author's own and the facts are as reported by him, and the publishers are not in any way liable for the same.

Devashish Dhar asserts the moral right
to be identified as the author of this work.

All rights reserved. No part of this publication may be reproduced, stored in a retrieval system, or transmitted, in any form or by any means, electronic, mechanical, photocopying, recording or otherwise, without the prior permission of the publishers.

Typeset in 10.5/13.5 Adobe Caslon Pro at
Manipal Technologies Limited, Manipal

Printed and bound at
Thomson Press (India) Ltd

This book is produced from independently certified FSC® paper
to ensure responsible forest management.

To my parents, Neelam and Ashok
To my partner and friend, Shruti
To Nehru
To all the lives we lost to Covid-19

Contents

	Foreword	ix
1.	Cities: Humankind's Longest-running Experiment	1
2.	Indian Cities: At the Centre Stage for Global Trends	25
3.	Urban Economy: Making Cities Engines of Growth for Everyone	55
4.	Urban Equity: Bridging the Infrastructure Deficit	102
5.	Urban Transport: Moving People, Ferrying India	149
6.	Urban Land: The Next Frontier of Urban Growth	172
7.	Urban Planning: Old Wine in New Bottle	196
8.	Urban Safety and Inclusiveness: Putting People at the Centre of Cities	219
9.	Urban Resilience: Preparing for the Worst, Hoping for the Best	254
10.	Urban Governance: The Fountainhead of All Maladies	278
	Epilogue	309
	Acknowledgements	311
	Bibliography	317
	Index	371
	About the Author	395

Foreword

I am privileged to be the Member of Parliament for Thiruvananthapuram, a thriving hub of innovation and culture, and home to a diverse metropolitan population nudging 1.7 million. This means I spend a great deal of my time thinking about the unique rewards and challenges of the modern Indian city—a fascinating and deeply complex institution.

The share of Indians employed in the agricultural sector has declined steadily over the past several decades. With this decline, India's cities have swelled in size and importance; millions have moved from rural areas to urban ones, transforming urban economies and bringing huge benefits. India's internal migration system is free of official restrictions such as China's constrictive *hukou* model, allowing Indians to move as they choose, taking with them their talents, reshaping their new homes. But this phenomenon has not been trouble-free. Urban infrastructure, and resources from schools to hospitals, have struggled under the strain of surging populations and limited public finances. Above all, perhaps, the Covid-19 pandemic swept through crowded cities and exposed the limitations of urban design. Some had written off the Indian city as obsolete and beyond salvation.

Devashish Dhar, while mindful of the immense challenges that threaten urban India, is more optimistic. *India's Blind Spot* combines an incisive diagnosis of the problem with an unabashed faith in the resilience and potential of the city. He traces the development of urban centres throughout history before focusing on India, the manifestation and effects of our seemingly unstoppable urbanization, urban economies, and the impact of Covid-19, while touching on the many threats posed to cities, natural and man-made alike. Dhar's nuanced analysis leaves much to be considered: we have a great deal to do if our cities are to survive and thrive in the long term.

This is a rich and thoughtful look at one of India's defining challenges by a young man who worked with me at an early stage of his career. I believe that policymakers, planners and urban residents would do well to read it and take heed of its lessons.

Shashi Tharoor
MP for Thiruvananthapuram, Author
Former Under-Secretary-General, United Nations

1

Cities: Humankind's Longest-running Experiment

AS I write this book, the Covid-19 pandemic has been raging for over two years and at one point had brought human life virtually to a standstill. Since the majority of cases were clustered in urban areas, countless people wrote the obit of cities (especially rural apologists who found a convenient target). The truth can't be further from this misconception. Cities are human civilization's longest-running experiment. We will see throughout the book how and why they are resilient and what more can be done to make Indian cities more robust.

Cities are not merely complicated spatial entities, but an evolving system that continues to improve upon itself. By facilitating the formation of clusters of industries, firms and people with specialized skills and occupations, cities enable firms and people to learn from each other and in the process increase productivity and innovation. This is the single largest factor why Covid-19 has not been able to fundamentally shift the nature of cities. This also explains why Covid-19-related lockdowns were enforced with great reluctance by Indian companies. People couldn't wait to get back to their workplaces. The only exception was a tiny, privileged section of people who operated with internet connectivity and would have had little marginal benefit from workplace interactions to boost their productivity. However, the presence of technological solutions for physical distancing could be a short-term escape (not a solution), as collaboration and competition requires intense, meaningful and physical proximity.

The function of cities is to provide growth, jobs and wages, and solve irritant social problems. Cities thus tackled the problem of Covid-19 by providing an environment that helped create the solution—the vaccine and eventually herd immunity. Secondly, the mortality rate of Covid-19 fell way short of the benefits that come from cities and thus, cities remained resilient. The pandemic proved that Covid-19 cannot fundamentally change the nature of cities and this is what we call resilience. If a shock doesn't change the basic nature of a person, we call her resilient; likewise, if a shock doesn't effectively change the nature of our cities, we can safely say that cities are resilient. Plague, black death, influenza, cholera, malaria, typhoid, severe acute respiratory syndrome (SARS) and now Covid-19—all temporarily halted the progress of cities, but none was devastating enough to halt the onward march, since in the progress of cities lies the progress of humankind.

CITIES HAVE ALWAYS BEEN RESILIENT

History shows that cities have bounced back from every epidemic they have faced. Within the last 200 years, London suffered from a cholera epidemic (1854), and the world suffered from the Spanish flu (1918–19). More recently, (SARS) hit the world in 2003, H1N1 influenza in 2009, the Ebola crisis in 2014, the Zika outbreak in 2016 and in 2020, of course, the Covid-19 pandemic, which captured the minds of policymakers worldwide (Acuto, 2020).

Cities have survived and are resilient *because* of the way they respond. And these responses invariably emerge from the clusters of specialists they house. During the London cholera epidemic in 1854, 'physicians such as Jon Snow from England saw the connection between poor living conditions, overcrowding, sanitation and disease,' and London invested heavily in its modern sewer system, which continues to serve the city to date (Puliyel, 2020). This information helped public health advocates elsewhere, such as Dr Stephen Smith who helped establish New York's Metropolitan Health Board in 1866, which helped improve the city's sewerage and water systems (Glaeser, 2020). The role of open and green public spaces, broader streets, and decongesting parts of the city was also recognized; in fact, New York's legendary Central Park was created in 1858 to function as the 'lungs of the city' (Puliyel, 2020).

On the Indian subcontinent, the city of Bengaluru (then Bangalore, and a part of the princely state of Mysore)—having suffered bouts of plague in the nineteenth century—created new areas such as Malleswaram and Basavanagudi, to enable citizens to live among open spaces with access to better sanitation (Aruni, 2013). In 1918, when the Spanish flu hit India, Bengaluru was better off than many other parts of India (Prasanna, 2020). In 1898, the Bombay Presidency set up the Bombay City Improvement Trust following a serious bout of bubonic plague. It focused on providing housing to the poor, improving ventilation, and decongesting slums (Puliyel, 2020).

Sounds like today, right? Likewise, when the plague broke out in Surat in 1994, the city underwent a series of reforms and an administrative clean-up; within two years it had become one of the cleanest cities in India (Wangchuk, 2021). Twenty-five years later, it continues to rank as India's second cleanest city, the first being Indore (Bansal, 2020).

City Life over the Rural Idyll

All over the world millions long to live in beautiful rural surroundings, with all that such an idyll seemingly has to offer. 'Leave your family and friends and go over the mountains and valleys into the country,' advised Leonardo da Vinci—one of the world's greatest luminaries, a brilliant polymath, artiste and visionary (Isaacson, 2017). Did da Vinci himself quit the (then) plague-ridden towns of Italy? Far from it. From the 1480s to the 1510s we find him at his most prodigal, based out of the densely packed and vibrant cities of Rome, Florence and Milan. Isaacson notes he flourished in these 'crowded centres of creativity and commerce, usually surrounded by students, companions and patrons' (ibid.). It was no coincidence that da Vinci prospered in urban centres.

Why do billions continue to leave behind a rural idyll to suffer pollution, endless hustle, cramped apartment-living, threats to life and countless other issues in cities? Why don't they stay put and enjoy all the space, fresh air, greenery and sunshine that a rural life offers? What is the everlasting allure of cities? It is simply that they exemplify the best of what human civilization has to offer—a clustering that leads to interaction, trading skills and goods, seeking opportunities; a place where a human can experiment, and has better facilities to do so, to innovate relentlessly to improve the quality of life; where the promise of prosperity is more real than the often harsh and dead-end reality of village life; a place where the historically marginalized can shed their identity or wear it as a badge, but—either way—come out from the shadow of being at the periphery; a place where the world comes together, for each other and to make a better world. Cities are all of this (and more).

The year 2007 marked a special tipping point in the history of humankind—50 per cent of the world's population now lived in urban areas. As per estimates, 180,000 people continue move to cities every day and by 2050, 75 per cent of the world's population will be living in urban areas (Hollis, 2013). It is perhaps the last, greatest and widest human migration story of mankind.

WHAT IS A CITY?

Experts define cities variously. Eminent sociologist Louis Wirth defines it as a 'relatively large, dense and permanent settlement of socially heterogeneous individuals' (Fox and Goodfellow, 2016). Another definition by Lewis Mumford is more elaborate: 'The essential physical means of a city's existence are the fixed site, the durable shelter, the permanent facilities for assembly, interchange and storage; the essential social means are the social division of labour, which serves not merely the economic life but the cultural processes' (ibid.). As per the United Nations (UN), out of 233 countries/territories, 30 per cent use specific administrative criteria, 21 per cent only use population size, and 4 per cent do not use specific criteria, to define urban areas (ibid.).

Even after centuries of experience with cities and urbanization, there remains a consensus deficit on what classifies a city. Within India too there is lack of consensus on what is urban and what is not, and Indian states use varying definitions of urban centres. We will explore later how this has serious policy implications for India and how we can resolve this discrepancy. For now, it is good to acknowledge that different countries have different criteria when we mention their urbanization rates.

There are various words associated with modern urban habitats, the most common being urbanization, urbanism, urban growth and urban expansion (the latter two sound synonymous, but are not, as seen below). Sean Fox and Tom Goodfellow define urbanization as:

> [A] demographic process involving a shift in the proportion of a population living in settlements defined as 'urban' as opposed to 'rural'. The level of urbanization refers to the proportion of population which is living in urban areas at any given point of time. Rate of urbanization is the pace at which the relative proportion of the urban population is changing over a period of time (Fox and Goodfellow, 2016).

The same authors define urbanism as simply 'the way of life associated with habitation in a city'; urban growth as 'an increase in the absolute size of an urban population'; and 'urban expansion' as, 'an increase in the built-up area of a settlement or collection of settlements' (ibid.).

CITIES: A BRIEF HISTORICAL OVERVIEW

Ancient and Pre-Modern Settlements, Towns and Cities

Globally, there has been much and continued debate on which was the world's first or most ancient city. There is considerable literature to support that Damascus in Syria was inhabited in the second millennium BCE (Hollis, 2013). Claims put the onset of Mesopotamian cities at around 4000 BCE—Uruk was established between the fourth to third millennium BCE and is considered to be the greatest and earliest Sumerian city. It was the largest city in the world in 3200

BCE, home to 50,000–80,000 people (Rose, 2016). Ur, located to the south of Uruk, was one of the first cities to explore long-distance trade routes and flourished until the river Euphrates changed course (Clark 2016). Having lost both agriculture and trade (irrigation water and connectivity), Ur inevitably declined (ibid.).

Tony Joseph's book *Early Indians* provides a fresh, contemporary and detailed perspective on early humans, migrations, the first urban centres in Asia and on the Indian subcontinent (Joseph, 2021). Agriculture came into being in India, China and the Fertile Crescent—a crescent-shaped region in the Middle East comprising parts of modern day Iraq, Lebanon, Israel, Egypt, Syria, Iran among other countries—between 9700 and 5000 BCE (ibid.). Following the agriculture revolution, during the Early Harappan era (5500–2600 BCE), agricultural settlements grew into towns (such as Harappa, Mohenjo-daro and Dholavira) with their distinctive features (ibid.). Tony Joseph calls these cultures the 'First Urbanites'.

It is believed that the Harappan and Mesopotamian civilizations had trade contacts and each side influenced the other; this is also a trait of modern-day cities. Starting with the barter system and leading to the creation of currency, trade has been a primary factor in the growth of multiple areas necessary to trigger urbanization. The significance of trade as contributing to prosperity and well-being was recognized early on. Historian Romila Thapar points out that sites of cities were chosen with a focus on availability of resources and the potential to transport goods by river and sea (Thapar, 2002).

The Harappan civilization laid the foundation for city planning (an area that many cities have failed to master millennia later). Dholavira utilized advanced (for that time) water management techniques. The city had many interconnected reservoirs and its eastern reservoir was the biggest in the ancient world. The city also boasted stormwater drains. Houses in Harappa had different channels for water supply and sewage disposal. Joseph quotes Upinder Singh, author of *A History of Ancient and Early Medieval India*: 'Recent excavations in Harappa have uncovered toilets in almost every house. The commodes were made of big pots sunk into the floor, many of them associated with a small lota-type jar, no doubt for washing up' (Singh, 2009a; Joseph, 2021). India's

Swachh Bharat Mission has ancient antecedents; it was part of public policy and everyday living 4,000 years ago.

Looking northward to Europe, during the Roman Empire's rise, Vitruvius in the first century BCE, wrote *De Architectura*. These were ten books in all. The work provided a detailed treatise on urban planning and city-building (Rose, 2016). The books covered a range of important issues such as centralized infrastructure, separate areas for different uses and classes, building standards for safety, cultural elements and temples, streets, and highways, among others. The Roman Empire drew its power from a large number of revenue-generating cities, which were melting pots of cultural activity and were backed by wealthy patrons (Frankopan, 2015). Historians believe that such a flow of capital within Rome and outside strengthened trade routes and the villages along the route eventually grew into big cities (ibid.).

Back east, China's Silk Road network was created in 400 BCE and connected its east coast to Central Asia, the Middle East, and even the Mediterranean (Clark, 2016). Today that country's One Belt One Road initiative is a means to extend its hegemony in the region.

Perhaps one of the most important aspects of urbanization was the minting of coins, which gained swift currency in trade (Thapar, 2002). The first coins were minted around the fifth or sixth century BCE. This single development created a whole new ecosystem of urban-based financiers, provided trade stability within the country and with the rest of the world. After the ancient cities perished, urbanization found a hospitable area in the Indo-Gangetic plain, which saw the rise of new towns in different kingdoms from around 600 BCE to 300 CE (ibid.). The most vibrant centres were Rajagriha, Shravasti and Kaushambi in north India (ibid.). Around third century BCE, urban renewal received a boost on the back of the Mauryan Empire. This urban renewal provided resources and space for a new form of thinking and spiritual exploration. Not surprisingly, during this time of urban renewal in India two progressive religions emerged—Jainism and Buddhism. Can their emergence be attributed to the urban renewal of this era? Socio-culturally, the subsequent boost to trade had another unintended outcome. It led to the spread—locally, regionally and globally—of religions such as Hinduism, Islam, Buddhism, Christianity and Jainism, via the trade routes. Together, these religions have had a far-reaching impact on the world and most particularly on India.

The availability of currency intensified market activity, and in India it led to an important urban development—the rise of various shreni (guilds) of artisans, merchants and professionals (ibid.). It is pertinent to note that skills and specialization—the defining feature of a modern city—formed the foundation for these guilds. The shreni is thus a sophisticated classification of trade and highlights the onset of division of labour in an urban society, a factor that defines global value chains and cities of today. Division of labour in urban societies eventually morphed into the segregation of social roles, which in turn created separate physical spaces in the city for different occupations to live and work (Mumford, 1961). In India, it became exemplified in the rigid, occupation-based caste structure, which gives different living spaces to different castes. Today Indian cities provide an opportunity for emancipation from caste, as occupations available in the city do not align with rural occupations, gender roles or caste structures; merit takes precedence over everything else.

Thus, for ancient and pre-modern cities, we can generalize certain characteristics as described by Gordon Childe and quoted by Tony Joseph in *Early Indians*:

> A population that is often hundreds of times larger than any village; full-time specialists such as craftsmen, merchants, officials and transport workers; a ruling class that accumulates the surplus production of the peasants; monumental public buildings; systems of recording and writing; full-time artists; and foreign trade to get materials not available locally (Joseph, 2021).

Lewis Mumford also stresses how the inventions in villages predate cities: irrigation, ditch, canal, transport and storage. The house, shrines, public places, and the origins of law and justice too find their place in villages (Mumford, 1961). So could one say that cities are the last big inventions of villages and have undone their progenitor—the village—themselves?

Arrival of Modern Cities (1400–1945)

In 1492 Christopher Columbus crossed the Atlantic, paving way for connecting the Americas to Europe. In 1497, Vasco da Gama, backed by the King of Portugal, sailed down the length of western Africa, turning at its southern tip, the Cape of Good Hope, to sail north-eastward across the Indian Ocean and reach India in 1498. His arrival left a deep impact, and ports in south India were soon competing aggressively for trade, using tax concessions and other instruments to beat their competition (reminds you of the modern day Special Economic Zones!). Cochin, for instance, gave tough competition to Calicut—the city that Vasco da Gama had reached after spending ten months at sea (Frankopan, 2015).

By the mid-1600s Europe was experiencing a relatively stable period after the Peace of Westphalia was signed in 1648, following the end of the Thirty Years' War. The treaty had emerged out of multiple factors including the intense competition among ambitious urban merchants and the need to protect the lucrative tax revenue base of the cities involved. This treaty ushered in the system of sovereignty in international relations, which is the key principle of global governance and state-to-state relations that continues to this day.

From 1500 to 1800, the rise in territorial conflicts cascaded into a sophisticated transaction between rulers and urban financiers and elites. In return for capital, new claims in terms of education, city planning, pensions, assemblies, among other features were added to the state. This, in turn, gave rise to nation states (Fox and Goodfellow, 2016). It was seen that European cities run by merchants were better managed than those run by monarchs, as the merchants had developed legal rules to protect private property and commerce. The economic gains were higher in countries that had large towns that generated greater tax revenue (Frankopan, 2015).

In India, a new dynasty had risen to power at the end of the 15th century, when Babur, a descendant of Timur, got control of Kabul and from there launched an attack successfully defeating the Lodis. Before their decline, the Lodis did play their role in laying the foundation of Agra (Chandra, 2020). Europe was leveraging riches from the Americas to import Chinese porcelain and silk, and spices from India. This flooded

Indian markets with money, which was used to buy horses from Central Asia (Frankopan, 2015), which in turn also witnessed a major boom.

In the sixteenth century, Babur's heir Humayun built a new city in the area that we know as Delhi (the city has been rebuilt/expanded several times, starting from the eighth century) and called it Dinpanah or 'the Asylum of Faith' (Sultan, 2018). The main part of this city that survives to this day is the Purana Qila (Old Fort), work on which had been continued by Sher Shah Suri, after he had briefly snatched power from the Mughals. Sher Shah also constructed another city in the (present) Delhi area, called Shergarh. He is credited for many things, including the road between Punjab and Bengal, which was called Sadak-e-Azam (Sanyal, 2013a). We know it today as the Grand Trunk Road and it is still in use. It was the precursor to our modern highways, and thus important for the growth of urban centres along its route. Connectivity, as we have seen all along, remains key to urban growth.

The Mughal empire peaked under Akbar, who created the city of Fatehpur Sikhri, near Agra. His grandson Shah Jahan moved the capital back from Agra to the Delhi area and in 1639 started building another city (and if we are keeping count, the seventh version of Delhi). He called it Shahjahanabad (Banga (ed.), 1991). He also built the Red Fort, which is now used by Indian Prime Ministers to give their speech on Independence Day on 15 August, every year.

Meanwhile, European ambitions were reaching new heights and this ambition shaped their cities. The city that best encapsulates this pursuit is Amsterdam—the capital of Holland. It started as a fishing village in the twelfth century, but due to constant flooding, its people came together to build dams, dykes and canals. Leo Hollis mentions how the creation of the city was an innovative effort, as concentric canals around the River Amstel created a city out of a wetland (Hollis, 2013). The city grew in importance in the seventeenth century due to its strategic location, connecting the Hanseatic states in the north to the Mediterranean states in the south (ibid.). Given that merchants had begun to undertake long arduous and risky journeys, they created joint-stock companies such as the East India Company (EIC) which allowed them to share risk. Most of these companies did not have great success (Frankopan 2015). However, the fortunes of the Dutch East India Company, started in 1602, fared better. Within twenty years, it controlled the majority share of the Asian spice trade.

Big cities like London and Amsterdam made some astonishing innovations—banking, promissory notes, financial leveraging of stocks. As EIC controlled more territory, it created international laws to protect its interests. English and Dutch commercial success was to an extent interdependent, but they also had commercial rivalry (Frankopan, 2015). The Dutch gained a foothold in Masulipatnam in 1606 (Chandra, 2020). This helped them expand their presence in south India due to their growing interest in spices and Indian textiles. Major European powers also set up factories in Surat in the early seventeenth century (ibid.).

Masulipatnam and Fort St. George (later Madrasapatnam, then Madras, and now Chennai) became major ports of trade (ibid.). However, as the English developed their naval capabilities on the lines of Dutch in the second half of the seventeenth century, their volume of trade began to soar. The EIC entered into a pact with the local ruler of Madrasapatnam to trade free of customs duty. Within the next seventy years, Madrasapatnam was transformed into a vibrant metropolis. Founded as the trading post in 1639, it continued to the very end to be dominated by functions of trade and administration.

Meanwhile, the advent of the industrial revolution gave the European nations a huge technological advantage (hence economic boost) over the rest of the world. European cities underwent a demographic transition, experiencing low birth and death rates. The creation of industry provided jobs to the rural populace, which flocked to cities in search of economic opportunities, leading to an explosion in the urban population:

> In 1800, the world population was roughly one billion, only 3–5 per cent of which lived in towns and cities; by 1900 the world population had grown to 1.6 billion, with about 14 per cent residing in urban areas. By the turn of second millennium world

population had reached six billion with nearly 50 per cent living in urban settlements (Fox and Goodfellow, 2016).

In 1800, no city in Europe had a population of over a million, London was inching towards it and Paris housed a little more than half a million people (Mumford, 1961). England's urbanization level jumped from 20 per cent in 1800 to 62 per cent in 1890 (Sanyal, 2013a). By 1900, the world had at least nine cities with a population of over a million—Berlin, Chicago, New York, Philadelphia, Moscow, St. Petersburg, Vienna, Tokyo, and Chicago (Mumford, 1961). The industrial revolution had changed the face of urban centres in Europe and the US. In Europe—from 1800 to 1910—the urbanization rate in France jumped from 12.2 per cent to 38.5 per cent; Germany went from 8.9 per cent to 48.8 per cent; in Belgium it increased from 20.5 per cent to 56.6 per cent; and in the UK it surged from 19.2 per cent to 69.2 per cent. In North America, during the same period, Canada's urbanization rate increased from 6.5 per cent to 41.6 per cent and in the US it increased from 5.3 per cent to 41.6 per cent (Bairoch and Goertz, 1986). Within the umbrella of colonialism, many nations also developed a global network of cities that have gone on to become the leading cities of our times: London, New York, Hong Kong, Singapore, Sydney, Mumbai, Shanghai, Toronto, Cape Town, and Boston (Clark, 2016).

In the context of Britain, the role of Mumbai (then Bombay) and Kolkata (then Calcutta) stand out. It would be not too far-fetched to say that Mumbai is still an unholy alliance between royalties, reclamation and corruption. In 1661, the seven islets that comprise Mumbai were gifted as dowry to Charles II on his marriage to Portuguese princess Catherine of Braganza. Given the inhospitable condition of the islands, they were leased out to EIC for a paltry sum of 10 pounds. The islands became a contiguous area only by 1838, when all seven—Colaba, Old Woman's Island, Bombay, Mazgaon, Parel, Mahim and Worli—were connected and Bombay was born.

The story of Kolkata is very passionately narrated by Sanjiv Sanyal (2013a). When Job Charnock was charged by the EIC to consolidate its presence in Bengal, he found a place near Hooghly River's Sutanuti village. The city derives its name from the village Kalikata which, along with Sutanuti and Gobindapore villages, formed the area where Calcutta was to be founded. The city was home to many EIC employees. Over the coming decades, it transformed into a major trading hub, drawing trade from all over the world. It emerged as a cosmopolitan centre and attracted reformers like Ram Mohan Roy who brought about major changes in Indian society.

Urban centres can safely be said to have played a role in creating a more modern society with space for all. In south India, after the Vijayanagar empire crumbled, the successor states reverted to existing as (the towns of) Thanjavur, Madurai, Vellore and Mysore (Banga (ed.), 1991). The other city-specific changes that occurred in the eighteenth-century peninsular India include: the political centre being moved to Hyderabad from Bijapur, Golconda and Raichur Doab; a new state Mysore (later) created; and an increase in economic activity in the ports of Madras and Pondicherry. Also by the 1850s, Bangalore emerged as a major cantonment city and Vellore reclaimed its role as an entrepôt. Nevertheless—barring the cases of a few port cities and cantonments—the colonial era, particularly in the nineteenth century, was marked by rapid de-urbanization. In fact, the urbanization level had been higher at the end of the seventeenth century (ibid.).

An indicator of de-urbanization is the dominant existence of primacy, i.e., when there is a high difference in population size or commercial activity between the largest city and the second-largest city. Calcutta had emerged as the primate city in colonial India by 1921. Between 1872 and 1921, cities that grew the fastest were those that were part of colonial economic activities, such as centres of British industrial enterprise (Kanpur and Howrah), railway junctions (Nagpur, Jhansi, Darbhanga), agriculture marketing and collection centres (Gaya and Mubarakpur), centres of sugar manufacture (Basti), mineral belts (Ranchi and Hazaribagh), cantonments (Dinapur and Jhansi), and resorts (Darjeeling) (ibid.). Thus, in colonial India, urbanization remained subdued in the majority of the districts (ibid.).

Following the first war of Indian Independence in 1857, the British aggressively changed the layout of cities, creating a 'dualistic city'—the British lived in demarcated Civil Lines and cantonment areas, while the local population lived in older parts of the city (Shaw, 2012).

Shaw has summarized the key impact of colonial rule on cities: 1) the creation of Civil Lines and a cantonment area, both of which had better amenities and more open space than the older parts of the city. The Civil Lines were located in administrative centres of tehsils and provincial capitals, while only major towns had cantonments (in all, in 114 towns). 2) European-style architecture became commonplace in such cities. 3) Colonial rulers created many such towns, including hill stations, to suit their needs. 4) The new developments of rail, factories and ports were introduced by the British to keep running the empire more efficiently. 5) The elite in such towns was plugged-in to 'western modernity'—law and education (ibid.).

The British also commissioned Edwin Lutyens and Herbert Baker to design a new city—the eighth and the current version of Delhi—New Delhi. At its heart was the Viceroy's House, now known as Rashtrapati Bhavan and home to the President of India. During the famous Durbar of 1911 where King George V was coronated, it was read aloud that the capital of British India had been moved from Calcutta to Delhi (Kazmi, 2018). During 1912–31, the city buzzed with activity as the British poured in resources to project power from the jewel in the crown, as they created this city of New Delhi.

Indian Cities after World War II and Colonialism

As soon as World War II ended, the fate of the world lay within the contest between the Western democracies and communist Soviet Union. Churchill said in 1946:

> From Stettin in the Baltic to Trieste in the Adriatic an iron curtain has descended across the Continent. Behind that line lie all the capitals of the ancient states of Central and Eastern Europe. Warsaw, Berlin, Prague, Vienna, Budapest, Belgrade, Bucharest and Sofia, all these famous cities and the populations around them lie in what I must call the Soviet sphere, and all are subject in one form or another, not only to Soviet influence but to a very high and, in some cases, increasing measure of control from Moscow (Churchill, 1946).

Drained by World War II and under heavy-debt, the British hastened their withdrawal from the Indian subcontinent. The 1857 fight for independence had been led by the sepoys in the urban centres, supported by the local population (Banga (ed.), 1991). After this 'mutiny' was crushed, a new class of Indian leaders arose from among the local civil servants and lawyers trained by the Raj. They were the new urban elite and were at the forefront of the fight for Independence. The arrival of the charismatic and politically astute Gandhi, married this urban movement to the rural hinterlands to mobilize a major share of the Indian population. The major mobilizations—such as Rowlatt Satyagraha and the Non-Cooperation Movement of 1920–22—fomented the nationalist sentiments of the urban classes (ibid.). The participation of urban classes was important, since the Raj's control over the Indian subcontinent was largely based in urban centres. When the British finally did quit India, they transferred a modern urban governance structure to this England-educated urban elite.

INDIA'S INDEPENDENCE AND ITS LOVE-HATE RELATIONSHIP WITH CITIES

When India became independent, its share of urban population was 17 per cent as compared to 12 per cent in China (Sanyal, 2013a). Calcutta's population stood at 2.6 million, Bombay's at 1.5 million, Madras at 0.8 million, and Delhi at 0.7 million (ibid.). The first official census of India had been conducted in 1881 and revealed that India had eighteen cities with a population of more than 100,000 people. Six of these cities were in the United Provinces (it dominated the charts because of the preponderance of railway lines and troops stationed in case of a military contingency) (Ghurye, 1953). Bombay province had four such cities, and the other provinces had one each. In 1901, only 11 per cent of the Indian population (around 26 million people), lived in urban areas (Shaw, 2012). In the 1891 census, India had twenty-two such cities. By 1941, this number had gone up to forty-seven. However, in 1951, only 6.8 per cent of the Indian population lived in cities, the corresponding figure for 1941 was 5.3 per cent.

After Independence, the new government was led by Jawaharlal Nehru for seventeen years. For a fledgling country, with poor socio-economic indicators, irritant neighbours and secessionist and communal interests, cities did not qualify as Nehru's top priorities. Policies must be adjudged in the context of the political economy of the times, rather than the high seat of the benefit of hindsight. Post-Partition, the influx of refugees led to the creation of fourteen new towns during 1947–51 (ibid.). The 1942 famine, followed by the refugee influx and the reorganization of states in 1956, accelerated the movement of people to cities.

Between 1951–61, India's urban population increased by 26 per cent (ibid.). By 1971, 112 new towns had been built. Some of them were created in the wake of new heavy industries projects such as the towns of Bokaro and Rourkela. Most of these towns were paid for by the government. The few exceptions were towns like Jamshedpur and Modinagar, paid for by private capital (ibid.). Le Corbusier was commissioned by Prime Minister Nehru in 1950 to design a greenfield city and he created Chandigarh (Sanyal, 2013a).

During the first two Five Year Plans (1951–1961), the Indian state created institutional structures, such as the Ministry of Urban Affairs, the School of Planning and Architecture in Delhi, a Regional and Town Planning Department at the Indian Institute of Technology (IIT)-Kharagpur, and the Town and Country Planning Organization (Shaw 2012). Shaw highlights that 500 master plans were made but couldn't be implemented, as the urban population increased from 61 million in 1951 to 217 million in 1991 (ibid.).

The Second Five Year Plan saw the enforcement of the Slum Areas (Improvement and Clearance) Act. During this period, parastatal agencies—such as the Delhi Development Authority and the Madras Metropolitan Development Authority—were set up to direct the development of these major cities. The Third Five Year Plan (1961–1966) focused on establishing industries away from large congested urban centres, controlling the price of land and its physical planning, minimum standard for housing and other services, and strengthening municipal administrations (Shaw, 1996). During this time, the states had to pass the town and country planning legislation and then create master plans for their cities, starting of course from large metropolitan areas. Unfortunately, the planners had developed a distaste for congestion and crowded cities, and preferred order and homogeneity (ibid.). Shaw notes that the state became heavily involved in the use, control, sale and lease of land and promoted single-use neighbourhoods.

The Fourth Plan set aside funds for the development of new state capitals and also set up the Housing and Urban Development Corporation (HUDCO) to support the development of housing (ibid.). The Fourth to Sixth Plans (1969–1985) focused on decentralizing urban development and raising revenues from the urban centres. They did not succeed at either. The Central government provided funds for the development of large urban centres, but the amount was too small (ibid.). In the 1970s two major initiatives were undertaken—Integrated Development of Small and Medium Towns (IDSMT), 1979, and the Urban Land (Ceiling and Regulation Act) 1976 (ibid.). The former focused on developing smaller and medium-sized cities and the latter focused on controlling the ownership of vacant urban land.

The Seventh and Eighth Plans (1985–1997) made serious attempts toward the devolution of funds and the empowerment of local bodies. While legislation toward this had been introduced in the Seventh Plan, the 74th Constitutional Amendment Act was introduced in the Eighth Plan in 1992, to empower the urban local bodies (Shaw, 1996; Batra, 2009). The *India Infrastructure Report* (Deb 1996) completely changed the dialogue on the creation of major infrastructure, including the urban infrastructure (Shaw, 1996). It passionately argued for engagement of the private sector and the use of innovating financing schemes like Municipal Bonds. It also advocated privatization and deregulation of infrastructure sectors.

By 1992, there was a significant change in the distribution of urban population. The population share of Class I towns increased to 65 per cent in 1991 (from 44 per cent in 1951 and just 26 per cent in 1901). On the other hand, the population share of smaller towns, with less than 20,000 people, declined to just 11 per cent in 1991 from 29 per cent in 1951, down from 47 per cent in 1901 (Shaw, 2012). The Ninth Plan (1997–2002) admitted the failure of IDSMT (Batra, 2009). It focused on encouraging urban local bodies (ULBs) to raise funds; for smaller cities, it recommended an 'Urban Development Fund'—a pooled finance scheme (ibid.). This plan continued the focus on housing, repealed the Urban Land Ceiling and Regulation Act (ULCRA), 1976, and introduced 100 per cent foreign direct investment (FDI) in integrated townships. The Tenth Plan gave a greater nudge to ULBs to raise their finances and become independent. The 2002 Union Budget also announced a fund to encourage states to undertake urban reforms (ibid.).

The first Prime Minister to extensively highlight the role of urbanization in India's growth story was Manmohan Singh. On 15 August 2004 he outlined urbanization as one of the seven pillars of India's development in the coming decades (Jha, 2020). In 2005, the government launched the Jawaharlal Nehru National Urban Renewal Mission (JNNURM), which focused on urban governance, reforms and infrastructure. It was launched in sixty-three cities (Batra, 2009). After the Bharatiya Janata Party (BJP)-led National Democratic Alliance (NDA) government came into power in 2014, the mandate for urban development was raised exponentially.

Prime Minister Modi launched various schemes to tackle urban issues—Swachh Bharat Mission (Urban) focusing on sanitation, Atal Mission for Rejuvenation and Urban Transformation (AMRUT) of urban infrastructure, Smart Cities Mission (SCM) for technology-led improvement in quality of life in cities (focusing on specific areas of a city), and Housing For All (to provide housing to everyone by 2022), among others. This change in the narrative on urban development and the government's approach to it was initiated in JNNURM and taken to new heights by the gamut of these schemes post-2014.

INDIAN CITIES: A COMPLEX UNRESOLVED AGENDA

India is at a tipping point on its urbanization levels, given the increasing role of urbanization in its economic development and the massive movement of millions of people from the rural hinterland to urban centres and from towns to cities. These two factors—along with the lack of preparedness at the city-level and technological advancements worldwide—make it uneasy for anyone to imagine what Indian cities might be like in the coming decades. Indian cities of the future have two daunting tasks ahead of them. First, they have to play catch-up in terms of key urban infrastructure and services, in which they lag compared to not just developed countries but also many developing countries. They will have to also catch-up on present-day standards on local governance and reversing trends in local environmental damage. The currently successful cities have suffered most of these gaps in the past but with their economic growth, could overcome these challenges.

Second, there are certain attributes that would remarkably distinguish the Indian cities of the future from their present situation. The future shape of these attributes cannot be conclusively defined; but yet, India can identify these attributes and adopt the agility to follow, and wherever possible beat, the global trends on these attributes. One such attribute is urban transport: though the nature of public transport will largely be the same, the nature of personal travel is fast changing due to developments such as vehicle-sharing systems, electric vehicles, underground tunnels and the hyperloop rail, among others. Our city planners should look towards issues such as this.

Historically, with the majority of the population living in rural India, urbanization has not received the attention it deserves. Nevertheless, it is time to recognize that it is one of the key areas critical to the transformation and modernization of India. As per Census 2011, 377 million Indians comprising 31.1 per cent of the total population live in urban areas. The *UN-Habitat World City's 2016 Report* estimates that the urban population in India reached 420 million in 2015 (UN-Habitat, 2016). According to one projection, the country's urban population would reach 590 million by 2030 (Sankhe et al., 2010). In 2011, India's urbanization rate stood at 31 per cent as compared to 45 per cent in China, 54 per cent in Indonesia, 78 per cent in Mexico and 87 per cent in Brazil (CII, n.d.). Therefore, there is substantial potential for accelerated growth in productivity through higher urbanization levels.

The factors driving urbanization in India are also undergoing change. During 1981–2001, India's urbanization was caused by: a natural increase in the population of cities (around 60 per cent); followed by rural–urban migration; expansion of boundaries of cities; and re-classification of rural areas into urban areas (MoUD, 2011). However, during 2001–2011, the share of natural increase in the population of cities declined to 44 per cent (still a predominant factor), while the share of reclassification of rural areas into urban areas strengthened, and the share of rural urban migration increased to 24 per cent (Panagariya et al., 2014).

Moreover, due to land mismanagement and faulty policies, Indian cities are at present witnessing unfettered expansion along their outer boundaries. This urban sprawl is putting ever-rising pressure on their infrastructure. Lastly, 70 per cent of India's urban population is concentrated in Class I cities (cities with 100,000 people or more). During 1951–2011, the number of Class I cities increased from 77 to 468. Out of these 468 Class I cities, fifty-three are metropolitan cities (cities with a population of one million or more) (Shaw, 2012). During 1951–2011, the population share of metropolitan cities increased from 18.9 per cent to 42.6 per cent, and the number of metropolitan cities jumped from five to fifty-three. As per website of the Ministry of Housing and Urban Affairs India added eighteen metropolitan cities in the last decade alone (2001–2011). Today India has three megacities (a population of 10 million or more)—Mumbai, Delhi and Kolkata.

India's renewed orientation towards transforming urbanization coincides with two primary global development agendas—the UN's Sustainable Development Goals (SDGs) and Urban Habitat III. These two agendas have successfully changed the policy discourse on urbanization worldwide. The SDGs were adopted at the UN's Sustainable Development Summit in September 2015, wherein the world leaders adopted the 2030 Agenda for Sustainable Development which includes a set of seventeen SDGs covering 169 targets. Of the seventeen Global Goals, Goal 11—'Sustainable Cities and Communities'—focuses on making cities and human settlements inclusive, safe, resilient and sustainable. Moreover, Goal 11 is not a standalone goal and is interlinked and interdependent on several other goals. The Second Agenda, the 2016 UN Conference on Housing and Sustainable Urban Development is often referred to as Habitat III and is considered as an extension of SDG 11. This conference concluded with the adoption of the 'New Urban Agenda' which focused on sustainable urbanization for the next twenty years up to 2036.

India has been a leading participant in both these agendas. Under the context of urbanization, India recognizes their importance and has absorbed these agendas in its national and sub-national policymaking. The SDGs that pertain to urban life are SDG Goal 1: 'End poverty in all its forms everywhere'; Goal 3, Target 3.6: 'By 2020, halve the number of global deaths and injuries from road traffic accidents'; Goal 6: 'Ensure availability and sustainable management of water and sanitation for all'; and Goal 12, Target 12.5: 'Substantially reduce waste generation through prevention, reduction, recycling and reuse', among others.

However, given the status of growth and development in India, urbanization policies focus on national priorities, along with balancing them with the two global agendas. For instance, Indian cities have to prioritize infrastructure development, provide good governance, facilitate growth and create jobs in the near term to further achieve their goals on resilience, safety and inclusiveness. Another illustration is the national priority on facilitating domestic migration more than international migration. Thus, it can be said that the urban vision and strategy focuses on national priorities, but works in tandem with the global urban development agenda.

To resolve above challenges, India needs a national urban policy. Such a policy would serve multiple purposes. For instance, in Australia, the national urban policy outlines issues of productivity, sustainability, liveability and governance as important objectives in framing the agenda for cities (Sanghi and Dhar, 2018). Such documents bring everyone on to the same page in terms of issues, role of stakeholders, objectives, key outcomes and new economic entities in cities (ibid.). Such a policy at the national and state levels, is pertinent and a prerequisite to resolving India's complex urban agenda.

GLOBAL CITIES: AT THE TIPPING POINT

Looking back at the past 500 years, it is now widely accepted that industrialization and urbanization mostly happen concurrently. Urbanization is considered a function of industrialization. The work of Arthur Lewis points out this relation. He notes that low-productivity rural labour migrates to urban centres mostly engaged in industrial production, in search of higher wages (Fox and Goodfellow, 2016). Europe, North America and Japan in the eighteenth and nineteenth centuries, followed by countries in East Asia in the mid-twentieth century (with China closing in, following the reforms of the 1990s), have all seen this happen. India and Africa are in the process of joining this group of regions, which would lead to greater prosperity in these countries.

Before India, China's urbanization was the one big trend that dominated all aspects of the global political economy. Since its liberalization until 2014, China added 500 million people to its urban population (*The Economist*, 2014a). China's urban population share increased from 12 per cent in 1950, to 50 per cent in 2012. The first Special Economic Zone that attracted global attention was Chinese intervention in Shenzhen in 1980, which was then a group of fishing villages with a population of 30,000; now transformed into the world's largest contiguous urbanized area with 11 million people—a model initially tried in 1959 in Ireland's town of Shannon (Kennard and Provost 2016). With its 11 million population, Shenzhen is now part of the world's largest urbanized area of over 60 million people, called the Pearl River Delta composed of eleven cities—Guangzhou, Foshan, Zhaoqing Shenzhen, Dongguan, Huizhou, Jiangmen, Zhongshan and Zhuhai, apart from Hong Kong and Macau. The area shows the twin narratives of China—export-led growth and dizzying urbanization in which migrants have been an illegal but integral part.

Urban China is built on one of mankind's most entrenched institutionalized inequality mechanisms—the Hukou system of household registration. Only if you have an urban hukou can you access urban services at subsidized costs. Millions of Chinese rural hukou holders live in cities in an informal set-up and have developed an entire ecology where they can access urban services. China now plans to ensure that 45 per cent of its population gets an urban hukou, and doing that means granting new registration to 100 million people. However, the problems are not completely ironed out even then. For instance, the points-based system of urban hukou is different for different tier of cities. It is more relaxed for smaller cities, but due to variety of complexities it also discourages rural hukou holders from applying for urban hukou registration (Sheehan, 2017).

At this juncture, in the history of humankind, the world is most urbanized. The urbanization wave that took the West through a transition that lasted from 1750 to 1950, urbanized 400 million people. The ongoing wave of urbanization as per the Organization of Economic Co-operation and Development (OECD) will last from 1950 to 2100, but will urbanize close to 8 billion people (OECD, 2015). As per the UN, 55 per cent of the world's population is living in urban areas. As per UN Department of Economic and Social Affairs, level of urbanization across regions varies greatly with 82 per cent in Northern America, 81 per cent in Latin America and the Caribbean, and 74 per cent in Europe to 50 per cent in Asia and 43 per cent in Africa (UN-DESA, 2018).

By 2050, the global urban population share is bound to clock 68 per cent. The UN's World Urbanization Prospects report predicts that by 2050, 2.5 billion people will be added to cities. And 90 per cent of this increase will happen in Asia and Africa. This growth can be further pinned down to three main countries—India (416 million), China (255 million), and Nigeria (189 million) (UN-DESA, 2018).

Interestingly, city populations are shrinking in some parts of the world. These cities are located in East Asia (Japan and South Korea) and Europe, where the Total Fertility Rate (TFR) is on a constant decline. Economic contraction and natural disasters contribute to such decline. As mentioned earlier in this chapter, the rate of urbanization and population size of cities is on a constant rise. By 2030, as per UN Department of Economic and Social Affairs, majority regions of the world will be largely urbanized and there will be proliferation of million-plus cities across the world, mainly in Asia and Africa. Notably, as per 2018 estimates, there will also be a surge of 10 million-plus cities across India and on the eastern side of China by 2030 (UN-DESA, Population Division Fund).

We have seen how the fortune of cities is closely intertwined with the progress of human civilization. Despite this, over and over again, the city has been relegated to the backwaters. In fact the city is the last and greatest innovation of the village, and has since been humankind's longest running experiment. In the success of the city lies our progress. No ideology, crisis, and even countless public health crises over millennia can halt its success. Yet, in India, we have been unfair to the idea and merits of urbanization. So much so that it has become our greatest, biggest and, perhaps, the most fatal blind spot. We must visit the merits of Indian cities to understand what they can offer for the Indian and global political economy. We must find a way to promptly, systemically and efficiently make up for the lack of priority given to our own cities since Independence.

2
Indian Cities: At the Centre Stage for Global Trends

URBANIZATION is a work in progress that continues to baffle, disappoint, encourage and inspire humankind. Cities are melting pots of innovation that are on constant boil to improve the quality of life of their inhabitants. Unarguably, the world's greatest events have taken place in cities: the start of large-scale infrastructure projects, the birth of many new religions, the study of natural sciences, creation of the nation state system, sophistication in technology and commerce, onset of financial transactions, printing and dissemination of information, creation of colonial ambitions and colonies, new forms of travel and interaction, globalization leading to high specialization of the workforce, the advent of social media, advances in medicine, the journey to space, journeys to the depths of the seas and oceans—and much more. If it were not for cities and what they have given us, we would have progressed from nothing to even less. Much of what we see and live with is a function of urbanization and cities.

In understanding the world's longest-running experiment—urbanization—we stumble across facts and themes that run contrary to the popular imagination on cities. Indians, for instance, have a romanticized view of rural areas, coupled with uninformed disdain.

This romanticized view finds acceptance globally, even among the most evolved minds. It comes from a good place though—a longing for clean air and water, for greater prosperity (minus the forces of congestion, competition and housing and population density), and the need for being in harmony with nature. The fact is that cities—birthed out of villages—can also offer some hope and reconciliation to these desires. However, more than meeting some of these desires, we must realize that cities are our only hope for a broader and deeper prosperity given the ever-growing population globally—and more so in India.

City-dwellers do not welcome rural migrants. They look at slums (that house most migrants) as one would a wall with peeling paint and exposed bricks at home: an embarrassment. They want the rural population to stay home in the village and are willing to dole out subsidies and charities to make this happen. They want to continue to earn exorbitant incomes in the city, but want villagers to live on a pittance in rural hinterlands and deal with millennia-old social and gender roles. This apathy and selfishness of the urban elites—an apathy that masquerades as some 'higher calling' to preserve rural structures—is reason enough to explain why hundreds of millions in India remain stuck in a reality that can only be called archaic. This asymmetry needs to be corrected once and for all. India (and Indians) should encourage healthy urbanization, and must be supported in this by nations across the globe, because the impact of urbanization will have reverberations far beyond India's own geographical boundaries. History is testament to the far-reaching impacts of urbanization.

As the world's fastest-growing large economy (we hope Covid-19 recovery doesn't change that), India, with its 1.3-billion population, has recognized that it is at the cusp of a major urbanization boom. It is time the world sat up and took notice. India's urbanization will change the world forever, whether for better or for worse only time will tell. Globally, the impact of Indian cities will endure for decades. These cities will birth global trends, not just in growth or business opportunities, but in everything under the sun. With the sheer tyranny of numbers on India's side, it is only natural that this country will influence global dialogue, development and the understanding of everything important. Besides this advantage of numbers, India also carries a millennium-old legacy of institutions, skills, religions, culture, geopolitical position and scholarship, all of which accentuate the ability of Indian cities to dominate and steer global discourse to new and different heights. It is important for India and the world to notice how these cities will influence the discourse and, therefore, leverage them to gain the best possible advantage.

The world of snake charmers and elephants is a distant memory. To continue to stereotype India, reducing it to a country of the poor, the peasants, gaudy billionaires, political dynasties, religious revisionism, and as an outsourcing hub, is almost criminal. If India continues to carry this image, it has no one but itself to blame. The country has grown slowly and organically, but as it grows conscious of the power of its cities, this growth will be sustained and bolstered in unprecedented ways. In the process, India will evolve and leave an indelible impression on the world. For now, if the stereotypical image of India continues to prevail globally, it simply means that India has yet to learn to capitalize on its cities to project power and a positive image.

In the last chapter, we saw how Europe's cities provided the world with sea-based trade, modern urban planning, colonization, rail and postal networks. Likewise, cities in the US gave us skyscrapers, modern urban transport, a modern financial system, and even global governance structures. China's urbanization, a more recent phenomenon, has provided a strong market for the last three decades, hyperactive clusters of modern industries and new-age infrastructure capabilities, among other things. Likewise, Indian cities too will make their presence felt worldwide. Let's deep dive into the major themes in which we expect Indian cities to touch the lives of people living in far corners of the globe, as the cities and the nation morph into a force to reckon with.

INDIAN CITIES: FUTURE EPICENTRE OF GLOBAL VALUECHAINS

Since ancient times, cities have been centres that were born out of (and survived on) agricultural produce surplus. Cities have traditionally been the main consumers, as the most prosperous classes (royalty, merchants, artisans, trained professionals, etc.,) lived there. The trade in silk, horses, spices, textiles and even slaves happened in cities. Cities are truly the market of the world and the majority of the world's produce is focused on consumption in cities. This holds even more true in the case of goods and services of high value, since only cities are capable of paying the high price of such products and services. For the foreseeable future, Indian cities are expected to emerge as the consumer (market) and producer (basket) for the world.

As per official estimates India is home to around 8,000 towns, of which fifty-three are metropolitan towns—however, these are under-reported figures. India is more urbanized than these numbers indicate and we will see, later in the book, how to address this issue. As India continues to grow from a USD 3 trillion economy—within a decade expected to breach the USD 6–7 trillion mark—it will serve as both the market and basket for the world. Every industry worldwide will be influenced by India's changing demographics—a growing young, middle-class population carrying a smartphone, with access to cheap data and improving health and education outcomes. The social, religious and political leanings of this population will have an impact far beyond the nation's geographical boundaries.

As per the *Global Cities* report from Oxford Economics, the world's top ten growing cities during 2019–35 are all in India (Whiting, 2019). This study assessed 780 cities globally. While the major urban economies are expected to grow by 2.8 per cent a year, leading Indian cities are expected to grow by much more—Surat (by 9.17 per cent), Agra (by 8.58 per cent), Bengaluru (by 8.50 per cent), Hyderabad (by 8.47 per cent), Nagpur (by 8.41 per cent), Tiruppur (by 8.36 per cent), Rajkot (by 8.33 per cent), Tiruchirappalli (by 8.29 per cent), Chennai (by 8.17 per cent) and Vijayawada (by 8.16 per cent)—during 2019–35. These cities are thus expected to become four to five times their present size. Surat's GDP will cross USD 126 billion, Bengaluru will breach USD 280 billion and Hyderabad's GDP will touch USD 200 billion.

This is just the tip of the iceberg. There are other major urban growth centres that are already economic powerhouses, such as the Delhi National Capital Region (Delhi-NCR) and Mumbai. As more people move out of agriculture and into cities for better opportunities, India's urbanization rate is going to increase.

Prasanna Mohanty has produced strong evidence on the role that cities play in growth. He stresses that there is an almost perfect correlation between urbanization and a nation's prosperity. As the share of the urban population increases by 10 per cent, the per capita output rises by 30 per cent (Mohanty, 2019). Moreover, per capita income is approximately four times greater in countries where the majority of population is urban, as compared to countries with predominantly rural populations (ibid.). People living in metropolitan areas, even when controlled for a range of variables, are 50 per cent more productive than are people from smaller metro areas (ibid.).

This high growth is likely to lift India's per capita income from the lower middle-income bracket to the upper middle-income bracket. The high purchasing power is likely to influence all sectors globally—from mobile manufacturers to realty companies, from apparel companies to the consumer goods industry, and from automobile giants to the services sectors. India will be the growth market for Indian and global companies. The higher purchasing power of its urban residents will influence the call that a chairman of a top multinational bank or a tech company takes on its business model. The influence of Indian cities will be location-agnostic; where an MNC is headquartered—New York, London, Mumbai, Singapore, Beijing, Geneva, or Kigali—will no longer matter. Just as the world knows about the average American consumer and China's new middle class, the Indian middle class has all the makings of becoming an influential force.

A 2012 study by McKinsey Global Institute stated that the global consuming class—people with a daily disposable income of more than USD 10 at constant 2005 PPP (purchasing power parity) dollars—would more than triple during 1990–2025 to 4.2 billion and around 2 billion of these people would be residents of cities of emerging economies (Dobbs et al., 2012). Such urban households could create an additional spending of USD 20 trillion up to 2025 (though this might be delayed by a few years due to Covid-19). As per a WEF report, *Future of Consumption in Fast-Growth Consumer Markets: India,* upper middle-income and high-income households constituted one in four households in India in 2018, and by 2030 this number could increase to one in two households with a total of 200 million households falling in this category (WEF, 2019a). Covid-19 may have pushed forward the year of this outcome, but the broad trend will hold. The world should be ready for the great Indian middle-class based out of its cities.

Apart from consuming, the Indian cities will also produce for global consumption. The salience of this factor has increased particularly due to the ongoing US–China trade war. Moreover, China's growth is expected to moderate and the world will look to India to do business. China has also lost legitimacy—a currency that matters most in the international order—due to the vicious spread of Covid-19. Many countries are now supporting their businesses financially and politically to move out of China. This has expedited the diversification of global value-chains. While countries like Bangladesh and Vietnam have taken a lead in attracting such firms, India's fundamentals and large domestic economy will mean that we will continue to be globally competitive.

Our leaders should see the global spotlight on India for what it is. First, that the world has faith in India's business fundamentals. Second, that this is an opportunity for Indian cities to become suppliers to the world. Our leading product exports include electronic goods, organic and inorganic chemicals, petroleum products, engineering goods and drugs and pharmaceuticals (PIB, 2021). Our leading services exports include telecommunications, computer and information services, travel, transport and financial services. Some other sectors play a dominant role too—India commands a 95 per cent global share in diamond polishing; it is the world's second-largest mobile market, footwear producer and steel producer; the third largest exporter of textiles and apparel; fourth largest in-vehicle market; fifth largest in terms of passengers travelling by air; and the sixth largest globally in chemical sales (Invest India, n.d.).

The Indian government has further identified twelve 'champion sectors': technology & information technology-enabled services (IT & ITeS), tourism and hospitality services, medical value travel, transport and logistics services, accounting and finance services, audiovisual services, legal services, communication services, construction and related engineering services, environmental services, financial services and education services (PIB, 2018a). In manufacturing, India is providing impetus to the sunrise sectors of food processing, electric vehicles, battery storage, among others.

Around three-fourths of commercial activity in any major economy is concentrated in its cities. As India urbanizes and takes cognizance of the growing importance of its cities as hubs of economic activity, removes logistical and congestion bottlenecks, leverages its youth, creates an English-speaking, trained urban workforce, its cities will become suppliers to the world. As China did with Wuhan (not the virus) and Shenzhen, it is highly likely that India will impact the global value chain and also global consumption patterns. In India's case, with 1.3 billion people living under a democratic regime, the reverberation will only be stronger, wider and last longer.

Any discussion of the changing nature of global value chains must include a discussion of the role of international politics. China received a boost as far back as 2001, when it joined the World Trade Organization (WTO) and global governance institutions provided legitimacy to its production capabilities. It emerged as the world's factory in the 1990s and now produces goods at a speed and scale very difficult to emulate. The role of producing for the world, economic growth and global governance, all find their roots in the post-World War II order led by the US. The Bretton Woods systems provided the much-needed stability to the post-War global order and changed the growth trajectory of nations. In a landmark paper, 'Power and liberal order: America's post-war world order in transition', international relations-and-US foreign policy expert John Ikenberry observed that the features of a US-led international order after World War II were 'organized around open markets, security alliances, multilateral cooperation, and democratic community' (Ikenberry, 2005). Part of this arrangement included providing asymmetrical access to American markets, which helped the erstwhile West Germany, countries in East Asia, and later China.

Post Covid-19, coupled with the inching together of international interests, India is gaining traction that will bolster the production capabilities of its cities. During the Covid-19 pandemic, the country went from being a zero producer of personal protective equipment (PPE) kits, to one of the leading exporters of PPE kits and N95 masks. India also produces seven out of ten vaccines worldwide (Upadhyay,

2020). India is also a member of an important and relatively new grouping of four maritime nations (the other three being the US, Australia and Japan), called the 'Quad', short for Quadrilateral Security Dialogue. While India has gained legitimacy, China has lost its edge. There is every likelihood that this legitimacy, coupled with the changing nature of strategic interests, will help Indian cities produce and gain asymmetrical access to world markets. To better leverage this opportunity, Indian cities need to deliver on making it easier for small and large businesses to function within their peripheries.

LIBERALISM VERSUS CONSERVATISM IN INDIAN CITIES

India is a vibrant democracy of 1.3 billion, with 900 million voters in the 2019 general elections. Clearly, it is the world's largest democracy, and how it imbibes certain values and principles will have global influence. With a history that dates back to antiquity, the old ways linger on and are slow to disappear. India remains one of the last countries where shrinking groups of communists adhere to the original principles, fight elections (and sometimes win). Even the Communist Party of China has long abandoned the communist ideology and embraced capitalism, and how! It should also be noted that communism is the only major political movement to lay great emphasis on the rural constituency. As is globally evident, it is undergoing a multi-organ failure now, living out its last days in a few remaining pockets around the world. Capitalism—an essentially urban political movement—on the other hand continues its onward march.

Urbanization has always been an unstoppable juggernaut; can one attribute it as a force that contributed in bringing communism to its knees? And that it naturally led to the spread of capitalism? Defining the exact boundaries of conservatism and of social and economic liberalism is difficult. Yet, it is these boundaries that define the rural–urban political divide and vote share. Liberal politics envisages the choice of the individual as paramount, whereas conservative political thought upholds social norms and traditions. Therefore, a politically conservative individual would show stronger belief in caste and religious practices, be opposed to the lesbian, gay, bisexual and transgender (LGBT) rights movement, and see a more traditional role for women; while economic liberalists would focus on individual action, less government regulation and strong property rights.

Cities, being a function of economic liberalism, usually become a bulwark against political conservatism. However, the dual play between these two forces causes serious friction. Bigger metropolitan areas are more economically and politically liberal, while smaller cities, towns and rural areas are in a flux. Moreover the inability of politicians and global commentators to sense the palpable current among smaller cities is proving a factor in their undoing. For instance, in the US presidential elections in 2016, global commentators and many American citizens dismissed the possibility of billionaire and former TV personality Donald Trump ever becoming President, given his disparaging views on women and gay rights, that he seemed not in the least statesmen-like, and many such issues. Hillary Clinton, a favourite of democrats based in American coastal cities, failed to win despite being a seasoned politician, an administrator and the wife of former President Bill Clinton. The answer to this surprise twist lay in the rural areas of America and the sun-belt region, comprising the states of Alabama, Arizona, Florida, Georgia, Louisiana, Mississippi, New Mexico, South Carolina and Texas, among others. It also lay in America's commitment to its version of economic-liberalism-plus-political conservatism.

This dichotomy can today be clearly seen across Indian cities. The norm of economic liberalism had been well established after the 1991 reforms. Successive governments were largely aligned towards greater foreign investment, privatization, engagement of private players, reduction in government size and unleashing of market forces in the sunrise sectors. Despite this, Indian cities are at present divided on major issues such as the role of religion in state policy, special rights of certain states, dietary preferences, inter-caste and inter-religion marriage, the death penalty, women wearing jeans, women having a career, social structures, and the role of caste, among others.

Going back several years to the US election of 2012 can provide us some key insights. An article in *The Atlantic* states that people didn't make cities politically liberal but cities made people politically liberal (Kron, 2012). It further added that since 1984 and up to 2012, more cities had voted 'blue' (synonymous with liberal politics), and in 2012, twenty-seven out of thirty major US cities had voted for the Democrats—the US party based on liberal politics. In 2008, eighty-eight of the hundred most populous US counties voted for Barack Obama and in 2012, eighty-six voted for him (Desilver, 2016). Urban voters in the US tend to vote Democrat at the national level, whereas urban voters in India predominantly voted for the BJP in the 2014 and 2019 elections. This is fairly intuitive too, your location, particularly your city, has an overwhelming influence on your voting choices.

India's urban voters are thus quite different from their US counterparts. Research findings reveal that as education and income levels rise, they engage less with the state perhaps because national growth and economic policy are not on their agenda (*Mint*, 2018). Research also proves that so far Indian voters have voted saffron when income and education levels have risen (ibid.). Fighting the 2019 national elections on the twin planks of 'Minimum Government, Maximum Governance', the BJP won 61.7 per cent (fifty-five out of eighty-nine) highly urban seats (those with 1 million or 1 million-plus urban population) (*The Economic Times*, 2019). The BJP has long been labelled as the party of urban constituencies, and these continue to be largely in its favour. Its vote share in such constituencies had gone up by 5 per cent.

Policies of the United Progressive Alliance (UPA) government that did not sit well with urban voters included affirmative action, rights-based policies, greater government involvement and higher taxes—indicating that urban voters prioritize economic liberalism. However, once a certain economic potential has been achieved, there is a possibility that Indian cities might favour political liberalism too. Did Congress, the Grand Old Party of India, fail to understand the change in the country's demographics? And did this lack of insight lead it down the path to defeat? At this stage this is just speculation; it would be worth noting how urban Indian constituencies vote in the coming decades.

India is currently a USD 3 trillion economy. If and when we become a USD 10 trillion economy with a 1.5 billion population, it will translate to a per capita income of USD 6,700. My own assumption is that Indian cities—with the majority of their citizens belonging to different parts of the country and with considerable disposable income—will demand liberal economics. This will create tension as, in the words of my Professor, Dr Razeen Sally, politics tends to centralize whereas economic growth decentralizes. These new numbers will also consolidate India's position in the world of global politics. Its economic power, huge market, strong diasporic presence, a largely English-speaking workforce, a long legacy of reputed educational institutes and strong domestic institutions may prove a strong bulwark against conservative politics, first in the region and eventually globally.

Another impact of Indian cities on global politics will be through power projection. The rise of every global and regional hegemony is characterized by institutes incubated and sustained by the support of hegemons. The role and longevity of the World Bank, the International Monetary Fund (IMF) and daughter concerns of the UN nurtured the Bretton Woods system—also known as the Washington Consensus. The recent rise of China has led to speculation about the rise of the Beijing Consensus with new institutions mushrooming, the most notable being the Asian Infrastructure Investment Bank and the Belt and Road Initiative. None of these would have crystallized if China's cities had not performed well. Cities are engines of growth and add to the economic heft of any country. When people talk of the United States of America (USA), the United Kingdom (UK), Germany and China, they do not imagine an entire country. What people visualize in their head is their version of its leading cities—Washington, New York, London, Berlin, Shanghai and Beijing. Cities are mascots of a country's global power.

If India plays its cards right, there is every likelihood that it will be among the top three world economies, while deriving the economic strength of its more than fifty major cities. As India's global clout increases, one can speculate on the rise of the 'Delhi Consensus'—on the lines of Washington and Beijing Consensus—wherein the leadership of these countries has had a considerable impact on global politics, international finance and global governance. In fact, the Delhi Consensus is not a distant dream. It is firming up in our times. From playing a significant role in existing multilateral institutions to creating new international coalitions such as the International Solar Alliance and the Coalition for Disaster Resilient Infrastructure, the changing role is palpable. The Delhi Consensus has also begun to exert influence through its own home-grown dialogue. The most recent example is the Raisina Dialogue, jointly organized by the Ministry of External Affairs (MEA) and the Observer Research Foundation (ORF), which brings together the who's who of global politics and foreign policy. In the global order, countries use economic clout to project power. The clout—the clustering of ideas, hard and soft power—is concentrated in cities. Thus, cities literally project power.

When India gained freedom from its former colonizer, it was a country of 340 million, with a GDP of USD 30.6 billion. In 2018, it had a population of over 1.3 billion and a GDP of USD 2.7 trillion (Guruswamy, 2017). In 2019, it surpassed the economy of the UK and France to become the fifth largest economy with a GDP of USD 2.9 trillion (*Business Today*, 2020). The majority of nations now want to do business with India and gain access to its large market.

Today's global workforce cannot be imagined without India's skilled, English-speaking workforce that has given the world top executives like Indira Nooyi, Satya Nadella, Sundar Pichai, and many others who are leading the global pack in innovation and research. Members of this Indian workforce work in different roles across different professions all over the world. From business owners to scientists, from pop culture icons to innovators, they take up all sorts of roles. They also influence global culture and propagate Indian soft power.

When cities are successful, the country accumulates hard power of economic resources and defence might. When cities are successful, domestic culture is exported worldwide through labour movement and migration. For global politics, this mix of hard and soft power matters the most. Given how cities define this growth of hard and soft power, the growth of Indian cities will influence global politics in the foreseeable future in much more concrete ways.

CITIES: EMANCIPATION FROM CASTE- AND GENDER-BASED SEGREGATION

Cities are all about economic efficiency driven by division of labour and agglomeration of firms, people and skills. Any force that stratifies society runs contrary to the purpose of cities. In the Indian context, there are two such forces—caste-based segregation and gender-based segregation. Both are the legacy of a rural political economy that has no space in the urban context.

People left behind due to caste and gender segregation find a voice in democracy. Unlike in other countries where land-ownership and privilege initially determined the right to vote, India adopted universal adult suffrage right off the bat at Independence. Communities left out of political decision-making for hundreds of years (barring a few exceptions), found a voice in parliamentary democracy and constitutionalism—both of which are pioneering products of urbanization. It is heartening to note that studies have revealed that cities are 'privileged places for democratic innovation' and that urban centres might very well be the reason behind the spread of democracy (Fox and Goodfellow, 2016). Political mainstreaming is a promising start and though a lot is left to be desired, the underlying forces of cities will resolve these unmet expectations.

The father of India's Constitution and India's first law minister, B.R. Ambedkar, came from a disadvantaged background as he belonged to the Dalit caste (then deemed 'untouchable'). His determination, and academic brilliance supported by merit-based scholarship, led him to study at the world's best institutions. Through the force of his vision and his brilliant achievements, he mobilized people and resources around the anti-caste movement and became a towering political figure. He often tried to marry the rights of women with caste issues. He lent his support to urban centres which he felt were centres for the emancipation of the oppressed. His view was that villages had, 'no room for democracy. There is no room for equality. There is no room for liberty and there is no room for fraternity. The Indian village is the very negation of the Republic' (Jha, 2020).

A 2007 report by the UN Population Fund (UNFPA) stressed that 'the best recipe for a life without poverty is still to grow up in a city' (Hollis, 2013). This is more so the case in India, when we talk about historically oppressed groups. Cities concern themselves with the division of labour. Ambedkar, in his book *Annihilation of Caste*, pointed out how the caste system inherently contradicted economic efficiency (Ambedkar, 1936). He highlighted three key arguments: first, caste was not a division of labour but a division of labourers; second, he said that such division was unnatural and that there was a 'hierarchy in which the division of labourers are graded one above the other'; and third, that such division was not based on aptitude but was artificial (ibid.). In other words, the system does not encourage the free development of mental faculties nor the free use of them; careers are thrust upon one trapped in this system, not chosen.

Cities prevent this grab of power. What matters in a city is how skilled you are and how you perform in the labour market. It can be argued that Indian cities are far from perfect. There is ghettoization of certain castes, and they do not get full representation in the private sector. Nevertheless, in cities, they can depend on education as a great equalizer—both primary and higher. True, they have to work to support families, continue to face discrimination and yes, the learning outcomes are not perfect in government-run schools, but we are not comparing city life with perfect city life. We are assessing what cities can do for these communities as compared to a life spent in the village. After education, they have a considerably better chance of getting a job of their choice in the city, because firms seek talent and not a background per se.

In a few decades, the forces of urbanization will overpower and overwhelm the forces of caste segregation. Cities are a way more powerful force than are outdated norms such as caste and caste-based segregation. Suraj Yengde in his moving book *Caste Matters*, presents compelling evidence on how Indian corporate boards, positions in media and seats in the Central Cabinet are overwhelmingly dominated by Brahmins and have little to show for diversity (Yengde, 2019). Another research report shows that Dalits are concentrated in urban slums: 'one in every three Dalits living in urban areas was settled in a slum; and one in every five slum-dwellers in urban India was a Dalit. This clearly indicates how Dalits are more concentrated in slums' (Konda, 2020). A study of neighbourhoods shows that caste-based segregation exists in a city such as Bengaluru (Bharathi et al., 2018).

Clearly a lot needs to be done, but well-functioning cities are the light at the end of the tunnel for India's oppressed castes. The world's mightiest forces have, in the past, crumbled in the face of the force of a city. Caste segregation is bound to collide with city laws and if our cities function well, we can beat this archaic system too. Ambedkar's contestations against caste vis-à-vis economic efficiency can apply to gender-based oppression and segregation as well. The gender bias cuts across religions, geographies, caste, languages and educational backgrounds. It is sad to note that gender bias is one of the more common features across all sorts of divisions and diversity in India. Ideally, cities should be gender-agnostic as labour plays a major role in the productivity and efficiency of cities. The theatre for reclaiming gender parity will be the city. The legacy of the village with its rigid gender roles, prohibited yet practised regressive traditions of child marriage, sati and prohibition of widow remarriage, the archaic practice of holding a khap panchayat (community-based arbitration as per community norms), countless hours wasted in unpaid or low productivity labour, and lack of education and livelihood opportunities—have all led village women in India to remain trapped in their archaic, unchanging reality.

The tide is turning and the flow has begun to hammer cracks into such institutionalized gender bias. When the #MeToo movement gained movement worldwide, Indian women in cities came forward with stories which brought many men of wealth, influence and power under intense scrutiny. Many such names may have been forgotten by public memory, but most are now aware that given a chance Indian women (at least in cities) will not let oppression and abuse pass by. There will be repercussions. The horrific rape of Nirbhaya and the similar case in Hathras awakened the nation's conscience, not because of the terror of these crimes or the benevolence of humanity, but because these episodes stood out since women led the campaign for justice. With education and financial empowerment, Indian women get a voice and are able to mobilize and sway opinions. However, this is seen mostly in cities and not so much in villages.

Health outcomes in the city bode well for women, as compared to outcomes in villages. India's fourth National Family Health Survey (NFHS) conducted in 2015–16 offers startling insights on this matter (NFHS-4, 2017). Four out of five urban women use hygienic methods for menstrual protection; just one in two do so in rural areas; the average age of marriage in urban areas is higher (than in rural) by 1.7 years; the urban total fertility rate (TFR) is 1.8, against 2.4 for rural; more urban women (than rural) have access to modern methods of contraception such as the pill, intrauterine devices (IUD), post-partum intra-uterine devices (PPIUD) and condoms (ibid.).

The fact is, urban Indian women are more informed, empowered and independent, and have an equal, if not greater say in the matter of reproduction. The cost of raising children in a city is also a factor for moderated TFR. More urban women (than rural) deliver their babies in the care of a skilled healthcare provider in a health facility; more rural than urban women are likely to experience emotional, physical, and sexual violence and marital control (ibid.). As per NFHS-4, more urban women (than rural) find meaningful occupations working mostly as production workers (30 per cent), service workers and professionals (20 per cent each), among others, while more than six out of ten women living in villages are employed in low productivity/wage agricultural labour (ibid.).

Globally, cities operate on skills and connectivity. Access to both unlocks opportunities for both genders. This is particularly liberating for women, as they come from a more disadvantaged background. Their artistic expression, physical presence in public spaces, claiming their own sexual identity, and the manifestation of their fashion and culture are all in collision with the men's upbringing and notions of acceptability. Violence against women and the push back against their independence is a manifestation of this collision. Even some of the most urbanized countries have failed to address these issues. Nevertheless, women are in greater control of their lives in cities and have a better opportunity to recourse in cities, as compared to villages. The fight on issues of marital rape, workplace harassment, gender budgeting, acceptability of divorce are being sustained in urban areas. This is not to say that urban areas do not have safety and inclusivity concerns regarding women. We will look at some of these issues and how to resolve them later in the book;

but the overarching point remains that cities offer a better chance for emancipation of women than do rural areas.

For both caste and gender oppression, there is a lot left to be done. How India urbanizes will impact the lives of more than a billion people who fall in into one or both categories. Cities offer them their best chance at parity and of correcting a history of atrocities and oppression. The world should pay heed to how these movements are fought and sustained. Global movements against oppression will find solace in and partner with these Indian movements.

DOMINATING THE GLOBAL LABOUR MOVEMENT

Migration is a companion of human civilization since the beginning of time. From migration out of Africa about 70,000 years ago, to distressed reverse migration from cities to villages in the wake of Covid-19, the human urge to search for stability, food, shelter and prosperity has been a constant. The ability to move has defined human civilization and the arc of cities too. 'Migration is an expression of the human aspiration for dignity, safety and a better future,' said UN Secretary-General Antonio Guterres in 2017. 'It is part of the social fabric, part of our very make-up as a human family' (WEF, 2017).

Our forefathers lived in villages, at some point migrating to cities and now we embellish ourselves as 'city residents'. Migration remains the core of what and how the world changes. The way the movements of tectonic plates define the topography of the world, human migration likewise defines civilizations and different eras. No story would ever be complete without the joy, pain, agony and turmoil unleashed by migration. In this context, cities become more critical because they are magnets for those looking for a better quality of life, job opportunities and a different world.

The WEF report, *Migration and Its Impact on Cities*, focused on all forms of migration—internal and international, voluntary and involuntary; international migration stood at 244 million and internal migration at 763 million (ibid.). In India, we have over 100 million internal migrants, intercity as well as rural to urban. If this migrant population were to form a nation, it would be the fourteenth largest in the world. It is also to be seen how Indian migration abroad will impact other nations and their cities. The migration of people from other countries to Indian cities is an important factor too, but not too much of it is expected to happen in the foreseeable future as people will prefer cities in the Americas, Europe and East Asia owing to the higher liveability factor of these cities. When the three migrations (village to city; city to city; migrating abroad) influence Indian cities and global cities, multiple sectors will shake up, which, in turn, will define and influence these cities. Impacted sectors include housing, education and employment, health, transport, utilities, sanitation and waste, social cohesion, and safety and security (ibid.).

As India continues to urbanize, the pace of migration will only swell and Indian cities are less than prepared to handle this movement. Moreover, as Indians migrate abroad, we will influence global migration flows, making them either levers of pain or growth for other global cities. It depends on how we prepare our population and how destination countries are prepared to handle such an influx of Indian migrants.

Economist Chinmay Tumbe, in his book *India Moving: A History of Migration*, has provided a name to the Indian migration phenomenon from 1870 to 2010—the Great Indian Migration Wave (Tumbe, 2018). According to him this migration, 'semi-permanent, male-dominated and remittance-based, is the world's largest and longest voluntary stream of migration. Thus, urbanization in India will invariably influence the cities worldwide' (Tumbe, 2019). Though he details domestic migration, he has left no stone unturned in discussing the movement of the Indian diaspora. His book *India Moving* richly weaves factual and anecdotal evidence of multiple stories of international migration from India to different parts of the world such as Southeast Asia, Africa, Latin America, Europe, North America and the Gulf. It is a telling work of how this migration has influenced the source and destination locations.

The cities in the developed world are facing the issue of shrinking cities, which means the population of these cities are declining; 35–40 per cent of the US cities are classified as 'Shrinking Cities' (Florida, 2019). As per a study, over 5,000 cities worldwide were shrinking during 2000–2019. These cities are primarily located in Europe, East Asia and North Eastern USA (Meng et al., 2021). Such decline happens due to two main reasons. First is migration, city to city (same or another country) or suburb. Second is demographic change, wherein the TFR falls below the replacement-level fertility (RLF). The RLF rate is defined as the number of babies per woman to sustain the population level without migration, and is roughly 2.1 children per woman (Searchinger et al., 2013); however, when the TFR falls to below the RLF rate, population size declines.

The WEF report highlights the willingness of people to migrate and how national policies are encouraging or discouraging this global migration (WEF, 2017). There are considerable parts of Europe and Asia that intend to invite greater migration to 'counter long-term population decline', 'address population ageing' and 'meet labour requirements' (ibid.).

Much as hardcore nationalists may revile Thomas Babington Macaulay—the British historian and bureaucrat who brought western education to India and overlooked the merit of India's indigenous education and culture—his influence spans far and wide across India. It has been established that proficiency in English played a key role in India's freedom movement, as most major leaders were English-speaking barristers who hard-negotiated with the British Government and presented India's case globally. They also helped unite a country that speaks hundreds of languages. After the railways and post and telegraph, the English language played a critical role in uniting India against British rule. After the long painful struggle for freedom, the Partition and subsequent division of states on linguistic grounds, English lost its sheen for some decades. However during the 1980s, and certainly in the 1990s—when India liberalized its economy and its economic transactions with the rest of the world increased and deepened—English again gained currency.

India is now home to an over 125-million-strong English-speaking workforce, second only to the US (Masani, 2012). This estimation is a decade old, so in all likelihood, we may have breached the 200-million mark. The use of English is so predominant that 'Hinglish'—a combination of English and Hindi—is a real thing in the northern belt, and every year many such hybrid words make their way to Oxford Dictionary (ibid.). As India continues to skill its manpower, its English-speaking abilities will come in handy in increasing global interactions. Undoubtedly, this will put a friendly face to Indians, making them a more amicable and acceptable choice for global migration (thereby, influencing the world outlook towards India and vice versa), and will shape the workforce across the countries.

Migration is the core that drives urbanization but it is also often at the receiving end of rapid urbanization. China is the most compelling case of the latter. It continues to practice the hukou system of household registration, as discussed in the previous chapter. As per this system households in rural areas and their residents cannot access amenities in urban areas, unless their registration is changed to urban. Meanwhile, urban residents continue to look down on migrants and discriminate against them.

The Europeans and Americans in the Brexit and Trump eras were just as suspicious of migrants. A new wave of nationalism found a breeding ground over the 'othering' of migrants; the battle of Us versus Them, pitted migrants against citizens of the host country. Tony Joseph in his work *Early Indians* shows that we are all mixed and we are all migrants, with our traces to parts of Africa (Joseph, 2021). Host nations intend to control sovereignty and foreign influence and save jobs, but knee-jerk policies to control migration is not the best way forward.

As per WEF, countries of the OECD have 120 million migrants, 30 per cent of whom are highly educated—the largest number (around 3.12 million) in this group come from India (McCarthy, 2020). While a considerable share of migrants still go to work in Gulf countries in the construction sector, improved education outcomes will increase migration towards countries welcoming skilled talent. India remains the top country in terms of remittances. This year, despite the Covid-19 slowdown, India is expected to receive up to USD 76 billion in remittances (PTI, 2020a). Globally, countries may implement policies to reverse the trend of shrinking cities; while Indian cities will be a constant source of global migration and, over decades will influence the face of the global workforce.

PROSPERITY FOR ALL: THE KEY TO DELIVERING SDGS

The SDGs are highly ambitious goals articulating the global development agenda. Some of them are extremely tough for countries to achieve. An entire generation has been impacted by the global financial crisis, followed by the European Union's (EU's) debt crisis, the US–China trade war and—at the start of a new decade—the spread of the global pandemic. This renders too many SDG goals rather difficult to achieve, particularly those pertaining to zero poverty and reduced inequalities. Those on slum reduction and proper housing, access to toilets, access to transport and electricity and better healthcare and education opportunities are bound to face a bump. The post-Covid-19 world has a difficult and long path to economic recovery. National and individual trajectories have taken a serious hit. Cities and regions will have to find new ways to grow at the local level and find innovative ways to deliver on SDGs at their level. Cities are now stepping forward to report their progress and New York has been the first city to submit its progress to the UN on the SDGs.

The SDGs have set out a 'common language', 'clear diagnosis', 'concrete objectives' and encourage 'concerted action' for cities (Pipa, 2018). While national adoption of SDGs happened at one go, countries like India have already adopted the SDG at the sub-national level. The effort by NITI Aayog, the Indian government's think tank, to localize SDGs has gained traction from all state governments and multilateral agencies. The localizing of SDGs in Indian cities is a matter of when and not if. Besides, given the burden of overpopulation, the power of a young population, the curse of poor socio-economic indicators, and the scope for catching-up, Indian cities are sitting at a cusp that can make or break the SDGs, particularly in the context of developing countries.

With the multilateral institutions becoming ineffective and fractious and the declining role of the US as a global hegemon, cities globally have picked up the mantle to serve the causes within their control and those that they deem urgent. Homelessness, jobs, poverty eradication, environmental sustainability, safety and reduced violence, inclusive societies, and resilience against climate change are few such actions. Leading Indian cities have joined the fray and are paving the way for other cities to follow their actions and create a better life for millions of people.

Now existing as a different project, Rockefeller Foundation's 100 Resilient Cities (100 RC) was a global network of 100 cities trying to build resilience at the city level and they worked with some Indian cities too. Similarly, the C40 platform brings together city leaders to take forward the work of the Paris Agreement on climate change. Bengaluru, Chennai, Delhi, and Kolkata are already part of this network. Urban95, an initiative by the Bernard van Leer Foundation, focuses on creating child-friendly cities from the perspective of a three-year-old with a height of 95 centimetres. Bhubaneshwar and Pune are part of this initiative. Likewise, the City Alliance, which works in multiple areas of migration, gender and resilience, continues to grow. The ICLEI-Local Governments for Sustainability network also brings together over 1,750 local and regional governments to work towards sustainability, and they have a deep network with Indian cities. India recently also joined the G20 Global Smart Cities Alliance on Technology Governance, which was established in 2019 and brings together fifteen leading city networks and technology governance organizations to work on smart cities (PTI, 2019a). These organizations bring together over 200,000 cities and local governments. There are numerous such networks and there will be many more. With large resources, high growth opportunities and significant challenges, cities are stepping up to deliver on SDGs and when we look back in 2030 this will not seem like a conjecture or speculation.

In India, villages have done a commendable job in terms of providing basic common infrastructure and subsistence income. Their work stops at that. India and China both have been able to lift hundreds of millions of people out of poverty since they delivered on growth, which has a direct correlation with urbanization. We would need cities in the developing world to deliver SDGs. With India taking over the mantle from China in terms of moving the highest number of people to urban areas, almost the entire set of SDGs will be at stake, not just those pertaining to urbanization. The dense clustering of Indians at such a scale when the country is taking measured steps towards doubling the economy within a decade, and the opening of new avenues of growth through Reforms 2.0 announced during the pandemic in 2020, make for a compelling case on the fate of SDGs. We have lost a handful of years of progress to Covid-19. In the scale, density and economic potential of cities, lies the prospect of meeting the global development agenda.

WINNING THE BATTLE: ENERGY, ENVIRONMENT AND CLIMATE CHANGE

In *The Sixth Extinction*, a book that won her the Pulitzer prize, Elizabeth Kolbert writes that the earth has undergone five big extinctions over the last half a billion years (Kolbert, 2015). These extinctions radically changed the biodiversity of the earth. She says we are in the middle of the sixth, caused by humans, and we may well be a casualty of it too. The last five extinctions were all due to natural causes, while the sixth extinction is completely human-made. She quotes an anthropologist as saying, 'Homo Sapiens might not only be the agent of the sixth extinction, but also risks being one of its victims', and adds a hopeful note, saying 'human ingenuity will outrun any disaster human ingenuity sets in motion' (ibid.).

The issue of how humans consume and live and prosper is exemplified in cities. Even the ingenuity of humans to outrun any danger to themselves is at its sharpest in cities. As India continues to urbanize, with hundreds of millions of people, we need to assess how that might influence the global battle against climate change. Cities influence the environment and climate change at three levels—how they consume resources, what the by-products are and how they deal with them. The misguided apprehension of the adverse role that Indian cities might play in climate change is pregnant with heavy costs. Urbanization will happen whether we like it or not. Only two questions matter—how can we urbanize more sustainably; and, are we are giving people a lifestyle in cities, which is not environmentally degradable as compared to their lives in villages.

Climate change thus sits uncomfortably at the nexus of cities, energy and the environment. In urbanizing and growing the economy, what matters the most is how energy-intensive the country's economy is. The ranking of Indian cities by pollution levels will also depend on the national and sub-national economic structure. If India continues to be part of global value-chain activities that require cheap labour and have lower value addition, the overall pollution levels emanating from Indian cities will only rise. However, if India moves towards cleaner, higher value-addition activities in the global value chain, Indian cities might be able to restrain the emission of greenhouse gases (GHGs). Even countries with greater urbanization can have lower energy consumption patterns and lower impact on the environment and climate change.

Another important factor is how cities embrace the idea of resilience and climate change. This essentially means understanding how cities are able to bounce back from a climate change related shock, how they relate to their ecosystem and what the costs of the choices—exercised by individuals, private companies and governments at all levels—are. Once this is done and risk response is accounted for, the battle against climate change will be well fought in the cities. A coalition of cities against climate change will be the key. Even small understandings and exchanges of best practices on climate change will go a long way in addressing this issue. For instance, the focus on keeping the population density low has led to distorted benefits for houses and trunk infrastructure at the periphery of cities, which encourages car use. High density in cities with appropriate infrastructure reduces car use and is better for the environment.

Edward Glaeser goes to great pains to explain in his book *Triumph of the City* that cities are our greatest invention that make us greener too (Gleaser, 2012). Only one-third of New Yorkers drive as compared to 86 per cent of other Americans, and the city relies heavily on public transport (ibid.). Clearly, all urbanization cannot be painted with one colour. It matters how we decide to urbanize. Cities have a bearing on the environment. The cognizance of this factor led to an understanding of the ecological footprint of a city, which is calculated by converting its 'resource needs and pollution into the equivalent land area that would be required to offset or produce these' (Fox and Goodfellow, 2016). For instance, London's footprint is 125 times the size of its surface area of 158,000 hectares (ibid.).

This is understandable given how cities are centres of economic activity and pack larger population in smaller areas. Depending upon how cities decide to focus on public transport, cooling systems, population density, water and sanitation practices, waste reduction and disposal, urban sprawl, and other such factors will influence how big will be their ecological footprint.

If both China and India rise to the US's per capita levels, global carbon emissions will rise by 139 per cent as against a 30 per cent rise if their emissions follow the levels achieved by France (Gleaser, 2012). How we choose to urbanize will have a far reaching and wide-arrayed impact on global energy use, environmental costs and the battle against climate change. Glaeser has a word of caution: 'If billions of Chinese and Indians insist on leafy suburbs and the large homes and cars those suburbs entail, then the world's carbon emissions will soar' (ibid.). Thus efficient urbanization, a term fast gaining currency in India, will hold the key to how Indian cities will impact global energy use and climate change.

Globally and in India, cities are focusing on being resource-efficient, carbon neutral and greener than the countries that are already urbanized. When Donald Trump withdrew from the Paris Agreement, mayors of leading cities wrote an op-ed which said that a grand alliance of 7,400 cities was taking shape that would try to uphold the targets of the Paris Agreements (Swiney and Foster, 2019). They will do their best.

So far 150 cities have declared their intent to follow up on the Global Compact on Migration and the Global Compact on Refugees. As multilateral organizations stagnate and climate summits such as Rio+20 and Kyoto turn out to be duds, the mayors are taking on the responsibility to reduce carbon emissions and deliver more environmentally-friendly cities. The C40 group, mentioned earlier, is a coalition of cities to fight the menace of climate change. It has already identified eight areas—building, energy, lighting, ports, renewables, transport, waste and water (Hollis, 2013). There are already examples of the same—Buenos Aires aims to reduce its emissions by one-third by 2030, Chicago wants to reduce them by 80 per cent by 2050 (ibid.). New York City recently announced the Climate Mobilization Act. As 71 per cent of the GHG emissions come from the city's buildings, the new laws aim to reduce GHG from buildings by 40 per cent by 2030, and 80 per cent by 2050.

Cities are filling in the gaps as they know they cannot lose this battle. They also know that they will be at the receiving end of the climate-change battle. Extreme heat waves, rising shorelines, drought and flood, pestilential air pollution, and crime against water resources are all coming to bite back Indian cities. As per the International Finance Corporation (IFC), cities in developing countries can attract as much as USD 29 trillion in climate-related investments, with a focus on six sectors—green buildings, public transport, electric vehicles, waste management, water treatment and renewable energy. Of this, the major investment will go to green buildings (USD 24.7 trillion), electric vehicles (USD 1.6 trillion), public transport (USD 1 trillion), water (USD 1 trillion), clean energy (USD 842 billion) and waste management (USD 200 billion) (Taylor, 2018).

Indian cities are already making a significant gain on reducing their energy use and carbon footprint. India's Intended Nationally Determined Commitments (INDC), submitted to the UN Framework Convention on Climate Change (UNFCCC) in 2015, hopes to reduce India's energy intensity by 33–35 per cent by 2030 as compared to the 2005 levels. As per the *Climate Transparency Report*, India is the only G20 country (a grouping of world's most economically powerful nations) that is on target to reduce the emissions intensity of its GDP by 33–35 per cent by 2030, from the 2005 level as per the Paris Agreement (Climate Transparency, 2020).

By 2030, India aims to have 450 gigawatts (GW) of renewable energy capacity (Frangoul, 2020). Its National Solar Mission has done tremendously well. There is a high possibility that India will achieve this target earlier and the government may increase targets for 2030 (Saran, 2019). Two other India-led international organizations that focus on climate change and adaptation—International Solar Alliance and Coalition for Disaster Resilient Infrastructure—are paving the way for sustainable urbanization.

India's effort to curb the carbon footprint of its industries through the Perform, Achieve & Trade Scheme has outperformed its targets. India achieved an energy saving of 8.67 million tonnes of oil equivalent (MTOE), which was 30 per cent more than the target (PIB 2018b). Likewise, India's focus on using energy-efficient LED bulbs all across the country has not only made energy consumption more efficient but has also converted India's once tottering power sector into a strategic advantage (Dhar, 2018a). By 2016, India's energy intensity declined to 0.122 kilogram oil equivalent (kgoe)/\$ from 0.158 kgoe/\$ in 2005, which is an efficiency gain of 22.8 per cent (NITI Aayog, 2018). The Ujjwala scheme to provide LPG cylinders to prevent solid biomass cooking has shown tremendous results, with 80 million connections.

India's City Gas Distribution network will make Indian cities greener. We have already launched our actions to move towards electricity-powered vehicles or EVs, and the government at all levels is focusing on public transport more than on private vehicle ownership. Indian cities are doing well on this front, at present 22 people out of a 1,000 own a car in India (Abbas, 2018). The same ratio is very high in other countries—US (980), UK (850), New Zealand (774), Australia (740), Canada (662), Japan (591), and China (164) for every 1,000 people (ibid.). If India can mainstream its public transport better and limit the growth of private vehicle ownership, it can make a huge dent in favour of climate change and energy conservation.

In 2017, buildings globally accounted for 30 per cent of final energy-use and 28 per cent of energy-related CO_2 emissions (World Resources Institute [WRI] India and MoHUA, n.d.). In India, in 2018, buildings accounted for 25 per cent of the total electricity demand. If the current scenario continues, the final energy consumption will jump by three times between 2020 and 2050, driven by demand for cooling and heating in buildings (ibid.). The Bureau of Energy Efficiency has introduced the new Energy Conservation Building Code (ECBC) for both commercial and residential buildings in 2017 and 2018, respectively. This is an ambitious code under which each ECBC-compliant commercial building will deliver minimum energy savings of 25 per cent. The buildings can get higher ratings—ECBC Plus, and Super ECBC—if they show further energy savings of 35 per cent and 50 per cent, respectively. The code for commercial buildings is expected to achieve a 50 per cent reduction in energy use by 2030, translating into 250 million tonnes of CO_2 reduction (Greentechlead, 2017). The code for residential buildings is expected to lead to an energy saving of about 100 million tonnes of CO_2 emission (PIB, 2018c).

Cities such as Pune are already taking steps to become carbon neutral. Indore has done a phenomenal job in changing the way cities worldwide could reduce their carbon footprint and, in the process, has created a template for other cities to follow. Indore is ranked as India's cleanest city for over four years straight. It has also been selected for India's smart city project. Three projects have already been registered—a bio-methanation plant, a compost plant, and a 1.5 MW solar plant—under the Verified Carbon Standard programme of the UNFCCC (Nitnaware, 2020). These projects reduce carbon emissions in Indore by over 1.7 lakh tonnes and one tonne of carbon is considered to be one carbon credit. The city was paid USD 0.05 per tonne of carbon as it sold these carbon credits. The city generated INR 5 million for itself in the process, and the amount will be ploughed back into the city's development. This is just one of the many ways in which Indian cities are dealing with their role in mitigating the impact of climate change.

With this multifaceted approach, Indian cities are avoiding the mistakes of the cities of developed countries. We are charting a resource-efficient, carbon-neutral path for our cities. In the global fight against climate change, Indian cities will prove to be the most able, honest, determined, and reliable ally.

URBAN INNOVATION: SPOILS FOR ALL

Innovation in cities is a natural outcome of the clustering of people, firms and skills. Clusters generate agglomeration effects that lead to positive externalities. Innovation is one such externality that has been the defining feature of cities and their role in the development of humankind. In the previous chapter, we saw how different cities worldwide, when they were at the top of their game, created innovations that were plugged into human civilization forever. The use of currency, democracy, trade, tax collection, guilds, water and sanitation infrastructure, printing press, use of rail and cars, lifts, and now information and communication technology—all have their origin in urban melting pot.

As Indian cities grow, they will reproduce patents and innovations at a high rate, many of which will solve some of the pressing issues of our days. English economist Alfred Marshall in his work, *The Principles of Economics,* stated that in dense concentrations, 'the mysteries of the trade become no mystery but are, as it were in the air, and children learn many of them unconsciously' (Fitjar and Rodriguez-Pose 2016). As per Edward Glaeser, the patents, skills, wages and relevant experience all increase due to concentrations (Glaeser, 2012). As Indian cities continue to become integrated with global value chains allowing for free flow of brain power and capital among countries, they are likely to fuel urban innovation at an unprecedented scale. Tel Aviv, Seattle, Austin, Silicon Valley, Beijing, Boston, London, Berlin and New York are some of the most innovative cities and what happens there in one cluster spreads across other clusters in no time. This reverberates in further innovation across these clusters. Put together, they change the nature of transactions across the globe.

London and New York are known disruptors. Let's look at the new player in town, China. It went through an extensive urbanization wave since 1980 that continues till date. One of the consequences of this urbanization was the rise of start-ups and innovation in Chinese cities. No wonder China created a Unicorn—a start-up with the value of a billion dollars—every 3.8 days in 2018 (Yang, 2019). Beijing created the 'Zhongguancun' hub thirty years ago to replicate the success of Silicon Valley, and has been able to partly achieve this goal. This area is home to 9,000 tech companies. Shanghai comes second in China in terms of start-up creation. It has been offering 'business start-up visas' to invite international talent to create start-ups (ibid.). China is also aiming to create a 'Greater Bay Area', an innovation corridor involving the cities of Hong Kong and Macau along with nine others in Guangdong province—Shenzhen, Guangzhou, Dongguan, Zhuhai, Zhonghan, Foshan, Jiangmen, Huizhou, and Zhaoqing. These cities offer various incentives on tax, visas, domestic market access, as well as world-class infrastructure, and extensive research capabilities.

Innovation has become highly localized and cities are vying to gain the lead. India has already started to rake in the benefits of innovation. It jumped twenty-nine spots in the Global Innovation Index to climb to fifty-two in 2019, up from eighty-one in 2015 (Lalwani, 2019). While reducing the regulatory risks in 2019 it ranked third in terms of attracting investment for technology transactions. Gone are the days when people used to wait for months for a telephone connection and cosy up to important people to get ahead of others. India has around half a billion active internet users, which is approximately 40 million more than the users of entire Europe put together (Gupta, 2020a).

Mobile data is available at USD 0.26/gigabyte (GB), which is the cheapest in the world. By 2023, India is expected to have 800 million active users (ibid.). With the world's third biggest start-up ecosystem, India had twenty-six start-ups valued at more than USD 1 billion in 2019 (Lalwani, 2019). As of September 2021, this number jumped to sixty-six unicorns! (*Business Today*, 2021).

The nation knows the importance of urban innovation. For the same reason, it has launched the new National Education Policy, which heavily focuses on inculcating and encouraging innovation capabilities. Lalwani adds that India already ranks eighth on the number of students graduating in science and engineering. However, he also cites employability reports and these suggest that a lot more needs to be done in ensuring that students have the right skills for innovation, tech-start-ups, and capabilities to absorb frontier technologies such as the Internet of Things, Artificial Intelligence and Machine Learning (ibid.).

While the national initiatives of Start-up India, Digital India, National Logistics Policy, attracting marquee investors, lower tax rates for start-ups and changing the definition of medium and small-scale enterprises (MSMEs) will help at the broader level, the real contest will happen at the city level. Bengaluru, Hyderabad, Delhi and Mumbai share the majority of the innovation pie. How cities develop higher educational institutes, attract talent, provide services and a high quality of liveability will define how Indian cities provide innovation to the rest of the world. India is already changing the landscape of bioscience, pharmaceuticals, the auto industry, ed-tech, telemedicine and digital payments at scale. American and Chinese investors have sensed the potential of Indian start-up ecosystem and innovation capabilities and that is the reason they are contesting to get a higher stake in India's start-ups through investments. Clearly, they foresee the Indian urban innovation ecosystem as the next frontier of innovation for the world.

3

Urban Economy: Making Cities Engines of Growth for Everyone

SINCE ancient times cities have traditionally been the main consumers of surplus agricultural produce, as the most prosperous classes live there. Trade in silk, horses, spices, textiles, even slaves, happened in cities. Even today cities remain the markets of the world and the majority of the world's produce is consumed in cities. Cities, which began as consumers, have gone on to become consumers-and-producers—a fundamental change that has remained unchanged over the last 8,000 years. In fact, if it wasn't for their ability to generate growth, cities would have no takers. All the issues that come with living in a city are bearable because the opportunities make it worth the fight.

For a city to capture global attention today, it must be liveable, sustainable, competitive, carbon-neutral, dynamic, smart, inclusive and innovative, before anything else. Above all, it needs to perform its primary function—that of generating jobs and economic growth for itself and the surrounding rural areas. Say 'city' and popular imagination *will* link it to economic growth, opportunities and better wages. Experience worldwide indicates that two factors—growth in city-based employment opportunities and the mechanization of the rural economy—attract people from rural areas in search of higher wages (Fox and Goodfellow, 2016). As the country prospers, the concentration of growth also spreads to other cities. While fine-tuning the relationship between cities and national development, it has been found that in countries like India, with sub-national variations of economic prosperity, cities are a more appropriate unit of economic analysis (ibid.).

We have seen in the first chapter that the growth of empires and nations was accompanied by urbanization. Empires—the Byzantine, the Ottoman, the Abbasid—Magadha, the Guptas, Cholas, Pandayas, Pallavas, and Cheras, the Italian-city states, the slave dynasty in north India, the Mughals, the European colonial powers, particularly the British, the American Hegemony and now the Chinese resurgence—are all characterized by their cities and growth therein. Studies have shown that there is an almost perfect correlation between urbanization and a nation's prosperity.

Prasanna Mohanty notes that as the share of the urban population increases by 10 per cent, per capita output rises by 30 per cent (Mohanty, 2019). He also highlights that per capita income is approximately four times higher in countries where the majority of the population is urban, as compared to countries with predominantly rural populations (ibid.). A study by Kala Sridhar finds that for every kilometre that a small city is away from a large city, it (the smaller city) sees the reduction of INR 1,088 in non-agricultural output per capita (Sridhar, 2011). In another paper, she reiterates that there exists a strong positive relation between urbanization and per capita income and also between national income and urbanization (Sridhar, 2016). This is now unfolding in India. India's urban centres contributed 29 per cent to national GDP in 1951, 45 per cent in 1981, 60 per cent in 2011, and were expected to breach 75 per cent by 2020 (Jebaraj, 2018). The pandemic may have temporarily hurt this prospect, but it is just a matter of when and not if.

As per the *Global Cities* report by Oxford Economics, which has been discussed in the previous chapter, the world's top ten growing cities (2019–35) are all in India (Whiting, 2019). It is no coincidence that those Indian states which have high economic growth also have a higher rate of urbanization (Bhagat, 2011). Consider this, all the southern states—along with Punjab, Haryana, Gujarat and Maharashtra—have higher urbanization levels than the national average. The state with highest urbanization rate (over 48 per cent urban) is Tamil Nadu. The least urbanized states are Himachal Pradesh (10 per cent), Bihar (11.3 per cent), Assam (14 per cent) and Odisha (16.6 per cent). States like Uttar Pradesh, Rajasthan, Madhya Pradesh, Chhattisgarh and Jharkhand also have low levels of urbanization.

Indian policymakers and citizens have come to realize the importance of cities only recently. In the past, measures taken by the Indian government to control the growth or pace of urbanization overlooked its positive impacts on economic growth. In 1977, for instance, the Central government decided to not issue industrial licences to applicants from metropolitan areas and large cities. Investment was instead channelled to government enterprises in smaller cities, rural areas and low-income areas. Other policies also focused on channelling government subsidies and assistance to smaller industries in smaller towns (Sridhar, 2016).

There are some 'experts' who still hold that rural areas should be job providers and centres of growth, so as to prevent migration to cities. As stated above, it is only recently that India has started appreciating the benefits of urbanization for national and state prosperity. At the mass level though, this understanding has still not been mainstreamed. This can be attributed to a hangover from the pre-1947 freedom movement, which focused on rural and agrarian issues. It was justified then; but not now as the global and our national economic structure has evolved. Even at present, we see intensive discussion on village issues and agricultural income, but very little on the issues that cities face and that need to be discussed.

It is pertinent to understand how the local economy plays a pivotal role in the national economy. In India, the local urban economy contributes to the national economic growth through three levers: local economic development; jobs and livelihood; and the contribution of the informal sector. Policy recommendations made later in this chapter use these attributes as a backdrop for the local economic development approach. This is defined as the process by which public, business, and non-governmental sector partners work collectively to create better conditions for economic growth and employment generation.

The aim is to improve the quality of life for all (Rodriguez-Pose and Tijmstra, 2007).

The local economic development approach differs from broader economic development strategies on three issues: 1) it uses a territorial rather than a sectoral approach; 2) the approach is more bottom-up than top-down; and, 3) it focuses on the development potential of each area (ibid.). This differentiation is important, since most confuse city-level strategies with national economic policies. There is a significant overlap, but how well (or poorly) cities function and deliver on their core capability to generate jobs defines how successful cities are. If strong growth is clustered in just one or two major cities, it doesn't bode well for a country in the long-run, nor does it reflect well on the future of its cities.

AGGLOMERATION: KEY TO URBANIZATION

Why do margin-conscious firms invest in cities, where they have to deal with high costs of land, labour and congestion? The plausible explanation is because they have far too much to gain by doing so. The link between growth and urbanization, established by the economic benefits of urbanization, points to agglomeration—the coming together of people, institutions, businesses and infrastructure in a geographical space. The tension between the benefits and costs of agglomeration determines how growth will remain concentrated. This understanding—previously used to understand why in the past firms did not move to the global South—also explains the growth of cities. Firms tend to move towards geographies that provide substantial productivity gains (cities) and achieve these gains by being at the centre of the activity (the area that is the city's business hub or even at the peripheries of cities). Urban economies gain on grounds of these agglomeration benefits.

Scholars such as Porter, Marshall, Arrow and Romer believed that 'knowledge spillover in specialized, geographically concentrated industries stimulate growth' (Glaeser et al., 1992). This refers to productivity gains when firms from the same industry are located in the same urban area. However, scholars such as Jane Jacobs believe that the best knowledge spillover occurs when different industries are located within the same city and there is economic diversification (ibid.).

To understand the benefits of agglomeration, the key is to understand types of benefits of urban economy. Prasanna Mohanty documents urban economics in detail in two books, *Cities and Public Policy*, and *Planning and Economics of Cities* (Mohanty, 2014; Mohanty, 2019). He notes that agglomeration are driven by: 1) internal economies of scale within the firm; and 2) by external economies of localization and urbanization (Mohanty, 2014). Economies of localization refer to productivity gains due to spatial concentration of firms along with firms in similar businesses. They provide the gains accrued due to learning, sharing and matching; while urbanization economies refer to productivity gains due to the spatial proximity of a diverse range of producers and service providers. They increase with the size and diversity of the urban economy. This is an externality of agglomeration (ibid.).

As per Mohanty, the size of cities can explain the type of agglomeration economies (ibid.). Small towns have scale economies for agricultural inputs and outputs. Medium-sized towns gain from localization economies of manufacturing and specialization. Larger cities leverage urbanization economies, which bring with them size, innovation and diversity. As the size of the city grows, urbanization economies tend to matter more. Mohanty's research on developed and developing countries focuses on the jump in productivity corresponding to the size of cities (ibid.).

The growth of any country depends on how it continues to increase its productivity. Cities are important because they are the key enabler of productivity gains, which, in turn, is the sole driver to catapult countries' economies.

Paul Krugman's remark is quite revealing in this aspect: 'Depressions, runaway inflation, or village war can make a country poor, but only productivity growth can make it rich' (Moretti, 2012). The presence of 'knowledge spillovers'—a new idea, product, or design, developed by an individual or a firm, spreading more rapidly in denser places—explains why certain experts or industries want to cluster only at certain places and are willing to bear the other transaction costs. India's diamond merchants want to go to Surat, software developers to Bengaluru, and financial wizards to Mumbai. Globally, the tech industry has clustered in Silicon Valley, the financial industry in New York, London and Singapore, and manufacturing in Chinese city-clusters.

Working against agglomeration are the forces of congestion, such as mega traffic snarls and poor infrastructure that bleed a city's economy because people, goods and ideas take more time to move and percolate and interactions become more expensive in terms of higher transaction costs. Forces of congestion thus blunt the synergies that emerge out of agglomeration economies. All cities that became big have dealt with such congestion forces at some point or other in their growth. They did so by investing in infrastructure development to reduce the impact of congestion, thereafter they were successfully able to transform into agglomeration economies.

Tale of Three cities, two countries: Bengaluru, Kanpur and Detroit

The changing fate of these three cities, located in two very different countries, has a lot to teach about the role of cities in development, why certain cities succeed and when they do, what the essential ingredients are.

Bengaluru: A city that most non-Indians are able to associate with India (the others are probably Mumbai, Delhi, Varanasi, Chennai and Hyderabad). Edward Glaeser's stunning economic biography *Making Sense of Bangalore*, notes that in 2010 the city was home to more than 10,000 millionaires and the per capita income of the city was twice the national average. The city is India's software capital and its rise is synonymous with India's rise (Glaeser, 2010). It is to India what Shenzhen is to China. The city also symbolizes the agglomeration effect of cities. Ask any software engineer where they would like to work and Bengaluru is sure to find a mention. The preferred choice of tech innovators in India, it offers a classic urbanization economy with a diversified base that Jane Jacob would have approved of. However, Bengalureans do complain about two things—the painful travel between

Kempegowda International Airport and the city, and traffic congestion within the city. It wouldn't be wrong to say that the flying time from Bengaluru to Delhi is about the same as driving from Kempegowda airport to Bengaluru city.

What brings people to this city, despite its congestion, the acute pressure on public services of water and sanitation, and its diminishing wealth of lakes? In 1901, Bengaluru's population was close to 160,000. From 1941 to 1971, this number quadrupled from 420,000 to 1.6 million. Glaeser attributes this rise to two factors: the city being named the capital of Karnataka; and the creation of heavy industry in the city, with the location of firms such as Hindustan Aircraft Ltd (now Hindustan Aeronautics Ltd), National Aerospace Laboratories, and Bharat Electronics (ibid.). During this time, the city was also home to a considerably strong textile industry and chemical industry.

Before Independence, Bengaluru was part of the princely state of Mysore. The state's rulers, using the wisdom of their dewans (prime ministers) such as K. Seshadri Iyer, Mokshagundam Visvesvaraya (better known as Sir MV) and Mirza Ismail, chose to invest in roads and dams, rather than spend their wealth on themselves (as many Indian rulers did). For instance, in 1902 they commissioned the building of a dam on the Kaveri River at Shivanasamudra, to provide electricity. This and other similar projects eventually led to the availability of enough power to fuel growth. In fact, Sir MV's motto was 'Industrialize or Perish', a strategy that also had a major focus on promoting education (Gleaser, 2012).

In 1948, Indian Telephone Industries was founded in Bengaluru and in 1954, the foundation of Bharat Electronics Ltd was laid. The city soon became a hub of engineers, and this bestowed on it a focus on education as well as a bubbling economy. Presciently, Jawaharlal Nehru's government planned to set up multiple universities, engineering colleges, and polytechnic schools (Hollis, 2013). By the 1980s, Infosys and Wipro were already operating out of Bengaluru. And after IBM was shunted out of the country, Wipro transitioned from a being a company that manufactured vegetable oil to becoming a software firm. Infosys was founded in 1981 and moved to Bengaluru in 1983. Today, with offices worldwide, both Wipro and Infosys employ thousands of people and are stars of India's software export industry. In 1985, Texas Instruments set up its first multinational software design centre in the city, to leverage the lower wages of the city's skilled, English-speaking workforce. Since then there has been no looking back for Bengaluru.

A simple Google search shows that the world's leading tech firms and countless tech-based start-ups are located in Bengaluru. But why do they choose to live in a city with rising wages, fractured public services and high congestion costs? The answer is agglomeration. People learn software-industry skills that give them jobs in this city, like nowhere else in India. They learn at the job and they learn from each other. This enables them to access better-paying jobs, they are ensured upward mobility. Firms locate here because they find high-powered talent within their reach, which enables them to stay globally competitive. Bengaluru's talent is the coal that feeds the ever-expanding fire of Silicon Valley. No wonder, Infosys founder Nagavara Ramarao Narayana Murthy said: 'Our assets walk out of the door each evening. We have to make sure that they come back the next morning' (Gleaser, 2010).

The story of Infosys is a microcosm of how cities create wealth for all and generate capabilities that have a ripple effect. Narayana Murthy founded the company with six others, all of whom worked at the Pune office of Patni Computers, which was an early starter on the offshoring business model. Most of the founders were educated at the prestigious Indian Institutes of Technology (IITs), and the Indian Institute of Management (IIM). Thirty years before they started their businesses, Bosch (founded in 1886), had already opened a subsidiary in Bengaluru in 1954, due to the availability of engineers. By the 1980s Bosch subsidiary MICO (Motor Industries, Co. Ltd.) had become a major client of Infosys (ibid.). In fact, it asked Infosys to shift to Bengaluru (which they did). Many Infosys employees have since left Infosys to start their own ventures. The founders created wealth for themselves and for others too, and now their former employees are following suit.

Let us now look at the growth trajectory of the other Indian city in this comparison, Kanpur.

Kanpur—in the nineteenth and early twentieth centuries—had emerged as a major cluster for textile and tannery. Mumbai (then Bombay) also hosted similar clusters. However, with passing decades, one city was able to transform into India's financial capital while the other remains a shadowy 'has-been'. Kanpur is now notorious for its poor public hygiene, poor law and order, power outages so long that they have become part of urban folklore, and extremely poor road conditions. The city is also known for its family businesses that, with little motivation to compete and innovate, took over polluting industries and struggled to deal with modern compliances. None of this helped to create the right business environment for firms to come, or to compete.

The city was known as Cawnpore before Independence. The British built a large cantonment there and also set up two mills—Elgin Mills and Muir Mills—which became the anchor for the textile industry (Sen, n.d.). Soon the city attracted the industries of leather, engineering and ordinance. The nationalization of the textile industry in 1974 seems to have triggered a downslide in the city's fortunes. The city failed to invest in upgrading the infrastructure of these now nationalized mills and to ensure that they remained competitive. Much of the revenue the city earned for itself was invested in the state's political capital—Lucknow. Seven out of the nine mills in Kanpur closed and thousands lost their jobs and moved out of the city.

In the 1980s the Rajiv Gandhi government introduced a new policy towards liberalizing. It resulted in reduced worker strength, but gave a boost to power looms and decentralized production (Mahaprashasta, 2016). As a result, the nation's textile hubs, like Mumbai and Kanpur, lost out to smaller players. By the 1990s, most of these textile units were declared sick and only two were provided support for revival (ibid.). Unlike Kanpur's entrepreneurs, those from Mumbai showed remarkable ability to pivot towards new business, such as financial services and now IT. The presence of the Reserve Bank of India (RBI), the Bombay Stock Exchange (BSE), and being the state capital with its own port, all helped Mumbai sail through the mill strike and closure of such mills in the 1980s and 1990s (Agrawal, 2017).

From its heydays as the 'Manchester of the East', Kanpur has now become the 'Detroit of the East'. Mills that once met supply needs during World War II—Lal Imli, and Juggilal Kamlapat Cotton Spinning and Weaving Mill—today operate at a fraction of these levels (Mahaprashasta, 2016). The city is still a considerable player in India's leather and footwear exports, but struggles to meet environmental compliances. Even the presence of India's first premier technology institute, IIT, built there in 1959, failed to pull up the city's growth momentum. If you replace Kanpur with Detroit, you would probably find a similar narrative.

Detroit, like other cities in the US, and most other cities in the early twentieth century, derived its value from its waterways. It was first set up as a French fort and its subsequent growth was a function of growth in waterways built by the US. As it was situated on Detroit River, it leveraged its location for the movement of goods and people (Gleaser, 2012). During the nineteenth century, Detroit's population grew exponentially and large amount of goods moved through the city. Such economic advantage attracted many entrepreneurs hoping to leverage agglomeration benefits. One of these enterprising figures was Henry Ford who produced the Ford Quadricycle in 1896, the Model N in 1906, and the Model T in 1908. He soon moved into building Model Ts using an assembly line. After he set up operations in 1899, other auto players such as American Motors, General Motors and Chrysler moved into the city. In 1917, Henry Ford started his River Rouge plant which had 7 million square feet of workspace. By 1930, the city clocked a population of 1.7 million (Hollis, 2013). As the car industry matured, the urban ecology of Detroit—initially bubbling with a variety of small firms—saw these being absorbed into large behemoths.

In the words of Edward Glaeser, 'the tragedy of Detroit is that … supersize, self-contained factories were antithetical to the urban virtues of competition and connection' (Glaeser, 2012). Rising urban wages on the back of powerful labour unions, and high crime rates, further contributed to the decline of the city which had already become a single-industry city. By 2008, Detroit had lost over 58 per cent of its population, one-third lived in poverty and the median income was half of the national average. It had one of the highest murder rates in America and in 2009, the unemployment rate was 25 per cent (ibid.).

Towards the end of the twentieth century, hundreds of thousands of low-skilled people were employed by a single industry in three major vertically integrated companies.

Competitiveness is a fickle feature with constantly shifting characteristics. What is competitive today may not be so tomorrow. This was the case with Detroit and its automobile industry. Sophisticated models from Europe and Japan (the latter also more fuel-efficient), the oil shock of the 1970s and the asymmetrical access of the US market given to the Japanese led to the eventual eroding competitiveness of Detroit's economic model. Greater reliance on one industry, lack of information exchange and entrepreneurial energy and poor innovation, all led to the decline of the city and with it the model of industrial city. This is not to say that the city cannot revive its economy. It is currently trying multiple initiatives to regain its economic momentum.

RETHINKING THE ROLE OF MIGRATION IN URBANIZATION: POLICY SOLUTIONS FOR URBAN INDIA

It is now widely accepted that in developing countries the concentration of growth in a handful of cities, rises with development and eventually falls with development. It follows an inverted U-shape, with the development trajectory on the horizontal axis and concentration on the vertical axis (Elgin and Oyvat, 2013). This largely happens to best leverage the scarce resources of infrastructure and skilled manpower, but as countries grow, they can invest in these resources and growth spreads to other cities (ibid.). The concentration largely happens at either the political capital (where the businesses can extract the best deals), or in port cities (which have been in use for centuries for waterborne trade). Mumbai and Beijing are classic examples of such cities.

Fears of over-concentration are valid for cities in those countries that display a tendency to concentrate on a few cities. Given India's three-tier governance structure (Central, state and local) the issue of the cost of locating to new cities is currently being addressed through the democratic process, as new state governments focus on creating their own urban economic powerhouses. We can expect to see competition among states in terms of attracting the maximum number of productive firms and people. Urban governance will ensure that city mayors and councillors are held accountable to provide for better ease of living, ease of operating a business, and solutions will be provided for local problems. The creation of Navi Mumbai and Delhi-NCR are a response to such democratic processes. We will see later in this section how many Indian cities are touted to become economic powerhouses in their own right.

In order to deliver inclusive growth and a decent quality of life to its citizens, India needs to sustain robust economic growth over the next two decades. This must be accompanied by massive job creation. Clearly, such a high level of sustained economic growth would essentially come from industrial and services sector growth. Also, global experience shows that such a high level of growth is achieved as an outcome of increasing urbanization, which leads to mutually reinforcing agglomeration economies, gains in productivity and innovation in cities. It is critical to manage the economic, social and environmental dimensions associated with rapid urbanization well. If this is not done, diseconomies—in the form of increased traffic congestion, water and air pollution, housing shortage, lack of clean water and sanitation, proliferation of slums and urban poverty, crimes and social unrest and other negative externalities—may adversely impact urbanization and economic growth.

Now that we understand why and how cities deliver growth, we should look at some policy solutions that can work on the ground.

As we discussed in the last chapter, India's migration will have global reverberations, while also influencing and defining Indian cities. International migration to Indian cities is a smaller issue. Who makes our cities function are our domestic migrants. This category of migrants has produced luminaries in almost every field, whether A.P.J. Abdul Kalam and Dhirubhai Ambani or Nawazuddin Siddiqui. This category also provides the urban workforce—whether a worker engaged in a daily-wage job at a factory in Noida, a domestic help in Navi Mumbai, a software engineer in Bengaluru, or a woman engaged at a construction site in Hyderabad. Domestic migrants literally run the city. It is on their blood and sweat that a city builds its skyscrapers.

Those who argue in favour of stopping migration need to understand that this is a mistake at multiple levels. First, let us realize that most of us are migrants. Someone in the family tree had migrated at some point, which is why we have a comfortable life in a city now. Second, people come to cities in search of better opportunities. They want to make a life for themselves and their families. Stopping them is nothing short of a human-rights violation, as you are preventing them from seeking a life of choice. However, those migrants who have decent jobs and businesses from the get-go, do not have to deal with the shocks that an Indian city imposes on migrants engaged in informal work, which brings us to the third point—the failure of cities to function efficiently or the presence of slums, are not a migrant's doing (that slums are not entirely bad for cities, is a separate discussion). It is the failure of cities to function as optimally as they should.

This was most clearly seen when Covid-19 struck and the government issued a diktat late in the evening of 24 March 2020—a nationwide lockdown, effective from the morning of 25 March. The economically most vulnerable groups—mostly migrants—were stranded. They did not have enough rations to last even a few days, let alone a few months. Their jobs and wages took a hit. Many did not know where the next meal would come from. Gut-wrenching images of the biggest exodus India has seen since the Partition showed how they walked hundreds of kilometres. Their home states did not have a clue on how to get them home, nor the resources to do it; the cities in which they were based and which ran on their labour, failed to respond.

The reality is that the poorest Indian migrant has always remained invisible to all—the city, its rich, upper-middle and middle classes, and the state and Central governments as well. As per one estimate, over 10 million migrants moved back home when the lockdown was imposed (Nag, 2020). They walked carrying their spouses, children and belongings with them. How could so many stakeholders have not thought about this group of 10 million, while imposing such strict restrictions?

The lockdown also unmasked a deeper problem, mentioned above—that focusing only on consumers and the affluent, Indian cities had never been prepared for migrants. Had these migrants not returned to these cities, their economies would have been adversely affected. Had cities planned for migrants, perhaps the lockdown may not have triggered the exodus. The only good to come out of it was that it awakened the state machinery and better-off citizens to the plight of migrants who worked in the informal sector in cities.

City initiatives pertaining to migrants should have a threefold focus: 1) an enabling environment which helps mainstream them; 2) increasing their human capital formation; and 3) providing them avenues for upliftment.

Migrants in India: What Does the Evidence Say?

A World Economic Forum study notes that cities thinking about migrants is the right thing to do, as it compels cities to focus on issues such as housing, education and employment, health, transport, utilities, sanitation and waste, social cohesion, and safety and security (WEF, 2017). But when cities are barely empowered to run themselves, they just keep postponing the urgent need to look after their migrants.

The WEF report, quoting a recent economic survey, points out that the interstate migration rate in India doubled during 2001–11 as compared to the previous decade, growing 4–5 per cent annually (ibid.). The annual interstate migration averaged about 5–6 million migrants a year. The key driver for internal migration in India is state-level economic inequities. India is home to a quarter of the top 100 fastest-growing cities. As per the report, there is considerable variation of in-migration in Indian cities. Proportion of in-migrants in cities such as Faridabad, Ludhiana and Surat is as high as over 55 per cent, whereas for cities such as Agra and Allahabad this ratio is less than 15 per cent.

Economist Chinmay Tumbe, in his book *India Moving*, estimates that the size of domestic Indian migrants might be close to 100 million (Tumbe, 2018). However, he highlights in another paper on 'Urbanisation, Demographic Transition' that such migration is 'mostly male-dominated, semi-permanent and remittance-based in nature' (Tumbe, 2016). It is worth discussing his paper in detail before we go on to understand what cities can do for their migrants. The paper highlights that the sex ratio (the number of females per 1000 males) is worse in urban areas, as women stay back in rural areas (while the men migrate to the city) due to cultural reasons or due lack of proper housing in the city. This has seriously dampened urbanization in India. He also outlines that the economic structure of major cities is in favour of the services sector (over 50 per cent of the urban workforce in the majority of districts is engaged in this sector), because more manufacturing units are moving to rural areas.

Another revealing observation Tumbe makes in his paper is that we are at least 10 per cent less urban than our per capita income levels indicate; another country with the same income levels would have been at least 40 per cent urbanized (ibid.). Lastly, Tumbe explains that the natural growth rate—the difference between the birth rate and death rate—has been higher in states with a lower urban population. This implies that non-urban populations are growing at a higher rate in these states. As per his research, de-urbanization is also linked to rural prosperity, including agricultural productivity and rural literacy (ibid.).

As we are failing our migrants in cities, fewer people are moving to cities, as compared to other countries. During 2001–11 a key factor driving urbanization—the net rural–urban migration—stood at 20 million people. It is reported that in China, 177 million people moved to cities in the first ten years after 2000 (Randolph and Gandhi, 2019). The same analysis quotes that the net rural–urban migration has remained stagnant since the 1970s. This gives a fair bit of idea of when Indian cities stopped being an attractive option for people living in rural areas.

Look at China—despite its stringent hukou system (compulsory registration as urban or rural resident) that prevents rural hukou holders from availing urban services—migrants totalling half the size of India's current urban population have moved to the city. About a decade ago (in 2012), the number of internal migrants in China stood at 262 million (WEF, 2017). The Chinese have accepted that the hukou model is not sustainable, since they now intend to drive growth up by increasing urbanization, fuelling domestic consumption and raising standards of living.

Solutions That Still Need Working On

Housing: The foremost issue for migrants and cities is the housing conundrum. In previous chapters, we have seen India's straight record in failing to meet the demand for housing. The issue lies with plans that only park resources for the formal economy while trying to shoo away migrants and wipe out slums, so as to maintain a misplaced picturesque notion of an ideal city. Slums are good because they indicate that migrants are thronging to cities. We still have hundreds of millions of people waiting to come to our cities in the coming decades; our slums are not going anywhere, they are here to stay. However, we should focus on providing avenues for people to escape slum life with its poor provision of urban services. This brings us to housing and planning for the informal sector.

In the wake of the migrant crisis triggered by Covid-19, the Central government announced the Affordable Rental Housing Complex (ARHC) scheme for the migrant population. Under ARHC, it engaged the private sector to retrofit, develop and operate vacant government housing as rental dormitories. After a specified period of use by migrants, these would be transferred back to urban local bodies (ULBs). Gujarat was the first state to float the proposals and Surat was the first city to provide 391 such units, which makes sense because the city is one of the fastest growing, has a large migrant population, and witnessed unrest during the Covid-19 lockdown.

Though this is too little, but hopefully, it is not too late. The ARHC is a well-placed notion but we should scale it exponentially. A few 100 rooms here and there will not help. As millions move to cities, we will need commensurate dormitory housing. Chinmay Tumbe's work shows that it would be better still if we had a higher share of such housing for women. There is enough data generated at the city level to plan for key intra-city travel networks and to build dormitories at a scale that matches the ambition we have for our cities.

One untapped resource for migrant welfare—that came to light during the Covid-19 exodus, and can be used in this direction—is a mandated requirement for construction projects, under the Building and Other Construction Workers Act, 1996, to provide a cess to states that register workers. The cess goes into a fund to meet the needs of the workers. But states have not been very good at spending this money, and the unspent funds amount to a whopping INR 31,000 crore (Roy and Manish, 2020).

In the wake of Covid-19, it is these unspent funds that the state governments have been asked to utilize for the welfare of returning migrants. Registration for such schemes and other areas of engagement of migrants should be available in all twenty-two languages listed in the Eighth Schedule of the Indian Constitution (Chandrashekhar and Naik, 2020), as migrants are often not familiar with the language of the host state, nor with Hindi or English. Language supremacy is good for politics, but not for cities and growth.

The question then arises on how to use this money. One way this money can be spent is through housing rental vouchers that can free migrants from dependence on government housing and slums, by helping them move to a location that is closer to work, provides basic services and reduces their transport expenditure. Research on migrant housing—in areas such as Udyog Vihar on the Delhi border, Industrial Model Township (IMT) Manesar (located on the border of Gurugram district), and RIICO Bhiwadi (located on the border between Rajasthan and Haryana)—has been termed 'blackboxing' by experts who have studied these areas. They note that such housing is pushed into rural areas, the infrastructure is abysmal, the residents do not receive proof of residence and have to shell out high rents (Bathla, 2020). The focus on rental housing will have to ensure that cities do not create such abysmal living conditions for migrants.

Education: While there is a separate section focusing on what can be done in the education sector to drive up the economic potential of our cities, there are migrant-specific approaches as well.

Public schools should be deployed, using evening and weekend classes to teach migrants English and the local language—this will increase their access to both work opportunities and better wages. This could become their anchor to the city and also provide upward mobility. However, experts highlight that teaching the local language in schools should not be made mandatory as that may hurt the children of the migrant population (Chandrashekhar and Naik, 2020).

Skilling programmes can be mapped to the economic cluster around which the migrants are floating. For instance, a guard in an automobile factory can be trained in skills pertaining to automotive assembly to provide him or her avenues for a better future. Women who are able to join their husbands, could enrol in such classes as well and thus be financially empowered; this would eventually reflect in fertility rates.

Food: The lack of identity is the source of a domestic migrant's various vulnerabilities, especially when it comes to getting household rations. The history of accessibility to foodgrain is useful in understanding the challenge that migrants face. In the middle of World War II, the Food Department (the precursor to the present Indian Public Distribution System or PDS) was set up in 1942 for food rationing purposes. Post-Independence, it became a tool to provide foodgrain to all. After undergoing many changes it, finally, was revamped in 1997 to target the poorest households to provide them foodgrains at affordable prices and to enhance nutrition and food security through Fair Price Shops (FPS). Despite all the good work, one of the primary concerns with the PDS was the non-portability of the Ration Card, with its unique number; this meant the migrants could only purchase rations at the location where the cards were issued, i.e., the home village/town/city/state they had just left.

The PDS system had been conceptualized when India was predominantly rural, a time when migration to urban centres was not at the centre of mainstream discussion. At present, when India is industrializing and urbanizing at a rapid pace, it is necessary to ensure that migrants are able to access foodgrain anywhere in the country and not just back home at their permanent residence. During Covid-19, food security and keeping a roof over their heads had become the two primary concerns that triggered the reverse migration.

The Central government launched the 'One Nation, One Ration Card' scheme in August of 2019 in four states, but with the onset of Covid-19, rapidly expanded its coverage to thirty-three states and union territories from March 2020 onward. The scheme has ensured nationwide portability of the ration card. Once again technology has come to our aid, in resolving the issue of data redundancy, non-portability and population pressure. The card is standardized and bilingual. Using this card, migrants can get their ration through biometric identification at any Fair Price Shop across India. Their family members can also access the remaining ration at an FPS back home.

On the back of the data generated from the One Nation, One Ration Card scheme, cities can do a lot more for migrants. Their migration patterns, month of migration (showing patterns of seasonal migration), key migration corridors, gender-disaggregated data and other such information can be accessed. Based on this data, Central, state and local governments can work together to provide social security and welfare benefits to migrants, providing them a conducive environment to stay.

Access to credit: Another vulnerability of migrants is their inability to access credit. Non-banking finance companies (NBFCs) and banks should be encouraged to provide credit to these migrants, using data from ration cards and employment data for them to be able to purchase titles for the land they are living on, even if it is a slum. Credit must be provided even if it starts at the micro-credit level. Such initiatives bode well for migrants who can use credit to venture into self-employment, upgrade housing and skills and even afford to access local transportation. In the US, for instance, the Bank of San Francisco is an initiative run by the city of San Francisco to mainstream the financial inclusion of immigrants, even the undocumented ones, into the city by helping them open low-maintenance bank accounts and teach them about financial literacy (WEF, 2017).

Healthcare: The role of civil society is important, as even the most well-meaning and resourceful cities can't reach out to all potential beneficiaries. Toronto engages civil society organizations to provide housing and employment opportunities to Syrian refugees (ibid.). There is no reason why city governments should not engage civil society to reach out to beneficiaries living in some remote slum, or working on a construction site with children in tow and limited resources, to help them understand and access the welfare benefits cut out for them. There are already some hopeful stories from around the country. For instance, Disha Foundation has engaged more than 15,000 migrants on issues of sexual and reproductive health in Nashik, and 45 per cent of these migrants are girls in the five-to-twelve-year age group (ibid.). The Foundation's community leaders refer migrants to health services and help them get timely access to healthcare.

The National Aids Control Organization has also done a phenomenal job in raising awareness around the issue of HIV/AIDS through its Red Ribbon Express (ibid.). The organization Mobile Creches in New Delhi has been providing day-care facilities for the children of migrants since 1969. As per the WEF report, they run 700 such centres, have reached out to 750,000 children and trained 7,000 women as childcare workers (ibid.). Similarly, Ajeevika Bureau has been providing an entire gamut of support services—registration and photo ID, skill training, social security and financial services, among other services, at both source (Rajasthan) and destination locations (Gujarat and Rajasthan). These efforts, though eminently laudable, are a drop in the ocean; government policies and functionaries need to pick up their game. Migrants make cities work, let's make cities work for migrants.

GLOBAL THINKING ON URBAN CLUSTERS

Clusters, as a unit of economic analysis (pioneered by Michael Porter), have become a standard and widely accepted model of economic development. Clusters are defined as 'geographic concentrations of interconnected companies, specialized suppliers, service providers, firms in related industries, and associated institutions in a particular field, which compete but also cooperate' (Fox and Goodfellow, 2016).

As per McKinsey, between 2012 and 2025, around 77 per cent of India's economic growth will come from forty clusters of districts with metropolitan cities at their centre (Kaka and Madgavkar, 2016). Some of these city clusters will outsize present-day, middle-income countries, in terms of GDP. For instance, the GDP of Ahmedabad in 2030 will be more than that of present-day Vietnam and Mumbai's GDP in 2030 will outstrip Malaysia's present-day GDP (ibid.). It is imperative that India focus on removing bottlenecks in the way of the development of these clusters and cities act as facilitators for these clusters.

As discussed in detail earlier, clusters provide economies of scale, knowledge spillover and positive externalities (Moretti, 2012). Enrico Moretti is a professor of economics at the University of California, Berkeley and has written a seminal work—*The New Geography of Jobs*—on the role of innovation, economic growth and cities. He slices

American geography between cities that are delivering growth and that are not. On clusters, Moretti says:

> Larger clusters are more efficient because they have a thicker labour market, a more specialised supply of business services and more opportunities for knowledge spillover. The effect can be amazing: while individual companies in a cluster do not necessarily become more efficient as they grow in size, all companies taken together become more efficient as the cluster grows (Ibid.).

Moretti notes that once clusters form it is difficult to remove them. This bodes well for India. However, we should look at creating new clusters that can focus on sunrise sectors. Cluster-level analysis is pertinent because it goes beyond geographic or administrative boundaries and provides benefits to all who are part of such a cluster.

A cluster is formed by market forces and is the most natural categorization. While administrative boundaries are easier for administration, they do not often bode well for growth. Porter lists down the key benefits of a cluster and notes that:

> Clusters affect competition in three broad ways: first, by increasing the productivity of companies based in the area; second, by driving the direction and pace of innovation, which underpins future productivity growth; and third, by stimulating the formation of new businesses, which expands and strengthens the cluster itself (Porter, 1998).

All of this bodes well for city economies that host these clusters. Indian cities—especially those that are on way to become or have already emerged as clusters—should establish a transparent certification system for enterprises, labour rules and employee skills. They should also create an environment to facilitate synergies between private enterprises, educational and research institutions to improve skill development and human capital investments in the cities. The cities could also work on setting up single windows for starting businesses at the cluster level.

This would require uniformity at the cluster level; perhaps the next big step after having achieved the city-level single-window clearances.

We must also keep in mind that new urban stories may emerge out of this cluster-focused economic development approach. In 1980, Shenzhen had around 30,000 people living in a group of villages, but its story changed when Deng Xiaoping launched China's first Special Economic Zone (SEZ) at Shenzhen (Sala, 2016). By 2030, China plans to create nineteen massive, planned city clusters which will contribute 90 per cent to its GDP (*The Economist*, 2018). Each cluster would be anchored by a major city-region. Out of these, three are already functioning—Pearl River Delta, adjacent to Hong Kong, the Yangzi River Delta around Shanghai, and Jingjini around Beijing. The average population size of its top five such clusters would be 110 million (ibid.).

Clusters spill beyond the geographical boundaries of cities. Successful clusters of mobile (such as Noida), auto (such as Gurugram and Chennai), and textile manufacturing (such as Tiruppur) will help Indian cities. However, as such clusters grow in India and elsewhere, they also call for caution. Economist Enrico Moretti points out that while innovation leads to a rise in productivity and lower prices, it leads to the loss of jobs for the same reason (Moretti, 2012). Therefore, it is to India's benefit to find new horizons of growth. For instance, over the last five years, India has added 200 mobile phone manufacturing units, making it the world's second-largest mobile phone manufacturer (Chaudhury, 2020). The Indian Government's recently announced Production Linked Incentive (PLI) scheme will strengthen such clusters and will create new clusters. The scheme has been extended to sectors such as Advanced Chemistry Cell (ACC) Battery, Electronic/Technology Products, Automobiles & Auto Components, Pharmaceutical drugs, Telecom & Networking Products, Textile Products: man-made fibre (MMF) segment and technical textiles, Food Products, High Efficiency Solar photovoltaic (PV) Modules, White Goods (air conditioners [ACs] & light-emitting diodes [LED] and Speciality Steel (PIB, 2020a).

This scheme is bound to create new clusters and also preserve the dominance of existing clusters. This, in turn, will create a comparative advantage for India in new sectors; comparative advantage advocates that when countries focus on areas in which they are more productive, they tend to benefit more (Moretti, 2012). The creation of new clusters and continued consolidation of existing clusters will also help India create enough jobs for people trying to leave agriculture, which is a low-paying, low-productivity engagement. All major economies have undergone this transition. One and a half centuries ago, around half of all Americans were engaged in agriculture (ibid.), but now only 1 per cent remain, the rest have been absorbed by jobs created in urban areas. How we treat our cities will have the single most important bearing on how we want to look at technology, innovation and high-tech jobs.

Metropolitan integration through large infrastructure projects is key to leveraging these clusters of growth. One of the most cited examples of this is the use of bullet trains in China. Since their introduction in 2007 in China, the country has used these trains to connect Beijing, Shanghai and Guangzhou with neighbouring cities (*The Economist*, 2013). It is a win-win for all—the labour pool remains aggregated, firms and houses are able to access affordable real estate, dwellers can choose the quality of life they want and neighbouring cities also successfully tag along with the economic growth of metropolitan areas. However, the opposite is not true! Creating massive infrastructure may not necessarily fuel demand. For India, the metro rail and metro-lite are more sustainable options than bullet trains. Sometimes, it is better when promises remain unfulfilled.

Another initiative to scale clusters is to create a platform to bring together key stakeholders of the local economy. This is a time-tested approach. Prince Henry founded Munich in 1157 and Lübeck in 1159. He emphasized city-driven prosperity and he created what Jonathan Rose calls 'Europe's first economic development zone' in Lübeck (Rose, 2016). The prince granted political and economic freedom to allow people to conduct their business freely. Twenty businessmen were elected to the city council in Lübeck and served for two years. This council also elected executives, including a mayor, and all operated under a city charter. With time, this charter, also known as Lübeck's Law, was adopted by 100 cities and eventually led to the formation of the Hanseatic League—a multi-city and national trade alliance that dominated trade in the Baltic region for centuries (ibid.). Scholars note that Lübeck's Law led to the ascension of Amsterdam and later New York (New Amsterdam), cities that achieved the acme of economic prowess and cutting-edge technology—Amsterdam in the sixteenth century and New York in the twentieth and twenty-first centuries.

India's Urban Cluster Deficit

As of now in India, the states lead the efforts in terms of attracting investments and solving sector-related issues. However, very few cities, if any, have the institutional platforms to help industries voice concerns across a range of issues. The idea is to bring together ULB representatives, trade associations, local legislators (members of parliament, and of legislative assemblies [MPs and MLAs]), and representatives from local colleges and key administrators, among others. Such platforms can help businesses voice concerns and help policymakers understand what is holding local clusters back.

The associations of flower growers in the Netherlands—the Dutch Flower Council and the Association of Dutch Flower Growers Research Groups—have created specialized auction and handling facilities that contribute significantly to the competitiveness of the Dutch Flower Cluster (Porter, 1998). Porter stresses that such associations should represent clusters and not just industries. This should be considered at the city/regional level with a cluster-level approach. We can't keep on changing the boundaries of cities, and clusters also go through changes. We should also focus on ensuring the success of economic clusters that transcend administrative boundaries. For instance, a new association—MassMEDIC—was formed by the Massachusetts medical-devices cluster. It successfully worked with US Food and Drug Administration on a range of issues, including the approval process for medical devices (ibid.).

Since smaller cities are relatively more intimate than metropolitan areas, it would be worthwhile to create such platforms that show promise in cities with manageable population size. India's National Urban Policy Framework also suggests the creation of City Economic Councils that would act as, 'a clearing house between business and governments to hasten progress of specific projects, remove bottlenecks hampering economic productivity, improve ease of doing business and catalyse investments into the city' (MoHUA, 2018a).

Moretti and Glaeser: Ripple Effect of Education on City Economies

The work of Enrico Moretti on American cities shows that cities with a higher share of college graduates tend to have a more vibrant local economy (Moretti, 2012). This is intuitive too. His work also shows that high school graduates earn more in the top performing cities than do college graduates in poor-performing cities. This ties in well, given that college graduates in top performing cities create enough jobs in the local economy. He also highlights that: 1) earnings of high school graduates increase in tandem with the share of college graduates in such cities; and, 2) workers in such cities get the benefit of higher salary increases in cities with a high share of college graduates. A person's income increases by 8 per cent if the share of graduates in the metropolitan area of the person increases by 10 per cent. People flock to cities that have a population with higher education and skills (Glaeser, 2010).

Essentially, the mere presence of skilled workers can have a cascading impact on city economies. The presence of skilled workers helps others in three ways according to Enrico Moretti: 1) complementary; 2) adoption of technologies; and 3) human capital externalities. The policy implication of this is that we should subsidize quality education (Moretti, 2012). If the rhetoric on subsidized education in India in recent times translates into withdrawal of such support, it will subvert our potential in the long run. As more people—and so much the better if they come from disadvantaged backgrounds—can receive higher education, it will help the unskilled workers around them, their own career trajectory, society and the city's economy. Besides, Moretti's research proposes that the presence of a university can be associated with a better educated workforce and higher wages. His work focuses on the role of higher education and its benefits.

His research quotes studies by other researchers in terms of the inflation-adjusted annual return of college education. College education offers returns of 15 per cent, followed by stocks (7 per cent) and bonds, gold, and real estate (3 per cent). Though, he makes a strong point that the presence of universities is an essential but not a sufficient condition to forming a cluster. This is seen in the case of Kanpur, which has an

IIT. Across India, we have 993 universities and close to 40,000 colleges which are attended by 37.3 million students (AISHE, n.d.).

Enrico Moretti's work also explains the importance of a city's ability to attract academic stars in starting and anchoring a cluster, especially the case of high-technology sectors—researchers in private companies should be closer to frontier academic research, and many of these star researchers also anchor the setting up of companies (Moretti, 2012). This can be seen be seen in the case of one of the world's most renowned clusters, Silicon Valley.

Edward Glaeser cites a telling story about the impact of Stanford University on Silicon Valley and beyond (Glaeser, 2012). The university was set up in an 8,000 acre horse-farm by Senator Leland Stanford, who had earned his fortune in the railroad business. The son of the senator's head coachman, Francis McCarty, died at an unripe age but not before devising a 'spark telephone' that could send voice seven miles over water. McCarty's backers looked for new talent and eventually spotted Cyrill Elwell who was also studying at Stanford. With some travel and financial backing, he used the Paulsen Transmitter to set up Federal Telegraph Corporation (FTC), termed as the pioneer firm of Silicon Valley's radio industry and set forth a chain of events that bear fruits to date.

One of FTC's employees, Fredrick Terman—whose father also worked at Stanford as he did later in his life—decided to set up an industrial park near Stanford. He attracted talents such as David Packard and William Hewlett, apart from tenants such as Lockheed, General Electric, Westinghouse and Shockley Semiconductor Laboratory. Shockley Laboratory was founded by William Shockley who, along with two others, won the Nobel Prize in physics for inventing transistors in 1956. William Shockley's father also taught at Stanford and he had worked at the Bell Labs in the past. He brought bright people to work with him but due to his fickle behaviour, eight of them left. They, with support from Sherman Fairchild, founded Fairchild Semiconductor which patented the first integrated circuit. They would eventually move out from this company as well. Two of them founded Intel and another created the Venture Capital Kleiner Perkins, which would eventually bankroll many innovators in the Silicon Valley.

Hewlett and Packard founded their own company and two of their former employees set up Apple. An Apple employee would later go on to create eBay in the 1990s. Even Google and Yahoo were founded by Stanford graduates at locations close to their university. Gleaser concludes, that like major successful cities of our times, Silicon Valley was built on high-skill human capital, 'nurtured by Stanford University and attracted by economic opportunity and a pleasant climate' (ibid.). It is only a matter of time before some of India's institutes produce such a legacy of entrepreneurs, mushrooming from a single education institute. The IIMs, IITs and the Indian School of Business (ISB) Mohali, are producing entrepreneurs at lightning speed. Such a story is in the making in India.

Further, research and development (R&D) investments by private companies have led to important benefits for not only the company but also the industry (Moretti, 2012). Enrico Moretti suggests that the government support for R&D should be higher as the knowledge spillover and consequent productivity increase have benefits for the local economy. Cities with universities in the vicinity which are engaged in R&D will benefit from the mere presence of it. This is already the case in some Indian cities.

As per a study, the alumni of the top four engineering colleges in India have produced over 1,066 start-ups, whereas these institutes produced 914 start-ups from 2000 to 2015 (Dalal, 2019). IIT Bombay alumni created the largest number of start-ups, but the most successful ones came from IIT-Delhi. Some of the known businesses that came out of these start-ups are: Grofers (now BlinkIt), Udaan, Zomato, Flipkart, Delhivery, Ola, InMobi, Snapdeal and Shopclues, among others. They are net job creators and have triggered a chain of events that will continue to fuel the start-up and innovation space in Indian cities. Thus, India should continue to focus on higher education with strict quality control. It should tap R&D capabilities as there are significant firm-level and social benefits of such R&D activities.

As per the cluster development approach, it is pertinent that the workforce, academic institutions and industries are in close proximity to each other. We have already discussed how they provide agglomeration benefits. They not only boost innovation but also usher in the best global and local talent, create more employment, provide an exchange of ideas and skills and even increase income levels. This is contrary to how Indian universities have been set up post independence and how they continue with the same model. India's leading institutes such as IITs Kanpur and Kharagpur, IIM Lucknow, even ISB Mohali are outside the periphery of main cities. Thus, they fail to generate value from each other and for each other.

I remember when I gained admission to Shaheed Sukhdev College of Business Studies, University of Delhi—one of Asia's premier undergraduate business schools—I found it extremely confusing as to why it was located in a part of Delhi surrounded by slums and unauthorized colonies. The dust of unchecked construction mixed with the stench of animals squatting on the road. Even the ride from the Metro was painful as one got down at Shahdara and then had to bear with the painful fifteen-minute rickshaw ride that took one through an area that was a toxic mix of urban village and slum. Folklore peddled on the campus was that the first principal wanted the school away from all distractions so that students could study in peace. Well, he was proven a little too right; even recruiters, or teachers from other centres for skills and training refrained from coming to our campus though they went to other colleges in Delhi University.

Many contemporary cities are fuelled by the presence of universities. Sanjeev Sanyal highlights the example of Singapore—wherein the foreign campuses of universities coupled with Nanyang Technological University (NTU), National University of Singapore (NUS) and Singapore Management University (SMU) have played a crucial role in helping the country transition to a knowledge economy. New York University (NYU) too played a similar role in the 1990s, regenerating Lower Manhattan.

India's National Urban Policy Framework also makes the case for hosting institutes of higher education within city parameters. Sanyal lays down the reasons to avoid creating universities with industrial factory-like infrastructure, closed walls and at a distance from city limits. His concerns are to the point: he highlights that this leads to conversion of farm and forestland, and the creation of expensive infrastructure. He also expresses concern that the selection of such remote locations do not take into account the personal and professional life of the families of the faculty and staff, and do not lead to knowledge spillover from academic and research work (Sanyal, 2018).

India has recently opened its cities to international universities. This bodes well for Indian cities. Though we have a lot of space to increase our domestic productivity, the incoming skilled and entrepreneurial global workforce to India will further push up productivity gains, which, in turn, will help city and national economies. Subsidized education for women and R&D will bode well for individuals, businesses and cities. Cities should focus on new frontiers of growth when it comes to education. For instance, medical tourism is a high-performing sector for Delhi-NCR and it will benefit from investing in making the sector further competitive. Surat is already investing in gems and jewellery related education and skills. Bengaluru continues to add jobs and create unicorns as an array of quality higher education institutes are consistently providing the firepower for skilled talent. Similarly in Chennai, the investment in education has resulted in rise of multiple clusters of medical tourism, automobile and software services. The spending in science and social sciences need not be a trade-off.

The infrastructure of cities and their round-the-clock activity have huge untapped potential. Evening and weekend schools to improve adult literacy and will have many takers, as Indians appreciate the value of good education. Consider this: America's ability to make high school education universal in the twentieth century (way before any European country), played a critical role in its becoming a world power. Moretti cites Goldin and Katz's (2008) reference to the twentieth century as the 'human capital century' (Moretti, 2012). During this time, the average American was way more productive than any other worker elsewhere. The dominance of the US in the twentieth century has a lot to do with the average school education of its workers.

This has two lessons for India. First, India needs to focus on the learning outcomes of its students and make them more productive. We have already achieved the accessibility issue of school education through the Right to Education and now we have rightly zeroed on the issue of improving learning outcomes. Second, India can do little to attract international migrants, but it must ensure it doesn't lose its own highly skilled labour that will drive its local economy. An improvement in the literacy and learning outcomes of the informal sector and vulnerable sections of society will also have a promising impact on the fortunes of cities.

THE GREAT INFORMAL SECTOR: INDIAN PARALLELS AND SOLUTIONS

Informal urban employment is defined as 'informal wage employment and self-employment in informal enterprises, as well as informal wage employment in formal enterprises and households' (Chen and Raveendran, 2014). Elgin and Oyvat have established an inverted-U relationship between informality and urbanization levels, indicating that the informal sector's share grows as urbanization increases in a country and declines once the urbanization level reaches advanced stages (Elgin and Oyvat, 2013).

Clearly, the Indian urban story is following this inverted U-relationship trajectory. Chen and Raveendran highlight that the Indian informal sector is growing fast instead of getting formalized (Chen and Raveendran, 2014). Their paper on 'Urban Employment in India: Recent Trends and Patterns' shows that in 2011–12, of the total urban workforce in India, only 18.4 per cent worked in the formal sector on a salary, 39 per cent were wage workers in the informal sector (of whom 38 per cent worked in formal offices and factories), while a larger share (42 per cent) operated as an informal self-employed workforce (with 53 per cent working at home or in open public spaces). The paper highlights the growing importance of domestic workers, home-based workers, street vendors, and waste-pickers in the urban informal economy, who constitute three out of every ten urban informal workers (ibid.).

That India's informal sector does not stand in competition to the formal sector, but plays a complementary role, can be seen from the fact that the role of contract workers in many industries has been on the rise (Chandrasekhar and Ghosh, 2018). The hiring of informal workers in the public sector has also been on the rise. The share of contract workers in the registered manufacturing sub-sectors has risen to over 30 per cent in 2009–10, from 15 per cent in 1998–99 (ibid.).

The informal sector constitutes a significant share of non-agricultural gross value added (GVA). Scholars from the Centre for Policy Research highlight that working in unorganized sectors leads informal workers to be self-employed without social welfare benefits, be part of unregistered establishments and also be part of establishments that are located in areas where the industry is not allowed (Mukhopadyay and Kunduri, 2019). They highlight a high degree of economic exchange between planned and unplanned industrial areas and also a fair share of 'labour circulation' (ibid.).

As the pace of India's urbanization increases, policy-level solutions must be found for the informal sector. We should provide more opportunities for the sector, in addition to our work on formalizing the Indian economy. City clusters should map the informal sectors, and their respective skills, operating in and around the city. This exercise aims to create a comprehensive directory of skills and training. Such mapping will also help in creating a roster of city activities. It would be enormously helpful if cities could create a roster of year-round activities, which should dovetail with regional and national tourism calendars, linked with surrounding tourism circuits, and focus on the informal sector in the region. Creating such a roster will attract local talent, provide informal workers multiple avenues of income generation during the year and create a legacy of such events over the years. Such a move will help in reinvigorating the contribution of creative arts—which sends a high share of people to the informal workforce.

India's Street Vendors

This group of informal workers has taken a huge beating in the aftermath of Covid-19. While the Central government is providing them a one-time working capital loan of up to INR 10,000, it is now time to take a long-term approach to their role in cities. Defined as, 'Anyone without a permanent shop is a street vendor', Indian cities have close to 5–6 million of them and they constitute 14 per cent of the total non-farm urban workforce (Divya, 2020). Close to 1.2 million households are dependent on street-vending (ibid.). The government passed The Street Vendors (Protection of Livelihood and Regulation of Street Vending)

Act, 2014, but this has done little to improve the state of affairs. Its idea was noble to create Town Vending Committees in districts that could identify such vendors and accommodate them in designated vending zones (ibid.). This legislation has had limited success.

Street vendors are an important part of Indian urban life—they are 'eyes on the roads' to increase safety, they maintain the vibrancy of day-to-day urban life, they reduce the consumer's commute for small transactions and they provide an avenue for migrants to enter the city's informal workforce. However, the problems they face are humongous—less-than-minimum-wage earnings, harassment by local authorities and the police, social stigma associated with their work and high susceptibility to income shocks (as in the case of Covid-19) (ibid.). Given India's population, the number of street vendors is not going to decrease. There have to be solutions to their problems.

Of the estimated 6 million street vendors, close to 3 million have already reached out to the Central government for loans under a special micro-credit facility for street vendors, called 'PM Street Vendors AtmaNirbhar Nidhi' or SVANidhi for short (pmsvanidhi.mohua.gov.in). This database should be used to match them with other social welfare schemes and increase sensitization of their entitlements. Second, the sanctioned limit for licences to be issued to them should be increased to match the actual number of street vendors in the city—Mumbai has 15,000 licences as against 0.25 million street vendors (ibid.).

A one-time mandate for smart cities throughout India to provide licences, can help street vendors find a legitimate and visible place in city life. The diversification of growth centres should alleviate cities' concerns about the proliferation of street vendors. Third, the plans need to provide places for street vendors—such as food trucks in the US or hawker centres in Singapore. The hawker centres of Singapore boast a Michelin Star rated restaurant, provide affordable meals and are highly vibrant places for social exchange. You see the most elderly enjoying drinks and Singapore's famous street food in such centres. Early morning and lunch queues include the rich and the middle class. A place for street vendors in Indian cities is the least we can do.

Besides, the informal sector will gain from public investments to create more efficient urban-rural links. Owing to a large number of factors, non-agricultural informal sector workers either reside on the periphery of cities or in the nearby rural areas. It is suggested that cities focus on public investment to create efficient linkages between rural and urban areas. This will not only reduce transaction costs for the informal sector, increase their income and prevent unsustainable migration, but will also create much needed jobs.

Female Workforce in the Urban Economy

Apart from focusing on the informal sector at the broader level, it would be useful for economic growth to boost the female workforce participation rate (FWPR). It is believed that along with the high urbanization rate, the increase in FWPR was one of the key drivers of the East Asian economic 'miracle'. However, presently in India, the urban FWPR remains low. In 1993–94, the FWPR for rural and urban areas was 33 per cent and 16.5 per cent, respectively (Jha, 2021a). In the last Periodic Labour Force Survey (PLFS) prior to the pandemic, for 2018–19, the FWPR was 19.7 per cent for rural areas and 16.1 per cent in urban areas. The LFPR for men for the same year was 55.1 per cent for rural areas and 56.7 per cent in urban areas (MoSPI, 2020). The work on WFPR in the urban areas will have to focus on the women, especially in the informal sector. This is because the biggest employer for urban women as per PLFS 2018-19 were manufacturing, (24.5 per cent), trade, hotel and restaurant (13.8 per cent), and other services (45.5 per cent) (Ibid.).

As per the International Labour Organization (ILO), India ranks 120 among 131 countries in terms of FWPR (Venkatesh, 2017). Some of the obvious reasons for women dropping off the workforce include: the lack of safe and quality public transport accessibility; support to companies to set up crèches and other childcare infrastructure; transport expenditure support for working women; and increased investment in female-only dormitories and hostels, among others. Besides, city governments can undertake bolder yet proven successful initiatives such as launching on-the-job training for females and job-matching services (ADB, 2015). Scholars from the Centre for Policy Research provide a nuanced view on the FWPR in the informal sector (Mukhopadyay and Kunduri, 2019). They highlight that women prefer to work in unplanned industries closer to the urban periphery or an urban village, as working closer to home provides them the flexibility to attend to their children during breaks. Mukhopadyay and Kunduri stress that unplanned and planned agglomerations in industrial areas create home-based work opportunities for women that span a whole range of activities. The important policy imperative is that instead of pushing such unplanned industrial areas to outside cities, thereby crushing FWPR, we should regularize such industrial areas and ensure that they conform to regulations on environment, safety and labour (ibid.).

LEVERAGE CITIES FOR WHAT THEY DELIVER BEST: INNOVATION

Enrico Moretti notes that the local economy jobs 'are the effect, not the cause of economic growth' (Moretti, 2012). While India remains at the periphery of manufacturing-led growth—and has had limited success in replicating the success of East Asian economies and China, to boost manufacturing to spur growth—the country's growth has largely bypassed traditional manufacturing-led growth to use services to drive growth. This is the age of using information technology as a tool for innovation, which accounts for the major productivity growth and competitiveness of local firms.

The next enabler of growth is innovation and, as argued previously, the cities are the fountainhead of innovation. As India climbs the innovation ladder in the world, it needs to address city-level issues. Moretti argues that getting good jobs (jobs that are highly skilled) with high salaries, trigger a multiplier effect that generates enough local jobs (ibid.). He categorically mentions that as per his research, using data on 11 million American workers in 320 metropolitan areas, for every high-tech job, there are five new jobs created outside the sector—these include skilled jobs (doctors, lawyers, health workers) and also semi or unskilled jobs (drivers, household help, nurses.) (Ibid). Moretti notes that innovation has the largest multiplier effect, which is three times that of the manufacturing sector (ibid.).

Economic growth is driven by innovation, which is, in turn, a function of cities. As per some research, patent citations are geographically concentrated (Gleaser, 2012). There is also evidence that the productivity of firms is higher when they are closer to the centre of inventive activity pertaining to their industry (ibid.). The agglomeration effect and clustering of people and firms is what drives innovation.

Worldwide, there are new indexes that track innovation at the city level. The Creative Class Index focuses on cities in the US and Canada, whereas the Innovative City Index (by the Melbourne-based data analytics company 2thinknow) assesses 445 cities as per their potential for innovation economy (Fan, 2018). As per 2014 rankings for China and India, Shanghai was one of the nine 1-tier innovative cities called the 'nexus'; three Chinese cities—Beijing, Shenzhen and Nanjing—along with Mumbai, were 2-tier cities called 'hubs'; and eleven Chinese cities (Suzhou, Chengdu, Guangzhou, Hangzhou, Changchun, Tianjin, Dalian, Dongguan, Xi'an, Xiamen, and Wuhan) and four Indian cities (Bengaluru, Delhi, Chennai and Pune), were termed 3-tier innovative cities, called 'nodes'. Bengaluru remains India's most innovative city with 8,557 US patents during 1970–2015, followed by Delhi, Pune, Hyderabad, Mumbai, Chennai, and Kolkata (ibid.).

It is pertinent to see that agglomeration fuels innovation and sustained growth momentum is driven by innovation. This makes the innovation economy of cities very important for national growth and even strategic positioning. Indian policymakers need to consider this value addition by our cities in allocating resources. Can we allow Bengaluru, India's most innovative city, to bleed with the thousand cuts of congestion, infrastructure deficits, poor governances, and other countless issues? Many of the policies suggested in this section and in the book will act as enablers of innovation in Indian cities. However, city administration and state-level policymakers must be aware of the innovation potential of their cities. This should be an important factor while they make policies for such cities.

SMALLER CITIES FOR GREATER STRIDES

By 2025, 56 per cent of the world's urban population will live in cities with a population of less than a million. Thus, the small and medium cities of Asia and Africa will be absorbing the incoming deluge of urbanizing population from rural areas (Fox and Goodfellow, 2016).

This population inflow will happen as people leave rural areas for jobs and better wages and are attracted to nearby smaller cities. We have already seen how 400+ Class I cities (population with more than 100,000) other than metropolitan areas, act as magnets for migrant influx in India. Clearly, we need to focus on fostering economic activity in smaller cities to not only decongest over-concentration of economic growth in few cities, but to create many more growth centres as the US did in the twentieth century. Vibrant economic activity will ensure that migrants have enough city options to choose from, so that the key metropolitan areas do not suffer a sudden population surge just because other cities could not provide opportunities.

As we have studied earlier, concentration benefits are a critical gain of urbanization. Yet, at a reasonable stage of development, national policies should aim at decongesting cities (but not with the use of force). Given the infrastructure deficits, lack of affordable housing and high costs of living and transportation, the rural-urban migration towards smaller cities is witnessing acceleration. As per research, around half of the industries are moving towards rural areas and the unorganized sector is fast becoming urbanized (Ghani et al., 2012; Naik, 2019). These rural areas will soon be urban areas and would require investments of all kinds. Moreover, these cities also require lesser financing to provide adequate urban infrastructure and services as compared to retrofitting infrastructure in larger cities. There is merit in indulging the thought of increasing the share of the economic contribution of smaller cities without losing sight of the malaise that plagues metropolitan cities. This is already happening in various Indian states, wherein Tier 2 and 3 cities are emerging as hubs for IT services such as mobile application development, website designing and web development.

Some of these cities include Hubballi, Mangaluru and Belgaum (Karnataka), Coimbatore (Tamil Nadu), Bhubaneshwar (Odisha) and cities in Tripura (TNIE, 2018). One-third of the fastest growing cities are smaller cities with a population of less than 100,0000 (Naik et al., 2019). Partha Mukhopadhyay and Mukta Naik, who are scholars studying urban India, note that 'half of India's rural-urban migration is to smaller cities, and half its manufacturing located in areas classified as rural, which also produce over a third of non-farm output' (Mukhopadhyay and Naik, 2018). They make a compelling case that while metropolises remain fraught with crisis after crisis, it is of consequence to channelize our focus on smaller cities as well. They make the point through Kishangarh, a city of 150,000 people in Rajasthan. It was a market for marble quarries but has now emerged as a marble and granite market, with supporting infrastructure built or planned to be built, including an airport, a nearby dedicated freight corridor and a logistics park.

While such moves are important, it is pertinent that we understand how such vibrancy of economic activities in smaller cities can change the fortune of the local and regional economy. With Covid-19, many start-ups have moved their base to smaller cities to contain their operating costs at a time when demand is jittery and risks remain high. Even before Covid-19, the rise of tech start-ups boded well for India in the sense of how it would percolate to multiple cities, rather than being concentrated in a handful of cities.

Moretti's book *The New Geography of Jobs* explains how Seattle was very similar to Albuquerque on a range of economic, social and infrastructure indicators; however, when Microsoft moved to Seattle in 1979 from Albuquerque it triggered a chain reaction that made Seattle into a high-tech cluster (Moretti, 2012). Eventually, other Big Tech companies gravitated towards the local cluster created and anchored by Microsoft. Besides, he notes that 4,000 new companies have been started by former Microsoft employees. This is in addition to the estimated 200,000 jobs created for the services and skilled sectors. He calls this phenomenon *'multiple equilibria'*, where high-performing clusters continue to strengthen further as highly-skilled people cluster there and not so attractive cities continue to lose (ibid.). Likewise, India needs its cities to compete to get such vibrancy. We do not want smaller cities to lose out. We do want them to step up their game. This shift should not come through mandate or regulation but enabled through the right interventions. The companies will be able to pick the signals and the city will evolve to attract and ensure their stay.

To make a sustainable plan to leverage these smaller cities, it is advised that we start with identifying cities and regions with high growth potential and mapping their core sectoral competencies. The states can then work around this identification to provide appropriate infrastructure and an enabling business environment. For example, in Telangana, the state has partnered with Tech Mahindra and Cyient to open new centres in the Tier II city of Warangal. The state also plans to encourage more industries in Tier-II cities of Karimnagar, Khammam, Nizamabad and Mahbubnagar (Mukhopadhyay and Naik, 2018). Though, this is a good move and helps solve the problem of congestion in bigger cities, there are some essential ingredients needed before such endeavours become a success.

According to a paper by the National Bureau of Economic Research (NBER) in the US, which studied the concentration of skills and wages in cities of three countries (Brazil, China and India), the top paying jobs and skills are concentrated in bigger cities (Kwatra, 2019). This is instructive for emerging countries. While it may not be surprising, it tells us that there is a window of opportunity in terms of what can improve the economy of smaller cities.

Many believe that education centres should be created in areas where the industry is already present, but that is a self-fulfilling path that favours big cities. The creation of quality universities and colleges within smaller cities can have tremendous positive externalities. These cities can be picked by shortlisting through a variety of filters such as growth in wages and population, changing spatial patterns, proximity to major infrastructure projects, and entry of any new marquee investor. The idea is to invest in cities that are already showing some promise. India currently does not have the fiscal space wherein it can create universities to revive/jump-start the economy of an inert city. That may happen in a couple of decades but not now.

INDIAN CITIES AS INVESTMENT DESTINATIONS

The following is an excerpt from an article the author co-authored in 2018, on the subject:

> It is interesting to note that cities around the world have now started coming forward to promote themselves as a destination for skilled labour, investments and trade. Various cities have set

up dedicated investment promotion arms that actively engage with potential investors, businesses and skilled personnel from around the world. Examples of such promotion agencies include Hamburg Invest, London and Partners, Invest in Cardiff and Invest in Manchester, among many others. Some of these agencies have representatives in various regions and cities around the world. Apart from promotional efforts, these agencies and their representative offices serve as a local point of contact for existing and prospective investors and businesses, sometimes hand-holding them as they plan their strategy for engaging in the city.

Against this backdrop, it is imperative to see how India attracts investment—do states take precedence, or do cities matter when it comes to attracting investment. Invest India, the national investment promotional body, is structured by states and sectors. At the state level, the large-scale, summit-style model of attracting investments was mastered by the then chief minister of Gujarat, Narendra Modi. The event 'Vibrant Gujarat' had sort of become an annual ritual watched by the entire India. The big Indian business houses and global corporations, year after year, pledged billions of dollars' worth of investment. After the wide acceptance of successive editions of Vibrant Gujarat, now, at least half a dozen states hold similar summits—Resurgent Rajasthan, Bengal Global Business Summit, Invest Karnataka, Happening Haryana, Progressive Punjab, Magnetic Maharashtra and UP Investors Summit. Besides the high political dividends that these events yield, there is little evidence of how much actual investment has been received as a follow-up. This leaves us to the question of why there is no single city in India—including Mumbai, Delhi and Bengaluru—that has undertaken an initiative to attract global capital.

The answer is twofold. First, present urban governance in India is a hodgepodge of administrative overlap among mayors, development authorities and parastatal agencies. Very few cities have directly elected mayors with a stable tenure, a clear mandate and sufficient power to undertake initiatives focusing on cities. Second, the non-fulfilment of promises of the 74th Constitutional Amendment Act (CAA) is a key obstacle. The 74th CAA provided for further decentralization in city governance by providing constitutional status to urban local bodies and mandating devolution of 18 critical functions as defined in Schedule 12. However, the reality is that states have not fully, or even significantly, devolved these functions to the cities. Indian states, and not Indian cities, are in control of land, labour, power, water supply and infrastructure-related issues. All these are critical requirements for cities to attract long-term investment. In the absence of control over such issues, cities continue to remain introverted when it comes to reaching out to the world.

We must recognize that India is a complex and vast country. Investors, both domestic and foreign, could be overwhelmed by the sheer scale and size of India. Investment promotion by cities could be a great way to help them focus their efforts and give them confidence about the ease of doing business given the support of the local administration. With the global audience looking upon India as the beacon of future growth, it would be opportune for states to unshackle their cities so that they can step up and reach out to these investors and businesses proactively (Dhar and Kapoor, 2018).

DISCOVERING INDIA, EXPLORING HERITAGE AND GROWING THROUGH TOURISM

Tourism is a low-hanging fruit for any city, gaining revenue from both domestic and international tourists. Tourism is best measured not only by the number of tourist arrivals, but also by the length of their stay which is a key determinant for tourism growth. India is a destination that offers sites of early civilizations and urban centres from 3000 BCE, to new thriving urban centres. It thus has a huge potential for city-level growth. The best aspect of tourism is that it generates local jobs and preserves history for future generations.

As of now, India has thirty-seven world heritage monuments as recognized by UNESCO (Kirpal, 2019). The Archaeological Survey of

India (ASI) has under its protection around 3,650 sites, however the number of unprotected sites is not fully known and could be in the range of 35,000 to 700,000. In Delhi alone, we have 1,000 such sites. Sites forever lost are termed as 'missing'—one cannot be sure of the number of missing monuments lost due to encroachments and modern-day development projects.

However, it is time for us to make a move to change this poor state of India's heritage to not only rediscover India but also make economic gains in the process. The India Lost and Found Foundation has started a project to create a heritage map of India (ibid). It has involved a range of volunteers to map these unlisted sites, click their pictures, upload them on Google Maps and make them accessible for everyone. This project has also involved known experts such as William Dalrymple, Laila Tyabji and others. The Government of India also launched a scheme called HRIDAY (National Heritage City Development and Augmentation Yojana) for twelve Indian cities—Ajmer, Amaravati, Amritsar, Badami, Dwarka, Gaya, Kancheepuram, Mathura, Puri, Varanasi, Velankanni and Warangal. While the projects are at different stages of development, India needs to focus on creating a pan-India approach for city-focused tourism. There will be significant gains in converging projects of India Lost and Found Foundation, HRIDAY, and the city infrastructure schemes. Think about the history of India, hundreds of wars, hundreds of languages and dialects, dozens of cuisines, different forms of architecture, dance, textiles, mythology and folklore. If all this is mapped well at the city level, we can generate growth and job creation on a large scale.

One example of this is the city of Hiroshima in Japan. Hiroshima was bombed at 8:15 a.m. on 6 August 1945. The 16-kilotonne bomb called 'Little Boy' killed over 140,000 people (McCurry, 2016). Within seconds, the heatwave reached 3,000-4,000 centigrade and 90 per cent of Hiroshima's 76,000 buildings were partially or completely destroyed. Today, the city's Peace Memorial Museum has extensive remains of that tragic day, from human remains to clothes, from tattered buildings to stones with shadows cast as an impact of the bomb blast. I had an opportunity to visit Hiroshima and hear centenarian Keiko Ogura recount the affairs of that day—she was a first-hand witness to that horror. In restoring the remains and telling the story through human and non-human cues, Hiroshima has translated a tragic episode in its history to a living tale which not only sustains the tourism economy but also falls within the broader national narrative.

Likewise, in the centre of Washington DC, you get to see the Holocaust Memorial Museum. Upon entering the Museum, you are given a card with the actual name of a Jewish person imprisoned by Nazis. Spread over two floors, you walk through the entire narrative—how the Nazis started the Fascist regime, started chipping away parts of Europe and started World War II. You get to see the wagons in which the Jews were transported, how they were treated, how they ate and what they wore. There are two moving sights: a container filled with countless shoes of Jews and one with a huge amount of human hair. The Nazis used them to earn some profits on the side. Audio-visuals and a small model (similar to the shows on the bombing of Hiroshima) explain what depravity occurred in Auschwitz. When you come out of the tour, you get to know whether the person whose name was on the card given to you, survived or not. It is extremely tragic but a moving and humbling experience.

Washington DC Mall offers a tour in which you get to see the Lincoln Memorial, Washington Monument, National Air and Space Museum, National Museum of Natural History, Vietnam Veterans Memorial, Martin Luther King Memorial, Korean War Veterans Memorial and the Franklin Delano Roosevelt Memorial, among others. The Vietnam, Korean War, and Lincoln Memorials are pregnant with symbolism and closure for the national and international audience. This tour and these museums generate large tourism revenue and footfalls, while projecting power to the world.

India could do well by replicating such exemplars. Hundreds of historical wars, mutinies, countless religious sites, success in various sports, wide-ranging geography, and incidences of violence are scattered around India. If capitalized well, this could very well be a tool of strategic posturing for India and also provide closure to Indians. But we lack the creativity and guts to go about it. Look at Amritsar. While the Golden Temple is a humbling sight and very well maintained, we have done a shoddy job of maintaining the site of the Jallianwala Bagh tragedy.

Likewise, we have not done a good job of telling the stories of Tibetans in Dharamsala.

We are focusing on the policy side of tourism—visas, budget, marketing, and so on. City-level tourism will not kick off if we do not create such experiences at the city level. We have not done a great job with the Police Memorial. There are various experiences that we could create for local and international audiences—the Gandhi Circuit—taking people to places where Gandhi spent key moments of the national struggle. Lucknow should have a museum on the 1857 Mutiny. We must provide closure to victims of the anti-Sikh riots, the Godhra riots and to the Kashmiri Pandits by creating places of communal harmony. We can provide a tour of the Mughal footprint across India. We could turn around the British oppression by highlighting the sites of colonial control and violence. We can provide experience of Sikhism by telling the stories of all Sikh Gurus. The opportunities are limitless.

UNESCO has launched a network of creative cities which throbbing with cultural activities in countries worldwide. The UNESCO Creative Cities Network (UCCN) presently has 246 cities (PIB, 2019a). The idea behind this network is to mainstream the creative economy. The seven categories for recognition under UCCN include Crafts and Folk Arts, Design, Film, Gastronomy, Music, Media Arts, Literature. Till 2019, there were only three Indian cities part of this network—Jaipur (Crafts and Folk Arts; 2015), Varanasi (Creative City of Music; 2015), and Chennai (Creative City of Music; 2017). In 2019, two more Indian cities became part of the network —Mumbai for Film and Hyderabad in the field of Gastronomy. This is an encouraging development. These cities are moving towards creative economies as can be seen with the showcase of Indian talent globally, the proliferation of haats (traditional markets) and melas (fairs), and growing domestic demand for creative products and services. We should continue to support such endeavours at the city level and as discussed previously in this chapter—local businesses and administrators can identify the local creative talent. There is no reason, when cities eat away our villages, why we should lose the talent. The former is inevitable, the latter is a choice.

There are already some initiatives that are looking to channelize this creative economy. The start-up Khoj.city (www.khoj.city) was started with the motivation to identify and build a community of artists and creators from all over the country (*Hindustan Times*, 2020). This is one way to support the local creative economy. UNESCO also awards heritage-site status to locations, buildings and monuments of incredible heritage value. Of India's twenty-nine World Heritage sites, one-third are in cities. In 2018, the Victorian Gothic and Art Deco Ensembles of Mumbai (which has ninety-four such buildings), and the Oval Maidan were given UNESCO World Heritage status (Seetharaman, 2019). The Mumbai Art Deco project is a good example of how cities can partner with citizens to revive heritage sites. Similar efforts are going on in different cities such as Delhi, Hyderabad and Jodhpur. In fact, in 2017, Ahmedabad received the world heritage site status. As per experts, less than 10,000 heritage sites are under the purview of the Central and state archaeological departments (ibid.).

Given the size of India, this is too little. Besides, the government alone cannot be responsible for the identification and upkeep of these sites. Private players and citizens will have to do their bit too, because the gains are socialized across the city. In many cities such as Delhi, Kolkata, Mumbai and Bengaluru, citizens conduct heritage walks all across the city. There are also success stories, where the revival of such sites using civil society has brought local economic and social benefits. The Aga Khan Trust for Culture worked with authorities to revive the garden of Humayun's Tomb between 1997 and 2003 and it has now become a major tourist attraction. Likewise, the revival of the Sunder Nursery Complex in New Delhi by them has yielded similar results.

The other way is to undertake large projects. This was successfully done in the city of Bilbao, Spain. From the nineteenth century till the 1970s, Bilbao was a major industrial city. However, there was little that was known about its cultural scene in other European cities. Bilbao in the 1980s had high unemployment, as many of its industries had moved to Asia. In the 1990s, the Guggenheim Foundation was scouting for a location for a European Museum. The city expressed its interest. An LA-based architect Frank Gehry was commissioned for a USD 100 million project. This project has immensely transformed the once-dying city. The roads have been made pedestrian-friendly and water bodies are less polluted. The abandoned and 'rusty dockyards were replaced by green spaces and promenades' (Wünsch, 2017).

The project paid for itself in the first seven years. In 2010, 60 per cent of its visitors came from abroad. They generated employment for 3,000 local workers and provided as much as 26 million euros in tax revenue to the municipality (Hollis, 2013). In 2017, the project had completed twenty years and had accounted for 20 million visitors. This project led to the rise of the term 'Guggenheim Effect', also known as the 'Bilbao Effect'—implying how art and culture turned around the fate of a region and its failing economy, using a large architecture project. However, there are many projects worldwide that have failed to generate the same kind of success (Wünsch, 2017). Again, there is futility in suggesting which approach to follow. The cities should try and use a mix of these approaches, especially depending upon the political will, financial strength and capacity of local administrators.

NIGHT ECONOMY AS THE NEXT FRONTIER OF GROWTH

We imagine and see our cities working through days and resting through nights. There have been some exceptions that have allowed a night-time activity. Gurugram made global headlines as it offered Business and Knowledge Process Outsourcing (BPO) to firms worldwide, and hosted Indian firms that allowed English-speaking, tech-savvy, aspirational youngsters to make a good living for themselves. While the offices worked through the night, there were no major restaurants open. The BPO/KPO workforce took pride in hanging out at dhabas—roadside eateries, which were once an exclusive offering of Indian villages but had found a fond place in Indian cities such as Gurugram.

The other such exception was Mumbai—where a lot of eateries were open till the early hours of the morning. Many people in Mumbai work two to three jobs, or travel long distances on the local trains (called 'locals') that start operating as early as 4 a.m. I have taken a Mumbai local at this hour and it had considerable occupancy, brimming with people who were dressed for a good day's work. Many Indian cities have hubs with shops and eateries open throughout the day, especially in places that house organizations that work round-the-clock such as hospitals and the railways. Recently, a third-generation politician Aditya Thackeray, the then tourism minister of Maharashtra, announced a pilot would be run in Mumbai, allowing shops, eateries and malls to stay open twenty-four hours of the day for all seven days of the week. Is this a giant step towards boosting cities' economy or just a small incremental step?

Think about it in terms of equity and efficiency, wherein you treat the city as a company. The city offers both—opportunities for all, and jobs. The city's economy hinges on major infrastructure projects such as highways, major offices, buildings, roads, shopping complexes and urban transport. In the daytime, people work and study and by around midnight almost everything in cities shuts down. The majority of places do not open till 10 a.m. the next day. Suppose you allow people to work and provide them the option to eat out through the night. Since it is a choice, people and firms will do what they think is better for them—financially, emotionally, and socially. This in turn will help increase the utilization of cities' fixed assets. People can work more jobs. The occupancy of many commercial buildings is zero at this time so they can lease out part of offices to other firms/start-ups with low rents. Someone trying to make more money or making ends meet can look for jobs in different sectors. The city will have to only worry about variable costs—offering public services such as transport which it can do by hiring more people which will be good for the economy. The good thing is that you would not have to invest in fixed assets at all.

People may worry about the safety of women and the distraction of youngsters as a reason to resist the night economy. These are naysayers, because cities that are safe for women and youngsters who want to study, do not look at hours. By this logic, we should disband cities altogether. Is that possible? No. But there is also no harm in offering more choices to people. In the process, it is even better for cities that can mop up more revenue, offer more jobs and boost the local economy. Nitin Pai's telling quote is loaded, and rightly so: 'If cities are engines of growth, we're operating them, at best, only three-quarters of the time' (Pai, 2019a). According to Pai, of the total workforce in London, one-third or about 1.6 million people worked during the night. The top three sectors in which they worked were health, professional services and nightlife. Transport, automotive IT and education were the employers; thus 6–8 per cent of the economy of London stemmed from its night-time economy and this was reason enough for the appointment of a 'Night Czar' by Mayor Sadiq Khan (ibid.).

China too has encouraged its malls, supermarkets and convenience stores to stay open till late. As per Nitin Pai's calculation, if the top ten Indian cities work through the night, they could add USD 24 billion to the GDP (0.8 per cent of GDP) and pull 2 million people out of poverty (ibid.). With India's cities brimming with people and Covid-19 encouraging staggering hours, there is a case to consider it for 100 cities. This could be done with a good, control experiment to see how the night-time economy could play a role in unlocking the value of our cities.

4
Urban Equity: Bridging the Infrastructure Deficit

THE promise of cities doesn't only lie in better wages or higher productivity. If one were to imagine a social contract at the city level—this is but one part of it, wherein city governments and businesses benefit. The other part of the bargain lies in higher prosperity and quality of life for a city's residents. Cities fulfil this promise only if they have the appropriate infrastructure. In fact, the best cities in the world today were, at some point in the past, baptized by fire, i.e., threatened by a major crisis that could wipe them out. These crises arose due to the lack of appropriate infrastructure and led them to, and through, the tough phase of providing commensurate infrastructure—London (after the plague and the fire); Singapore after it was separated from Malaysia, to name two. It is the provision of urban infrastructure and services that has, over centuries, maintained social cohesion and the legitimacy of rulers and governments.

Post Independence, the planning process in many formerly colonized nations, including India, failed to prioritize urban development and provide this infrastructure over time. Cities build infrastructure over generations, one of the rare exceptions is Paris. Its transformation was led and delivered by Baron Georges-Eugène Haussman, and its infrastructure created within a generation. Haussman, a civil servant by profession, was appointed to undertake this urban renewal work by Napoleon III who wanted to clear the haphazard streets of Paris of revolutionaries, win popularity and secure his place in history. The city was home to over a million people in 1846, up from 759,000 people in 1831 (Willsher, 2016).

BARON HAUSSMAN'S PARIS

Turning Paris into a construction site for seventeen years, Haussman cut through swarms of slums, cleared more than 12,000 buildings and laid wide avenues that connected major locations in the city. He spent 2.5 billion francs, evicted thousands of poor people, and tore down ancient landmarks (Gleaser, 2012). The city's most spectacular infrastructure was created by Haussman during 1853–1870, when he built an elaborate underground sewer system to separate wastewater from clean water and gave the residents of Paris access to clean drinking water (ibid). He installed newspaper kiosks, lampposts and railings in twenty-seven parks and squares (Willsher, 2016). Glaeser points out that the buildings, the opera house, the streets, are all Haussman's work (Glaeser, 2012). Soon enough, the city became known for its beauty and attracted tourists, artists and diplomats from the world over.

Haussman's critics say he quelled civil unrest in working-class areas by segregating high-income and low-income households (Willsher, 2016). However, even at that time many (and many more today) considered him a brilliant modern urban planner. His construction accommodated later inventions such as the omnibus, steam engine-driven rails, and created public spaces that have remained in use centuries later (Glaeser, 2012). However, Haussman's legacy will continue to remain contested due to the means he used to achieve his ends. It cannot be a way out for Indian cities.

Around a hundred years after Haussman's Paris turnaround, another leader in the global South started an experiment on urban infrastructure that continues to inspire to date.

WE CAN'T DO A PARIS, BUT WE CAN PULL OFF A SINGAPORE

In terms of city infrastructure, Singapore is a case study in proving naysayers wrong. It is one of the few nations to have jumped from 'developing' to 'developed' within two generations. Many say that it is not right to compare Singapore to Indian cities, given that it is a city-state with power and resources and is home to a far smaller population, but I beg to differ. Since it is a city-state, it also has more sovereign responsibilities. Its population of 6 million is still greater than the majority of Indian cities, and lessons can be drawn from the manner in which it has provided access to services.

The island city came into being in 1819 as a trading post of the East India Company (EIC) before changing hands briefly more than a century later, when the Japanese colonized it from 1942 to 1945 during World War II; the British regained it in 1945 (Nations Online Project, n.d.). However, the desire for self-rule had grown strong among Singaporeans. By 1954 Cambridge-educated lawyer Lee Kuan Yew had founded People's Action Party (PAP), and in 1955 the British rulers were pushed to recommend 'partial-self government'. The first elections held in May 1959 resulted in victory for PAP and Lee became the first Prime Minister of Singapore (ibid.). In 1963, he declared complete independence from British rule and chose to merge Singapore with Malaysia. The merger collapsed in 1965 for various reasons and the Republic of Singapore was born (ibid.).

Though now an independent city-state, Singapore had a tough road ahead. It had no access to drinking water (it depended on Malaysia for a water supply pipeline connection), had hardly any natural resources and was covered in slums that bred poor hygiene. Economically, the short-lived merger with Malaysia had failed to boost Singapore's economy (and this was one of the reasons the merger had fallen through). World Bank's website notes on its page on Singapore that 'Singapore was confronted with severe unemployment, poor infrastructure and a housing shortage. Today the city-state is ranked as one of the most liveable cities, boasting one the highest levels of human capital development in the world'. Hank Lim of the Singapore Institute of

International Affairs notes in his paper on 'Infrastructure Development in Singapore': 'From the experience of Singapore, infrastructure is clearly central to socio-economic advancement' (Lim, 2008). He adds that 'An efficient infrastructure facilitates delivery of information, goods and services, supports economic growth and assists in achieving social objectives such as raising the living standards and educational levels' (ibid.). All of this Singapore has certainly achieved.

What the city-state did on infrastructure is pertinent to India too. The government led by Lee Kuan Yew identified two key areas at the very outset—housing and unemployment—and set up two entities that could act autonomously: the Housing Development Board (HDB) and the Economic Development Board (EDB) (ibid.). The HDB achieved its target of providing 10,000 houses in the 1960s, and as of date has sold more than 1 million units and homes to 80 per cent of Singapore's population (www.hdb.gov.sg). Singapore is a melting pot of Asian ethnicities (primarily Malay, Chinese and Indians) and Lim notes, 'Along with the nation-building social goal, is the attempt to foster racial harmony by allocating flats in every areas to have a balanced multiracial makeup so that there is a growth of vibrant, thriving multi-racial communities' (Lim, 2008). This target too has been achieved.

Another area where the city-state has achieved remarkable success is in securing water security for its people. In 1965, at independence, the little nation faced lack of perennial surface water sources, dealt with flooding and polluted waterways, had limited groundwater availability with a risk of seawater intrusion, and had (until then) depended on Malaysia for drinking water. Today, Singapore has four sources of water—'four national taps comprising of harnessed rainwater, recycled water, desalinated seawater and surface water', that provide a sustainable supply (Gupta and Dhar, 2020).

On the economic front we see that soon after independence, Lee Kuan Yew was able to keep a small government with economically astute advisors. The economy remained open, transparent and effective (though, press freedom was curbed and opposition leaders were sued to bankruptcy—which are not desirable features of a functioning democracy). Lee and his team used the EDB to leverage low labour costs, create business-friendly laws, and low taxes to encourage firms to set up headquarters in Singapore. In the 1980s, when Singapore started facing competition from Malaysia and Indonesia, it changed its economic model to boost entrepreneurship, market its tourism potential and attracted more hi-tech and knowledge-based industries; and, of course, it leveraged its unique position on the Malacca Strait, and continues to gain richly as a hub of maritime trade. Singapore was marketed through EDB offices in other countries; India's award-winning investment promotion agency 'Invest India' is created on the lines of the EDB.

What factors underpin this success story? Kishore Mahbubani, Distinguished Fellow at the Asia Research Institute, National University of Singapore, and eminent former diplomat with the Singapore Foreign Service, attributes the achievements to its 'three remarkable leaders: Lee Kuan Yew, Goh Keng Swee and Rajaratnam'; and to the three principles behind Singapore's success: meritocracy, pragmatism, and honesty. In an online interview he states, 'By accident of history we had three brilliant leaders who were also exceptionally honest, even when Singapore was a very poor country and the salaries were very low. If any country can implement these three principles, I guarantee you the country will succeed' (Infrastructure Channel, n.d.).

Let us begin with water security. India's status on each of the four areas that Singapore has leveraged shows that we have a long way to go.

- **Rainwater harvesting**—only a few Indian cities have bye-laws that mandate this. This will need strong legislation and engineering interventions.
- **Recycled water**—a great resource that is climate-change resilient and can be reliably produced using advanced treatment technologies. Singapore's recycled water (called NEWater) complies with the highest water quality standards, is fit for human consumption and has high demand among industries. Additionally, NEWater is also blended with a surface water source to augment water supply during droughts (ibid.). In India, as of now, only a few states such as Tamil Nadu, Karnataka, Gujarat and Haryana mandate recycled water and usage for industrial purposes (MoJS, 2020).

- **Desalinated seawater**—happens to be Singapore's third source of water security. India, with its massive coastline, has come up with some desalination plants in some coastal cities. It can capitalize on Singapore's strong experience in seawater desalination in bringing down the per-unit cost of water and developing seawater as a sustainable water source.
- **Surface water**—India is more richly blessed with riverine systems than is Singapore. Yet it is Singapore that is water sufficient, while India—as per the Global Aqueduct Water Risk Atlas—stands at 'Extremely high level of water risk. The Atlas bases this on thirteen parameters, 'including water stress, water depletion, groundwater table decline, drought risk, flood risk, untreated connected wastewater and unimproved/no drinking water, among others' (www.wri.org/aqueduct). As per the WRI this is the highest level of risk. A long-term Water Master Plan should gain higher importance within the Master Plan of each Indian city.

As of 2021 Indian cities still severely lack basic infrastructure and services such as clean, piped drinking water, sewerage, sanitation, solid-waste management, stormwater drainage, affordable housing and public transportation. In other words, Indian cities are unable to provide basic amenities even at current population levels. When cities fail to provide such services, they hurt India's growth story—the productivity loss is immense. People spend hours in fetching drinking water from a source far from home, the poor queue up at water tankers to access higher-priced water because they have no other alternative, roads are regularly flooded due to lack of stormwater drainage, and the disease burden of untreated faecal sludge adds to the burden on our cities.

Besides, the poor bear an additional cost of having to access these services through the private mafia in cities. If India's rural urban migration rate accelerates, then our cities would have to create basic amenities at a faster rate than they have until now. In fact, lack of such effort and investment has created huge urban inequities. Those with purchasing power can procure essential services while the urban poor, including the migrants and other vulnerable sections, are left to fend for themselves. On a relatively brighter note, successive Central governments and most state governments have been trying to catch up.

As per the High Powered Expert Committee's (HPEC) Report to the Ministry of Urban Development (MoUD), the estimated requirement for urban infrastructure investment over twenty years (from 2012–13 to 2031–32) stands at Rs 39.2 lakh crore at 2009–10 prices (MoUD, 2011). Twenty per cent of this investment is to go to water supply, sewerage, solid-waste management, and stormwater drains. This estimate was made by the MoUD in the context of the JNNRUM scheme launched in 2005. Since then the dialogue on urban infrastructure has drastically evolved. Let us look at what Indian cities can and must do on the three sub-sectors of infrastructure: water and sanitation, solid-waste management, and urban housing.

BUILDING INFRASTRUCTURE: WATER AND SANITATION

In 2019, India's sixth-largest city, Chennai, faced one of its worst monsoons and its four reservoirs began to dry up. Called the 'Detroit of Asia' because it is the chief automobile export cluster of India, water demand in Chennai outstrips supply by 200 million litres per day (MLD) (Kubernein Initiative, 2020). In the months preceding the monsoon of 2019, storage in two of Chennai's reservoirs—Cholavaram and Chembarambakkam—had fallen as low as 2 per cent and 6 per cent, respectively (Sengupta, 2018). Hotels, businesses and residential areas bought greywater (contaminated water) at high cost. Businesses were shut for days (and Covid-19 had yet to come). The city receives water from a desalinization plant, but that too wasn't enough to meet its daily needs. The city relies on 4,000 private water tankers to deliver 200 MLD; 66 per cent of households have their own wells which are fast depleting the groundwater tables (Kubernein Initiative, 2020).

At the peak of the 2019 crisis, daily trains ferried in 2.5 MLD of water for the city every day (ibid.). Chennai is not alone in this battle; various cities, large and small, are facing acute water shortage. Bathinda, Lucknow, Jaipur, Mumbai and Nagpur have started water rationing (Sengupta, 2018). This becomes severe in the summer with many cities supplying citizens with water for less than an hour/day. The popular hill station, Shimla, had to recently turn away tourists as it had run out of drinking water. India could face up to 6 per cent of GDP loss by 2030, the same as Mumbai's contribution to the national GDP in 2018, if it fails to manage its water resources properly (Kubernein Initiative, 2020).

As per the National Sample Survey Organization's (NSSO's) seventy-sixth round, only 40.9 per cent of urban households have access to a piped water connection (Kapil, 2019). A new report highlights the demand-supply mismatch in the cities of Bengaluru, Chennai, Delhi, Kolkata, Mumbai and Surat (Kubernein Initiative, 2020). In Bengaluru, a city of over 12 million people, the demand of 1,900 MLD far outstripped the supply of 1,440 MLD in 2019. The current 32 per cent gap is estimated to reach 80 per cent by 2030, with demand reaching around 4,000 MLD. Tankers supply water to 50 per cent of Bengaluru's residents. In Delhi, the demand of 4,353 MLD is met by the supply of 3,159 MLD. In Kolkata, the demand-supply mismatch is to the tune of more than 500 MLD, with demand at 2,989 MLD. In Mumbai, the demand is 4,849 MLD, while the supply is 4,128 MLD. Surat has one of the better supply scenarios, with supply meeting most of the 1,363 MLD demand. We can imagine the scenario for the other cities in India. They also face additional issues such as poor water quality, erratic water supply, untreated sewage, depleting groundwater table, and dilapidated storage capacity.

As per Census 2011, only 32.7 per cent of urban households are connected to piped sewerage systems, while 38.2 per cent dispose waste into septic tanks and around 7 per cent into pit latrines. Even though a considerable proportion of these urban Indian households depend on on-site sanitation facilities, safe disposal of septage/faecal sludge continues to remain haphazard. Private sludge operators largely operate in the unorganized sector, with no regulation or monitoring. Untreated waste poses considerable health and environmental risks. A workshop on 'Gaps in Sanitation: An FSM Point of View', jointly conducted by the Environmental Management and Policy Research Institute (EMPRI) and Centre for Study of Science, Technology and Policy (CSTEP) on 11 September 2016, revealed that an estimated 0.12 million tonnes of faecal sludge is generated in India per day. Natural water bodies are thus getting polluted. Another threat water bodies face is of encroachment by builders who drain them to reclaim land.

India's water-supply infrastructure being in poor shape has led to a high share of non-revenue water (defined as water that is lost due to technical reasons such as leakage, meter or data error, non-metering; or due to poor governance leading to successful theft and non-payment). The most vulnerable sections are left at the mercy of the water mafia which supplies water through tankers at exorbitant rates. The painful irony is that the more comfortably off—who can afford to buy water at much higher rates (as charged by the tanker mafiosi)—get piped water water supply at home at the very nominal rate charged by government bodies. The irony cannot be overemphasized. Let us deep dive into ways in which we can address these issues.

As per the *Handbook of Urban Statistics 2019*, only a third of India's urban population had access to tap drinking water within the premises, another third had access to tap water outside the premises, and over one-fifth of the population was dependent on tube well/borehole (MoHUA, 2019). As of 2020, no Indian city supplied round-the-clock water to its residents. This—2020—was the year that many leaders and opinion thinkers had heralded as the milestone when India would take the world by storm!

The fact is that India—with 4 per cent of the world's freshwater resources—has to provide water to 17 per cent of the world's population. Strong regional disparities exist across India in access to water, in daily hours of water supply, in per capita supply and in share of non-revenue water. NITI Aayog has highlighted that the water demand may outstrip supply by 2030 (Wheeling, 2019).

There is no way out of this but to build the right infrastructure—providing a round-the-clock, year-round piped water supply, universal coverage of the sewerage network and sewage and wastewater treatment plants. The HPEC Report brings out that a key input for round-the-clock water supply is the replacement of the distribution network (MoUD, 2011). About 80 per cent of the network in cities needs to be replaced.

To treat wastewater too we need to collect it through universal coverage of sewerage. Indian cities suffer from a massive gap between the wastewater generation and treatment. Barring a few cities, there are hardly enough wastewater treatment plants in Indian cities. In Delhi, only 78 per cent of the city's population is served by a sewerage network (Rumi, 2020a). As per a report, only half of the daily 6,200 crore litres of sewage water is treated before it is discharged (ET Bureau, 2018). Wherever there are such plants, they are in extremely poor condition, with silting, leakage, out of operation, poor flow of sewage, blockage, unconnected areas and tattered sewer lines (Rumi, 2020a). We have seen Singapore meets 40 per cent of its demand through wastewater recycling. There have been many welcome initiatives on these lines. The Central government has created a new water-resources ministry called Ministry of Jal Shakti (MoJS). It is a welcome step but the ministry is overwhelmingly inclined towards rural water resources for now. The AMRUT scheme covers 500 cities, around 60 per cent of the urban population. It aims to provide universal coverage of drinking water supply and substantial improvement in coverage and treatment capacities of sewerage and septage, along with stormwater drainage, non-motorized urban transport, and green spaces and parks.

Cities, when empowered, are able to take the lead on this front. Pune was the first city to raise money through municipal bonds after new regulations on the 'Issue and Listing of Debt Securities by Municipalities Regulations, 2015' were introduced (Kumar et al., 2018). The city aims to establish round-the-clock water-supply capacity and has a detailed project report for it. The project has multiple components such as construction of reservoirs, computerised billing, monitoring of water system, and maintenance of water lines, etc (Kalaskar, 2019). Lucknow too has recently issued municipal bonds to provide round-the-clock piped water supply. There is no shortcut to this. It is going to be a long effort but we should remain focused on creating this infrastructure. Post Covid-19, wherein regular handwashing and sanitization was one of the most effective methods to prevent infection, the need for access to universal supply for water and sewerage network has been further highlighted. London and New York built their water and sewer networks after they suffered from cholera. Will Covid-19 cause Indian cities to do the same?

Water Efficiency in the Agriculture Sector

Aquifers, flow, contamination and stress do not follow man-made administrative boundaries. It would be well to remember this. Of the total rainfall of 4,000 billion cubic metres (BCM), 53.5 per cent is lost to evapotranspiration, leaving us with 1,869 BCM. Of this, 1,137 BCM is utilizable, comprising 690 BCM of surface water and 447 BCM of groundwater (NITI Aayog, 2018). The agriculture sector accounts for 80 per cent of the entire water consumption (Sen, 2018). The majority of it is consumed through flood-irrigation. Therefore, the irrigation efficiency of surface and groundwater needs to increase to 60 per cent and 75 per cent respectively, from 30 per cent and 55 per cent currently (Mishra and Dhar, 2018).

As per an analysis, micro-irrigation is 40 per cent more efficient than flood irrigation techniques (Likhi, 2019). States with greater exploitation of groundwater resources need to move towards micro-irrigation technologies like drip irrigation which has 90 per cent water efficiency, unlike surface irrigation which has 60–70 per cent efficiency (Mishra and Dhar, 2018). The Government of India is already operating a scheme called 'Per Drop, More Crop' that uses micro-irrigation systems such as sprinklers, drips, pivots, and others to increase water-use efficiency in the agriculture sector. As the urban political economy continues to gain more sway over policymaking in India, it should push for such irrigation methods rather than those that are depleting groundwater resources leading to water stress and contamination.

Another area of intervention is the cropping pattern in India. The minimum support price (MSP) set by the government, though set for twenty-three crops, is largely enforced only for wheat and rice (Suhag, 2016). Growing these two crops is highly water intensive. Providing incentives for the cultivation of pulses and millets will increase cash income as well as reduce water usage in the countryside (Kant, 2019). However, as Amitabh Kant points out, through our exports of Basmati rice alone we are virtually exporting 10 trillion litres of water (ibid.). Plus, there is huge variation among states as well. He notes that Punjab uses three times the water used by Bihar for growing one kilo of rice (ibid.). Our crops—paddy and sugarcane—are immensely water-guzzling. The water consumption in the sector can be influenced by separating the power feeders for agriculture so that the water consumption related energy use can be tracked and effective responses can be raised; Gujarat has achieved a fair amount of success on this issue, says Kant (ibid.).

On overall water efficiency, Singapore and Israel are important examples since they both recognize water as a national security issue and have mobilized resources and policies accordingly. We have studied the example of Singapore already. The Israel Water Authority sensitizes school children on the importance of water and how to save it. With 60 per cent of the country covered by desert, the country has excelled by recycling 90 per cent of its water and 80 per cent of its drinking water comes from recycled or desalinated water. Israel's drip irrigation techniques are being used in India since the 1990s and only now have begun to be mainstreamed (Malka, 2019).

Water Efficiency: Groundwater Depletion and a Colonial Legislation

India is heavily reliant on groundwater resources for irrigation. In fact, 25 per cent of the global groundwater use is accounted for by India (Kant, 2019). Of this, 89 per cent is for irrigation, 9 per cent for consumption, and 2 per cent for industrial use (Suhag, 2016). As per government data, in 2017 groundwater withdrawal in more than 110 districts was not made up for by recharge through natural and artificial processes (Balachandran, 2019). Groundwater resources, which constitute 40 per cent of the water supply, are clearly fast depleting. Indian cities are lined with thousands of tube wells and boreholes. In fact, a Central government survey found over one-fifth of the population was dependent on a tube well/borehole for water supply (MoHUA, 2019). Kolkata alone officially has 17,000 water hydrants, 12,00 hand-operated tube wells, and 2,500 large tube wells, and has seen a significant drop in its groundwater levels (Kubernein Initiative, 2020). In Parliament, it was reported that for every 100 units of groundwater recharge, 137 units were withdrawn, up from 58 in 2004 (Suhag, 2016). It was also reported in Parliament that 50 per cent of urban water consumption and rural domestic water consumption also relies on groundwater (ibid.).

There is one single reason behind this indefatigable exploitation of groundwater resources—a colonial legislation, the India Easement Act of 1882. It marries the rights to accessing water under one's land indiscriminately. The law allows, 'every landowner with the right to collect and dispose, within his own limits, all water under the land and on the surface' (ibid.). So landowners can dig wells as deep as they want and keep extracting water as per their wish. Besides, they are also not liable for damage to water resources due to their activities. This has led to a massive crisis.

A Bill on Indian Easement, 2018, has been introduced, but has not been legislated yet. Besides, water is a state subject so states will have to amend this Act. The Bill says that state governments, municipalities and gram sabhas can make rules to regulate the use of groundwater, prevent its exploitation, and *ensure equitable distribution* (italics mine).[1] The text in italics is important since people without land cannot easily access groundwater. The Amendment Bill observes that 60 per cent of India's districts face issues of groundwater availability or of its quality, or both. The National Water Policy, 2012, and previous observations advocated a 'public trust doctrine' for groundwater management (advocating that the government is the ultimate guardian of natural resources), to prevent overexploitation.

Since water is a state subject, the matter has to be legislated. My guess is states where the urban population becomes dominant—and as a consequence see a huge shift of agricultural workers from farming to non-farm jobs—would be the first to bite the bullet. No one would want to lose an enormous amount of rural votes by passing such

---

1   The Indian Easements (Amendment) Bill, 2018, was introduced by Dr Kirit Premubhai Solanki, and the text of this bill—Bill No. 106 of 2018—may be found at: http://164.100.47.4/billstexts/lsbilltexts/asintroduced/289LS%20AS%20INTRO.pdf

legislation, but the time will come sooner than we imagine. For instance, Maharashtra passed the Maharashtra Groundwater Development and Management Rules, which make it compulsory to register borewells—you need a permit to install a new well and also have to create a recharge structure (Kant, 2019). This is some progress. Round-the-clock water connectivity and sewerage network connectivity is a prerequisite to pass such legislation.

Water Efficiency in Urban India

There is immense scope to create a water-frugal society. Recycled wastewater is our best hope to meet at least two-fifths of our urban demand. There is immense scope to launch a water efficiency scheme for industries in urban areas on the lines of Perform, Achieve and Trade (PAT) scheme that was launched for energy efficiency. This scheme generated immense value for energy-intensive industries resulting in considerable energy and costs savings, while significantly reducing CO_2 emissions. There is also a Bureau for Energy Efficiency (BEE) in India to steer the efforts on energy efficiency. As a consequence, a new ecosystem of energy efficiency has been created in India that includes Energy Saving Companies (ESCOs) like Smart Joules.

Since the creation of MoJS (the water resources ministry), there is merit in focusing on the Bureau for Water Efficiency (BWE) and Water Saving Companies (WSCOs). This should also allow for trading mechanisms such as for CO_2 emissions, as that would spur innovation and investment in the sector. Why don't we have RO systems that use less water? At present RO water purifiers cause considerable loss of treated water, as close to 3 litres of water is wasted for 1 litre of purified water (Rumi, 2020a). Another considerable loss is due to the use of treated water for non-potable purposes, including gardening, washing cars, flushing and filling coolers. In Delhi, as per one estimate, 40 per cent of water is used for non-potable purposes (ibid.). There have been city-level initiatives already to provide for smart meters for large industries, water-efficient devices like water purifier systems, and no-water urinals.

Hedging Risks by Expanding Water Resources

The process of rapid urbanization-led encroachment and misuse of water is eating away the benefit of creating cities near large water bodies. All major cities in the world have been built near water bodies—from Varanasi to Venice, from Amsterdam to successive cities of Delhi, from New York to Lucknow, and from London to Chennai. Empires crumbled and cities have perished when water resources were not managed. Even the mighty Mughals had to act according to the demand of water resources. When Akbar took over, he initially declared a new city Fatehpur Sikri (near Agra) as his capital. But he was forced to return to Agra as the water supply was not sufficient to sustain a capital city (Sanyal, 2013). Reservoirs like Hauz Khas and the various baolis (step-wells) in Delhi are a few of the hundreds of structures that rulers used for centuries to ensure water security through storage.

This method of maintaining a steady water resource has been continued in modern cities as well. Any risk to the storage of these reservoirs reflects poorly on the survival of nearby cities. Currently, two-thirds of India's reservoirs are holding less than average water levels as per the Central Water Commission (CWC) (Yeung et al., 2019). As per the CWC, 'The overall storage position is less than the corresponding period of last year in the country as a whole, and is also less than the average storage of last ten years during the corresponding period'; in fact, live storage in the 91 reservoirs was at 17 per cent of total storage capacity (Abbas, 2019). The government has taken steps to recharge these reservoirs, but this information should stand as a steady reminder about the poor state of operations and maintenance of water levels in reservoirs.

Many Indian cities are home to lakes that act as a steady source of water resource rejuvenation, storing water for situations like draughts, acting as a catchment area for rainfall, preventing floods, and reducing pollution. However these water bodies are under threat due to encroachment. The state of Uttar Pradesh alone has lost 100,000 water bodies due to illegal encroachment (IANS, 2019a). As per a survey by the Lucknow Municipal Corporation, the city had 964 ponds in 1952, by 2006 the number had reduced to 494. It is said that water bodies within the core areas of the Lucknow city have almost completely vanished. Experts believe that another 300 water bodies around the city are facing an existential crisis due to indiscriminate construction. This is making the city extremely prone to flooding. In fact, the city has faced four major floods in the last decade alone (ibid.). The Supreme Court had passed a judgment in 2006 that the protection of natural water bodies was in line with Article 21 on the Right to Life in the Constitution of India. It is time we abide by that. Urban planning and local administration should be held accountable for this. As per Central Pollution Control Board (CPCB), India had 150 polluted river stretches in 2008 and that number more than doubled to 302 in 2015 (Jadhav, 2019).

The situation is no different in other cities. In a very passionate article, scholar Ritu Rao narrates the horrific tale of the fate of the Najafgarh Jheel (lake), located on the Delhi–Gurugram border. The lake was embanked on Delhi's side in 1964 and Gurugram has since built property after property on the natural catchment area of the lake. Once spread over 220 sq km, Najafgarh Jheel is now reduced to 7 sq km and looks like a wastewater drain (Rao, 2010). The pollutants that drain into the lake contaminate its aquifers. A 308 per cent increase in groundwater extraction in Gurugram, from 2014 to 2018, has further adversely affected the lake's fate. Borewells have to go as deep as 91 feet now, as against 21.6 feet previously, to get water. In its current condition the lake cannot play a role in groundwater recharge. All this collectively has led the lake to become a deprived version of itself. Another case in point is Bengaluru, which had 260 lakes in the 1960s. By 2019 only eighty were left and most had become dumping grounds for industrial waste (Kubernein Initiative, 2020). In Chennai, the area of water bodies declined from 12.6 sq km in 1893 to 3.2 sq km in 2017. During the same period, the surface water storage capacity declined from 37.8 billion litres to 9.5 billion litres (ibid.).

Water storage capacity can be increased using three tools at a city's disposal. First by investing in building material for footpaths and roads that allows the seepage of rainwater; the concretization of ULB areas has been the bane of urbanization, but not all is lost. We want water to seep through to the aquifer levels. The second is to invest in a stormwater-drain network. Studies have shown that during the monsoon in India rainy days are fewer, but with increased precipitation (Udas-Mankikar, 2020a). The Observer Research Foundation points out how India's water drainage systems are outdated and cannot deal with present realities. As per government standards, drainage systems are designed to handle 12–20 mm of rain per hour, but many Indian cities have received more than 50 mm of rain in an hour. Data from an IIT study shows that many Indian cities receive more than 50 mm of rain per hour and some even 100 mm per hour, multiple times a year (ibid.). Every monsoon, the Indian media plays and replays visuals of flooded cities and tries to fix accountability. This is easy. The solution, however, lies in the long process of increasing the capacity of the drainage system in Indian cities. To address this problem, the Central government released the 'Draft Manual on Storm Water Drainage Systems' in 2019, but it needs to be adopted by ULBs and states.

The second issue is that of managing solid waste that blocks the existing drainage system. Indian cities are making good progress on this issue and should continue to work on proper management of solid waste, which we will study in the next section. Drainage systems across Indian cities need to be mapped, upgraded, desilted and unclogged. Frontier technologies can help in the prefabrication of drainage pipes which can be laid down quickly. Lastly, the ULBs need to ensure that they separate the drainage networks for stormwater and sewerage. This is a problem that further exacerbates the pollution in water bodies.

The third measure is harvesting rainwater. A major component of planning that can help augment water resources in ensuring the installation of rainwater harvesting (RWH) structures in all houses above a certain threshold and in all government buildings. Delhi revised its laws in 2019 to enable Delhi Jal Board, Delhi's water agency, to help increase the water resources of the city (Rumi, 2020b). It has taken a mix of measures—financial rebates and penalties, regular inspections, standard operating procedures as developed by Delhi Jal Board and sensitization activities—to nudge the creation of harvesting structures throughout Delhi. As of now, a considerable share of buildings (even government buildings), do not have RWH structures (ibid.). Rumi reveals that though many major public buildings have installed RWH structures, a lot of work remains to be done in terms of maintenance and in engendering behaviour change among the residents (ibid.). Rainwater harvesting structures were introduced in Chennai 2003 but most of them are now in poor condition. Hyderabad also has RWH structures, which are poorly maintained. Bengaluru and Mumbai also do not comply with the local laws passed in 2009 and 2002 respectively concerning RWH structures (Rumi, 2020c).

After toilets, housing, electricity connection and now drinking water supply, the Central and state governments will have to work together on creating a dedicated mission for sound water drainage systems and rainwater-harvesting infrastructure.

India's Urban Water Sector: Poor Quality, Leakage, No Revenue and Mismanagement

A survey conducted by the Bureau of Indian Standards (BIS) studied piped drinking water quality in twenty-one cities. Hardly was any city found to have water that was safe for drinking. Delhi's water failed on nineteen parameters (including ammonia, turbidity and pH levels). Mumbai met all parameters, but none of the samples from thirteen state capitals was of drinking quality (IANS, 2019a). The figures on water supply are also telling in the HPEC Report (MoUD, 2011). While it may be a decade old, not much has changed. As per the report: 1) the duration of water supply in Indian cities ranges from one to six hours while it is twenty-four hours in Brazil and China and twenty-two hours in Vietnam; 2) per capita supply of water ranges from 37 litre per capita per day (lpcd) to 268 lpcd for limited hours, Paris, for instance provides 150 lpcd (ibid.).

The issue of non-revenue water is also a major problem. This is water that is lost either due to technical reasons (leakage, meter or data error non-metering) or poor governance (theft and non-payment). India's non-revenue water is as high as 50 per cent, as compared to 5 per cent in Singapore (Ibid.). The situation hasn't really improved a decade later. Delhi Jal Board reported up to 40 per cent distribution loss due to a variety of factors including leakage, illegal tapping and misuse of water tankers (Rumi, 2020a). In Bengaluru, 20 per cent of the water is non-revenue water (Kubernein Initiative, 2020).

These are long-standing problems and will take considerable resources to be solved. A research paper by the Observer Research Foundation highlights non-invasive technologies that are already being used across India, which help in detecting and preventing such leakage and loss of water. Sensor-based technologies such as SmartBall® and Sahara® (used by the Kerala Water Authority), helium gas-based technology (used by the Municipal Corporation of Greater Mumbai, and by the Bangalore Water Supply and Sewerage Board) and sound-based technology (used by the Vadodara Municipal Corporation) are examples of such technologies that can be used to solve the issue of leakage (Rumi 2020c).

Cities must be able to raise revenue for operating and maintaining their water and sanitation systems. Local governments must know how to collect revenue efficiently and citizens and industries should learn to pay for potable water. Unlike the energy sector, which has been reformed since the 1990s and households are less likely to resort to power theft (called *katiya* in North India), the governance structure is the root cause of non-revenue water. We have read how we can attend to the technical side of non-revenue water. Sound governance remains to be unlocked.

Just as the energy sector has privately managed utility companies that ensure universal coverage and efficient revenue collection, we need to do the same for the water sector. The HPEC Report mentions the case of Cambodia's Phnom Penh Water Supply Authority which is a publicly owned and managed company (MoUD, 2011). In 1993, only a quarter of the city was serviced through a poor distribution network. Reforms took three years and tariffs were also revised in a step-wise manner in those three years. The turnaround by 2006 was phenomenal. From 1993 to 2006, the share of non-revenue water declined from 72 per cent to 6 per cent. The coverage area jumped from 25 per cent to 90 per cent, metered coverage increased from 13 per cent to 100 per cent, and supply duration zoomed from ten hours per day to twenty-four hours. The collection ratio doubled to 100 per cent and the revenue generated increased from 0.7 billion riels (Cambodian currency) to 34 billion riels.

Water issues are solved through governance innovation at the city level. India's Draft National Urban Policy Framework, 2018, cites the success of Dhaka Water Supply and Sewerage Authority (DWASA) in providing quality and affordable water in Dhaka round the clock (MoHUA, 2018a). The authority divided the city into zones with a focus on managing water flow and pressure and bringing down non-revenue water. The share of non-revenue water fell from 40–50 per cent to 15 per cent, and in some zones to less than 2 per cent. The reason behind the success was bureaucratic efficiency, deployment of performance-based contracts, focus on universal metering, use of important tools (bulk-flow meters and SCADA systems), and use of trenchless technology for faster laying of pipes.

Sanitation beyond Toilets: Thinking beyond Sewers

The cities of the world have to deal with the issue of waste management at some point. The issue of waste management comes up once cities reach a certain scale of economic prosperity and population growth. The mainstreaming of this issue marks the arrival of an emerging urban political economy that demands cleaner cities. The sight of waste hurts the environment, health, economy, and is an assault on the senses. The piles of waste also exacerbate other issues in the city—they increase health and income inequalities, since marginalized sections cannot afford private solutions; cities are flooded when stormwater drains (however few) are clogged by this waste; they hurt the resilience of cities, as the risks of natural hazards increases with the rising pile of garbage; the quality of life (especially of the urban poor) is subject to deterioration and also prevents effective utilization of urban land.

Swachh Bharat Mission was launched by the NDA government to free India from the menace of defecation in open spaces. Previous governments had run similar campaigns of Nirmal Bharat Abhiyaan but the scale of the Swachh Bharat Mission has been unprecedented. This is perhaps the first time that sanitation and solid-waste management became a political issue. Since its launch, the urban component of this scheme has created over 62 million household toilets, 6 million community and public toilets, apart from making serious progress on solid-waste management.

It is not enough that people are not defecating in the open. It is as important that such human waste and household waste is getting treated before finding its way to the streets and eventually to the water bodies including rivers. This is fatal as it contaminates both water and our sources of food. Even before the entire India was covered through the availability of toilets, the situation of faecal sludge management was in a poor shape. The connection and operation of the entire city through sewage lines, pumping stations and sewage treatment plants is a capital-intensive process. As per the government, this is the reason why more than 7,000 towns in India do not have comprehensive sewerage systems (MoUD, n.d.). Only 400 cities in India have sewage treatment plants (STPs) with a capacity of 25,000 MLD. Two-thirds of these, only operate at 50 per cent capacity; many of them are not functional (Mishra and Chary, 2020). As per one estimate, India generates over 120,000 tonnes of faecal sludge a day (Sivaramakrishnan, 2019)! But since most toilets aren't connected to the sewerage network, the waste remains uncollected, untreated and unattended. This causes serious waterborne diseases such as diarrhoea and dysentery, killing 350,000 Indian children every year (MoUD, n.d.). Every day only 10–12 per cent of the 40 billion litres of wastewater generated is treated (Rath et al., 2020). While STPs would be needed in the long run for hundreds of more Indian cities, they are time and cost consuming so we have to find other solutions in the meantime.

The Government of India has already prepared the National Urban Faecal Sludge and Septage Management (FSSM) Policy and, at the earliest, the states and ULBs should create state- and ULB-level plans for execution. Besides, since only one-third of the households are connected to sewer lines, the remaining use on-site sanitation (OSS) tools of pit latrines and septic tanks. Since faecal sludge is different from wastewater, the same plants can't be used as to treat faecal sludge. Traditional solutions for safely collecting and disposing of human waste, through a vast water- and energy-intensive infrastructure of sewage pipes and treatment tanks, are no longer the most appropriate options for today's cities. However, one way out of this is to create co-treatment plants that help treat both wastewater and faecal sludge. Hyderabad has been able to achieve success on this by converting many of its STPs into co-treatment plants and based on their success it has commissioned more such plants (Mishra and Chary, 2020). Hyderabad also provides a 'dial-a-desludger' service, wherein you can request desludging services. The city has received an 'open defecation free' (ODF)++ status due to these initiatives.

Though septage/faecal sludge is more concentrated than domestic sewage, its constituents are similar to municipal wastewater. The unutilized capacity at sewage treatment plants may be used to accept the septage without hampering the functioning of the sewage treatment plant. Supporting frameworks need to be developed to ensure regular payments to service providers for de-sludging (through potential taxation modes, i.e., a septage tax) and absorb other models of faecal and septage treatment such as 'honeysuckers' (vacuum trucks that use suction power to clean up sludge) (Vishwanath, 2012). Centralized sewerage networks are not able to address the needs of small and densely packed settlements, or small cities with fragmented settlements. Decentralized, non-sewered treatment solutions need to be expanded and can be appropriately designed for different topologies and environments.

At present, the legal framework at municipal level is oriented entirely towards the sewer approach and fails to establish the responsibility of civic bodies. There is a need for a legal framework that establishes civic responsibilities of public authorities, and provides legal backing for a non-sewered approach, to ensure universal and equitable sanitation service-delivery with adequate service-level benchmarks across the service chain. The improper disposal of faecal sludge by private tankers has to be banned and severely penalized, but not before giving them a chance to become part of the city's faecal sludge-management chain through proper training, licensing and registration. Devanahalli in Karnataka is an example that stands out for successfully adopting the decentralized approach to treat faecal sludge.

The Devanahalli plant has been built over a former waste dumping site. The operators of the plant have given a few reasons for their success: the plant is close to the city leading to efficient operations; the plant creates a pleasing site that is green and odour-free to create wider acceptability; timely land approvals were sought and received; a conducive regulatory environment exists; a centralized call centre has been established; and vehicles are GPS-tagged. Low-cost plants, like this one, run thanks to effective use of financing measures such as raising property taxes, selling manure, advertising, and collection fees for desludging. The community of farmers, residents and self-help groups has been engaged to increase the acceptability of the FSTP. Devanahalli Town Municipal Corporation (Bangalore Rural District) governs a population of 30,000 people and collects faecal sludge through honeysuckers that carry the sludge to faecal sludge treatment plants (FSTPs) (Dasra India, 2017; Rath et al., 2020). The solid component is used to produce biogas using the anaerobic digestion process and is later used for co-composting with the organic municipal waste, which is then sold to farmers. Human waste is rich in nitrogen (N), phosphorous (P), and potassium (K)—the three nutrients that form the basis of the majority of fertilizers (Kapil, 2020).

As of now, the majority of the human waste is untreated and when it is treated, it is not plugged back into the economy. However, there are numerous instances wherein human waste has been treated, turned into co-compost and sold to farmers at a lower price. One such example is Nilgiris District in Tamil Nadu (ibid.).

MANAGING SOLID WASTE

What is the extent of this problem? Globally, 2 billion tonnes of solid waste is generated annually, with India contributing a tenth of it as per a 2018 World Bank study (TNN, 2020a). The report states that India generated municipal solid waste to the tune of 277.1 million tonnes in 2016. This figure is expected to breach 287.8 million tonnes by 2030 and 543.3 million tonnes by 2050 (ibid.). Global waste generation is expected to reach 3.4 billion tonnes annually by 2050. However, as per estimates from India, Indian cities generate waste in the range of 62–72 million tonnes annually (Patel, 2019). By ICRIER's estimate, this can go up to 121 million tonnes by 2031.

Eighty per cent of the entire waste generated in South Asia comes from India. The cities that generate the highest waste in India are the usual suspects—Delhi, Mumbai, Chennai, Hyderabad, Bengaluru, Ahmedabad, Pune, Surat, Kanpur and Jaipur. The urban population is quite under-reported so the numbers may be considerably higher than the government estimates of 60–70 million tonnes. As per World Bank numbers, the average waste generated in India is pegged at 0.57 kg per person, as against the global average (0.74 kg), US (2.24 kg), Russia (1.13 kg), Japan (0.95), but curiously higher than China's average waste generation (0.43 kg per person). The 2050 figures are based on the assumption that an average Indian will generate 0.9 kg of waste (TNN, 2020a).

Going ahead, it is pertinent to note that the waste generation will increase with greater urbanization, increased consumption higher purchasing power, percolation of further consumerism, and change in consumption patterns. The older habit of repair and use is already giving way to use and throw. All this, with a rising population, portends problems. Notably, the nature of waste also evolves with increasing prosperity. As of now, over 50 per cent of the waste in developing countries, including India, is food and green waste (also referred to as wet waste/biodegradable waste). In the developed countries, the share of these two types of waste declines to 32 per cent (ibid.). In India, another 10 per cent is plastic waste and 7 per cent is paper (Patel, 2019). The remaining is made up of textile, glass, metal, street sweepings and others (ibid.).

In terms of classification for processing, waste can be divided as: 1) close to 50 per cent biodegradable waste or organic waste (food and kitchen waste, green waste [vegetables, flower, leaves, fruits], paper, etc.); 2) 32 per cent inert and non-biodegradable waste (construction and demolition waste, dirt, debris); and 3) 17 per cent recyclable waste (plastic, paper, bottles, glasses) (Singh, 2020a).

As per the Central Pollution Control Board (CPCB), of the 1,43,449 tonnes of municipal solid waste generated per day (TPD) in India in 2014–15, only 80 per cent was collected, of which only 20 per cent was processed or treated. Furthermore, the 2015 'Report of the Sub-Group of Chief Ministers on Swachh Bharat Abhiyaan' brought out that collection efficiency of municipal solid waste ranged between 70–90 per cent in major metro cities, and below 50 per cent in several smaller cities (NITI Aayog, 2015a). The ULBs spent about INR 500 to INR 1,500 per tonne on solid-waste management—about 60–70 per cent was spent on the collection of waste and 20–30 per cent on transportation, but almost nothing on treatment and disposal (ibid.). These figures will have changed considerably by now, as the report came out in 2015.

Municipal solid waste is one of the issues on which we have come to our senses just at the right time. The role of Swachh Bharat Mission had been critical in kickstarting work on the management of municipal solid waste. As per the government, 96 per cent of the wards have door-to-door collection, whereas 65 per cent of the total waste is processed (PIB, 2020b).

But not all is waste (pun intended!). Achieving this level of cleanliness is not only doable but also has been achieved in one of India's big cities—Indore. Not only it has been rated as India's cleanest city for three years in a row, but it is also showing ways to convert waste to wealth (Barnagarwala, 2019). The mass movement to clean India's cities should learn from the Indore model. Making it a clean city was no easy task. Sustaining this milestone was even more difficult. In studying the Indore model and successes from other cities, we have a ready model for solid waste management for Indian cities. We just need to emulate it.

Waste Segregation: First and Foremost

Indore, with a population of more than 2 million, now generates 1,150 metric tonnes of waste, 60 per cent of which is wet waste. Indore Municipal Corporation (IMC) engaged Basix Municipal Waste Ventures, a Hyderabad-based firm that conducts programmes on solid waste management, and NGOs for door-to-door collection and segregation of dry, wet, and hazardous waste (ibid.). If the waste is not segregated, waste collection is not carried out and this uses the shaming technique to influence behaviour.

Tamil Nadu's excellent progress on solid waste management also highlights the importance of segregation. The state is most urbanized and has done a commendable job at the state level. Its success, as documented by Dr Isher Judge Ahluwalia and Almitra Patel, shows that solid waste management can have a predictable story. By 2019, the state had achieved 50–60 per cent at-home segregation of waste (Ahluwalia and Patel, 2019a). The state has deployed over 3,000 communicators for sensitizing the people on waste segregation and they visit at least 200 houses per week.

The success of solid waste management in any city hinges on how well it segregates waste. Indore has aced it and many cities have already adopted it in their daily practice. In fact, Tamil Nadu has implemented segregation and solid-waste management at the state level. It is imperative that Indians inculcate the habit of intuitively segregating waste on-site into biodegradable and non-biodegradable components. This should not only happen at the household and commercial levels, but also at community resources such as toilets, schools and hospitals. Certain waste disposal technologies can only consume dry waste and hence, this segregation will have to be adopted at the ward/neighbourhood level depending upon the waste management technology adopted for the area. Swachh Bharat Mission's momentum should be carried forward to embed such behaviour changes.

Varying Forms of Collection and Transportation: Local Context Is Key

As Indore city got 800 vans covering 1,000 houses a day to collect and dispose of waste, it faced friction from ragpickers who were contracted to collect this waste (Barnagarwala, 2019). The city acted promptly to add 1,000 ragpickers and garbage collectors to make them part of the 8,000 *safai-mitras* or 'friends of cleanliness' (ibid.). The city installed 700 new toilets and urinals along with 3,000 roadside bins (ibid.). It also uses a live tracking system to monitor the garbage vans. If the vans are late regularly, the drivers are discharged from duty. Even common citizens track the vehicles (Santdasani, 2020). Garbage transfer stations have been installed at strategic locations for vehicles to offload garbage and return to their route (ibid.). The city also sells bottle-shaped dustbins at low prices that fit into the car doors and prevent people from throwing garbage on the roads. Such effective planning ensured that there is no need for secondary/community-level collection bins (ibid.). The city has also changed the shape of the vehicles carrying garbage, so that while following the traffic rules, they can carry thrice the load and service 1,000–1,200 households, up from 400 households previously. This has generated significant savings (ibid.).

In Tamil Nadu, the waste is transported using e-rickshaws and light commercial vehicles (Ahluwalia and Patel, 2019a). Pune has the world's first co-operative of waste pickers and urban poor called SWaCH (Solid Waste Collection and Handling)—2,700 waste-pickers collect segregated waste from households institutions and businesses (Kaza et al., 2018). Its cost of waste collection was the lowest in the country in 2015.

In Ambikapur in Chhattisgarh (population 1.25 lakh), 623 women from economically weaker sections have formed self-help groups and collect waste from forty-eight wards. This has been already segregated at source, before the women collect it. They deposit the waste at seventeen Solid Liquid Resource Management (SLRM) centres at the ward level (Das, 2017). They use e-rickshaws and garbage pick-up vans. The city has also launched a café wherein a person who brings in a kilo of plastic waste gets a full meal, and half-a-kilo gets breakfast free (ZeeBiz, 2019). Collection and transport are key processes, since they involve the use of technology, can generate savings and, most importantly, offer a chance to mainstream the marginalized sections of society.

Treatment of Waste Is Not All Waste

Key waste-processing methods include composting, biomethanation (a process that uses microbes to convert biodegradable waste into biogas and manure), recycling, refuse-derived fuel (or RDF; used for non-recyclable and non-biodegradable waste which converts the waste into pellets to be used later for combustion), incineration, and waste-to-energy (waste is not particularly segregated, but incinerated to generate energy) (Singh, 2020a). Composting is a method to convert biodegradable waste into organic fertilizer. As of 2016, there were ninety-five composting plants with an installed capacity of 2.3 tonnes/year (Ahluwalia and Patel, 2018). Many cities have now created their own plants. Likewise, few cities had bio-methanation, RDF plants, and waste-to-energy plants. Pune has had reasonable success with the use of biomethanation plants (ibid.). The RDF method has not taken off much in Indian cities.

Indore has ten Transfer Stations for waste collection and compression from where the waste is sent to the Central Processing Unit in Devguradiya (Barnagarwala, 2019). Indore has installed compost pits in 585 municipal gardens. The waste is also converted into methane which is tapped for city transport. The waste from markets such as Choithram, Nandlal Pura and Rajkumar has been particularly used for this process (Mohan, 2018). The plastic waste collected from all over the city is converted into pellets, a raw material for various plastic products. Indore has also cleared a 148-acre dumpsite in Devguradiya using bioremediation and biomining measures. Biomining uses machines to separate soil from recyclable items in the dumping ground. After this separation, items are sent for recycling and the process of bioremediation is used to further break down the soil (Barnagarwala, 2019).

To keep the road-dividers, railings and the city's fifteen statues dust-free, every night from 10 p.m. to 4:30 a.m., ten hose pipe-equipped vans, and fifteen road-sweeping machines wash, sweep and hose them down (ibid.). No wonder that 600 city corporations have visited Indore to learn how it has transformed itself and how the population has changed its behaviour around the issue. It is a turnaround story. Indore ranked 180 in the first Swachh Survekshan (Cleanliness Survey) in 2015, rose to the twenty-fifth rank in 2016, and has since ranked first for the last three consecutive years.

Other cities have also deployed the similar processes. In Ambikapur, organic waste is turned into compost whereas the inorganic waste is further segregated into 158 categories after cleaning (Das, 2017). Tamil Nadu, too, has put its weight behind the micro-composting centres—700 of them, each with 4.8 tonne capacity, and farmers are encouraged to take up the compost from these centres for free. Tamil Nadu also conducted a ten-day, state-wide survey on waste generation and found municipalities generate 250–300 grams of waste per capita whereas municipal corporations generate 320–375 grams per capita (Ahluwalia and Patel, 2019a).

Behaviour Change and 3R Mantra Create Impact at Scale

Historically, the Indian way of life has laid emphasis on sustainable living and consumption. However, in recent decades, as India recovered from economic stagnation and widespread poverty, waste generation has increased manifold but waste management has failed to catch up. As India continues to grow and urbanize, it would help cities' ecosystems to imbibe the 3Rs—reuse, reduce and recycle—to limit waste generation in India; the 3Rs, coupled with behaviour change, could prove highly effective.

In Indore, children in school are being taught about waste segregation, the community is encouraged to clean up after any major event (marriage, rally or festivity), and a pledge on cleanliness has been added to the traditional seven pledges of a Hindu marriage (Barnagarwala, 2019). The city enforced behaviour changes by modifying bye-laws on littering/spitting and non-segregation, to impose heavy fines. These fines range from INR 100 to INR 100,000 (Mohan, 2018). In Tamil Nadu, dry waste is collected every Wednesday. If it has not been segregated, the waste-pickers segregate it right at the doorstep on a plastic sheet (Ahluwalia and Patel, 2019a).

In Ambikapur in Chhattisgarh, an entire road has been constructed using plastic and granules (ZeeBiz, 2019). The city makes INR 12 lakh a month just by selling plastic granules and recycled paper (Kaur, 2019). Indore recycles different types of waste—polythene, cloth and glass (Barnagarwala 2019). In Karjat, Maharashtra, there is a ban on plastic carry bags and they instead sell bags worth INR 6, made of old saris. The municipal commissioner has been encouraging people to give away thirty-six different kinds of waste on different days (Ahluwalia and Patel, 2019a). The recycling rate of plastic in India is higher than the global average, but given the impending rise of our cities, there is a huge amount of work to be done in the coming decades (Ahluwalia and Patel, 2018). For paper, however, our recycling rate (27 per cent) is considerably lower than that of other countries—Germany (73 per cent), Sweden (69 per cent), Japan (60 per cent) and the US (49 per cent).

What Indian cities are trying to achieve through behaviour change and focusing on the 3Rs is part of a broader strategy called the circular economy. A circular economy eliminates waste, reuses raw materials and goods, deploys renewable sources of energy in the process, resulting in lowered resource consumption overall. It is called circular, as opposed to a linear economy that gets resources, goods are produced and consumed, and thereafter the end product is thrown out as waste. In some aspects, Indian households have been using the circular economy very well for many decades and the most common example is of clothes. When new clothes are bought, they are worn on special occasions and after their value declines, they are used for home wear. After they further decline and are no good for daily wear, they are worn on Holi—the Indian festival of colours, which then renders them unusable for further wear. Thereafter they are cut up and used for other purposes such as dusting and mopping, placed in the family car for last-minute cleaning, used to shine shoes, folded and placed under a tilting cupboard to restore balance, used to hold mud for gardening, and whatnot. At the household level, this creative application is called jugaad (or making do) but at the national and city level, such creative use is called circular economy.

The circular economy is a step forward from the high-consumption lifestyles followed in some countries. For instance, if the entire world lived like the US, it would need five times the resources available on earth to sustain such consumption (Potocnik and Gawel, 2019). The numbers for Australia, Germany and the UK are 4.1, 3, and 2.7 respectively. Clearly, we do not want to go down that path. The way of living of the developed countries is not necessarily the best (ibid.). As per a WEF study, the world economy is only 9 per cent circular (WEF, 2019a). The study observes: 'concerted resource efficiency and sustainable resource management measures can reduce global resource use by 25 per cent and greenhouse gas emissions by 90 per cent, and boost gross domestic product by 8 per cent, as compared to historical trends scenario, on 2030–2060' (ibid.).

Resource decoupling, implying using lesser resources for economic growth, is a way forward that cities must take up. Jonathan Rose illustrates how consumers and producers can work on a circular economy. As per Rose, while we have consumption changing regulations and rules, and there is much that needs to be implemented, we have little to show for the responsibility of producers. When the EU passed the Directive of End-of-Life Vehicle for manufacturers to recycle and reuse 85 per cent of the parts, car manufacturing evolved in a way that made recycling easy (Rose, 2016). We need to create such standards for Indian industry and even peg it in international trade agreements that would distinguish India from other countries.

Another important ingredient is to provide regulations and infrastructure. A paper from ICRIER highlights how Japan focused on this policy and reduced its waste generation from 54.8 million tonnes in 2000 to 44.9 million tonnes in 2013 (Ahluwalia and Patel, 2018). Japanese producers are required to reduce waste by using less packaging material and charging for plastic bags. They are also required to recycle containers and packaging. Manufacturers of electric appliances are mandated to recycle waste; however, the cost of collecting and recycling waste, rests on consumers (ibid.).

The ingenuity of its cities reflects how India has already started to focus on the circular economy, though there are issues on which our cities can do a lot more—such as reducing waste, promoting the rental economy and encouraging service-based models (Potocnik and Gawel, 2019). We still have a lot of ground to cover in terms of reducing the nature and extent of waste. The move from plastic bags to cloth and jute is not universal. India is fast seeing the growth of bamboo-based products which can replace single-use plastics in many cases. A sustainable consumption pattern and resource efficiency as a way of life in cities, also promotes financial sustainability. The key financial transactions include user charges for waste collections, tipping fees to private operators, transportation costs, and pricing of recycled and reused products. It is advised that city- and state-level solid waste management plans should not ignore the financial cost element and should adopt appropriate models to ensure the financial viability of the city's solid waste management cycle. Indore alone generated INR 6 crore in 2019 and its user fees jumped sixty times from INR 60 lakh in 2014 to INR 36 crore 2019 (Santdasani, 2020). Being sustainable and clean is profitable as well.

Ridding Cities of Legacy Waste: The End of the Landfill

Cities like Indore and Ambikapur have been able to get rid of their landfills. Landfills are locations, usually outside the city. Since we paid little attention and committed few resources to treating and disposing of waste, much of it has ended up in landfills. Many Indian cities are lined with massive landfills which are a testimony to urban governance failure. It is estimated that 10,000 hectares of urban land is under waste dumpsites, some of which are over 50 metres high (such as those at Bhalswa, Ghazipur and Okhla in Delhi-NCR). Though Indore and Ambikapur have been able to address the issue of landfills, such successes remain far too few.

As per a 2014 report, 80 per cent of the waste was dumped at landfills and open sites which are a key contributor to GHG emissions (Singh, 2020a). By 2025, these waste dumps are expected to double in size (Livemint, 2018). Although Indian cities dump waste at the landfills; they would still need landfills to dispose residual waste left after segregating and using different methods to treat waste. Such dumpsites pose immense environmental hazards, including high GHG emissions. As per a 2016 estimate, CO_2 emissions from landfill sites in just three cities of India—Delhi, Mumbai, and Chennai—amounted to emissions from 137,000, 196,000, and 114,000 passenger vehicles respectively, annually (Ahluwalia and Patel, 2018).

Bioremediation and biomining are the preferred ways to deal with this legacy waste as we have seen in the case of Indore. On methods of final disposal, options such as biogas generation and composting are not sustainable solutions in larger cities since they generate by-products or large volumes of residue that these cities will find difficult to dispose of efficiently. Ideally, segregating, composting and recycling should handle most of the waste, but many big Indian cities still do not segregate their waste. As per an ICRIER study, Bengaluru and Pune were the only two cities out of the eight big cities studied that have a significant waste segregation process in place (ibid.).

The other processes are incineration (also called waste-to-energy), thermal pyrolysis and plasma gasification technologies. However, pyrolysis and plasma technology so far remain technically and economically unviable for the Indian market (ibid.). Hence, incineration is the best option. Singapore and other countries have widely used waste incinerators for solid waste management. The October 2015 'Report of the Sub-Group of Chief Ministers on Swachh Bharat Abhiyaan' also recommends waste incinerator plants for bigger municipalities and clusters of municipalities, and the use of composting for waste disposal for smaller towns and rural areas. The most important aspect of operating such incinerator plants is to ensure that they meet the emission standards. So far as they meet the safeguard measures, it could be an effective process to solve the issue of legacy waste (landfills) in India. In Germany, 35 per cent of the waste is incinerated and only 1 per cent goes to landfills; in Japan, 75 per cent is incinerated and only 10 per cent goes to landfills (ibid.). It would be wise to scale these solutions at the national level at a rapid pace in India.

Managing Biomedical Waste: Handling the Spike Due to Covid-19

The Covid-19 pandemic brought a spike in the amount of biomedical waste that needed disposal—PPE suits, masks, shoe-covers, gloves, among others. The 'Bio-medical Waste Management (BMWM) Rule, 2016' was already in place (PIB, 2020b). While the guidelines are in place, the enforcement at ULB-level remains weak and the common public remains largely uninformed. Some cities have charged hospitals high rates for disposing off such waste, as it requires different processes (Mascarhenas, 2020).

Civic bodies will have to construct hazardous waste treatment and disposal facilities in more districts, as transportation of such waste is an expensive process and hence an expensive part of the value chain. The good thing though is that the Swachh Bharat Mission-Urban has created value chains and systems that can be followed for this purpose. Any city which has a well-developed solid waste management value chain will be more than equipped to deal with the Covid-19-related biomedical waste. It is worth noting that much like construction and demolition (C&D) waste, biomedical waste did not receive enough attention from citizens and policymakers historically.

BUILDING INFRASTRUCTURE: URBAN HOUSING

When cities grow, slums increase. When London doubled in size between 1800 and 1840, its slums grew too, leading reformers such as Edwin Chadwick to conduct the first study on slums in the 1820s and '30s. The study identified a connection between poverty, housing and health (Hollis, 2013). The same happened in New York in the 1880s, as has been described by Jacob Riis in his book *How the Other Half Lives* (Riis, 1890). He recounted the same story that we see today in Indian cities—greedy landowners who exploit immigrants and labourers, forcing a large number of them to stay in small quarters. The same small quarters continue to house more and more people. This happened in Mumbai too as the city grew (by 43 per cent during 1971–81) to 2.2 million people. Dharavi came into existence and grew between the 1960s and the 1980s. Many schemes to revamp Dharavi have failed. They failed because their goal was slum removal. The government has finally realized that the only way forward is slum redevelopment (ibid.).

Leo Hollis rightly points out that people living in such informal and dilapidated housing do not call their colonies 'slums'. It is 'chawl' in Mumbai, 'bustee' in Kolkata and other parts of India, 'favelas' in Brazil, 'barraca' in Barcelona, 'tanake' in Beirut, 'shammasa' in Khartoum, 'colonias populares' in Mexico, and 'gecekondus' in Istanbul (ibid.).

The most common urban issue that people are likely to quote from the top of their heads is shortage of housing. This makes sense given how adequate housing determines every aspect of life—health and education outcomes, sense of being able to access the right opportunities, quality of life and chances of upward mobility, among others. Housing demand will continue to grow at a robust rate in India in the coming years, due to its high rate of urbanization, rising income levels, rural–urban migration and rise in nuclear families, among other factors. As per the Technical Urban Group on Urban Housing Shortage 2012–17, India faced an urban housing shortage of 18.78 million houses in 2012 (MoHUA, 2016a). Eighty per cent of this demand came from households living in congested houses, 12 per cent from households living in obsolescent houses, 5 per cent from households living in non-serviceable kuchha houses and a small share from homeless households (ibid.). Moreover,

76 per cent of the total demand came from ten states, and around 95 per cent from economically weaker sections (EWS) and low-income groups (LIG). Moreover, during 2001–11, the absolute housing shortage declined from 1.63 million in 2001 to 0.39 million (ibid.). Even though the absolute housing shortage is on a decline, the actual shortage is considerably high due to housing congestion and obsolescence (ibid.).

Startling new research points out that the shortage of housing in India has jumped from 18.78 million units in 2012 to 29–50 million units, of which 99 per cent stems from lack of housing for EWS (Roy and Meera, 2020). The study also estimates the number of inadequately housed households in slum areas. If this section is not considered, the corresponding figure for 18.78 million of 2012 would amount to 29 million in 2018 (ibid.).

We have seen how successive governments have launched housing schemes since independence. The current government also launched a 'Housing for All' scheme that aimed to build 20 million houses by 2022; a number that was eventually scaled down to 11.22 million houses (ibid.). In 2012, 80 per cent of the housing demand was due to congestion (defined as when a married couple does not have a separate room). As per the ICRIER paper, per capita consumption of floor area of congested households dwindled from 111 sq ft in 2012 to 83 sq ft in 2018 (ibid.). This reveals that the housing shortage has increased in Indian cities and that the majority of demand is coming from the EWS group. This may not necessarily turn into an actual demand (for a home) because it would depend on their income and personal choices. Driven by the congestion factor, urban housing remains a difficult issue to resolve.

What does this proliferation of slums and housing shortages tell us about cities? For one, national and sub-national governments have failed to create appropriate infrastructure commensurate with the growing needs of cities. Two, cities offer a plethora of opportunities, and cities that offer the greatest opportunities witness greater pressure from such housing deficits and slums. Edward Glaeser comments that 'Cities aren't full of poor people because cities make people poor, but because cities attract poor people with the prospect of improving their lot in life' (Glaeser, 2012). This tells us that we have missed the human element behind why slums and congested housing come about and what sustains them. No government can expect to just create housing in the middle of nowhere (to reduce land costs) and expect people to move there.

It takes time to understand and finance the varying needs of the local population, accommodating the needs of migrants swarming in for new opportunities and, above all, avoiding the haphazard expansion and growth of the city as has happened in many cities in India, and across the globe. Exacerbating this problem in many countries is the lack of inclusion of the informal economy, of migrants and of the urban poor. This has been India's blind spot too. Indian cities are yet to reach the point of redirecting the conversation to address these concerns.

To try to understand their dilemmas and choices, let us see what shapes the slums. There is one slum worth discussing, which tells a story of migration, struggles, poverty, urban centres and colonization. *The Hindu* newspaper shared an extract from Kalpana Sharma's book *Rediscovering Dharavi* (*The Hindu*, 2000; also see Sharma, 2000). It is a moving tale of Asia's second-largest slum, housing over a million people and spread over 175 hectares. Sandwiched between Mumbai's Central and Western suburban railway lines, Dharavi houses contiguous settlements with distinct identities that are separated by a nallah, a road, or even a poorly built wall. The original inhabitants of Dharavi were the Koli fisherfolk, who lived along the creek. The *Gazetteer of Bombay City and Island* (1909) listed Dharavi as one of the 'six great Koliwadas of Bombay' (Sharma, 2000). In the early eighteenth century, land reclamation projects connected the islands and swamps. A dam at Sion also accelerated the process of joining the separate islands into one long, tapered landmass. Unfortunately, in the process, the creek dried up and the Kolis lost their source of livelihood. The new land, however, provided more space for other communities to move in.

Modern Dharavi is built on two major chains of migration. First came the people who were originally from the Konkan coast and parts of Gujarat, and had been moved out of South Bombay's settlements and given land in Dharavi. One example of this is the potters from Saurashtra being relocated twice before they created 'Kumbharwada' (potters colony) on the land allocated to them in Dharavi. The second chain of migrants came directly to Dharavi. The author gives us examples of Muslim tanners from Tamil Nadu who set up the leather tanning industry, embroidery workers from Uttar Pradesh who started the ready-made garments trade. Some others who came were skilled in making treats and sweets. As Mumbai expanded, Dharavi ended up in the city's core areas from initially being on the periphery. As Kalpana Sharma puts it, 'Ironically, this heart-shaped settlement is now located literally in the heart of Mumbai' (ibid.). It houses people from all over India who have come to the city of dreams, to pursue their dreams; Suketu Mehta called Mumbai the *Maximum City* (Mehta, 2004).

Dharavi has existed as a slum for so long and hosts such a deluge of migrants (that still pour in each year), that it appears to be a living organism. It has its own local economy, societal ties, secular cultural fabric, and source of livelihood and support for everyone. Yes, the state of infrastructure, housing, sanitation and drinking water is abysmal in Dharavi, but slums cannot and should not be judged only upon their state of infrastructure. Yes, they may be illegal but they go beyond what meets the eye; slums offer—and have become—a way of life in Mumbai and in India. Slums have begun to have a cultural influence through the movies such as *Slumdog Millionaire* (2008) and more recently, *Gully Boy* (2019) that captures the life of real-life rappers Divine and Naezy. Both films are based on Dharavi.

Dharavi is bustling with energy and interactions and provides a vibrant local economic ecosystem. It is estimated that it has 20,000 small-scale enterprises and 80 per cent of Mumbai's plastic is recycled here in 15,000 single-room factories (Ratho, 2019). According to one 2015 estimate, the numerous micro-enterprises of Dharavi had a turnover of around USD 650 million and provided options for affordable housing to unending streams of informal workers with rents as low as USD 3 (Carr, 2015). There have been numerous attempts to rebuild and retrofit Dharavi since 1999. The current Dharavi Redevelopment Project is planned to be undertaken as a Special Purpose Vehicle (SPV) by the Dharavi Redevelopment Authority and funded by the government and a company in Dubai (Ratho, 2019). It is also a site for 'slum tourism'. Globally, every year around one million people go on 'slum tourism' trips to see slums in Cape Town, Mumbai and Rio De Janeiro, for instance. This is not to romanticize slum life. Life is difficult, infrastructure is poor and vulnerabilities are high. After Mumbai was hit by Covid-19, Dharavi recorded its first day of 'no new cases' only at the end of December 2020. People everywhere were worried that lack of space and sanitation might result in a human catastrophe for Dharavi. However, the study shows that 70 per cent of Dharavi already had Covid-19 antibodies by December 2020 (ibid.). We were really lucky that the mortality rate of Covid-19 was not too high then. We might not be this lucky when a new pandemic strikes.

The story of Dharavi reminds us of the human essence of the slums. Instead of treating urban housing and slum redevelopment/resettlement as an infrastructure exercise, we should appreciate why these slums are created, why urban housing shortage remains an issue and what nuanced approach can be taken to address what lies beneath this issue.

Urban Housing Shortage? Urban Land at the Centre of the Conundrum

The affordability of houses has declined as proved by many studies. As per an RBI study, the house prices have increased in thirteen metropolitan cities. Another estimate shows that housing prices have doubled over the last twenty years in the seven largest cities. One study in forty-nine cities, showed that households with an annual income of less than INR 6 lakh could only afford a house in any one of five cities (Roy and Meera, 2020). Some commentators believe that affordability is something that the government should not be concerned about. Nothing could be more wrong. The demand, from those who fall in the middle-income group (MIG) and above, has been mostly met by the private sector owing to the higher returns from the projects. However affordable housing has not received enough policy attention, given that the majority of demand is from sections that cannot afford properties delivered by the private sector. The government has moved away from its role of building houses and the private developers will not enter this space until the land is cheaper. Given that 99 per cent of the housing shortage is attributed to those in the lower-income group (LIG) and economically-weaker sections (EWS) of society, we ought to correct the land prices.

We will discuss urban land issues and strategies to unlock the potential of urban land in greater detail later in the book, but it is important to emphasize the role of land in determining the state of urban housing. Restrictive land policies, speculation and corruption in land markets, underutilized land parcels held by PSEs and railways, etc., have collectively, over the decades, drastically reduced the stock of land and led to a rise in land prices. Certain land policies in Indian cities have created an adverse environment for an efficient land market and, in turn, have negatively impacted the housing market. For instance, the restrictive floor space index (FSI) policy in Indian cities as compared to global counterparts, imposes one of the world's highest stamp duty and registration charges; tightly regulated land-use policies continue to limit the growth of the housing market in India (Abraham et al., 2017). Resolving these issues would soothe the price of land and further unlock private sector capital for building houses for EWS and LIG sections. For a flourishing housing market, it is important we first set the land market in order.

The Last Chance of Redemption for Urban Planning

The formal housing market has attended to the middle and upper-income brackets, but has been unable to meet the demand and needs of low-income households. Some blame it on the inability of urban planning to include their needs in the formal process (Roy and Meera, 2020). The most piercing adverse impacts of urban planning on housing are twofold: 1) making land unaffordable through complex policies that render housing for the masses unfeasible from the start; 2) overlooking the idea of informal housing and economy. In a way, it amounts to 'they can't address what they don't know'!

In being so busy giving a structure to a city, planners forget that structure follows people and economics, and not the other way round. Although urban planning does focus on urban housing at present, there is considerable scope for improvement. Going ahead, Indian cities should make it a practice of incorporating urban housing, particularly affordable housing, as a key component of the urban planning process. Urban planning needs to be more comprehensive and dynamic to ensure that urban housing seamlessly integrates with the other supporting infrastructure, transportation and land-use policies. There are key principles on urban housing on which urban planning needs to change its focus.

Emphasize access over ownership: India needs to step out from its conventional mindset of prioritizing ownership over access, which may not include ownership. Urban planning should lay more emphasis on access over ownership. Against this backdrop the confidence in, and right environment towards, rental housing is critical to ensuring housing for all.

Focus on affordable housing: Urban planning in India can redeem itself if it can play a constructive role in the rise of affordable housing in Indian cities.

Focus on vertical growth: Urban planning has so far focused on horizontal growth. This has stretched urban resources thin, leading to inefficient use of urban land, long commuter trips, and even contributed to high vehicular pollution due to increased motorization. Urban housing, fuelled by the right changes in policies such as FSI and rent control, should focus on vertical growth than horizontal sprawl.

Focus on mixed neighbourhoods: An important aspect is to ensure that neighbourhoods are not segregated. Less segregated neighbourhoods lead to better upward social and economic mobility. Mixed neighbourhoods are also good for the social harmony of cities. Experts point out that due to more segregated neighbourhoods the cities of Delhi and Ahmedabad see more communal tension than do cities like Lucknow and Jaipur (Bharathi and Ul-Huda, 2020). While informal segregation is difficult to deal with, legislation can ensure that there is no segregation sanctioned by the state—for instance, the US legislated the Fair Housing Act of 1968 and the Federal Fair Housing Act Amendments Act of 1988 to reduce segregation (ibid.). The foremost concern is to ensure that housing policies do not lead to segregation in cities and the creation of ghettos with inadequate infrastructure.

The United Nation's Urban Habitat III policy paper on Housing Policies highlights that the spatial inequality creates new poverty traps and people may face six challenges: 1) severe job restrictions; 2) high rates of gender disparities; 3) deteriorating living conditions; 4) social exclusion and marginalization; 5) lack of social interaction; and 6) high incidence of crime (UN-Habitat, 2017).

Dovetail housing with other aspects of daily life: The ICRIER paper by Roy and Meera notes that India has an estimated shortage of 50 million houses and recommends that if the housing initiative or even in-situ rehabilitation adversely affects the household's access to health, education, employment and other such benefits, it is likely that such a plan would fail and people would revert to the slums or to inadequate housing (Roy and Meera, 2020). This is the reason why Ahmedabad's rent-to-own housing programme failed to deliver. It moved people from the centre of the city to the periphery and as a consequence, 34 per cent of the selected beneficiaries did not relocate and 32 per cent returned to the slums (ibid.).

Treating cities as economic entities and not just spatial entities: Urban planning has approached the cities in the context of spatial entities, ignoring what is a common understanding now—that cities are economic entities and labour markets. Housing is an integral part of the urban economy and is a key factor in improving the quality of life. As per research, real estate projects in Mumbai take up to eight years to complete (Tandel and Gandhi, 2019). The high land prices make projects unviable and push developers to siphon off funds from one project to put into another. To address this, Maharashtra, for instance, has set up a Real Estate Regulatory Authority to ensure that projects meet procedures, funds are not siphoned off and there is adherence to the timeline (ibid.).

Nevertheless, the findings are alarming, given how the construction sector has a multiplier effect on the economy and has forward and backward linkages (direct and indirect) with around 250 industries. The success of cities will hinge on how well they can provide housing and associated services, as India continues to grow, urbanize and millions of people give their life a chance by moving to cities.

No Game Plan on Affordable Housing

There are essentially two components of urban housing: 1) affordable housing for LIG and EWS; and, 2) housing for MIG and above. Private developers have largely catered to demand from the latter, given its profitability. However, the majority of present demand comes from the affordable housing segment for LIG and EWS and therefore India should continue to make concerted efforts like the government's 'Housing For All' (HFA) scheme. While a lot may have been done by state and the Central governments on their files, the fact remains that an immense amount of unmet demand exists in the sector and it is going to rise, given the impending implosion of urban population and the setback caused by Covid-19.

There are some ways in which cities can make constructive interventions in the affordable housing sector. First, they have a critical role to play in lowering the costs. The study, 'India – Affordable Housing – An Inclusive Approach to Sheltering the Bottom of the Pyramid' highlights that construction costs, as a share of total costs, impact low-income/affordable housing more than luxury projects (J.L. LaSelle, 2012). It further mentions that for an affordable housing project, construction costs constitute around 50–60 per cent of the costs (ibid.). The use of prefabricated material is one of the ways through which costs are reduced under the HFA scheme. Indian states should continue to fund technical labs at institutes to find new ways of reducing construction costs. Another aspect of cost overrun is the long project approval time for such development projects. The delay in project approvals can lead to a significant rise in the project cost. State policies should focus on single window clearance with shorter approval time, as does Odisha's policy for 'Housing for All in Urban Areas 2015'. This will reduce the turnaround time and will make the sector more attractive to developers.

Second, the EWS and LIG segments suffer from a lack of financial access, which prevents them from either getting a new house or renovating the existing dwelling. As per the J.L. LaSelle (2012) report cited above, the majority of housing finance companies (HFCs) do not provide loan to people in the INR 3–10 lakh income bracket due to a perception that it would be a high-risk loan that could very well turn into a non-performing asset (NPA) for the HFC. Given that 65–70 per cent of urban workers are found in the unorganized sector (cash wages and no documentation), it is unlikely that they will witness any considerable increase in home loan lending without creative policy support from the Central and state governments.

Presently the Central government has undertaken various initiatives, such as interest subsidy and earmarking funds for housing credit. One strategy that has proved effective is beneficiary-led construction (BLC), a component of the HFA scheme of the Central government. The EWC households can claim a certain amount of subsidy from the government for the construction of a new room, along with a kitchen and/or toilet. A paper from ICRIER estimates that such kind of support can solve the issue of congestion and obsolescence in more than 22 million households (Roy and Meera, 2020). Policy measures such as using micro-mortgage financing mechanisms, leveraging existing SHGs, and providing documentation from city governments upon meeting some criteria could help this segment access more credit. Third, as highlighted previously, construction projects in Indian cities have to deal with a lengthy approval process and face higher transaction costs in registering property. Moreover, the policy issues on building bye-laws, FSI, zoning are all policies that hamper the growth of affordable housing in India. City authorities should work on easing the regulatory environments around the affordable housing market in their respective cities.

Concerted Efforts Toward Slum Redevelopment

As per the 2011 Census, 65 milion people (17.4 per cent of the total urban population) lived in slums. This amounted to 22.4 per cent of the people in the 2,543 cities which had slums. The Indian Census provides information on three types of slums: notified (36.1 per cent), recognized (27.6 per cent) and identified slums (36.3 per cent). It was estimated that 106.9 million people could be living in slums in 2018 in around 26.5 million slum households (ibid.).

Like most cities in the early stages of urbanization, Indian cities face the issue of an expanding slum population. The quality of living conditions greatly varies between slum and non-slum populations. The lack of healthy living conditions, lack of solid-waste collection, livelihood and tenancy vulnerability, lack of access to quality education and healthcare and congested living, among other issues, significantly mark slum life in cities. Despite efforts over the past few decades, India has not been particularly effective in housing its slum population in formal housing. However, the Indian government has taken a strong preventive measure in terms of accelerating affordable housing in Indian cities. This is an important first step, but we need to look at more holistic approaches. In addition to this preventive measure, states need to invest in curative measures of slum rehabilitation and resettlement.

Given the community bonds, established market exchanges and credit opportunities within slums and surrounding areas, the slum rehabilitation approach is better than slum resettlement. It offers the advantage of cost efficiency, community support and active engagement, and improvement in social indicators. The slum resettlement has given encouraging results in the cities of Kolkata, Mumbai, Jakarta and Manila (Panagariya et al., 2014). Moreover, cities should learn from the Gujarat model for slum redevelopment (ibid.). It differs from the Mumbai model, wherein the developer selects the slum for redevelopment and has to get approval; whereas in Gujarat, the builders are invited through open bidding. This approach reduces the irregularities introduced from the builders' end (Ashar and Shukla, 2014). For resettlement projects, city governments must ensure that transport connectivity (mainly rapid transit systems) and provision of basic services such as drinking water, electricity and sanitation are available. In all, Indian cities must pay serious and concerted attention to slum redevelopment.

One state-level initiative needs to be mentioned here, as it has adopted a more humane approach to slum redevelopment—Odisha's JAGA mission (also known as the Liveable Habitat Mission). This uses Odisha Land Rights to Slum Dwellers Act, 2017. Under this Act, technology has been used to map houses and grant land titles to slum dwellers. JAGA aims to give titles to as many as 200,000 households living in 2,000 slums in 109 small and medium towns of the state (Chakrabarty, 2020a). Then, such households are given support to upgrade their dwellings by converging schemes on drinking water, toilets, LED lights, use of permanent materials, among others (ibid.).

From Access to Ownership: Focus on Rental Housing

As per a report, there are 11.09 million vacant homes in India (Sharma, 2019). However, the Central government estimated that India needed additional 19 million houses in 2012 (Iyer, 2020). The share of owner-occupied households increased from 46.2 per cent in 1961 to 69.2 per cent in 2011 (Roy and Meera, 2020). This is a function of the obsession of successive governments at all three levels—Central, state and local—to build new houses, rather than resolving the supply-demand mismatch.

The Indian real estate market is skewed in favour of home ownership rather than access to homes. It nudges people to buy houses for tax revenue and growth purposes, and inadvertently discourages them from renting houses. The benefits of rentals—for the individual, the city, and the national economy—are thus lost. The key problem with rental housing is that unless the rental yields go up, the rental housing market will not improve significantly. As of now, the rental yields go up to 5 per cent, that too in a few cities (Chakrabarty, 2020a). The only way to improve yields is to correct land and housing construction costs, since rents are more market-determined. The importance of such correction increases further in the case of low-rent housing. We suggest strategies to correct land availability and prices in the 'urban land' section in this book.

In addition to the land prices, the regulatory environment around the rental housing market has been distortionary in favour of tenants. The Central government has drafted the Model Tenancy Act in 2019, and states would really benefit if they reformed their Rent Control Acts on the lines of the Model Act. For decades, the Indian rental market suffered because the various Rent Control Acts gave asymmetrical power to tenants. This prevented homeowners from freely renting out their homes and when they did, they shied away from renovating and redeveloping them. This has now created a large stock of poorly maintained homes-for-rent in India.

The Central government's twin moves: 1) the Model Tenancy Act; and, 2) the National Urban Rental Housing policy should provide a much-needed fillip to the rental market if the states adopt them in their state laws. The rental housing policy is aimed at increasing rental housing stock for both target groups: the urban poor and homeless through social rental schemes as well as for working, and high- and middle-income group individuals using institutional and public programmes. The policy uses a range of tools, including tax benefits for social rental housing properties, treating these properties as residential accommodations for the purpose of property tax and utility charges, and higher FAR for rental properties, among others.

Cities should undertake bold initiatives to encourage rental housing. For instance, it is estimated that around 3–5.5 million households live in slums on lands owned by urban local bodies (ULBs) (IIHS, 2015a). To address the issues of low municipal revenues, land insecurity and poor living conditions in slums, the ULBs can convert such land into social rental housing projects and charge nominal rent in a manner that can fund the provision of essential services to slum dwellers. Such projects are more feasible in smaller cities where slum populations are lower and the cost to provide essential services to them will also be lower.

We should also seriously look at launching a rental-voucher scheme. Harvard University examined the impact of 'moving to opportunities' in a study that covered a twenty-year programme that provided low-income households a housing voucher (Rose, 2016). This voucher paid the difference between the market rent and the rent paid by them. During the course of twenty years, 5 million households received the voucher. The results are not obvious but cannot be overemphasized—the households that moved to better neighbourhoods had a higher chance of upward mobility. Children raised in these households earned more as adults than those who continued to stay on in low-income neighbourhoods. Children raised in the better-off neighbourhoods scored better on key outcomes of education, health, lifestyle and economic trajectory.

The onset of Covid-19 could even act as a boon for rental housing in India. First, the uncertainty of jobs and incomes will compel many people to rent rather than buy houses. Second, homeowners might list their properties to realize income support in times of income vulnerability (Chakrabarty, 2020a). Third, the focus of all tiers of the government is now on rental housing for migrants. After India witnessed one of the biggest movements of internal migrants due to the severe lockdown, the Central government launched in July 2020 the Affordable Rental Housing Complex (ARHC) scheme (discussed earlier) for providing housing to urban migrants. Its aims were to: 1) repurpose the 1.08 lakh vacant houses under JNNURM and Rajiv Awas Yojana; and, 2) encourage public and private players to provide low-cost housing.

The ARHC scheme comes with a host of provisions and regulations but the success of any low-cost housing in a country like India will depend upon how well these rental complexes provide connectivity to the day jobs of the tenants and at what cost. A success on this scheme can decongest urban slums and give people an option to escape slum life while they transition from rural life to decent paying jobs in cities. Given that the EWS and LIG groups constitute the maximum population facing a housing shortage, the governments can look at using rental voucher schemes as an option to encourage people to move into such housing formats.

5
Urban Transport: Moving People, Ferrying India

CONSIDERABLE literature establishes the positive link between infrastructure development and an increase in output, productivity, growth and employment (Mohanty, 2014). Studies on similar lines attribute high growth in eastern and central Chinese cities to transport connectivity. The lack of proper connectivity also explains the high income disparity in multiple Chinese provinces. We have seen earlier in this book in the section on urban history how key historical urban centres, including in India, prospered due to transport connectivity. Venice, New York, London, Amsterdam, Mumbai, Chennai, Kolkata, Singapore, Beijing and San Francisco were all on major trade routes. Inland cities fared well, as road and later rail networks developed. Now, air connectivity is considered essential for any city to grow at a robust pace and sustain that momentum.

Even in rural India, one of the most successful schemes has been the Pradhan Mantri Gram Sadak Yojana—a village road-building scheme started by former Prime Minister Atal Bihari Vajpayee. The scheme has continued despite the changing fortunes of leading national and regional parties in every state. I have personally interviewed hundreds of people in villages impacted by it and asked them why they rated this scheme as the best. The simplicity of their answers holds boundless lessons for policymakers. They told me that this scheme connected their villages to nearby urban centres and thus provided them year-round connectivity to better livelihoods and healthcare services. They said they could manage the other challenges on their own, but connectivity to better wage and livelihood opportunities in urban areas had transformed their lives.

Transport plays an instrumental role in creating agglomeration economies, one of the defining features of cities and the key reason behind the success of cities. When combined with the tools of planning and urban land, transport can yield exponential gains. In the simplest terms, it can reduce commuter trips and commuting time, make it easier to do business, enhance functionality of labour markets and increase access to all services including employment. Thus, it reduces transaction costs and makes cities everything that we can imagine—growth engines, equitable, sustainable, liveable and resilient. If cities can be considered as living beings, transport is the blood that keeps our cities running. If it takes too much effort, cities may feel fatigued. If it clots, cities go into shock.

A good city-wide transportation system is critical to achieving the agglomeration economies that come with urbanization. An efficient transport system reduces transaction costs at all levels and becomes a facilitator for the economic growth and liveability of a city. It is the lynchpin that connects people to people, people to markets, people to places and people to services. If the transport system of a city is choked and congested, it renders the city inefficient and less productive. This is evident in many of the emerging cities in developing economies including India where citizens are spending hours daily commuting on congested roads and inhaling toxic air due to increased vehicular emissions.

Innovative thinking on urban transportation can unlock many benefits. Jaimie Lerner was the young mayor of Curitiba, in Brazil. He went at breakneck speed to convert some major areas such as the Rua Quinze de Novembro, one of the major streets of the city, into pedestrianized zones (Adler, 2016). He believed the area should not be deserted when shops downed their shutters and cars parked away. In manoeuvring to implement his plan, he outwitted the shopkeepers, who were initially against it. Next, he introduced new lanes for buses, which was against the global tide in favour of subways. He made a telling remark about urban works, 'If you want creativity, cut one zero from the budget. If you want sustainability, cut two zeros!' (Ibid.). As the bus movement succeeded, he found new areas to unlock the growth of bus transport—elevated platforms through which passengers could move into buses, longer buses, and prepayment for tickets. Now, 85 per cent of the city uses the Bus Rapid Transit or BRT system and more than 300 cities globally are experimenting with it.

Notably, BRT failed in Delhi. But that shouldn't stop other cities from championing it. Each city is different. While the BRT project failed to take off in Delhi, it has done remarkably well in the cities of Ahmedabad, which spurred adoption in other cities across India—Rajkot, Indore, Surat, the twin cities of Pune and Pimpri Chinchwad, and the twin cities of Hubballi-Dharwad (ITDP India, n.d.; Gupta, 2020b). Curitiba, at the same time as it was pushing BRT, was championing waste recycling and providing as much as 50 sq mt of green space per person. Not surprisingly, Lerner became a three-time mayor of the city. Similarly, in Delhi, the metro rail services succeeded when the Central leadership, the state leadership under Sheila Dikshit, and the managing director of Delhi Metro Rail Corporation, E. Sreedharan, came together. The success of Delhi Metro is so immense that cities all over India are now undertaking metro rail projects, even where it doesn't make financial sense.

If not done right, the costs of mismanaged and overlooked urban transport could be huge and far-reaching. The heightened urbanization levels and even higher acceleration in motorization levels does not bode well for urban transport in Indian cities. From 1951 to 2011, India's population grew at an annual rate of 3.8 per cent. In the same period, the number of registered motor vehicles went from about 0.3 million in 1951 to nearly 142 million in 2011—a double-digit growth rate. As per the Centre for Science and Environment, private vehicle ownership increased by 700 times, from 0.3 million in 1951 to 210 million in 2015

(PTI, 2019b). Half of this was added over a period of fifty-seven years from 1951 to 2008, the remaining was added over the next six years. Between 1981 and 2011, the total number of registered vehicles grew at an average rate of 11.5 per cent. This trend looks set to continue at the hands of a growing urban population with increasing purchasing power. If unchecked, this trend could cause urban transport to become a serious handicap for efficient urbanization. It could lead to choked road networks and further deteriorating air quality with serious public health implications.

The issue of urban transport becomes more complex because Indian cities have failed to address basic issues. Commute options and corresponding costs significantly vary for different citizens when they step out for work or leisure. An upper middle-income household prefers a different mode of transport compared to someone from the lower middle-income group, or a poor migrant. The preferred choice of conveyance is mostly an owned vehicle, with little predilection for public transport—unless one's means do not leave much to choose. Thereafter, congestion and pollution remain constant adverse companions throughout the commute.

Commute time and costs are not the only trade-offs. In our failure to integrate land-use planning and transportation we have exponentially lessened the quality of life in our cities. Given the convoluted and institutional fragmentation in city transport, if we attempt to reform urban transport, we fail to locate where the actual responsibility lies. Some major obstacles to unleashing the benefits of a robust and efficient transport system in Indian cities are the lack of substantial focus on demand side management, little focus on non-motorized transport, a declining share of public transport and the inability to raise finances.

It is pertinent to solve the issue of congestion while we are in midst of our transition to an urbanized country. As per a study, from 1990 to 2014, the share of 12-metre-wide roads has remained constant whereas the number of 4-metre-wide (narrow) roads have increased (Shah and Agrawal, 2019). Researchers have pointed out commuters in peri-urban areas travel through narrow roads to get to the wider roads to their workplace. This diminishes productivity (ibid.). This is based on Alain Bertaud's findings that productivity declines after twenty minutes of travel to work (Bertaud, 2018). This is a serious loss of efficiency in our cities.

The figures in some major cities are startling. As part of Master Plan 2031, estimates from Bangalore Development Authority noted that 1.18 crore citizens waste 60 crore person-hours annually in Bengaluru due to congestion. The combined cost to four cities—Delhi, Mumbai, Kolkata and Bengaluru—due to congestion, amounted to USD 22 billion (NITI Aayog and BCG, 2018). Can we fathom the loss that congestion continues to cause in thousands of Indian cities? The Traffic Index (peak hour congestion defined in terms of percentage of additional time to travel during peak hours) provides a telling picture of Indian cities. Traffic Index percentages for four Indian cities—Delhi (129 per cent), Mumbai (135 per cent), Bengaluru (162 per cent) and Kolkata (171 per cent)—are quite high as compared to an average of 67 per cent for other Asian cities. Another index, the TomTom Traffic Index by TomTom (an in-vehicle navigation company), covers 416 cities across fifty-seven countries on six continents. A recent edition showed that India is badly impacted by the forces of congestion; four out of the ten most congested cities in Asia are in India: Bengaluru, Delhi, Mumbai and Pune (Garg, 2020).

Indian cities should work towards the target that every citizen is within ten to fifteen minutes (or 400 m) of safe, reliable and affordable public transport. This is in line with the Government of India's 2014 National Urban Transport Policy (MoUD, 2014). This policy focused more on planning for people and vehicles and spelt out recommendations on a range of issues, including sustainable mobility, accessibility for all citizens at affordable cost and within a reasonable time. It detailed some key strategies on urban transport planning, public transport, traffic management, financing, governance and non-motorized transport among others (ibid.). Already, there have been some notable measures on easing urban transport in India—such as the Odd-Even Scheme, Traffic Signal Synchronization in Mumbai, Eastern Peripheral Expressway in Delhi and Intelligent Traffic Management Systems under the Smart Cities Mission. However, the political economy of states has led to an increasing obsession with metro systems in various cities which has diverted our focus and resources from more efficient solutions. We discuss some of the solutions that may help Indian cities solve the problem of urban transport.

INTEGRATED PLANNING AND SINGLE AUTHORITY

No city worldwide has reached its zenith without facing and then eventually overcoming the mobility conundrum. The fact that a city is facing a mobility challenge speaks volumes about the attractiveness of the city. One positive cause could be that more people are moving to the city because of the opportunities it offers. A negative explanation could be that planning has failed to deal with the influx of people.

Therefore, integrated and comprehensive planning becomes key to untangling the mobility conundrum. In the subsequent sections, we look at other specific interventions to ease the urban mobility. However, at the broader level, there are some major factors to be kept in mind. First, personal vehicles are one of the most inefficient modes of travel, with asset utilization of around 4–5 per cent (Reddy, 2018). This implies that your personal vehicle lies unused for 95 per cent of the time. Second, inefficient transport solutions lead to higher pollution. (ibid.). Third, the inability to solve mobility causes congestion. In most metro cities, the average speed is around 20–30 kmph (ibid.). Fourth, people should have options to choose when they want to travel from point A to B; a single option does not bode well for the city's transport. Fifth, travel options should focus on creating experiential value. We have seen in other parts of the book that women face maximum harassment in public transport and children do not feel safe in cities as they do not feel safe in public transport.

For Indian cities to achieve sustainable urban mobility solutions, it is critical that within the next few years all Indian cities with a population of more than 1 million people should integrate land use and transport planning. This procedure needs to be institutionalized and eventually be extended to all Indian cities. To further deliver on this strategy, all cities/metropolitan regions must have a single institution responsible for urban transport. Within cities, different modes of transport are planned for and operated in isolation by different institutions. This leads to considerable institutional fragmentation. Therefore, every city or metropolitan region should have a single institution with complete and comprehensive responsibility for urban transport. The institution's primary responsibilities will include planning, coordination, monitoring and evaluation—not actual operations.

A good example of the same is the New York Metropolitan Transportation Authority wherein this single agency has been successful in consolidating revenues from multiple sources. It has brought together revenues from federal, state, local governments and earmarked transportation taxes along with tolls (UN-DESA, 2015). Another case in point is the success of Stockholm, Sweden. StorstockholmsLokaltrafic was created as a single regional body to handle issues related to urban transport. It took over responsibilities previously shared amongst different municipalities. Other examples include the Toronto metro system, Transport for London and the public transport systems in Singapore and Hong Kong. These are examples of successful integration of land use and public transport. Urban planning, in tandem with transport planning, provides an opportunity to leverage locations to achieve successful transit-oriented development. This suggestion is explained in greater detail in the chapter on planning.

Whether we are using a rickshaw, the metro, a bus or our car, we should know which agency is responsible for our travel. A single agency responsible for all transport-related matters in cities with a certain population size and above, is critical for untangling the fragmented nature of commute within cities. The Department of Transportation in the US pretty much performs the same job at the city level. India envisaged a Unified Metropolitan Transport Authority but that exercise remained largely on paper. For instance, Chennai passed the Chennai Unified Metropolitan Transport Authority Act in 2011, but the authority is yet to come into existence (Kaveri, 2020). Presently in Chennai, public buses are operated by the Metropolitan Transport Corporation, the metro rail network is managed by Chennai Metro Rail Limited and the suburban and the rail-based Mass Rapid Transit System comes under Southern Railways. We can see the same distinction across all major cities. This fragmentation is financially costly, delays projects, creates duplication and cannibalization, while also failing to service under-serviced areas and people.

HYPER-CONNECTIVITY THROUGH MASS TRANSIT

Presently, the public transport industry in India either takes the form of public entities that plan and operate different modes of public transport services, or small private operators who operate these services. The global trend has been towards separating planning from operations, where a public entity plans the services and then contracts operations to private operators using a competitive procurement process. This is the model that needs to be encouraged as it effectively combines the efficiency of the private sector in operations with the public sector's responsibility of ensuring universal service. This means that state governments should engage private players to provide hyperconnectivity between major cities within the same state and different states.

Hyperconnectivity through mass transit should be the defining feature of Indian cities in the coming decades. I have strongly advocated looking at Indian cities as city clusters to drive growth. The agglomeration economies of clusters with a 'thick' labour market will kick in when the city clusters achieve hyperconnectivity. China and Japan have high-speed rail services such as the Shinkansen (Japan); we have just started using metro rail as one option. We will eventually need more metro-line connectivity, high-speed rail, suburban rail services (though not operating at current speeds) and buses. As an important aspect of urban transport, we have to provide such connectivity through multi-modal mass transit services—providing round the clock connectivity at a fraction of present travel times. This aspiration is just necessary to make our cities function as robust engines of economic growth and increase their liveability.

Another aspect of hyperconnectivity using mass transit is to focus on transport in a way that brings cities closer to their suburban areas and peripheries. Moreover, the core of the city should be identified with a dense, multi-modal transport system. This will ensure that people can stay outside the core of cities and travel to work in a cost-

and time-effective manner. This strategy will also positively impact the land and housing rental rates in the city. Moreover, cities will be more effective in planning the flow of people into the city and outside in a manner that will reduce the transaction costs. Since urban boundaries are spreading beyond municipal boundaries, transport networks need to be designed with a regional focus, integrating the need for suburban travel with the need for intra-city travel. Indian metro systems are trying to fill this gap.

The country launched the National Common Mobility Card and Automatic Fare Collection Gate Standards in March 2019. The metro has been customized for local conditions with the introduction of MetroLite and MetroNeo, which cost 40 per cent and 20–25 per cent less, respectively (MoHUA, 2020). In 2014, the country had around 250 km of operational metro lines, which increased to 702 km by December 2020, in eighteen Indian cities. Another 1,000 km-plus of metro has been sanctioned in a total of twenty-seven cities (ibid.).

Metro systems are extremely expensive and disrupt in an avoidable manner. However, politicians prefer the metro because it has been sold as one of the harbingers of a modern city. The reality is that there is a better option available—buses, even better if they are electric buses. A multi-modal mix of metros, buses, rickshaws, cycles and two/three-wheelers should help Indian city dwellers. A highly connected central urban core will also be good for the environment as people can transition to public transport. For other trips, they may not have to use their private vehicles as their trips for leisure, essentials and shopping are closer to their place of stay.

ALL EYES ON PUBLIC TRANSPORT

Over the past few decades, India has witnessed double-digit growth in the passenger vehicle segment, while the share of public transport—particularly for buses has declined. From 1951 to 2011, the share of buses in total vehicular composition declined from 11 per cent to 1.1 per cent (Planning Commission, n.d.). India has 1.2 buses for every 1,000 people, compared to 6.5 in South Africa and 8.6 in Thailand. Even among states, the disparity is large. Karnataka and Rajasthan have

3.9 and 0.7 buses per 1,000 population respectively, as compared to 0.1 in Odisha and 0.02 in Bihar (NITI Aayog and BCG, 2018). A Centre for Science and Environment report highlights that every car and two-wheeler trip causes seven to fourteen times more pollution than a bus trip made in Delhi (PTI, 2019b). There is a pressing need to arrest this decline and restore the share of public transport, as part of the urban transport mix. The over dependence on passenger vehicles is a cause of severe congestion, high local air pollution, long travel times, increasing incidence of road accidents and a rapid increase in the consumption of petroleum fuels.

Thus, going ahead, the strategy on public transport should be four-pronged: 1) increase public transport penetration to increase accessibility to all; 2) improve the quality of services, this means a quantum improvement in convenience, cleanliness, reliability and safety; 3) ensure affordability of public transport; 4) reposition the image of public transport (from a mode of transport for those who cannot afford private transport to the first preferred choice) by undertaking a sustained campaign. Although the first three goals of quality, accessibility and affordability run contrary to each other given the limited resources, in the long term the ability of ULBs to increase their revenue and to contract out operations to private players can help achieve these goals.

Stakeholders in India are already realizing the importance of public transport and have undertaken measures to reposition and reform public transport. Some noticeable examples include: the success of the Delhi Metro and the successful use of branded stations to meet financing needs, and the uptake of Bengaluru's Transport Corporation's AC buses and feeder buses. The rising use of bus rapid transit is good for Indian cities in the long run. Global examples also provide encouragement that similar cases can be replicated in India. For instance, the success of Curitiba in Brazil, the complementary role of rail and bus in Helsinki, and the success of Hong Kong Metro Corporation, all provide insights on how transit-oriented development, channelling development, efficient use of planning and, most importantly, the role of public transport, ensure the success of cities and regions.

One way to make public transport appealing and popular is by making it gender sensitive. So far, public transport has been designed through the lens of men or has been gender blind in the sense that women have different concerns when it comes to transport. Women are ready to downsize to low-paying jobs and enrol in poor quality institutions if they think that their daily commute will be safer by doing so. This is a damning indictment of our cities, let alone our society and urban planning.

Public transport has gone for a tailspin in the aftermath of Covid-19. Travel for discretionary and recreational purposes is mostly eroded. The metro re started operations around six months after the March lockdown, whereas buses started plying sooner. Nevertheless, the urban public transport in India and also worldwide is mostly a loss-making business. It is run for positive externalities of equity, connectivity, reduced congestion and a cleaner environment. Occupancy ratios in all forms of public transport have come down thanks to Covid-19, exacerbating their losses. Public transport is now facing a challenge, albeit with two possibilities. The challenge is that spread of a pandemic is greatest in places of public concentration such as public transport. The possibilities include that the pandemic comes with an expiry, sooner or later everyone will be vaccinated and people will resort to public transport. Overall, if positioned right, public transport can do wonders in increasing the resilience of cities.

In the light of Covid-19, many people have opted to use their own vehicles and those on the fence are leaning towards buying their own vehicles. Occupancy levels in public transport are low, losses are high and fear of infection is pervasive. During this gestation period, before life returns to normalcy, public transport authorities should focus on refurbishing buses and operating the metro rail instead of starting new metro rail projects. Such projects incur high expenditure and the money can be utilized more effectively elsewhere, mostly in buses that have lower costs.

Post Covid-19, the public transport system will not be able to pivot away from social distancing and sanitization. This in turn, will rid the urban public transport system of two prevalent malaises—over-occupancy and lack of hygiene. Buses would have to be sanitized when they stop for a break after completing their run. Even after mass vaccination, the infection will not disappear and a considerable share of the population will still be vulnerable. The public transport capacity needs to be expanded and investing in buses is cheaper than creating new metro lines, especially in cities where they are not financially viable. Investing in public transport might be costly, but is imperative for the larger battle of public transport versus private vehicles, import bill of crude oil, congestion and pollution.

Second, the staff should be adequately protected. The space around the driver could be cordoned off with a plastic sheet and buses should reduce contact by allowing interoperability of smart cards as envisioned in the One Nation One Card (National Mobility Card) launched in March 2019 (Philip, 2020). These cards are mostly used for metro rails but buses all over Indian cities need to upgrade to start using them.

AVAILABILITY OF PAID PARKING FACILITIES

Traffic congestion in India is a common sight mainly caused by vehicles illegally parked on roadsides. The majority of public places in cities don't have parking facilities, and in few cases where the facilities exist, parking fees don't reflect actual land costs. Given the parity in land rates of the central business district (CBD) in major Indian cities and world cities, parking rates in Indian cities do not reflect actual costs. The CBD parking charges in Chennai, Delhi and Mumbai are less than USD 1.5 per day as compared to higher charges in other cities: Bangkok (USD 13.2), Mexico City (USD 15), Singapore (USD 24.6), and New York (USD 41) (MoHUa, 2016b).

Indian cities should suggest that vehicle buyers present parking facility proof before vehicle purchase. Parking on roadsides and in front of shops is presently the common practice in the majority of metropolitan cities in India and this increases fuel consumption, road rage, traffic jams, road accidents, and transaction costs of travel. City authorities should adopt large- and small-scale PPP models to create parking spaces, and should work with neighbourhoods to create underground 'neighbourhood parking lots'. City authorities can provide the land-use permit and part of fixed costs, and encourage the neighbourhood to park cars in such parking lots following the purchase of a fixed yearly/

monthly/daily pass. This investment should be complemented by strict enforcement rules prohibiting illegal parking and encroachment.

NON-MOTORIZED TRANSPORT: A MODE OF CHOICE

The two important issues should be kept in mind regarding motorized transport (Glaeser, 2012). First, motorized transport leads to negative externalities, since every driver factors in her/his individual costs and benefits. The illegal parking and ensuing pollution, congestion, loss of productivity, adverse impact on climate change, and pushing pedestrians and other vulnerable groups such as street vendors to the sidelines of roads—are just few of the many ways in which motorized transport distributes the costs to people who are not even using it. Second, the creation of more roads and highways could lead to increased motorized travel. Scholars have found that the travel distance is closely correlated to the length of new highways (Stromberg, 2015). In India, we still need to build a considerable number of roads and highways to ensure the ease of movement of people and goods. However, we must remember that congestion is not a problem of the future and it cannot be solved by creating more flyovers. We will have to lay focus on non-motorized transport (NMT) concurrently; this would include NMT such as bicycles and cycle-rickshaws and of course, walking.

India severely lacks pedestrian-oriented planning and design with the provision of non-NMT infrastructure. There have been some piecemeal efforts in different states and cities. What India needs is a national-level focus on NMT and an entire range of ecology around it. The Central government can launch a national mission on NMT in partnership with state governments. It can also focus on creating infrastructure and using transport intelligence information to find ways to encourage NMT between places within cities, say within 20 km or less. Eventually, state and city governments can only allow NMT in all congested markets and public spaces while ensuring corresponding parking spaces are provided at different junction points of such markets. For instance in Lucknow, the congested Hazratganj and Aminabad markets can be provided with the right infrastructure and bikes at key connections for people to move to NMT for their shopping journeys.

Another policy can be what Sao Paulo has adopted—making its main street, Avenida Paulista, car-free on Sundays. This has not only led to lower congestion and lesser accidents but has created a public space that has spurred all sorts of social experiments.

Global lessons are encouraging and Indian cities could replicate their success. For instance, a quarter of the trips in the Netherlands are made using bicycles (van der Zee, 2015). This nation has developed a world-class standard on cycling infrastructure, which specifies speed limits, lane width and other details. Amsterdam is ruled by bikers and with good reason too. Between the 1950s and the 1970s, the share of bike trips declined in the city from 80 per cent to 20 per cent (ibid.). This led to a high number road fatalities and the kind of activism (that we are now seeing in India) swept through Amsterdam. People engaged in large numbers in this activism, especially after 400 children lost their life in the city in 1971. Increasingly, civil society was able to effectively lobby for the city to become cycle-friendly by creating speed bumps and bends that slowed the speed of cars. After the oil crisis of 1973, the Dutch Prime Minister advocated for car-free Sundays that we now see in cities such as Sao Paulo. Thereafter, more cities and more people moved towards using cycles. Presently, 38 per cent of all trips in Amsterdam are made using cycles (ibid.). In Australia too, the government of New South Wales has defined standards for footpaths and cycle lanes. Indian cities can quickly adopt these guidelines with modifications as per local needs.

There are three important concerns on NMT. First, comfort of pedestrians. Singapore's provision of sheltered walkways (from MRT to bus stations) made with non-slippery material ensures that a higher share of people use it. The other example is Winnipeg, Canada, where the Weather Protected Walkway System has created a large network of indoor pedestrian walkways. This has thereby led to mass-adoption of NMT. Second, the idea to make NMT make accessible to the elderly and the disabled communities is key to make any sort of meaningful efforts towards NMT. Third, we need to ensure that the incentives for NMT—both fiscal and physical—should be aligned with the long-term vision of promoting it. The costs of bicycles, infrastructure for NMT, private services for matching people to bicycles and cycle-rickshaws, investments for membership, and buying such transport should be incentivized at all levels.

The Covid-19 crisis has accelerated this change. Many cities like Milan, Paris and London, while unlocking, converted hundreds of kilometres of streets for use by NMT and public transport (Sadik-Khan and Solomonnow, 2020). Bogota has made a 75 mile stretch car-free, which used to be open for bikes once a week. It has added further 47 miles to it (Taylor, 2020). The use of NMT was imminent and Covid-19 has only accentuated this transition.

EMPHASIS ON DEMAND MANAGEMENT

When it comes to transport in Indian cities, the effort so far has been to enhance the supply of infrastructure and services to meet the growing demand. As Indian cities are staring at steep infrastructure deficits, it is wise to create appropriate infrastructure. Nevertheless, there is evidence that mere infrastructure creation is not the best way out of congestion problems. Evidence shows that if road capacity increases traffic during the peak period also increases until the road is again congested (Litman, 2018). Moreover, in a world moving rapidly towards hyperconnectivity in the physical and virtual space, this orientation towards demand fulfilment will change.

Indian cities of the future should focus on demand management to reduce demand in a manner that doesn't adversely impact the city's economy, society, or stakeholders. Cities will have to be creative in managing demand in ways that suit their needs. For instance, cities with a common Smart Card for all public transport can allow discounts on travel (directly credited to their cards) for non-peak travel. Other sets of policies could include careful integration of land use and transport plans, encouragement to companies that allow home-based work on some days, increasing the depth and breadth of public transport coverage, and finding ways of sharing freight carriers more efficiently.

A policy measure to manage demand is 'congestion pricing'—charging a small fee for driving in a certain location in a city. Such pricing is usually applied for a certain period during a day. One of the early proponents of the idea was Nobel Prize winner William Vickrey.

He noted that 'users of private cars and taxis, and perhaps also of buses, do not, by and large, bear costs commensurate with the increment costs that their user imposes' (Glaeser, 2012). Congestion pricing was first introduced in Singapore in 1975 and has now evolved into a very effective mechanism to keep the entire city congestion-free; it fetches the national exchequer more than USD 50 million a year (Marshall, 2016). London also adopted congestion pricing in 2003, introduced by Mayor Ken Livingstone. Within the first two weeks driving reduced by 20 per cent, and over the next two years declined by 30 per cent, providing a positive fillip to the public transit system (Glaeser, 2012). Mixed-use land planning can also ensure that one can either walk or use NMT to go shopping or to work.

The use of Intelligent Transport Systems (ITS) is also fast gaining currency in India and is used for varied purposes. The Smart Cities Mission is proving to be a critical catalyst of this change. Singapore is a classic case of the success of the use of an ITS. Other examples include the Los Angeles Department of Transportation, which reduced travel times by 13 per cent, delays by 21 per cent and stopping by 31 per cent, just by adjusting signals based on real-time demand (Niti Aayog and BCG, 2018). Automated vehicle ID and fines are already used in the cities of Delhi, Chandigarh and Bengaluru. We need to scale this capability to cities with more than 1 lakh population. Germany uses such models to give penalty points to drivers. Fines and redressal depend upon the number of points with drivers. The gathering of big data on travelling patterns by ITS can help public transport, planning and governance in a manner that can influence behaviour change, bolster revenues, improve utilization of a city's assets and improve the productivity of cities, while enforcing demand management to curb the need for travel.

AGILITY TO ABSORB NEW DEVELOPMENTS

Urban transport is undergoing rapid changes across the world. One such change has been the entry of companies such as Uber and Ola, which offer the triple advantage of the convenience of a personal vehicle, less space need for parking and lower fuel consumption. Another related change is the focus on alternative fuel technologies, particularly electricity. India spends considerable money on importing petroleum fuel but the focus on electric vehicles could lead to some reduction in import bill. A strong push towards electric vehicles, as in China, needs to be considered for the medium-term implementation. The return to NMT the world over also has health, social and economic benefits attached to it.

In essence, the urban transport authorities at the Central, state and, particularly, city levels need to be agile to absorb suitable new developments into their transport mix. Given the diversity of upcoming options, there can be no specific guideline on how these options should be absorbed. However, the guiding principle is to be agile in seeking and adapting to the right developments. The adaptation would entail action on financing, infrastructure, regulatory environment, behavioural change, creating an enabling ecology and accommodating new stakeholders, among others. The opportunity lies in creating that institutional agility of responding to such global changes on urban transport. Besides, Indian cities should create indigenous solutions to our local transport issues. One way to achieve this is to foster relationships and/or incubate centres at technical universities to stay on the cutting edge of transit technology.

The Indian transport sector has shown strong resilience in adapting to some of these changes. Shared mobility has created employment and consumer choices in Indian cities. Likewise, the focus on electric vehicles will help India exploit a sunrise industry to create employment, while moving towards the next phase of change in the automotive sector. This move will clean our city air and reduce our carbon footprint. Another major change that Indian cities are moving towards is the use of technology and data for better urban transport through ITS. We need to use data to provide seamless intermodal public transport. Hong Kong has six modes of travel and its Octopus Card can be used for all its modes (apart from retail transactions), and 95 per cent of those in the age group of sixteen to sixty-five use this card (Pisa, K. and Fleming, K., 2014). India launched National Common Mobility Card (NCMC) which focuses on 'One Nation One Card' in March 2019 (PIB 2019b). It has a debit card feature and a local wallet feature that can be used for contactless payments. The aim is to get one card for all local travel within India. India is moving at a pace that can be expedited. By

December 2019, only eleven transport agencies had started accepting NCMC (PTI, 2019c).

Sydney's Opal app and Helsinki's Whim app treat 'mobility as a service' (called MaaS for short). MaaS is a digital economy term that means that instead of owning and driving the asset, you will use more than one form of transport to travel from one place to another. This is fast gaining importance in urban mobility and deserves greater attention as we advocate how Indian cities should work on providing the right platform for enabling MaaS as a new movement. Multi-modal transport and digital connectivity are of the essence to MaaS. This move is happening as we speak.

If buses and feeder services of rickshaws and three-wheelers are connected with shared mobility apps, metro lines and suburban railways, we can cut down on vehicle ownership and increase the sustainability of our urban transport. This will lead to a shift from 'drive' to 'ride' (Shah, 2019). The state and city governments should focus on working with national governments towards moving to MaaS. Kochi in Kerala offers one of the early experiences of an Indian city with MaaS. The city introduced a digital platform called 'Kochi One' which brings together the Kochi Metro and feeder service with private bus operators, the state-run bus service, auto-rickshaw drivers, water-jetty service and the public bike-sharing service (Singh, 2020b). MaaS in Kochi has led to a welcome change in the city's transport sector. Singh adds that with regard to modes of traditional transport it, 'improves their operational capacity, solves territorial conflict and provides socio-economic support' (ibid.). Given India's economic status, the informal transport modes are here to stay but we also need our cities to grow sustainably while maintaining our growth trajectory. MaaS seems to be the way to achieve all these goals.

ROAD DESIGN AND CONTRACTING STANDARDS CAN SAVE COSTS

Change in how we build roads has had a major impact on cities worldwide. The small nudges of technology and regulations can go far in ramping up the work on infrastructure creation. For instance, as Haussmann was undertaking huge infrastructure creation of Paris, he realized that asphalt for roads provided a smoother and more manageable surface. This happened in the 1860s, and when New York's roads were to be cleaned in the 1880s, they were made of granite blocks over gravel (Gleaser, 2012). While this made sweeping easy, the issues of dirt and dust was resolved only when asphalt finally paved the New York streets. It helped because asphalt could bind together stones and gravel (ibid.).

In India, from 1981 to 2011, the urban road length went up from 123,120 km to 411,840 km, a 3.35 times increase. During the same period, the number of motor vehicles went up from 5.4 million to around 142 million, an increase of 26 times (Singh, 2005). However, growth in urban roads has not matched growth in vehicles and this is now one of the major reasons for traffic congestion, accidents and high travel times. No Indian city can claim to have road infrastructure that can justifiably accommodate the growth in the population, sprawl and vehicles. Roads not only carry people and goods, but also the infrastructure of stormwater drains and sewerage lines. The NYU-UN *Habitat Atlas of Urban Expansion* measured the quality of roads in several Indian cities in the pre-1990 period, compared to peri-urban expansion areas between 1990 and 2014. As per its assessment, the quality of roads takes a hit due to unplanned growth in peri-urban areas. For instance, the average road width in the Kozhikode expansion area (1990–2014) was 4.03 metres, compared to 9.84 metres in its pre-1990 area (Shah et al., 2020).

Moreover, roads in Indian cities continue to remain unsafe for pedestrians, suffer from poor design and surface quality and are constantly cut and/or modified to make way for utilities such as sewerage, electricity and internet. Given that a large part of Indian urban space is yet to be built, it will help Indian cities if we can establish national road design and contracting standards that drastically limit how are roads are repeatedly cut and dug by different agencies. This has been championed by think tank Janaagraha and was also recommended in NITI Aayog's three-year action agenda. The Tender S.U.R.E (Specifications for Urban Roads Execution) model implemented in Bengaluru uses this method. Municipalities can easily replicate national-level design standards and contracting standards.

NITI Aayog further stressed that 'Enforceable design standards can ensure that urban utilities are provided ducts under footpaths with inspection chambers, utility networks are mapped, and uniform lane width can be maintained' (NITI Aayog, 2017). It also recommended that a PPP model can be used wherein the private sector builds city roads and is paid usage charges by utilities for using the underground ducts for varying purposes. Utility companies will save resources as they would not have to spend on constructing these underground ducts; commuters benefit from not using roads that are very often cut and are pedestrian friendly.

WE NEED TO PEDESTRIANIZE ROADS

In my 2018 article for the Livemint titled 'Why there should be more pedestrians', I have highlighted that pedestrianizing roads have yielded multiple benefits in the West and the East. Indian cities have begun to use this approach, and one of the more recent instances has been barring motor vehicles in the 1.5 km stretch in Chandni Chowk from 9 a.m. to 9 p.m. (Dhar, 2018b).

This article highlighted how cities like Madrid, Paris, New York, among others have benefit from such moves. Copenhagen has achieved significant success since it started barring motorized vehicles since the 1960s. I have seen how Paulista Avenue, the most popular commercial street in São Paulo, Brazil, comes to life on Sundays when it is not open for motor vehicles. Residents, artists, performers, tourists and shops pop up on Sundays. The article highlighted the benefits of such policy: 1) improvement in air quality, 2) improved quality of life due to boost in physical activity and cultural expression, 3) increased use of bicycles such as in cities of Copenhagen and Paris, 4) rise in cultural expression as all kinds of artists have a venue to perform, earn, and learn from each other. Bogota hosts the cycling event Ciclovía on Sundays and public holidays and has been a huge hit, 5) increase in tourism and economic activity due to this increased cultural expression and emergence of cities' characters, 6) lower road accidents and deaths, 7) improved aesthetics of the city due to decline in all forms of pollution, and 8) cities becoming more equitable as all residents can use such streets without having to own a car or other motor vehicle to access such streets (Dhar, 2018b).

Apart from these long-standing merits, in the post-Covid-19 world, walking and cycling are becoming preferred choices in cities worldwide. Many cities are taking initiatives to pedestrianize roads to prevent loss of jobs, providing an avenue to socialize in these morose times and allowing people to move freely. Covid-19 will only increase the pedestrianization of roads, which should include the broadening of footpaths and cycle-lanes.

We have discussed how Bogota has done so well, focusing on cycling. The city has recently added 76 km of cycle-lanes to the already existing 550 km of such lanes (Adlakha, 2020). Berlin has created new 'pop-up' lanes and also marked cycle service shops as essential services. London and Dublin have widened their sidewalks using temporary cones. Though cities like Chennai and Pune have done well on creating cycle lanes, many more Indian cities should (and will) adopt this focus on pedestrianizing roads (ibid.).

I added a word of caution in my article though—blanket pedestrianization can cause serious harm to economic activity and mobility in the city. This low-cost measure has to be well-thought-out and used judiciously. Singapore has shown the way as it has balanced the Singaporean lifestyle and values with the economic needs of the city. It closes streets such as Club Street, Haji Lane, Bali Lane, Dunlop Street and Chander Road during different times of the week without hurting the economic activity and mobility in the city state (Dhar, 2018b).

BACK TO THE FUTURE: ELECTRIC VEHICLES AND AUTONOMOUS VEHICLES

As India continues to grapple with the most basic urban mobility issues, it cannot afford to turn its back on new solutions in the urban mobility space. The most notable developments include vehicles that run on electricity rather than on fossil fuel. Other such developments include driverless vehicles called autonomous vehicles (AVs) first produced by Google in 2009; unmanned aerial vehicles (UAVs, also called drones); flying cars that operate both on the ground and in the air; self-driving monorail pods using magnets; and the hyperloop, which is working towards magnetically levitated, high-speed train pods.

Problems such as road accidents, pollution, congestion and accessibility might be solved as we mainstream these inventions. G.V. Sanjay Reddy, vice-chairman of GVK, an infrastructure company, notes how countries are already making space for AVs. He has also mapped five stages of urban mobility in India (Reddy, 2018). According to him, we have moved from stage 1 (traditional transportation) and stage 2 (on-demand vehicles), to stage 3 (shared on-demand vehicles). Stage 4 will see the use of shared electric and connected vehicles (connected to the internet or to other devices and to different aggregator platforms which increase their asset utilization), and stage 5 (the use of automated and shared electric and connected vehicles), respectively. This seems to be the logical path of unfolding urban mobility. However, we need more action to accelerate this transition.

The adoption of AVs could be speeded up by setting national standards, amending the Motor Vehicles Act, 1988, to allow commercial testing; making requisite changes in the road infrastructure; tying up AVs with other related industries; engaging the private sector and also setting the policies on privacy, security and access. Drones (UAVs) truly leverage the third dimension of transport and have the potential for radical transformation of many industries, including home-delivery of non-large items, where it can slash costs (including fuel and manpower) and time, while increasing convenience and efficiency; UAVs also have the potential to change how we approach areas such as policing, fire safety and border patrolling. As of now, only a handful of countries have drafted regulations on UAVs.

Electric vehicles hit at the very root of air pollution/carbon emissions. As per some reports, carbon emissions in India could come down by 37 per cent by 2030 if we achieve a shared, electric and connected mobility future (Annapurani, 2019). Besides, the move to EVs will lessen India's excessive dependence on fossil fuel. Crude oil is one-fourth of our import bill. Crude oil imports jumped close to 500 per cent from 1998–99 to 2018–19, and the considerable share of petrol and diesel import is consumed by the transport sector (ibid.). While the Central government has taken some measures—low GST rates, providing charging infrastructure in key parts of Delhi, and allocating a higher budget to support EV roll-out—there is a lot of space to cover before we reach any comfortable position on EVs.

The first issue will be the business model, which Indian companies will have to significantly change to switch from vehicles using an internal combustion engine to EVs. We will have to scout for lithium, cobalt, nickel and rare earth minerals through trade agreements, particularly with countries in Latin America and Africa, as these metals are key components of EV batteries. More importantly, a fully charged EV can run for only one-third of the distance of a conventional vehicle with a full tank (ibid.). Again, we will have to wait for a technological breakthrough.

STRATEGY ON SHARED MOBILITY

Cars have historically been among the most underutilized assets. As of now, asset utilization of cars is about 5 per cent (Reddy, 2018). A NITI Aayog study notes that the launch of Uber and Ola in India and other similar app-based vehicle aggregators in various parts of the world have changed how we view and use cars (NITI Aayog and BCG, 2018). These privately owned, digital aggregator platforms offer shared mobility (ride-sourcing and ride-sharing); providing physical and digital safety and security to users and providers is of prime concern here (ibid.). These platforms have high employment potential and lessons from metro cities should be quickly replicated in smaller cities and towns for their benefit. It is important to maintain competition but also the welfare of users and providers. (ibid.). So far, Indian cities have aced shared mobility platforms.

Micromobility is also an emerging solution in Indian cities that is fast filling a gap, mostly using shared mobility. It refers to short-distance trips, usually covered at under 50 km/hour (Varma, 2019). Affordable public transport options are usually 1–3 km away. In Bengaluru alone, there is a demand for 9 million micromobility trips. As per a study, 500 start-ups in India have begun to address this issue (ibid.). It would be best for India that such mobility is shared, electric, and financially viable. Public transport could get a strong boost if such a market continues to flourish in Indian cities.

6
Urban Land: The Next Frontier of Urban Growth

CITIES are spatial manifestations of how humans became more productive and efficient and, in the process, more prosperous. Urban innovation can turn constraints upside down and create opportunities out of them. Cities have always been hotbeds of innovation and derive benefits from agglomeration, for which people and firms need to be closer to each other.

Just a few centuries ago people had no option but to reside as close to their place of work as possible, since the means of transport were fewer and slower. Two innovations of the nineteenth century—the elevator and the automobile—changed everything. Both Edward Glaeser, in *Triumph of the City*, and Leo Hollis, in *Cities Are Good for You*, present a gripping history of these two innovations (Glaeser, 2012; Hollis, 2013).

The advent of engines in the nineteenth century improved the speed and safety of elevators that were used to haul coal out mines. However, lifts as we know them came about due to an American citizen, Elisha Otis, who created the mechanical lift with an add-on—the safety brake. This ensured that even if the cable snapped the lift would not hurtle down, but descend safely. By 1870, the Otis Elevator Company had installed 2,000 steam-powered devices (Hollis, 2013). By 1884, they had opened offices in Europe and their lifts were serving London's underground stations and the Eiffel Tower. The world's first skyscraper (plus lifts) is said to be the 138-foot Home Insurance Building in Chicago built in 1885 (Glaeser, 2012). Incidentally, before the twentieth century, the top floors of buildings did not have many takers so buildings with more than six storeys were rarely seen.

Lifts have changed how we view and imagine cities and more importantly the introduction of lifts has changed the quantum of land available to mankind. Now, the world's biggest cities compete for the highest and largest number of skyscrapers. Even advertising changed in the twentieth century—success was occupying the top-floor office, with a window from where you could see the city's skyline. To date, the top floors of skyscrapers go to the highest bidder. Urban density derives its utility from these tall buildings which allow cities to give decent and even lavish space to a large number of people on a limited piece of land.

The other invention that shaped cities is, of course, the automobile. It is thanks to cars that city limits expanded. Glaeser paints a fast-paced picture in his book on how cars were mass-produced by Henry Ford and its impact on Detroit and cities in general (Glaeser, 2012). Assembly-line production meant cars could be produced faster, cheaper and more efficiently. Together, cars and trucks propelled the process of suburbanization—wherein people and factories moved to suburban areas. Today cars allow people to live away from dense urban areas and trucks allow factories to be built at a distance from railway lines and mines. The lesson from both these inventions, lifts and cars, is that land is a limited resource but its innovative use can unlock immense potential for cities and people.

Land is a prized resource; however, its use has been harmed by stringent policies and regulations. Indian cities inherited the colonial town-planning template which prevented efficient utilization of urban land. While other countries reformed their approach to urban land, we are still dealing with many basic issues—stringent regulations, focus on de-densification, lack of property titles, high inventory of unused public land and under-utilization of land due to the legacy of certain pieces of legislation.

Among the factors of production (land, labour and capital) there is an increasingly emerging consensus that land is the 'most distorted' factor market in India and poses significant challenges to growth (Kapur et al., 2014). The authors point out that though India was already relatively land-scarce as compared to other countries in 1960, by 2050 it will become one of the most land-scarce countries in the world (ibid.). In comparison to India, Brazil will have twenty times more land per capita and China will have four times land per capita by 2050 (ibid.).

The pressure on Indian land resources is driven by rising population along with sustained economic growth which is boosting demand for land from different consumers—commercial, residential, housing, and infrastructure sectors. Adverse land policies, particularly in the urban areas, are worsening the pressure on land resources. The time has come for us to look at the urban land differently. It needs to be viewed and treated differently as it has unique characteristics. Prasanna Mohanty (2014) succinctly outlines these attributes:

1. Every parcel of urban land has a unique location and development potential.
2. Urban land has both horizontal and vertical dimensions.
3. The right to develop urban land is not entirely a private right.
4. Urban land is an input for land assembly adopted by public authorities and affects the land markets.
5. The quantity of urban land is finite per se, but its supply can be increased using multiple policy tools.
6. Urban land is subject to environmental externalities associated with density.
7. Planned development can lead to unearned increments, making it an ideal resource to finance development.

Given this scenario, India needs to put in place highly efficient land management policies that will enable it to unlock the full potential of its land assets, thus contributing to its economic growth. However, before we study the policy solutions to urban land issues in India, we will first thread out the key policy lacunae in urban land management and their impact. Cities, host to half of human civilization, are built on just around 4 per cent of arable land (Kunzig, 2011); in India, with one-sixth of the world's population, the situation is worse. Inefficient building regulations further add to the woes of Indian cities by contributing significantly to escalation of land costs.

A study in the US on regulations and rising house prices focused on the cost that could be attributed to regulatory limits on supply (Glaeser et al., 2003). They found that this cost varied in the cities under study, including Washington, Boston, San Francisco and Manhattan. The latter two were found to bear the heaviest burden (50 per cent each). One can only assume what share of land costs in India can be attributed to the draconian regulatory laws. There is unfortunately no similar study on Indian cities, but we are known for: our rigid and static master plans, low floor area ratio (FAR; as compared to global peers), very limited success in monetizing land assets, and huge tracts of public land that remain under-utilized.

Limited supply and stringent regulations have made land in India extremely expensive and have forced people to move to cheaper places mostly to the city's periphery. Alain Bertaud summarizes this situation:

> In India, the combined effect of multiple layers of poorly conceived Central, state and municipal regulations contribute to an artificial urban land shortage. As a result urban land prices are abnormally high in relation to India's household income, and households consume less floor space than they could afford if the regulatory environment had been reformed ... [this] tend[s] to 'push' urban development toward the periphery (Bertaud, 2002).

A misdirected approach to urban land has left our cities weak on basic service provision, twin issues of vacant housing units and housing shortage (mainly for the economically weaker sections), rampant slum growth, high environmental degradation, financially bankrupt ULBs and unfettered peripheral growth, among others. The problem of housing (rental and ownership), soaring land prices and long travel times are driven by our continuous mismanagement of land resources. The present mismanagement of land raises serious concerns about India's economic growth and productivity increase. It is time that all of us understand the reasons behind these issues and their probable solutions.

LACK OF CONCLUSIVE LAND TITLING: AT THE HEART OF URBAN LAND ISSUES

One of the important acts of adult life in an Indian city is to buy land and/or property. It is 'peak adulting', so to speak. You pay for the asset, get it registered, and bask in the relief that you are now a landowner. What if people were to tell you that this assumption can be contested? You would be furious, right? Now imagine this at the national level. Take your imagination a notch higher and imagine the distress of poor people who, despite limited access to resources, buy land and find the title contested. Where are they to find the money to go through the judicial process?

This knot in the land markets has a dampening effect on a range of transactions—including loans from banks (your contested land cannot be used as collateral for loans), the long-drawn-out process of government taking over land (since your claim is contested) for infrastructure creation, burden on the court system (cases that go on for decades), and marginalized sections fighting illegal evictions. Hernando De Soto argues in *Mystery of Capital* that the problem of development can trace its roots to the absence of legal title to a property (De Soto, 2000). This prevents people from investing in improving their dwellings, and prevents the poor from leveraging the property as an asset for purposes such as a loan (ibid.). There are a few major issues with regard to land-ownership legislation in India:

1. The Transfer of Property Act, 1882, mandates that land or property can be transferred from one person to another (or entity) by a registered document (Mishra and Suhag, 2017).
2. However, the Registration Act, 1908, mandates that:
    a. the registration of this action is merely the registration of the transaction and does not imply that the government guarantees the land ownership (ibid.). So, any third party can come and challenge your right to ownership of the property/land; any

previous transfer of such property/land could also be challenged (ibid.).
b. Furthermore, the Registration Act, 1908, also does not mandate registration of all transactions.
3. As a result of the above, land records are not updated in real time as the transactions happen (ibid.).
4. There is no single document that guarantees a land title in India—there are various authorities that maintain records of different transactions. Thus, in India, we only have 'presumptive' land titling, not 'conclusive'. This, as mentioned earlier, opens the land market to various challenges and high transaction costs.
5. Another issue with the land transactions is that India's stamp duty rates are high and range from 4–10 per cent (as compared to 1–4 per cent in other countries). This, coupled with registration fees, discourages people from registering their properties (ibid.).

Since land is a valuable asset with no clear titles, there are an immense number of court cases on land and property disputes. Indians know the trouble of contested land titles and are willing to pay higher prices for dispute-free land. A study of transactions in Bengaluru during 2005–10 for around 2,500 properties showed that properties with clean titles (with no disputes) commanded a high premium of 4.3 per cent (Venkataraman, 2014).

Recent Initiatives to Resolve Land Titling Issues

The National Land Records Modernization Programme—launched in 2008 to computerize property records, the registration process, surveys, and maps—is a move towards conclusive land titling (ibid.). The scheme has now been revamped as the Digital India Land Records Modernization Programme (Sasi, 2016).

NITI Aayog has also drafted a model Land Titling Act. If introduced in Parliament as a Bill and passed, the Act will empower state governments to execute title registration of land and properties. People will be empowered to object to any such title registration by filing an objection with the Title Registration Officer. The objection will be taken up by the Land Dispute Resolution Officer and addressed at the Land Titling Appellate Tribunal. If there are no objections to a title registration, the title will be deemed conclusive after three years of the notification of title registration (PTI, 2020b).

The Rajasthan Urban Land (Certification of Titles) Act, 2016, is another progressive step forward in granting conclusive land titles. The state will set up an Urban Land Title Certification Authority, which will verifying the details and then grant a provisional certificate for two years. At the end of these two years, it will provide a conclusive land title. The state will act as a guarantor for such a land title and in case of dispute, will provide compensation (Sasi, 2016).

An important initiative—the Survey of Villages and Mapping with Improvised Technology in Village Areas (SVAMITVA)—was launched in April 2020, during the Covid-19 pandemic, to survey non-agricultural inhabited land in rural India and grant property rights (Bharti and Bindushree, 2020). This will not only be useful for people to access credit but will also help the urban land market, as more of these areas might be categorized as urban in coming decades.

The Odisha Land Rights to Slum Dwellers Act in 2017 is another very encouraging development. It not only grants land rights to slum-dwellers, but also helps in upgrading their homes. Covering close to 3,000 slums in the state, it benefits 400,000 households and over a million people. The state government calls it the JAGA mission. Using drones and GIS-based spatial technology, the state ensured that the mapping of 197,000 households (covering 1,886 slums under 109 ULBs) was completed within months—a task that would normally take years. By the end of 2020, the state government had provided land right certificates to over 51,000 families (jagamission.org).

The state government also converged benefits from various schemes to provide benefits worth up to USD 2,900 to upgrade dwellings. Issuing land titles and upgrading dwellings has ensured that slum dwellers no longer fear eviction and also have access to all essential physical infrastructure and services. The health, environmental and quality of life benefits are worth acknowledging.

Conclusive land titling thus unlocks the potential of the urban land market and allows reliable exchange once property rights are established.

It reduces delays and litigations, makes the land acquisition process easier, helps people use their land (their most prized asset) as collateral and also encourages them to invest in renovating their properties. Since land is a state subject under the Constitution, it is now time that the remaining states too move towards conclusive land titling and unlock a new frontier of growth for their state GDP, as has Odisha.

POLICIES CREATING AN ARTIFICIAL SCARCITY OF LAND

Urban Land Ceilings Act (ULCRA), 1976

One of the worst Government of India legislation to adversely impact the urban land market was the ULCRA, which allowed the government to take away a massive share of privately held land by imposing tight ownership ceilings, ranging from 500 to 2,000 sq m. Anyone who owned more land than this was made to surrender it to the government for a paltry amount in compensation. Arvind Panagariya has highlighted the damage of this policy in his works. Given the low compensation, the majority of the large landowners claimed exemption, while the remaining went to court. By 1999 an independent study had deemed ULCRA a failure:

> The state governments could physically acquire only 19,020 hectares of excess vacant land out of an area of 220,674 hectares estimated to be in excess of the ceiling limits. This works out to a mere 9 per cent of the total estimated excess vacant land. At the same time, as much as 56,640 hectares of excess vacant land were exempted under Sections [sic] 20 of the Act (on grounds of 'public interest' or on account of 'undue hardships') (Panagariya et al., 2014).

Thus, essentially, the land market was distorted, since neither could the government buy excess land nor could the sellers sell in the open market. Apart from blocking land for redevelopment due to legal disputes, the Act also gave undue power to government developers on land development. The states should ensure that such land blocked under ULCRA, if any, is released back into the markets and regularized for further development.

State-level Rent Control Acts

These have adversely impacted the supply of urban housing and prevented the rise of modern rental housing in urban India. Rent is a state subject and across states these Acts historically permitted a meagre 4–5 per cent increase in rent, while adopting acutely tenant-friendly provisions (ibid.).

As a result: 1) house owners were hesitant to let properties on rent, because the rent could not be increased and stayed the same for years; 2) it was even more difficult to get a tenant to leave (mostly as the rents once fixed remained the same, no matter the inflation); 3) since tenants continued to occupy the property, it was impossible to renovate or redevelop it; 4) this incentivized landowners to let their buildings become dilapidated, unsafe and poorly maintained so that the tenants would leave; and 4) all of the above discouraged the private sector from foraying into rental housing (ibid.). All this also led to the freezing of some of the major and important pieces of land in cities and made them unavailable for development.

As per Census 2011, the share of rental housing declined from 54 per cent in 1961 to 31 per cent in 2011 (Tandel et al., 2016). The study by Tandel et al. noted that Rent Control Acts were of two types: first generation (which fixed the rents), and second generation (which allowed for an annual increase of rent in percentage terms) (ibid.). In Maharashtra, the 1999 Rent Control Act capped the annual rent increase at 4 per cent (ibid.). The same study notes that such severe control has drastically reduced the supply of rental housing—as of 1961, around half the properties in Mumbai were self-occupied and half were rented; as of 2010, 82.4 per cent of properties were self-occupied, and a little over 17 per cent were rented. Thus, there is a strong need for us to reform the Rent Control Acts. The government has drafted a Model Tenancy Act and it would be wise for states to reform their Rent

Control Acts in line with this to create a level playing field between the tenants and landowners.

City Master Plans: Rigid, Deterministic and Technocratic in Approach

City master plans allocate land for different uses and use zoning tools—such as floor area ratio (FAR), land-use restrictions, taxes and fees, among others—to control the intensity of development in cities. However, master plans have shown the tendency of preferring low intensity of development and have thus tried to spread development across the master plan area.

We will see in detail, under the urban planning section, the pitfalls of such rigid, deterministic and technocratic approaches to planning. To cite an example, an early 1990s development plan for planned land use in one ward in Mumbai across different categories was as follows: residential (36 per cent), commercial (3 per cent), industrial (43 per cent), land for slums (nil per cent). Actual land use in this ward by 2010, was significantly different: residential (18 per cent), commercial (14 per cent), industrial (26 per cent), slums (17 per cent) (Pethe et al., 2014).

A few drawbacks of such planning include:

1. The approach focuses on the de-densification of cities, which leads to an urban sprawl that prevents efficient utilization of land resources in the city's core areas.
2. Unplanned development is likely to be classified as illegal.
3. There is zero inclusion of the informal sector within this type of planning.
4. Its twenty-to-twenty-five-year time horizon prevents land from being used as per the changing economic structure.
5. It fails to fully accommodate how public transport systems (such as BRT or MRT) can increase the value of land, which can then be used for financing infrastructure projects.

The National Urban Policy Framework, 2018 (NUPF)

The NUPF calls for a complete overhaul of this approach and allows for mixed and changing land use, which will help cities recycle the land for different purposes depending upon the efficiency. Another issue created by planning refers to the shortage of urban land for streets and public spaces. The IDFC Institute cites research by Bimal Patel which highlights that global practice suggests 30–40 per cent of city land should be for streets and public spaces, and the remaining for building footprints, i.e., the area under the buildings (IDFC, 2019). However, in India, Building Codes introduced the concept of private space—the area between the wall and building footprint.

In San Francisco, 61 per cent of the land is covered by building footprints and 36 per cent is covered by streets and public spaces. Compare this with Mumbai's Nariman Point: land under building footprint (22 per cent), land under public streets and open spaces (22 per cent), land under privately-owned open spaces (a staggering 54 per cent) (ibid.). We need to do away with such private open space for commercial buildings, at least. The FAR is a potent tool at the disposal of cities, but is used in a manner that has led to inefficient utilization of urban land. This needs a separate section for discussion.

PUBLIC LAND: A RESOURCE WAITING TO BE TAPPED

The government's central public-sector entities (CPSE) and other parastatal agencies own huge tracts of land, some even in the most expensive areas. These agencies cannot sell this land in the open market. These land assets thus become unavailable for urban development, and provide low to no economic returns to the owners. A survey of fifty-eight loss-incurring CPSEs in 2013–14 indicated that they held around 2.35 lakh acres of land (Siddhanta, 2015). A 2013 study claimed that in Ahmedabad alone the surplus public land could generate resources anywhere between INR 20,000–54,000 crore (Ballaney et al., 2013). A report by the Comptroller and Auditor General (CAG) 'Performance Audit of Defence Estate Management 2011' noted that the defence sector (government) held more than 81,000 acres of 'surplus' land—

meaning that the land is not currently used nor will be used anytime in the foreseeable future. Of this, around 52,000 acres are vacant and unutilized. Even when in use, these land banks are not most efficiently utilized. For instance, this includes ninety-seven golf courses spread over 8,076 acres of mostly urban land (Clarke Annez and Gangopadhyay (eds) n.d.). A World Bank 2013 report 'Unlocking Land Values for Urban Infrastructure Finance: International Experience', pointed out other large land-owning central organizations (Peterson, 2014). The Indian Railways named 43,000 hectares of landholdings as unnecessary for railway service; the Airports Authority of India owns around 20,400 hectares of prime land surrounding India's airports, and the major Ports Trusts have over 100,000 hectares of land, of which 6,300 hectares lies vacant (ibid.). Clearly the land allocated to these organizations, some from the British era, could be utilized more efficiently.

While putting this land on market or hiving off from the departments will not be an easy task. The political economy interests are bound to throw some pushback. The 'Panel of Experts on Reforms in Central Public Sector Enterprises (CPSEs)' headed by S.K. Roongta recommended in its report that a Public Sector Land Development Authority be set up for rationalizing the CPSE-owned land assets and unlocking their value (Planning Commission, 2011). The 2013 'Report of the Committee on Roadmap for Fiscal Consolidation' headed by Vijay Kelkar also stated the selling of public lands as a means for fiscal consolidation. However, India has a long way to go before its public land resources are utilized efficiently.

India should first create a policy focusing on managing public land holdings and finding ways to unlock their value. The report—'India's Public Lands: Responsive, Transparent, and Fiscally Responsible Asset Management'—has studied the international experiences and identified the steps ahead to use the public land more efficiently, especially under the urban context (Clarke Annez and Gangopadhyay (eds), n.d.).

1. First, the government should have an outlined policy that nudges towards active management of public land assets. It gives the example of Australia, which says that the government is not in

the business of owning land and its ownership of public land is to enhance the delivery of public services.
2. Second, the government should create an inventory of public land which will include ownership information, intended future use and current use, market value, and so on. This idea has been in discussion for years but no major steps have been taken on it so far.
3. Third, it advocates for a defined process for disposing public land rather than an ad hoc, case by case consideration—for instance, the Railway Land Development Authority (RLDA) identified 305, mostly urban, parcels of land suitable for development either through sale or joint venture; and the Land Policy for Major Port Trusts also identified lands (some of them urban) which will not be used. However, last-minute political intervention prevented such monetization.
4. Fourth, it suggests entrepreneurial management of land resources. This could be done through setting up a department with a strategic focus on managing such land such as Urban Development Investment Companies (UDICs) created at the local level in China and Canada Lands Company in Canada—which are responsible for the disposal of public lands that are not under any efficient use.

Presently, the Department of Public Enterprises in India is preparing a data bank of surplus landholdings of CPSEs. The government has also started the process of closing five sick PSUs—Hindustan Cables, Tungabhadra Steel, HMT (Watches), HMT (Chinar Watches) and HMT (Bearings)—which have a total land ownership of around 1,950 acres. Besides, there are another five shortlisted PSUs that have a total holding of 2,000 acres, and out of this list, Hindustan Papers Ltd alone has about 1,800 acres (Sai, 2016). It's a start but we have a long way to go before we correct the anomaly with the public land in the urban areas.

The report discusses China's success story. It has done extremely well in exploiting urban land for financing the development of urban infrastructure (Clarke Annez and Gangopadhyay (eds), n.d.). Reports claim that as much as 60–70 per cent of such financing came from urban land leasing (since the Communist Party of China owns the land). Many Chinese lessons do not hold good in the Indian context, such as buying land on the urban periphery by compelling farmers to sell. China's municipalities have funded 40–50 per cent of their budget through land leasing. The report mentions how Shanghai Municipality was able to generate USD 90 billion in the early 1990s, by buying and reselling land in Pudong Area in Shanghai. The majority of these funds were used to fund infrastructure projects in Pudong Area, which is now home to Shanghai's airport, luxury hotels, office spaces and manufacturing facilities. Chinese cities unlocked a lot of their land by relocating their inefficient public sector enterprises and municipal offices and selling the land to the highest bidder.

Another incremental measure that India could use is to begin taxing the property owned by the government in the urban areas—national, state, and local. The three benefits of such a policy are: 1) removing the property tax distortion between the public and private ownership of land; 2) boost the revenue realized by the ULBs; and, 3) discouraging the public sector from hoarding land, and encouraging an annual audit of their landholdings. South Africa was one of the first countries to implement such a policy (Peterson, 2014).

While the majority of these initiatives might be difficult to implement in India as of now, once local governments are empowered and there is a national consensus that such urban land parcels could unlock value for all, the momentum towards such policies would accelerate. The role of the private sector in wealth creation was once a taboo idea. It is not anymore. In efficiently managing urbanization, we have hit a roadblock. Unleashing the value of public land would be the way forward to tunnel through this roadblock.

SYMBIOTIC LINK: MANAGING GROWTH AND MANAGING FLOOR SPACE INDEX IN CITIES

In understanding and resolving the issue of inefficient utilization of urban land resources, the role of the urban sprawl remains extremely pertinent. The latter is an outcome of a movement that focused on marrying the city with the countryside. Many cities worldwide aimed to control urban growth by building greenbelts, water bodies and other structures around the cities (Kunzig, 2011). They did not succeed, as people continued to live outside these 'curbs'. Moreover, cheap transport and rising incomes allowed people to move further away from the city and travel to it for work every day.

An OECD report studied the issue of the urban sprawl and highlighted that that apart from average urban population density, the other important indicators to measure an urban sprawl are: 1) variation of population density across an urban area; 2) share of population living in areas with a density below specified thresholds; 3) share of urban land occupying areas where density is below these thresholds; 4) urban land fragmentation; 5) number of peak density areas within a city; and 6) a percentage of the population living outside these areas of peak density (OECD, 2018).

Urban sprawl has obvious environmental and economic costs and therefore needs to be checked efficiently. The study showed that all OECD countries are witnessing urban sprawls across most of the indicators stated above (ibid.). The costs of public good associated with an urban sprawl need to be balanced against the private benefits arising from it. In many sections of the book, including this one, I have tried to address some of these issues. For instance, achieving desirable population density and limiting an urban sprawl will generate numerous socio-economic benefits.

However, an insightful study by IDFC Institute tells that when a country urbanizes, its cities grow horizontally. New York grew nine-fold in size during 1900–1930 and Paris has grown thirty-fold since 1800 (as of 2020). More importantly, they explain that the density of Indian cities is already quite high, so as per OECD's measure we are not sprawling. Nevertheless, this growth is not managed well and is haphazard in nature with limited access to basic infrastructure (Lamson-Hall et al., 2020). So unlike the OECD, the urban sprawl is a lesser concern for India; managing geographic growth is a bigger concern.

The floor space index or FSI—the government-permitted ratio of the total built-up floor area and the plot size—was used as a tool to limit people from moving to cities. It was wrongly assumed that limiting city space would somehow stop people from moving to cities (ibid.). Indian cities have long enforced strict FSI regulations. For instance, an FSI of 2 for a 1,000 sq ft plot means permission to build a 2,000 sq ft built-up area on the plot (Guturu, 2015). However, cities are where the jobs are so people keep moving to cities and have to deal with the shortage of space and land, artificially created by the FSI policies. The IDFC has a telling insight on FSI, density of people, and density of buildings:

> Uniform and low FSI is meant to reduce or limit population densities in the centre of cities, but it ignores the fact that demand is higher in the centre; the policy likely confuses higher density of buildings with a higher population density. Consequently, artificial scarcity of space as a result of stringent FSI caps has led to greater density of buildings. Instead of relieving central city congestion, it has led to a large number of short buildings in urban cores that are still very crowded (Lamson-Hall et al., 2020).

Thus, judicious reform in the FSI regime is important to manage the growth of Indian cities. At present, the regime coupled with stringent planning, adversely affects availability of housing, public service delivery, congestion, air quality, and access to jobs, among other areas.

The imposition of FSI, particularly in the denser areas and in the central business district (CBD), limits housing supply and pushes up housing prices. Increased housing prices add pressure to the rentals as well. This leads to horizontal growth of cities, inefficient use of land, and suburbanization. For instance, Mumbai's CBD permits FSI to the tune of 1.33 maximum (as compared to 5 to 15 in CBDs in the world's major cities) and falling to 0.5 in the suburban areas (Sridhar, 2010). Apart from Mumbai, other major Indian cities also have been subjected to low FSI in both CBD and residential areas. A recent paper by IDFC Institute compares the stark difference between maximum permissible free FSI for Indian cities and global cities. FSI in Indian cities such as Thane (1), Pune (1.25), Mumbai (1.33), Nagpur (1.5), Jaipur (2), Indore (2), Lucknow (2.5), Chennai (2.5), Delhi (3.5), Bengaluru (4) is considerably low as compared to global cities of Shanghai (8), San

Francisco (9), Hong Kong (12), Chicago (12), New York (15), Tokyo (20), and Singapore (25) (Lamson-Hall et al., 2020).

In most cities worldwide, FSIs increase over time, which reduces unnecessary horizontal expansion, limits transport costs, and helps families consume more floor space with the resultant increase in their incomes. However, in India stringent and low FSIs have made redevelopment of key areas of cities implausible, public transport financially infeasible, rent per square foot too high, and the urban poor's liveability and transport limited. Not surprisingly, a middle-class family in Mumbai occupies 5 sq m per capita as compared to 55 sq m per capita in Manhattan (Guturu, 2015). Solution to the FSI issue remains the key to solving urban land woes.

Prasanna Mohanty explains the anomalies on the issue of FSI in Indian cities (Mohanty, 2014). First, the density of the population in Indian cities is quite high but FSI is equally low. Cities such as Delhi, Kolkata and Mumbai have a population density of 20,000 vis-a-vis 12,000 in New York. Yet, the FSI in Delhi is 1.2–3.5; and in the island city of Mumbai it is 1.33. Second, globally FSI tends to rise with increase in development. The reverse has happened in India. In 1964, the FSI in Mumbai was 4.5! Compare this to FSI in downtown areas in major world cities—Singapore (12–25), New York (15), Hong Kong (12), and Shanghai (8). Another paper showed that FSI in Delhi was higher on its periphery, which is a problem since providing infrastructure in the periphery is more expensive (Guturu, 2015). Third, FSI in Indian cities do not vary according to transport accessibility. New York's financial district, with an FSI of 15, is different from the FSI of 10 that applies along New York's main avenues. Similarly, in Seoul, a CBD FSI of 10 and a sub-centre FSI of 8 is complemented by one of the world's largest MRT networks.

Increasing FSI has solved/eased urban space and land issues in the world's major cities. In Hong Kong, an increase in FSI of government buildings from three to five led to increased per capita space from 3.2 sq m to 5 sq m. Similarly in Shanghai the increase in FSI, for in-situ development of old buildings, led to a rise in per capita space from 3.6 sq m in 1984, to 34 sq m (ibid.). However, an increase in FSI also means pressure on the surrounding infrastructure. To make planning simpler, FSI in India is accorded as per width of the roads and other indicators such as setback (area between the building and the start of the plot of the land), whereas in other cities globally it is based on the nature of building activity (Guturu, 2015). Clearly, we have taken the wrong path on the use of FSI. Used in the right manner FSI can serve as a useful tool in generating revenues for the municipality.

Urban planning guidelines of 2014 encourage liberalizing FSI, to enable the creation of mixed-use zones and transit-oriented development (ibid.). Since FSI is decided by local governments, the Centre and the state governments should mobilize support to compel municipalities to increase FSI, at least in the majority of the metropolitan Indian cities. The states should be encouraged to allow cities to follow a flexible and liberal FSI policy. For instance, FSI in New York depends on location and land use, but in Singapore it also factors in infrastructure availability. Further, Indian cities should be free to choose if they need any FSI regulation at all.

Higher FSI is desired around transport nodes and for commercial buildings (IDFC, 2019). Some cities in Gujarat such as Ahmedabad, Vadodara, Surat and Rajkot are already moving towards a more liberal FSI policy, which is an encouraging sign (*DNA*, 2019). As per research, a 10 per cent increase in densification in India also leads to a decline in commuting emissions by 10 per cent. India is presently the fourth largest emitter of CO_2 (1.8 tonnes of per capita emission), which is considerably lower than the world average of 4.2 tonnes (Koshy, 2019). Liberalizing FSI could also be useful for reducing the carbon footprint of our cities. Besides, FSI is a very useful tool for mainstreaming transit-oriented development as a tool for integrating planning and transport and is used in many other cities, as discussed in previous chapters.

BE CREATIVE IN RECYCLING LAND

Master plans of Indian cities have been trying, with very limited success, to segregate land use between a range of non-agriculture activities (such as residential, commercial and industrial). We have discussed already that for cities to be vibrant, economically relevant and safe, we need mixed-use and not segregated use. The failure to understand the extent of the futility of segregated land use, and the inability to enforce such plans is just half the problem. The remaining issue that prevents timely intervention in the land market is that of prolonged processes and laws and regulations that prevent land use change within the city.

Now, why is that important? First, the Central and state economic structure has an overbearing influence on the local economy, and land markets are way too slow to adapt to changes in the economic structures at the national and state level. Second, land use should not be static as it creates a highly inefficient market. Industries rise and fall. The local governance and infrastructure may nudge people to either leave the city or attract more people from surrounding and far-flung areas. People might prefer another part of the city and may desert a particular part of the city. There are so many reasons why planned land use may not work. So why freeze land use? Why not leave it free for use for some other purpose/s, before it is too late?

Third, changing the nature of land use can generate revenues for local authorities and may usher in new opportunities for the local population. This means if we could plan the change in land use with the local population, civil society and in tandem with the changing nature of the economy, we would effectively be recycling urban land for other purposes. We need to be creative and agile for such use. But a word of caution here—the higher frequency of recycling doesn't imply greater efficiency. It may reflect poor decision-making in prior instances!

Now, what sort of land can one categorize as being ripe for recycling? Vacant land, underutilized land, or abandoned land. It would be better if such recycling also benefits the communities and sections of people that may be adversely affected by such recycling (even if their loss is notional and in theory, and they are yet to come to terms with the fact that there is no going back). The point is that land use is not fixed by virtue of the nature of the land but by our own limitations in thinking. The more creative we get, the better it will be for us to effectively use land for multiple purposes after every set of several decades.

Some common examples of where this has been done are Beijing's 798 Art District (formerly a military factory), and the use of New York mills as design studios. Now the same is happening with the textile mills in Mumbai, and with the Cheonggyecheon river restoration project in Seoul, among others. There are numerous instances worldwide where derelict land has been converted into a public space, a green space, a place for cultural activity (a museum, centre for performing arts, centre for local arts), used for low-income housing, as a space for local retail activity, for new downtown centres and so on. The list is endless, but the point is that our ability to leverage land for our purposes is only limited by our imagination.

Globally, the major share of recycled public land has come from shuttered military bases. I want to mention just three cases. Canada closed most of its twenty-seven military bases (many near urban areas); the US closed more than 350 military installations to transfer land to local authorities; and the federal government in Australia, since the mid-1990s, disposed of 90 per cent of public land under military bases (Peterson, 2014). Yes, touching defence land is a sensitive issue in India, but by the defence ministry's own admission they have enough surplus land. If it is a win-win situation, a considerable share of defence land in Indian cities could be used for more efficient and inclusive purposes.

As per a recent estimate by a team from the Takshashila Institution, the value of land owned by the army in Bengaluru alone is INR 3 trillion (Pai, 2019b). The value of defence land in five big cities is INR 15 trillion. Such land in the next fifteen cities is close to another INR 15 trillion. They make a case that if land is instead given to the defence department around 40–100 km away from the city, if even five such projects are undertaken, it can create new cities as well as generate 7.5 million new jobs. Apart from this, there is another micro approach of using small parcels of land, leasing them to ULBs to build a museum, a public library, or an open space. Not all recycling has to be only about minting money.

Mumbai's eastern seafront, also called Port Trust Land, has been inaccessible to the city's population for a long time and it is now planned to be plugged into the city's economy. Its stretches for 28 km and has defunct 1800 acres of land that could very well be the new CBD in the making (Koppikar and Purohit, 2014). There is already a proposal for floating restaurants, museums, commercial centres, cruise terminals and other such mega projects (ibid.). The focus is on creating a well-connected, high-functioning commercial district. In so far we can attract the right firms and businesses, the employment generated will be enough to catapult Mumbai to the league of global cities. Sanjeev Sanyal has made a compelling argument in the past that this land is parallel to the city and thus offers a chance to grow public space, public transport and commercial space in an integrated way (Sanyal, 2013b). Architect Bimal Patel, whose company HCP is in charge of redeveloping this land, states that it will have 62 per cent of open public and streets, which is considerably higher than the Mumbai city which has 25 per cent of its space under open public space and streets (ENS, 2020). This form of better urban management is also a form of urban land recycling.

Another case that merits discussion is the recycling of land stuck under mills in Kanpur, Mumbai and many other Indian cities. Textile mills in Kanpur and Mumbai were brought to their knees due to political rather than economic reasons. Regardless of the cause, such industries usually choose to move to peripheries of cities and even rural areas as they want to lower costs associated with land and wages. If these textiles mills go on to become derelict, such derelict facilities—either in existing urban areas, or where the industries are absorbed in the expanding cities—should be made available to local city governments for recycling the land for better purposes.

The focus of such recycling would depend on what the local communities want, the type of financial resources they have, and the key outcome they are aiming for—economic gains, more public space, sense of community and culture, or hard infrastructure (housing, waste or sewage treatment plants). The understanding that the land will not continue to serve one purpose for an infinite number of years is key here. Policymakers need to understand how to 'keep flipping' the urban land through recycling, as this can lead to enormous economic and social gains.

So far as there is a broad understanding that if one can flip the land, there will be solutions to better their use. A very granular example is the government housing in the RK Puram area of South Delhi, which is one of the most expensive parcels of land in Delhi. The state of houses for government officers is poor. These flats have a ground floor and two floors above, poor infrastructure, chipped interiors, and too much wasted space around the flats. The government can use this land way more efficiently if it opens it up for more housing, for commercial establishments, or even just auction the excess land by creating the same number of units on a smaller parcel of land.

PROPERTY TAX MEASURES: WHY THEY NEED A RELOOK

Municipal finance is a topic of great concern for Indian cities. Municipalities have limited resources to fund their needs, let alone the city's ambitions. One of the prime contributors of a city's revenue—property taxes—has become more salient after the introduction of the goods and services tax (GST), wherein a city's local taxes have been subsumed but the city does not get a share of GST. The property tax is discussed under the land section, because it gives a fairly good indicator of the quality of urban governance when it comes to managing land and property assets.

As per an ICRIER study of thirty-seven municipal corporations, property tax revenue as a share of their total revenue was 36.5 per cent, making it an important source of revenue (ICRIER Team, 2019). Property tax collection in India leaves a lot to be desired and shows the limited ability of Indian cities to monetize their lands. As per a World Bank Report property tax revenue is 1.1 per cent of GDP in OECD countries, whereas in India property revenue only contributes 0.2 per cent to the national GDP. Some of the better performing countries are Spain (1.15 per cent), Poland (1.22 per cent), Australia (1.7 per cent), Japan (1.87 per cent), Israel (1.99 per cent), United States (2.47 per cent), France (2.6 per cent), Canada (3.05 per cent), United Kingdom (3.11 per cent) (Awasthi and Nagarajan, 2020).

The property tax revenue in Indian cities is marred by various issues. The *Economic Survey 2016–17* points out that property tax faces 'problems of low coverage, low rates, low collection efficiency and lack of indexation of property values, making it a non-buoyant source of revenue' (MoF, 2017). It goes on to say that cities such as Bengaluru and Jaipur collect only 5–20 per cent of their potential tax revenues. Moreover, some states have not permitted the municipalities to impose property taxes or have not framed the right regulations. Furthermore, the tax is calculated based on the annual rental value. This leads to lower buoyancy and the states also use their power to stall increase in rental value, sometimes even reducing it. The rental-based calculation encourages people to leave land vacant or underused, which then limits the land supply in the market. As a result, as per ICRIER, the average per capita property tax collection in India for 2017–18 was INR 421. As per the *Economic Survey 2016-17* and the Fourteenth Finance Commission state, there is an urgent need to reform property taxes. In countries like South Africa, the property tax collection rates are as high as 90 per cent whereas, in the thirty-six biggest municipal corporations in India, the property tax collection rates are at 37 per cent (Udas-Mankikar, 2019).

The Fourteenth Finance Commission highlighted that ULBs need to tap property tax as a key source of revenue for financing urban development. Municipal corporations in some cities such as Bengaluru, Hyderabad and Mumbai have had success in boosting their property tax base (ICRIER Team, 2019). They achieved this through mapping their properties using GIS, moving towards better methods of evaluation such as unit area value and the capital value method, allowing self-assessment, periodic revaluation, better payment processes and gateways, and stricter enforcement. Similar recommendations were made by the Fifteenth Finance Commission and the Ministry of Housing and Urban Affairs as well. Mumbai adopted the capital market value method for the assessment of properties and witnessed strong growth in property tax collection (Awasthi and Nagarajan, 2020). Pune city has been able to grow its property tax collection at an average rate of 30 per cent annually from 2010–11 to 2016–17. It used a mix of measures—a system based on capital value, GIS mapping, door-to-door collection, increased coverage of collection centres, introduction of digital payment platforms, and use of the amnesty scheme to facilitate payment from defaulters (ICRIER Team, 2019).

At the all-India level, it is suggested that the Central government mobilize the political support to increase property tax collection in all states and reconsider the exemptions given presently. They should also rebase their property tax calculations and create a system for regular revision to factor in inflation, strengthen systems for assessment, levy and collection and improve operational efficiency (GoI, 2015). Municipalities should be encouraged in updating urban property values and enforcing urban property tax collection. The efficient and effective collection of property taxes is critical to boosting the municipal share of revenue in GDP. Through successive finance commissions, or through matching grants by the Centre directly to the states, ULBs should be encouraged to increase the property tax coverage and revenue. Mapping using GIS has particularly helped many cities such as Raipur, and cities in Madhya Pradesh such as Burhanpur, Dewas, Katni and Khandwa, to bring more properties under the property roll and improve the collection efficiency (Awasthi and Nagarajan, 2020).

There are other measures that can help municipalities gain the maximum out of property taxes. There is also a case to tax government buildings. Currently, the Constitution exempts government buildings from paying property tax (Udas-Mankikar, 2020b). This must change. It reflects highly inefficient utilization of land and land assets. Another way to boost property tax is to regularly revise the rates and also the property assessment. A state-level authority such as a property tax board ensuring compliance from municipalities is the way forward to resolve this issue. States like Tamil Nadu, Andhra Pradesh and Maharashtra have constituted such boards (ibid.).

The property tax regime in India is a classic case of perpetuating complexity, which is inversely proportional to governance efficiency. It was estimated in 2008 that there might be 240 categories for property tax calculation all over India (Awasthi and Nagarajan, 2020). The calculation is also based on, among other things, the cost of construction, usage, whether rented or not, and zones. Rationalization of such categories and also probable rates will serve well for municipal finance revenue in India. A similar distortion is created due to varied exemptions across municipalities. For instance, in Chhattisgarh, properties of political parties are exempt and in West Bengal sick industries get this benefit (ibid.). It is as if we are encouraging inefficient use of urban land. In Madhya Pradesh, owner-occupied properties get a 50 per cent discount (ibid.). There are also private institutions of health and education that get such exemptions. Exemptions should be an exception, but the current application in cities is making property tax collection an exception.

7
Urban Planning: Old Wine in New Bottle

FROM the very start of cities anywhere, including those in the Indus Valley, the layout of cities has been given great importance. Archaeological digs prove that the location of the temple (citadel), royal seat/palace, the markets (bazaars), housing neighbourhoods and their clustering, the type of architecture, the layout of roads, and water and sanitation facilities were all paid close attention to even in ancient times. This amounts to the planning of cities, a spatial layout of the cities. Over the centuries, cities evolved on their own until urbanization, accelerated by the industrial revolution, faced a new set of problems—lack of adequate housing, pollution, inaccessibility of water and sanitation, higher crime rates, and issues of such order. City planning emerged to solve through spatial and geographic interventions, issues that arose from economic activities.

Planning today has evolved to define what you can do in a city and where, and what all compliances you need to do what you want to do. Done right, planning facilitates the best of urbanization (agglomeration, economies of scale, environmental sustainability, reduced risk, citizen empowerment and inclusive development). Done wrong, we do not know where the buck stops. In cities where planning has failed to deliver, the forces of congestion have weighed down the benefits of agglomeration economies.

For a country working overtime to scrub away all traces of its colonial hangover, it is remarkable that India has not revamped the colonial legacy of urban planning. Present-day planning in India traces its origin to the UK's Town and Country Planning Act of 1947, which states that all future land use will be in concurrence with the plan prepared by local authorities. As for the UK, it has long since moved to more decentralized urban planning, enacting the Town and Country Planning Act, 1968, and the Planning and Compulsory Purchase Act, 2004 (Mohanty, 2014).

Indian cities employ the 'master plan' approach. Master plans refer to 'spatial or physical plans which depict on a map the state and form of an urban area at a future point in time when the plan is "realized"' (Pethe et al., 2014). Planning essentially provides for: 1) land-use purpose—defining areas of cities as residential, commercial, industrial, recreational, among others; 2) zoning—defining land plot sizes, taxes and fees, and trunk infrastructure within different zones; and, 3) rules—such as the building codes and guidelines. Modern planning thus defines the land-use developments in the city as being planned/unplanned, formal/informal, and legal/illegal.

In India the negotiations, exemptions and notifications that accompany planning and its implementation are sources of corruption at the ULB level. Further, a city master plan usually spans a long period, a decade or more. This, coupled with a rigid plan structure, gives little or no space to the informal economy or the role of migrants. In most master plans, financing and transportation needs are not the main focus areas (though vital to a city's well-being). In India at least, we find that urban planning has failed to deliver on its original promise while also adversely impacting the key driver of cities—economic growth.

It is time to look at issues that need reform.

ISSUES THAT PLAGUE CITY PLANNING IN INDIA

The most detailed and passionate criticism of India's urban planning in its current form is outlined by Prasanna Mohanty (2019), who identifies critical drawbacks that I have clubbed here under core elements:

- **The master plan:**

i. States make their own master plans through development authorities, which work under bureaucrats (ibid.). The prerogative of people to plan for themselves has never been accorded to them.
ii. Has a twenty- to twenty-five-year horizon, its implementation is a long-drawn out exercise. For instance, the First Plan of Hyderabad began to be designed in 1965, came into effect in 1975 and the revised version was notified in 2008. Likewise, the second Master Plan of Mumbai was initiated in 1977 but was completed in 1994. It took Delhi ten years to complete the activity for its second Master Plan.
iii. Long duration freezes land use, doesn't allow cities to respond to changing structures in the economy, and fails completely to accommodate the social functions of the city.
iv. In separating land use, transport is seen largely as a means to connect different pieces of land use. Integrated transport land use, which unlocks growth, sustainability and inclusivity, has not been leveraged.
v. Does not encourage leveraging land-based financing solutions such as impact fee, betterment levy, transferable development rights and infrastructure cess, among others. The urban planning process looks to state/Central government for resources for development, while the city sits on a goldmine of urban financing—land.

- **The 1947 law:**

i. It 'separate[s] land development from ownership' (ibid.), so you cannot develop your land without approval from the planning authority.
ii. It gives sweeping powers to the planning authority. As mentioned above, negotiations, exemptions and notifications that accompany

planning and its implementation are also sources of corruption at the development authority level.

- **Fragmented local governance structure:**

i. A multiplicity of organizations and weak local capacity to plan and execute provides little help to alleviate city problems.

- **Land development:**

i. Restricted to construction and building.
ii. Focus on horizontal (and not horizontal *and* vertical) growth. It also fails to incorporate new models of development of inclusivity and sustainability.

A point not mentioned by Mohanty, but highlighted by many (including the National Urban Policy Framework), is the lack of gender-blind urban planning. Since the majority of planners are male, Indian cities are made for males and by males. Women seek out public spaces in the vicinity of mixed-use areas, where shops are open round the clock (Ratho, 2020a). Single-use areas make cities dead after work hours.

While these shortcomings have been discussed above in brief, their impact on muting the role of cities—preventing people from enjoying all that a city can offer, distorting democratic participation of local communities in shaping cities, and the stunting of the economic growth story of India—cannot be adequately quantified and justified here. Suffice it to say that such city plans and planning are a major setback for Indian cities, and state and Central governments can make a huge dent in changing the status quo.

Mohanty notes that some stop-gap arrangements have been made through schemes such as JNNURM, under which sixty-five cities were selected and asked to prepare a city development plan to get funding (Mohanty, 2019). This scheme tanked because: 1) these plans were prepared by private consultants and the local community had little say; 2) cities and states could not provide resources to execute the plan; 3) local capacity was not enough to execute the projects; and, 4) reforms mentioned under the scheme were not carried out (ibid.).

The new Urban and Regional Development Plan Formulation and Implementation Guidelines (URDPFI), 2014, have also not been completely internalized by all states. The guidelines also fall short of addressing the concerns of a multiplicity of plans from different authorities; they still continue to underplay the role of vertical land use; and still have limited flexibility to address the need for economic growth (ibid.).

Plans versus Outcomes

A research study by Pethe et al., of a development plan made in the early 1990s for land use in a ward in Mumbai found significant divergences between planned and actual land use across different categories in the ward (Pethe et al., 2014). Their findings showed the following outcomes as of 2010: residential land use (planned 36 per cent, actual 18 per cent); commercial land use (planned 3 per cent, actual 14 per cent); industrial land use (planned 43 per cent, actual 26 per cent); and, slums land use (planned nil, actual 17 per cent). This is fairly reflective of the issues that plague urban planning in India even today.

Many times a plan is made in a timely fashion but is not passed due to one glitch or another. For instance, even after twenty years of the formation of Uttarakhand the state capital, Dehradun, doesn't have a 2005–2025 Master Plan. It was prepared but was scrapped by Uttarakhand High Court in June 2018 as it did not have the approval of the Union Ministry of Environment, Forest and Climate Change (Joshi, 2020). At the regional level, planning is mandated by the seventy-fourth Amendment to the Constitution, which provides for a district planning committee and a metropolitan planning committee. Yet again, by failing to implement this provision the states have deprived citizens of the benefits of modern planning.

REFORMING PLANNING: LOCK, STOCK AND BARREL

When we notice the gaps in urban planning, it is clear what needs to be done. Apart from addressing governance concerns, we need to resolve the issue of inert planning in favour of building a dynamic urban economy. This change in orientation can be understood by illustrating the example of Chandigarh on the one hand and Singapore on the other. Chandigarh exemplifies the planned city approach whereas Singapore exemplifies flexibility as per changing times. The other key difference is that Chandigarh was a greenfield project, while Singapore had already been in existence for a couple of centuries when it became an independent city-state.

In the past six decades, Singapore has gone from being a British naval outpost, to a shipping port, to an electronics manufacturing cluster, to a financial centre and onwards—proactively determining the role it wanted to play in the global economy (Sanyal, 2017). Though Singapore is a city-state it is not inconceivable that India could adopt a certain degree of similar flexibility for its cities of the future, when local governance is empowered. This strategic flexibility could be one of the key drivers of efficient urbanization in Indian cities in the coming decades.

Flexibility is also entrenched in the anthropological paradigm of urban centres as living organisms with their own journey. The dogmatic pursuit of an end goal not only kills the present journey but also limits the possibility of reaching the desired outcome. Flexibility, on the contrary, allows the city to fully utilize its resources at any given point in time and to better adapt to changing conditions. With 70 per cent of urban India yet to be built, the reform of urban planning cannot be put on the back burner any longer (Puri, 2020). The Seventy-fourth Amendment Act empowered ULBs for local self-governance. As per this, eighteen functions were to be devolved to ULBs, under 'Urban planning including town planning' in the 12th Schedule (NIPFP, 1994).

The first and perhaps the key function—local self-governance—has been kept away from ULBs. This is in stark contrast to villages where the gram sabhas (village committees) have enabled villagers to determine the exact roads and basic infrastructure they want for their villages and it wouldn't be wrong to say that the Panchayati Raj Institutions (village-level local governance) have done a fairly good job in guiding the local development of the area. The question regarding the devolution of urban planning processes to ULBs is one of when and not if. When it happens, is our planning education equipped to deal with it? Twenty-five institutes produce 700 town planners per annum (Sridharan, 2015). As of now India has 5,000 town planners, but a government estimate notes that by 2031 India would need 300,000 town planners (Banchariya, 2019).

NITI Aayog is undertaking a deeper study of how to ramp up the number of town planners. One of the emergent themes of this ongoing work is to harmonize the terminology of education on planning, both at undergraduate and graduate level across institutes. Further, the course material will have to sync itself with the new successes of East Asia and China, along with keeping the lessons learnt from the West and the former Soviet style of planning. The other and more pressing concern is to reorient the study of urban planning around urban economics. The present premise is that cities are spatial entities that can facilitate economic exchange. The premise that should be taught is that cities are economic entities and labour markets, and planning is a spatial manifestation of such an entity. The moment this reorientation happens, economics and transport will no longer be taught as additional subjects, but as core subjects dovetailing with urban planning.

This would change the objectives of urban planning—housing access over ownership; public and non-motorized transport over private vehicle ownership; mixed land use over single land use; access to markets over access to homeownership; and building for sustainability and density, over building for horizontal growth.

WORKING WITH, AND NOT AGAINST, THE PRIVATE SECTOR

A lot can be said about what the system lacks, but how do we address the issues of those who enter the workforce with a degree in urban planning? Who hires them, at what wages, and who do they compete with? The answer lies in the conspicuous absence of the private sector in urban planning education and the urban planning process. Only a few private universities offer courses in urban planning. Urban local bodies don't get to make plans and state governments do not mandate the filling of vacant urban planning positions. This takes away the employability of urban planners. We need the presence of the private sector on both demand and supply sides. Scholar-practitioners such as architect Bimal Patel are big champions of this change, as we shall see below.

We need the private sector to offer urban planning courses to meet requirements and reorient education. The presence of private universities creates scale and modernization in education, as it would in any sector. The fields of engineering and management saw the quality of graduates and post-graduates soar in response to demand. Institutions that matched global skills were created to meet this demand and their graduates helped raise the standards of Indian industry. Likewise, as soon as ULBs are mandated to undertake town planning, they will work with the private sector to draft such plans (hopefully this exercise will be different from when, under JNNURM, the drafting of city development plans was outsourced to consulting firms). Once this happens, more institutes will enter the urban-planning education space and the standards and competitiveness of the urban planning industry are both bound to go up. In such an environment, urban planners will be able to focus on elements of equity, informality, transport, energy consumption, and the dynamic role of the private sector.

This change is much desired, as by 2031 India will have eighty-seven urban agglomerations with more than a million people (metropolitan areas), up from fifty-three in 2011 (Ahluwalia, 2019a). Growth in metropolitan areas reflects the changing nature of the economic structure in India, its transition from an agrarian economy to a service-based economy, with the largest share of people engaged in the informal economy. The metropolitan planning committee was envisaged as a channel for development of urban agglomerations with a million-plus population, and it would have elected representatives as members. Unfortunately, even in those areas (not many) where metropolitan planning committees do exist, they have not been empowered to work on a development plan for their metropolitan region (ibid.).

Thus far, planning has failed to deliver on the emerging role of the private sector and the informal economy. The city that best shows up this lack is Gurugram (formerly Gurgaon) located in Haryana on the that state's border with Delhi. At the beginning of the 1970s, Gurugram was largely a rural agricultural district, when some land was taken over by Sanjay Gandhi for his start-up venture 'Maruti'—a manufacturing plant for a small indigenous car. From that start Gurgaon/Gurugram has grown into a 'Millennium City', serving the aspirations of a growing economy, hosting the headquarters of the world's biggest companies, business-process and knowledge-process organizations, alongside roadside eateries and exclusive clubs that buzz with activity through the night.

Over the years many agricultural landowners in Gurugram have become millionaires overnight, their land bought at relatively exorbitant rates by real estate developers and by people who earned generous salaries. The city has worked round the clock to emerge as a residential and business counter-magnet to Delhi. The nightmarish traffic snarls on National Highway (NH) 24 from Delhi to Gurgaon, has not stopped people from commuting to and from the city. And guess what? Gurgaon never had a Master Plan till 2015, by which time it was already well-established in its present avatar and earning close to half of Haryana's annual tax revenue—INR 16,500 crore (Narayan, 2015).

Could the lack of a master plan explain the city's (haphazard) survival? Private-sector solutions to public failures in areas such as drinking water, electricity, safety, transport and so on, have saved the city and led it to thrive—I guess the absence of a master plan had to reflect somewhere. Indian cities have the option of collaborating with private players to plan well and see how the market, particularly the labour market, is functioning. As discussed previously, the movement of people is crucial for the success of cities, which are economic entities. Thanks to initiatives like Smart Cities and the world's overall transition to data and evidence-based policymaking, the cities are in a position to adapt in real-time. 'Movement', a website created by Uber, provides historical insights on a range of key indicators including travel duration, vehicle movement, route details and new transit-ways, among others (Balantrapu, 2017). The primary intention of this website is to assist officials with better city planning. By 2017 Uber had driven over 2 billon trips in 545 cities in 66 countries (ibid.). Given that the website (movement.uber.com) provides historical anonymized data for all days and all hours in the day, it's a goldmine for urban planners.

Data from Uber and similar service provider Ola can be as creatively used as our imagination. In association with other city data, city planners can use simulation from this actual data to identify the changing landscape of cities, the clustering of economic activities, bottlenecks and opportunities in urban transport, priority choke points for movement of people, and the impact of key events. These data insights and analytics can be used by urban planners for continuously improving the quality of life of citizens and ensuring efficient utilization of resources. The data can help them run experiments or study the impact of key policy changes at the city level—the impact of a new flyover, congestion at certain hours, launching a new bus service or route, changing land use, or liberalizing FAR in a market area, and so on.

WHY CAN'T INDIAN CITIES BE AESTHETICALLY PLEASING?

When you drive from Lucknow's Charbagh Railway Station to the other end of the city, why is there an incessant assault on the senses—constant honking, the obnoxious clutter of billboards of all sizes, the poor layout of markets, the deteriorated state of key places such as Hazarat Ganj market, Hazrat Mahal park, Kapoorthala and Aminabad, among others? This is the case in almost every city in India. Why does urban development and planning imply a divorce from a sense of belonging, a divorce from traditional architecture, and from our right to an aesthetically-pleasing city?

The reason lies in the almost tomb-like silence on an important urban planning concept—urban design. I looked for a very simple definition of urban design. I found it on the website of the San Diego government: 'Urban design is the visual and sensory relationship between people and the built and natural environment' (sandiego.gov). That is it. The city lists four elements of urban design: 1) contributing to qualities that distinguish the city as a unique living environment; 2) building upon existing communities; 3) direct growth into the commercial areas; and 4) preserving stable residential neighbourhoods. There is no need to complicate this as this is sufficient for us to achieve a city and a neighbourhood that doesn't rob us of our sense of belonging, community and aesthetics.

The everyday commentary on Indian cities rues the fact that they are mostly a pile of concrete and glass and that has made them generic and ugly. The problem is not with concrete or glass, the problem is how you use it and to what extent? When both aesthetics and a sense of belonging are high, people stay on in the cities that they may have moved to for work, or may have grown up and studied in—you prevent brain drain. Thus, urban design makes economic sense too. The opposite implies that if the city is ugly and chaotic, you might leave sooner—especially if you are living in a concrete box with standard amenities in a crowded locality. Second, we need to ask ourselves why are foreign tourist arrivals, as shown by World Bank data, the highest in France (over 89 million), Spain (over 82 million), the US (over 79 million), China (around 63 million), Italy (over 61 million) and Turkey (over 45 million)—as compared to India (over 17 milion)? (data.worldbank.org)

While the power of economic growth, tourism infrastructure, safety, connectivity and convenience matters, Spain, France and Italy score above India in terms of urban design. Foreign tourists come to witness the local culture and way of living—sitting in a café, drinking a local drink, sightseeing local touristy places but also walking around the neighbourhoods, absorbing the city's culture and history as an experience, and taking a walk through this history. In all these countries you witness the best of urban design in public spaces—museums, libraries, open spaces, vistas, etc. Private spaces at best can be asked to maintain their original façade and abide by some regulations. The magic happens in public spaces.

Even Singapore has more than 14 million visitors. The city has done a splendid job in maintaining the essence of its old neighbourhoods, the façades of its old buildings and residences; it has protected the natural environment, consolidated the sense of history, and preserved local experiences. At the state-level, Maharashtra and Tamil Nadu get highest share of foreign tourists, but that could be because of business activities; and Uttar Pradesh because of the Taj Mahal in Agra. In my view, the only Indian states that seem to have done a half-decent job in this regard are Rajasthan, Goa and Kerala. Their cities still provide for a feel of the local culture, and their houses, forts and palaces have been maintained, many as public spaces. Indian cities are older than Italian or French cities, and at the country level we have a lot to offer.

Third, the economic rationale of urban design is that it protects indigenous culture, language, arts and cuisine from slipping into oblivion. You go to Japan, you wear a kimono, hire translators, eat ramen, try yamazaki and sake, use chopsticks and visit the bamboo temple. You appreciate the reconciliation between the natural environment and the built environment. You don't fail to overlook Nagasaki city's preservation of the atomic bomb-site and the devastation it brought on the city. It is woven into the city's urban design. You cannot fail to notice their obsession with density, cleanliness, lack of noise and air pollution, and resource efficiency.

The one person championing urban design in India is Bimal Patel, an Ahmedabad-based urban planner and architect who has been awarded the Padma Shri. His take on the new parliament building signifies his focus on urban design: '[It] powerfully signifies who we are, how we view our past and where we see ourselves going' (Trivedy, 2019). He is designing the Central Vista too—the three-kilometre-long stretch between Rashtrapati Bhawan and India Gate in the heart of New Delhi. His other projects shine with the possibility of mainstreaming urban design—construction of the Kashi Vishwanath corridor in Varanasi, revamping the eastern seafront of Mumbai through the development of the Mumbai Port Trust, and the restoration of Ahmedabad's Sabarmati Ashram spread over 32 acres of land (ibid.). His success with the Sabarmati Riverfront in Ahmedabad gives us hope on urban design. Nevertheless, I would have been more hopeful if he were to be commissioned by the local government and not by the chief minister of the state.

There is massive criticism of Bimal Patel's approach to such projects but that is not the point here, the concern is that someone is willing to take up urban design as it should be. His take on the development of Mumbai's eastern seafront speaks of this pursuit:

> The current building regulations don't seem to be framed by architects, but by administrators or by architects who think like

administrators. Even the buildings in Ballard Pier were built at different times, but they have the same height and character. Across the world, this principle is followed to maintain the city's essence, but Mumbai has forgotten it along the way. We are trying to bring it back in our planning (Singh 2020c).

On the other hand, we have the case of Amritsar, where the area around the Golden Temple has been revamped. It's an experience to walk around the market area on the cobbled street, away from honking and air pollution. But Jallianwala Bagh, adjacent to the Golden Temple, bears the appearance of an afterthought in an otherwise solid urban design project. Though, there are some new projects implemented to rectify this issue.

In many former industrial hubs worldwide, the regeneration of former industrial districts has created a beautiful combination of urban economic activity and urban design, whilst also unlocking the value of land. Beijing's 798 district—a former district cluttered with military factory buildings has been turned into an art district (Smith, 2019). You can grab a coffee and soak in the emerging art and culture scene of China, in a place that was the melting pot of communist cooperation. The art and design studios and digital media housed in former mills in Mumbai and in New York are another such example. The way forward to achieve this is to use Form-Based Codes instead of conventional land-use regulation.

In India the tourists visit places despite the absence of urban design, and not because of urban design. A bureaucrat posted in a development authority has little time or space to appreciate the nuances of urban design. If we keep going the current way, Indian cities will keep producing ugly, generic cities devoid of character. Urban design is too multidisciplinary and nuanced a topic to be delivered through a special purpose vehicle (a new favourite of state governments to address everything). But if ULBs are given permission to plan, they might stumble at first, but they are the local people so they will invest and raise resources to hire specialists who will curate the experience of living and travelling in their cities.

TRANSIT AND PLANNING: TWO KEY TOOLS AT OUR DISPOSAL

Ancient cities were planned along major roads that intersected at right angles. The city's trunk infrastructure was laid along these routes, and housing lined these streets. Centuries later, post-colonization, India segregated cities based on amenities instead of planning them along urban transport nodes. This led to unplanned and informal urbanization, where the most vulnerable were either shooed off to the peripheries or were denied access to basic infrastructure. However, the world has circled back to the original idea behind the layout of cities—transit-oriented development. The simplest definition is given by the World Bank: 'Transit-oriented development (TOD) is a planning strategy that aims to concentrate jobs, housing and services around public transport stations' (Salat and Ollivier, 2017). Transit-oriented development is not a new way of planning. It is a reimagining of the old ways. Prasanna Mohanty in his book *Cities and Public Policy*, has made a very compelling case for using TOD as a planning tool (Mohanty, 2014).

This phenomenon has gained currency over the last twenty years, especially with its success in East Asian countries. TOD is an exercise in urban transport, land use, planning, financing and infrastructure development. But foremost, it is an exercise in planning. It aims at concentrating growth around one or more transit centres or within a transit corridor. It is to be noted that such transit nodes refer to public transport connectivity and not to an expressway, or to roads primarily used by private vehicles. South Korea decongested Seoul by creating five new towns and providing rail connectivity. The example of Copenhagen in Denmark and Curitiba in Brazil are well-established examples of TOD.

The role of differential FSI within the city and along the major transit points and nodes is a highlight of the world's most successful cities. We have discussed the issue of FSI in great detail previously, under the section on urban land. For instance, Copenhagen used the spatial strategy of 'the Finger Plan' which has been fairly successful in concentrating growth near major transit nodes. It is noted that around half the city's population lives within one kilometre from a railway station, and a quarter of the population within 500 metres of the railway station (World Bank, 2018).

Other such initiatives include the Oculus Station in New York, Shinjuku in Tokyo, and the entire city of Singapore. You can come out of a major station of the MRT in Singapore and immediately find a bus to your drop-off point. The same railway station houses many bank branches, restaurants, convenience stores and retail outlets. High-density apartments are at a walking distance and can be accessed using sidewalks wide enough to accommodate cyclists and walkers. The entire infrastructure is friendly for the elderly and specially-abled people. The announcements, arrival times of buses and MRT, route maps, ramps, and side rails make it a convenient experience for all. The city has dispersed immense green spaces between these nodes for people to walk through and pursue physical activities.

Put together, TOD encourages agglomeration economies, boosts liveability, increases land value, accelerates productivity gains, provides greater resilience and, most importantly for cities, helps finance local projects (Salat and Ollivier, 2017). World Bank has provided a basic but useful framework to assess if TOD can be applied to a transit node, since on an average 15 per cent of such nodes can support such development (ibid.). This framework focuses on: 1) node value, i.e., the importance of the station in the public transit network; 2) place value, i.e., the quality and attractiveness of the area around such nodes; and, 3) the market potential value, i.e., the unrealized market value of such areas (ibid.).

World over, all tiers of government grapple with the issue of financing—an area so critical and tough that the mere mention of it deflates the most idealistic and ambitious plans. However, under the broader action of planning, there has been considerable evidence where infrastructure development has accrued exponential benefits to governments. For transportation alone, the cases of Jubilee Line Extension in London, Mass Transit in Hong Kong and TransMilenio in Bogota provide examples wherein the creation of transport infrastructure substantially increased land prices and helped finance such projects (Mohanty, 2014). The Hong Kong Mass Transit Railway Corporation buys land from the government before undertaking development and then leases it out at higher prices after developing stations and properties around the stations (ibid.). As per World Bank, Hong Kong used land-value capture to earn HKD 140 billion in revenues between 1980 and 2005, while also unlocking land for 600,000 public housing units. Thus TOD makes financial sense too if done right.

India is in a unique position because its metro-rail line connectivity and public transport is undergoing a major revamp. In a country like the US, where cities are planned around automobiles, such a change is difficult to come by. However, as India continues to develop its public transport, it can very well dovetail its urban planning around this network to grow sustainably. TOD is a counter to the urban sprawl. It brings together people, activities and businesses around a public transport transit node that can be easily accessed using non-motorized transport. Delhi has already shortlisted five metro stations to be developed as TOD nodes and this bodes well for the city and the country at large (Chitlangia, 2019).

Since we are discussing the role of transit in planning, there is another initiative in India that merits mention. While many complain about the lack of infrastructure in India's expanding cities, one city stands out—Ahmedabad in Gujarat. It is a model that has been fairly successful in converting agricultural land into serviced urban land. It adopts a two-step approach—a macro-planning stage and a micro-planning stage (Ballaney and Patel, 2009). In the first stage the development authority draws up a statutory, decadal development plan for the town or city, identifying areas where the city is likely to expand. In the second stage, these areas of proposed expansion are divided into smaller areas, usually between one and two square kilometres each.

The development authority thereafter undertakes a town planning scheme in each of these small areas. Shirley Ballaney and Bimal Patel define this scheme as, 'detailed land reconstitution, infrastructure development and financing proposal rolled into one', which involves the following activities:

> Delimiting an area, and within it, reconstituting properties, appropriating land, levying betterment charges to finance

infrastructure provision, compensating dispossessed landowners, formally informing landowners of proposed plans, seeking a majority consent and recording their suggestions and objections, and empowering quasi-judicial officers for redressal of grievances (ibid.).

The scheme has enabled the city to manage the peripheral expansion. It ensures that landowners do not lose in terms of value of their land, while a street network laid in the periphery of the city ensures efficient urbanization as the population spreads outwards. As people start living in these areas, they already have access to trunk infrastructure of water supply and sewerage, road network and other public infrastructure.

As of 2013, 89 per cent of Ahmedabad's 2002 Development Plan was implemented, whereas cities hardly get to implement one-third of their development plans (Mumbai, for instance, has just implemented 15 per cent of its development plan) (Gaur, 2013). Ahmedabad has since seen rapid population growth and built-up area but that has not led to issues of congestion or a low-density sprawl (ibid.). The city has implemented hundreds of town-planning schemes, creating a win-win situation for all, as 40 per cent of private land is acquired for creating public utilities.

This town planning scheme does not limit options for industry but creates more options for them to locate. Such new areas that are developed are serviced through the city's Bus Rapid Transit System (BRTS). The ability of the town planning scheme to provide for roads has been a key factor in implementing the 2002 Development Plan, hence avoiding the hazards of haphazard urbanization. The city has been also revamping its central business district through liberal FAR, building bye-laws, and using self-financing (Patel, 2015). The most important factors behind the success of the town-planning scheme are: self-financing, amendments in the town-planning Act (GTPUDA) to provide infrastructure in a timely manner, and a quasi-judicial official Town Planning Officer who acts independently of local influence (Jain, 2019). The success of this approach can be judged by how different cities are now trying to learn from the Ahmedabad experience (*Hindustan Times*, 2019a and 2019b).

The town-planning scheme was also promoted as a pilot scheme at the national level for selected cities in July 2018 (MoHUA, 2018b).

The cities and towns covered under the pilot scheme will receive financial and technical expertise. This scheme will be implemented in convergence with the Smart City Mission and AMRUT and will cover 110 cities. Redevelopment using local area plans can solve the issues of more public space, higher FSI and street widening in inner-city areas. Similarly, it will also alleviate urban periphery issues of lack of public spaces, particularly adequacy of right-of-way for streets and street network, which also hinders the provision of basic network infrastructure.

DAVID VERSUS GOLIATH: JANE JACOBS AND ROBERT MOSES

After we have seen the India-specific issues pertaining to urban planning, I think we must revisit the most high-profile face-off over urban planning in the twentieth century. This actually covers a set of events that took place in the late 1950s and early 1960s, between an urban planner Robert Moses, and a journalist and activist, Jane Jacobs, over a highway Moses proposed be built through Washington Park. It makes for a master class on urban planning. Since India is gaining traction on urbanization, this battle of wills has lessons galore for us, and the more people know about it, the better it will be for our discourse on our cities. While many people have reported on it, I find Leo Hollis's lucid retelling in his book *Cities are Good for You*, very useful (Hollis, 2013).

Of the two main players, Moses was a product of Yale, Oxford and Columbia, part of civic government from early on in his career and by 1961 long acknowledged as USA's leading urban planner. He had a stellar career, at one point holding twelve government offices. Moses is also credited with turning New York around through his architectural vision, more than doubling the parkland in the city. Between 1920 and

1960, he added 658 playgrounds and developed seventeen miles of beach-front. He delivered some very high-profile assignments for the city such as making the city work around cars, replacing old blocks with high-rises, and even got the UN to build its headquarters (designed by Le Corbusier), in the city (ibid.).

On the other hand, Jane Jacobs started her career as a clerk and pursued a journalistic career, working at *Architectural Forum* magazine wherein she, along with her colleague William H. Whyte, began to question the lack of focus among citizens on the issue of urban planning (ibid.). This was after she took Moses head on by joining the opposition to Lower Manhattan Expressway (LoMex), which was proposed by Moses. It intended to connect the Hudson River tunnel and the two East River Bridges and would subject Lower Manhattan to automobile proliferation. In the process, it would dispossess 2,200 families, 365 shops and 480 businesses. It would have broken into the known and historic neighbourhoods of SoHo, Greenwich Village, Little Italy, China Town, Lower East Side and others.

Jacobs had succeeded in mobilizing common citizens, as well as public figures such as Lewis Mumford and Eleanor Roosevelt, in favour of her campaign. A frustrated Moses exclaimed, 'There is nobody against this, nobody, nobody, nobody but a bunch, a bunch of mothers' (ibid.). Though the system supported Moses, by 1969 the growing opposition ensured that in public Jane Jacobs won. The idea she proposed of building cities from the bottom up trounced Moses' hegemonic ideas of a top-down approach. By 1971, the Lower Manhattan Expressway (LoMex) project lost its funding (ibid.). Jacobs wrote in 1962 in her book *The Death and Life of Great American Cities,* cited by Hollis, that:

> This book is an attack on current city planning and rebuilding. It is also, and mostly, an attempt to introduce new principles of city planning and rebuilding, different and even opposite to those now taught in everything from schools of architecture and planning to Sunday supplements and women's magazines (ibid.).

For a country like India—where community relations are strong, education standards are not uniformly high, where there is a disdain towards migrants coming from all over the country, and where exists a fetish for the symbol of upward mobility (the automobile)—we need neither Moses' top-down approach nor Jacobs' bottom-up approach, but a mix of both. There is too much to be done and our best bet is to find best practices, while balancing issues that need to be resolved. Though the prescription here might seem to be a top-down approach, we will find our optimum solutions through experimentation.

Post Covid-19, people are baying for the blood of dense cities. They are claiming that dense cities had more infections. The most spirited contradiction has been raised by Reuben Abraham and Vaidehi Tandel of IDFC Institute (Abraham and Tandel, 2020). They show that cities like Taipei, which had the same density as New York, and other dense Asian cities like Singapore, Bangkok, Hanoi, and Hong Kong did not have a massive outbreak of Covid-19. Even New York's densest borough Manhattan had the lowest infection rates. The poor urban management, coupled with crowding of people and socio-economic factors are better explanations of the spread of Covid-19.

I think many lessons from Jane Jacobs' approach hold the key to some of India's most pressing problems. Primarily, I think hers is a lesson on how people's view of their city and its future holds much more value than the opinion of a bureaucrat sitting elsewhere in his office taking detached decisions. Detached, because the bureaucrat may not be invested personally in the city and fails to appreciate that a city is a living organism that needs facilitation to grow and prosper, rather than being bucketed in a straitjacket. Leo Hollis summarizes Jane's opposition as: 1) life on streets should be appreciated and is a good indicator of the vitality of a city; 2) public spaces of the city are more important than are traffic flow and efficiency; and 3) planning should be done from the perspective of how people use spaces (Hollis, 2013).

There are other countless lessons in Jane Jacob's book, some of which need to be articulated because they resonate in India of today. On lack of urban design, she said that 'Extraordinary governmental financial incentives have been required to achieve this degree of monotony, sterility and vulgarity' (Jacobs, 1992). On mixed use and inclusivity in cities, she emphasized 'the need of cities for a most intricate and close-grained diversity of uses that give each other constant mutual support, both economically and socially' (ibid.). She was a vehement and passionate supporter of sidewalks and streets. For her, these played the most important role in making a city safer and interesting. Safety in public spaces, she noted, 'is kept primarily by an intricate, almost unconscious, network of voluntary controls and standards among the people themselves, and enforced by the people themselves' (ibid.).

She advocated the benefit of 'eyes upon the street' in creating a sense of safety in cities. She opined how this could be achieved: 'the basic requisite for such surveillance is a substantial quantity of stores and other public spaces and other public places sprinkled along the sidewalks of a district' (ibid.). There is a reason why we feel the safest in areas of Delhi's Chandni Chowk, Lucknow's Hazratganj and Mumbai's Lower Parel area. This stands in such contrast with how current planning aims to tell how a person is living, working and spending her leisure time.

Such sidewalks are important to create contact among people. I choose to highlight this under a very drab section of urban planning, because it is the most potent tool to ensure this. A drive on Delhi's Nelson Mandela Road, zipping by three huge malls, fettered with the most high-end vehicles, leaves out an entire kilometres-long stretch between the colonies of Vasant Vihar and Vasant Kunj—a space that has zero scope for contact among people. Where there is no contact between people, there is distrust. On public contact, Jacobs has written, 'The sum of such casual, public contact at a local level is a feeling for the public identity of people, a web of public respect and trust, and a resource in time of personal or neighbourhood need' (ibid.). Such sidewalks lead to the wholesome development of children. The parks are important, she noted, but only if they were surrounded by spaces with different uses, which led to different people walking in and out at different times. She has provided insights on ensuring diversity in the city, regenerating the city, and the use of various strategies to salvage cities. They all tie back to Leo Hollis' summary of her lessons.

This brings us to the pressing role of public spaces and ways of reviving it. I wrote an article about it in the Livemint in 2018 under the title 'Realistic policies to revive public spaces'. It highlighted that the available public space per capita in Mumbai is as low as 1.28 sq m as compared to London (31.68 sq. m), New York (26.4) and Chicago

(17.6). No city can be successful without the availability of public space; but yes, all cities that do not have such spaces are bound to decline in the future. The article highlighted that the public spaces are defined by UN-Habitat as 'all places, including streets, publicly owned or of public use, accessible and enjoyable by all for free and without a profit motive'. I stressed that though global development agenda did highlight issue of public spaces such as Sustainable Development Goal 11 and UN-Habitat's 'Global Public Space Toolkit: From Global Principles To Local Policies and Practice'; but, we still lack broad consensus on realistic policies to achieve the goals on public spaces (Dhar, 2018c).

There are solutions I have discussed in the book and highlighted in the article to revive public spaces in India. First, we should direct focus and resources towards non-motorized transport (NMT), especially in areas of busy markets, roads, and transport junctions and only allow non-motorized transport during one day of the week in designated streets and junctions. Second, I cannot overstress the importance of opening public spaces for cultural expression. This could include areas of streets, sidewalks, neighbourhoods, marketplaces and places of historical importance. Third, I discussed the role of leveraging privately owned public spaces (POPS), such as malls. They are privately owned and managed but provide access to public. Is there a possibility of making them public spaces for a limited duration (even if few hours)? The inverse is also a question worth asking—can public spaces be privatized on a time-bound lease for maintenance? (Dhar, 2018c).

Fourth, the article highlighted that there is evidence that well-managed public spaces increase prices of nearby residential areas so municipalities may encourage private neighbourhoods to adopt nearby public spaces. Fifth, we need to replicate the success of countries like Italy and Spain in terms of reviving the existing inventory of public spaces such as parks, beaches, historical landmarks, places of worship, and centuries-old architecture. This can be achieved if we focus on four basic needs of infrastructure, hygiene, security and accessibility. Sixth, we should scale up our initiatives on converting old infrastructure, wastelands, landfills, and other such places into public places. Such an approach would involve reversal of encroachment of our water bodies such as ponds, beaches, mangroves and seafronts in urban areas (Dhar, 2018c).

Put together, these initiatives move into the direction shown by Jane Jacobs. It is worthy to close this argument by summing the benefits of functioning and vibrant public spaces—greater inclusion, safety, tourism, global power projection, democratic engagement, quality of life, gender parity, social cohesion, liveliness and economic returns (Dhar, 2018c).

8

Urban Safety and Inclusiveness: Putting People at the Centre of Cities

CITIES originally were not meant to perform the function of providing inclusivity and safety. They were meant for elites, who used the agrarian surplus to drive their professions and bring people together. However, changes in the global political economy changed the nature of cities too. From the fifteenth to nineteenth century, the industrial revolution ushered in agglomeration economies to such an extent that the world urbanized at a frantic pace, bringing more people together than ever before and allowed greater prosperity for more people. In 1800, no more than 3 to 5 per cent of the 1 billion people lived in cities, and no city in the West had a population of more than a million (Pethe et al., 2014; Joshi, 2020).

By 1900, the share of the urban population had reached 14 per cent of the 1.6 billion global population. By this time there were at least nine cities with over 1 million population—Berlin, Chicago, New York, Philadelphia, Moscow, St. Petersburg, Vienna, Tokyo and Chicago (Mumford, 1961). The urbanization rate in the US, France, Germany, Belgium and the UK became close to 50 per cent. In the second half of the twentieth century, dozens of countries came out of colonialism. East Asia, Latin America, Africa and South Asia were the major regions wherein independence movements gained desirable outcomes. However, as we have seen in the first chapter of this book, democracy was exported to other countries through colonialism—not as a conscious, direct, generous gesture, but indirectly—when elites of the colonialized world plugged into the new form of governance (democracy) devised by the Western world.

Democracy helped people worldwide become part of the mainstream growth and development process. Initially, democratic means to elect leaders were exercised by land-owning males. However, a churning in major urban centres allowed women and other marginalized sections to also vote and elect their leaders. There is a possibility that such an increase in democratic governance, coupled with the urbanization process worldwide, gave more people than ever before a chance to shape their destinies, including in cities. The buttressing of these two grand themes of the modern world—cities and democracies—shaped the development of both cities and democracies. For instance, functions cities were expected to perform evolved to include the provision of safety and inclusivity.

Safety continues to be one of the new social contracts between the city and the citizen, just like the chance for upward mobility provided by inclusivity and job opportunities. We have seen how cities perished and prospered from ancient times, depending upon how they were able to ensure safety and inclusivity for residents. The absence of safety and inclusivity tears down the understanding between cities and its dwellers. The safety construct existed even before the onset of democracy, but was not as comprehensive as it is in present times. In the past, kings ensured the safety of the guilds and merchants for the safe conduct of their business. Inclusivity, however, is a new concept that has been plugged into the functioning of cities as we know them today. The concepts of 'right to live and work in the city' and 'just cities' are a function of such an interaction between democracy and urbanization. Not surprisingly, worldwide, the lack of safety and exclusion are intertwined. This reflects in the disempowerment of economic opportunities, lack of access to key and basic infrastructure, higher time and costs to travel, inability to engage with key decision-makers and marginalization.

We have understood the reasons and probable solutions behind these issues in previous chapters. However, certain issues demand a separate mention, especially those exemplified in episodes that will remain forever etched in the public memory. For instance, will we ever forget what Nirbhaya went through in the city of Delhi, the capital of India? In 2022 we commemorated the fourteenth anniversary of the terrorist attack in Mumbai on 26 November 2008.

Will the sense of vulnerability ever leave us? When we leave for work, do our families forget to mention being mindful about road safety? Are we not aware of the consequences of deep inequalities and dramatic differences in access to resources among various communities and what that means for social cohesion? Do we not worry about seeing young people idling away on speeding bikes and often being pushed into petty crime? Don't we have a little apprehension when we venture into a public space with our loved ones? Anybody who has ever brooded over all these questions is clearly concerned about safety and inclusiveness in their cities. Pondering these questions and challenges implies that we are putting people at the centre of cities.

The UN's Urban Habitat III stresses the issues of safe cities by 'developing effective and humane crime prevention and community safety strategies and in creating and maintaining institutional frameworks for their implementation and review' (UN Habitat, 2015a). But it also highlights that urban safety stretches beyond crime prevention and also includes, 'enhancement of individual rights including the physical, social and psychological integrity of a person' (ibid.). The majority of the world population lives in cities wherein inequality has increased since 1980 (ibid.). Indian cities also show considerable variance in income and living conditions, mainly with the vulnerable population having to pay more for basic public services while living in informal and slum housing.

The safety and inclusivity of cities is now being measured worldwide. The most widely recognized is The Economist Intelligence Unit's (EIU's) *Safe Cities Index Report* (EIU, 2019a). It ranks sixty cities on fifty-seven indicators covering issues of digital safety and personal, health and infrastructure security. Ranked at the top are Tokyo, Singapore, Osaka, Amsterdam, Sydney, Toronto, Washington, Copenhagen, Seoul, and Melbourne. The Indian cities of Mumbai and Delhi occupy more modest positions, forty-fifth and fifty-third respectively (ibid.). The three lowest-ranked cities are Yangon, Caracas, and Lagos. The EIU report has an important insight, which it communicates using the quote by Leo Tolstoy: 'All happy families are alike: each unhappy family is unhappy in its way' (ibid.). The point it conveys is that the top five cities have performed well in all the important pillars—digital safety, and personal, health and infrastructure security.

Together with economic opportunities and robust urban mobility, safety and inclusivity makes for liveable cities. For instance, as per a survey, Hyderabad and Bengaluru were rated the top two most liveable cities in India based on commute speed, public transport availability, absorption of migrants, diversity in the city, affordable housing options, availability of dine-out options, presence of social infrastructure, greenery and per capita municipal spending (Mohanty, 2014). Indian cities are presently dealing with basic issues of infrastructure, public transport, housing, planning, safety and governance. However, given the policy orientation over the last fifteen years and resources, the nature of these issues will undergo considerable change.

The global rankings also focus on similar issues. For instance, the EIU's 'Global Liveability Ranking' uses thirty indicators across five themes to provide scores for lifestyle in 140 cities worldwide. There are other such rankings, where cities from Canada, Australia and Europe usually make up the top few ranks. While Indian cities cannot and should not compete with these cities on liveability, they should attempt to consistently improve their rankings. The business newspaper *LiveMint,* has its own Livability Index comprising of ten sub-indices: commute speeds, public transport, migrant flow, diversity, affordable housing, dineout, social infra, greenery, and municipal finance. If one were to look at these indicators, the relationship between safety and inclusivity is obvious. They reinforce each other. Safety and inclusiveness should be viewed concurrently, since the causes and solutions on these issues often converge. Gender, ethnicity, religion, physical ability, ageing groups, migrants and employment status (i.e., for informal workers) are all clear determining factors that influence access to the full benefits of urbanization. Safe cities are more inclusive; cities that exclude are often unsafe for more than one stakeholder.

Going back to EIU's Safe City Index, we have discussed most of the fifty-seven sub-indicators in other parts of the book—digital security in the chapter on governance as part of the discussion on smart cities; infrastructure security is part of a detailed section on urban infrastructure; and many aspects of personal security are part of the next chapter on resilience. The reason I mention this is because a couple of interventions cannot ensure that a city becomes safe and inclusive. Safety and inclusivity are outcomes of a multi-disciplinary approach, the consequence of many inputs and outputs. A lot has to go right for a city to become inclusive and safe. These two factors are highly influenced by national-level policies and social norms. Going ahead, the salience of these two issues will further increase, as it has after the onset of Covid-19.

In the context of Indian cities, there is one factor that demands separate mention: violence—individual and group violence. The solutions for both converge more often than not. Coming from Uttar Pradesh, I have seen conflicts being resolved through violence.

Group violence is something that can take over any city for a variety of reasons—socio-economic, political, migrant-related, and even fake news-driven. Many world cities have been subject to it and in India, cities small and big have suffered through mob violence. Communal pogroms are one aspect of Indian mob violence and are not new to India. The Partition of 1947 only heightened what has always existed. The pogrom against Sikhs in Delhi in 1984, the Mumbai riots in 1992, the the burning of a train in Godhra in 2002 which caused the deaths of 58 Hindu pilgrims and karsevaks returning from Ayodhya and subsequent violence in the streets of Gujarat in 2002, the Muzaffarpur riots in 2013, the recent violence in the streets of Delhi, the list goes on and on. There is no way cities can deal with such menace on their own. It is ignited and egged on by forces beyond their control. Cities are merely the screen on which communal hatred and bigotry play out their role. Yet it is important to consider this element—communal violence or bigotry—because it marries the issue of safety to inclusiveness. India is too diverse to force exclusion and/or religious, language and ethnic hegemony.

People who think this is a way forward must note that they will not be able to leverage cities for economic gains and quality of life if they believe they can marry exclusion with economic growth. The city of Kigali in Rwanda exemplifies this. The 1994 ethnic violence between the

Tutsi and the Hutu took the country back by several decades. Twenty-five years later, Rwanda and its capital Kigali are bursting with economic opportunities and quality of life as law enforcement had reduced such possibilities of violence. Such stability has made Kigali one of the most enterprising centres of Africa. On the other hand, those cities in South Africa that have failed to ensure safety and inclusion, have fallen behind Rwandan cities. Since 2000, Rwanda's GDP has increased by six times, its infant mortality rate has declined by half, and women constitute 61 per cent of its parliament. (Kamdar, 2019) Rwanda has the highest share of women parliamentarians worldwide, with over 60 per cent of the seats held by women (Thornton, 2019). While there remain concerns of political suppression and lack of democracy, the country turned a corner after the 1994 riots.

Going back to an economist's viewpoint, major stakeholders need to know that cities with a reputation for being notorious for lack of safety and inclusiveness bodes poorly for their growth and wealth generation. Not only does such a reputation prevent businesses and highly-skilled labour from coming to such cities, but residents of these cities end up paying for private security. One such example is private housing societies hiring security companies to provide guards for round-the-clock security. Not too far in the past (and maybe even now), certain Indian cities were known for people paying 'protection money' in return for protection from people and groups that perpetrated violence. In India, this was once common in the states of Bihar, Uttar Pradesh and Jharkhand. This exists elsewhere too, of course. In Brazil, for instance, 10 per cent of annual GDP is spent on private security and insurance (Fox and Goodfellow, 2016). Given below are some city-specific policies that are important for creating safe and inclusive cities.

RECLAIMING THE ROLE OF PUBLIC SPACES: REDUCING FEAR OF THE UNKNOWN

In this phase of rapid and haphazard urbanization, the critical element of social cohesion through public spaces has been left behind. Public spaces can take many spatial forms—parks, streets, sidewalks and footpaths, playgrounds, marketplaces, and even spaces between buildings and whole streets and beaches (UN Habitat, 2015b). A walk around Indian cities will reveal that they depend more on ad hoc infrastructure creation and on private spaces than on public spaces. Gurgaon is a classic example of the predominance of private spaces—malls, private housing, commercial spaces and amusement parks among others—over any meaningful public spaces. This stands in contrast to older Indian cities and cities worldwide which derive their unique characters due to their public spaces. As leading urban thinker and activist Jane Jacobs once pointed out—'eyes on the street', i.e., the neighbourhoods in which people are watching—make cities safer. Many traditional Indian public spaces, such as the 'nukkad' in north India, 'pol' in Ahmedabad, 'para' in Kolkata, 'chauraha' in Lucknow and Kanpur, and so on, have traditionally hosted a mix of gender and age, who were constantly there. Such public spaces are a key deterrent for anyone to consider committing a crime. Urban scholars such as Sanjeev Sanyal are constant champions of the role of public spaces.

Besides, public spaces in cities form a melting pot of equality, social cohesion, new ideas, city identity, creative expression, regular interaction between citizens, and increase trust between people and the government. There is also evidence that well-managed and planned public spaces have economic value and, in many instances, they have led to an increase in the price of nearby residential neighbourhoods. It is important that without the need of intervention by the Central or state government, cities place the agenda of public spaces at the top of their list of priorities. They should focus on design, functionality and location to create the public spaces that cities deserve. Moreover, public spaces need support of appropriate legislation and enforcement at the neighbourhood level, by city authorities. Indian cities should work with communities to provide a conducive environment for public spaces that encourage creative expression, increased interaction between residents and new economic opportunities for the poor. These spaces require creative thinking rather than intensive capital investment.

Apart from the benefits mentioned above, such spaces are a great equalizer. We usually talk of education as a great leveller, but the role of public spaces in making a city inclusive is hardly appreciated. The rich and poor, young and old, men and women, and skilled and semi-skilled all come to such places and feel that they belong. An outing to such a place can help reduce stress, make them feel part of society at large, and a constant interaction with people from other backgrounds and genders reduces the level of distrust.

There is a widely quoted example of just such a public space created in South Korea. Jonathan Rose has documented its story in detail (Rose, 2016). Cheonggyecheon is a tributary of the Han river, along which Seoul was founded in 17 BCE. Since the fourteenth century, the Cheonggyecheon river has been a source of economic growth for the city and the region. With the growing prosperity after the Korean War (1950–53), congestion and traffic grew. Cheonggyecheon river was covered by a road in the 1960s, and was eventually completely covered under an elevated freeway. Despite this measure, the issue of congestion was not resolved. This was when the city adopted a counter-intuitive approach.

Professor Kee Yeon Hwang suggested getting rid of the freeway. In his mayoral election bid, Lee Myung Bak took up this suggestion and proposed demolishing the expressway and restoring the river which once graced the city (Vidal, 2006). This brought down the volume of traffic. Jonathan Rose stresses that the Korean professor attributed the change to the Braess Paradox which essentially implies that 'adding capacity and connectivity to a user-optimized system such as a road network does not increase its efficiency if each user makes selfish choices' (Rose, 2016). The Delhi–Gurgaon highway is a classic example of such congestion.

As the Cheonggyecheon riverfront developed, the nearby area revitalized economically and culturally. Surface temperatures near the river fell significantly, particulate matter fell by half and biodiversity in the river increased fourfold (ibid.). Some similar initiatives in India include the development of the Sabarmati riverfront in Ahmedabad and the pedestrianization of Chandni Chowk in Old Delhi.

The Cheonggyecheon riverfront has become a public space that is enjoyed by office-going young people, families and artists. The project was able to revive the urban core, but its success on the ecological and biodiversity fronts is still contested. However, it has provided a space in a world-class city where people from all walks of life can mingle and reduce the level of distrust. This is the key function of a public space, in the absence of which people start 'othering' different sections of people as they do not interact with them on a one-to-one basis. Mumbai's beaches, Singapore's Hawker Centres, Washington's Mall, Delhi's Connaught Place, the Mall roads in India's hill stations, and centuries-old local markets in Indian cities are some examples through which the interaction among people and communities increases and distrust comes down.

PROVIDING AN ADEQUATE POLICE FORCE AND LAW AND ORDER IN CITIES

The South American country Colombia recorded eighty-four homicides per 100,000 people, at its peak (World Bank Data, n.d.). By 2018, the homicide rate had declined to 25 per 100,000 people (ibid.). Most of these homicides were triggered by drug wars and poor institutional capability. Bogotá and Cali were centres of such violence. When Bogotá elected Mayor Enrique Peñalosa in 2016, he promised to reduce crime in the city's 750 highest-crime streets (Blattman et al., 2017). He adopted the twin approach of increased policing and the other not so well-known approach of municipal clean-ups of the concerned streets. The local government studied the issue and provided services such as removing garbage and non-artistic graffiti, and repairing street lights (ibid.).

The second intervention used the 'Broken Windows' approach. Jonathan Rose has explained this initiative for neighbourhood-level safety (Rose, 2016). In the 1980s, two social scientists published an article 'Broken Windows', which has since become a theory of its own that is at the centre of urban safety. It suggests that when a neighbourhood has a few broken windows that remain untended, there is a high possibility that more windows will be vandalized and more trash dropped outside such buildings. However, if they are quickly mended, the likelihood of such crimes continuing declines dramatically. The idea is that a poor standard of municipal services reflects the lack of government attention on these areas and makes crime in such neighbourhoods more likely. Poverty Action Lab partnered with Bogotá to study the impact of these policies. The study proved that crime did not come down significantly where only one of the two approaches was used. Whereas, crime came down by 57 per cent in areas where the twin approaches were used (Blattman et al., 2017).

There are lessons for Indian cities in such an approach. One perception of the Indian police force is that instead of doing its job, it only follows the directions of the political masters, and engages in extra-judicial killings, is corrupt, harasses the weak and poor and does not cooperate with people who report crimes. However, this can be partly attributed to the fact that the police force is overburdened and understaffed. Reform and strengthening of the police force should also be at the top of the priority list of our cities. States would have to reform the state police act along the lines of the Model Police Bill. The police-to-population ratio recommended by the UN is 222 policemen per lakh population, but the average number for India is 192 policemen per lakh population (Kushwah, 2018). There is also a huge difference between sanctioned and actual strength. For instance, in 2016, the sanctioned strength was 181 police per lakh persons, but the actual police strength was 137 per lakh persons (Chaturvedi, 2017). This overburdens our police forces and it would be unreasonable for us to expect them to be effective and efficient. They are reluctant to even register complaints, never mind the intensive patrolling of hotspots.

The spending on police infrastructure is poor and includes slow acquisition of weapons, a shortage of police vehicles, lack of housing for the police force and their families, lack of complete integration of ICT among police forces and availability of ICT infrastructure in police stations. The 24 per cent vacancy in 2016 in state police forces—around 5.5 lakh vacancies—is alarming (ibid.). It is also an avenue for job creation and these vacancies should be filled. Besides, more than 85 per cent of the police force comprises of the constabulary, with limited pathways for promotion and growth (ibid.). The remaining share is made up of around 13 per cent of the upper subordinate ranks (i.e. inspector to assistant sub-inspector) and another one per cent makes up the officer ranks (DGP to the Deputy SP) (ibid.).

The people don't trust the police and the judicial process due to the low conviction rate (47 per cent in 2015 [ibid.]). Such low conviction is attributed to poor investigations, a direct function of understaffed and underprepared police forces. Thankfully by 2016, as many as fifty-three cities moved towards the Commissionerate system, where the police force is under the Commissioner of Police. This allows for quick decision making, rather than the dual system under which the power is shared between the district magistrate and the superintendent of police (ibid.).

Apart from the hard infrastructure issues the ICT infrastructure, the presence of CCTV cameras and smart-city projects, could help reduce crime using data-driven policing. The other important issue is to change the nature of the police force. From being a colonial tool of oppression and used for control of violence, it should move on to become a force of good at the neighbourhood level. The trust deficit between Indian society and the police force is deep and needs to be bridged before any other actions can be taken to make Indian cities safe. Many Indian states have started bringing the police closer to the community through various initiatives, including Kerala's 'Janamaithri Suraksha Project', Rajasthan's 'Joint Patrolling Committees', Assam's 'Meira Paibi', Tamil Nadu's 'Friends of Police', West Bengal's 'Community Policing Project', Andhra Pradesh's 'Maithri' and Maharashtra's 'Mohalla Committees' (ibid.).

We have discussed infrastructure and urban design issues in previous sections. Also important is upgrading and maintaining municipal services in areas that are crime hot spots to prevent them from succumbing to the 'broken windows' effect. Together with effective policing, such efforts can provide an avenue for cities to move from security to safety in the long run. Across Indian cities, leading political actors and administrators use safety and security interchangeably as they make tall promises on safe cities, and CCTV cameras have been unofficially declared as the panacea for solving all the urban safety-related issues. This only goes to show our limited understanding of the issue. In the policy life cycle, we ought to differentiate between inputs that translate into outputs and those that don't. This, sustained over a period of time, leads to outcomes. The allocation of the Nirbhaya Fund is an input, and installing of CCTV cameras is an output. If a city's children, its women, the elderly and other vulnerable groups are confident that no harm will come to them or their property—that will be the final result of outputs. This will be the sense of safety.

NO CHILD'S PLAY: THE ENDURING CHALLENGE OF CREATING CHILD-FRIENDLY CITIES[2]

Often it is the obvious that fails to make a case for itself. India's two predominant demographic characteristics—a high share of young population and surging urban populations—call on the country's urban policymakers to make cities more child-friendly. Yet the very concept of 'child-friendly cities' has still to be mainstreamed in India's policy lexicon. This may be understandable given the dire situation of Indian cities, overall they are mired in serious challenges such as acute pollution, rampant crime, infrastructure deficit, mobility congestion and environmental hazards. However, the lack of attention on creating child-friendly cities is no longer desirable or reasonable. Some fundamental statistics also make a compelling case for the need to make India's cities child-friendly.

Globally, of the entire urban population, one billion (23.7 per cent) are children (Voce, 2018). By 2050, 70 per cent of all the world's children will live in urban areas (Davies, 2018). According to a report from the National Institute of Urban Affairs (NIUA), 'Status of Children in Urban India Baseline Study 2018', India is home to 472 million children, comprising 39 per cent of its population (NIUA, 2018a). Every fourth child in India (27.4 per cent) lives in urban areas (ibid.). Given that globally, over one-third of children in urban areas are unregistered at birth, there would be many more children in urban areas than we presently know (UNICEF, 2012).

These figures leave little room for doubt that building child-friendly cities has become an imperative for India. The term itself found mention in the global urban development policy space only when the

---

2 This section is an edited and abridged version of a Working Paper co-authored by Devashish Dhar and Manish Thakre and published by the Observer Research Foundation (*ORF Issue Brief No. 415*) in October 2020. It is published here with permission from ORF.

'Child Friendly Cities Initiative' was first launched at the UN-Habitat II conference in 1996. According to UNICEF:

> A child friendly city is a city or any local system of governance that is committed to fulfilling children's rights, including their right to influence decisions about their city; express their opinion on the city they want; participate in family, community and social life; receive basic services such as healthcare, education and shelter; drink safe water and have access to proper sanitation; be protected from exploitation, violence and abuse; walk safely in the streets on their own; meet friends and play; have green spaces for plants and animals; live in an unpolluted environment; participate in cultural and social events; and be an equal citizen of their city with access to every service, regardless of ethnic origin, religion, income, gender or disability (UNICEF, 2009).

London-based engineering and design firm, Arup,[3] has provided a useful framework for studying issues pertaining to the creation of child-friendly cities. The same framework can be applied in the Indian context to understand what makes cities inhospitable for children.

1. Traffic and congestion. These issues are critical given the amount of time that children spend outdoors to travel to and from their school, play areas, markets and social gatherings. The roads, footpaths, crossings are essential in making cities safe and inclusive for children. Roads in Indian cities, for one, are occupied by cars and other motorized vehicles—a reflection of the lack of thought regarding children when these roads were being planned and built. Consider this statistic: Transport-related injuries ranked fourth as cause of death among five- to fourteen-year-olds in India in 2016.[4]

---

[3] Arup is an independent firm headquartered in London. It provides design, planning, engineering, architectural, consulting and technical services for all aspects of the built environment.

[4] Institute of Health Metrics and Evaluation (IHME).

2. High-rise living and urban sprawl. While residential high-rises tend to limit the interactions that children can have with their communities, the urban sprawl focuses on car-focused cities. Such living design also reduces the physical activity of children. In slum areas too, children live in conditions that are not clean, safe and conducive to their overall welfare. Data shows that over eight million children in the zero-to-six-year age group live in urban slums (NIUA, 2018a). It is not surprising that a survey (2017–18) on school health and fitness in eighty-six cities across twenty-six states in India found that two in every three children in the seven-to-eighteen age group do not have a healthy body mass index (BMI); and one in every three has inadequate lower body strength (ibid.). The problem of lack of physical activity has only exacerbated during the Covid-19 crisis as schools have remained closed and children are mostly indoors.

3. Crime, social fear and risk aversion. Children's mobility, especially for those in the younger age groups, is determined largely by the perception of the risk that their parents or guardians have regarding their environment. According to data from the National Crime Record Bureau (NCRB), the number of cases of crimes reported against children in violation of provisions of the Indian Penal Code and other laws in nineteen metropolitan cities (cities with >2 million population) increased from 19,081 in 2016 to 21,425 in 2019. The total number of victims in registered cases increased from 20,571 in 2016 to 23,107 in 2019 (NCRB, 2016–19). Poor infrastructure (including the absence of street lights, footpaths and safe public spaces) pose serious threats to the movement of children in these cities and thereby contribute to the stunting of their development.

4. Inadequate and unequal access to the city. This involves inequitable access to health and education facilities. For young girls, in particular, the problem can be disproportionately acute. According to Save the Children's *World of India's Girls (WINGS) 2018* report, travelling in public transport gave the highest sense of risk perception to girls in urban areas (47 per cent). This was followed closely by commuting to the local market (41 per cent), and using the narrow streets of the neighbourhood or near their school (40 per cent). The roads to their school, local market, or private tutor—were also largely perceived as unsafe (37 per cent) (Save the Children, 2018).

According to the Urban and Regional Development Plans Formulation and Implementation (URDPFI) Guidelines,[5] there should be one Anganwadi,[6] for every housing area or cluster of 5,000 population (MoUD, 2015). These guidelines, however, are not being followed. As per a Right to Information (RTI) query, only seven out of a hundred Anganwadi beneficiaries live in urban areas and the remaining are in rural areas (Chandra, 2020). This is primarily because of an acute paucity of Anganwadi centres in urban areas. The outcome is seen in the high incidence of stunting, missed immunisations and other health issues. For example, according to the 2015–16 National Family Health Survey (NFHS)–4, 38 per cent of India's urban poor children were found to be stunted (Kumar and Saiyed, 2019). Moreover, 36 per cent of children in urban areas miss full immunization; the ratio is as high as 58 per cent for the urban poor. The country also has some 2.27 million children in the zero-to-nineteen age group in urban areas, suffering from some form of disability (NIUA, 2018a).

The other issues that impact children in India's cities include single-use neighbourhoods that make the movement of children after certain hours risky, lack of age- and gender-disaggregated data on children living in slums and non-slum households; the limited orientation programmes for municipal and planning officials who incorporate the needs of children in planning and design; and the negligible participation of children in the municipal affairs that directly affect them.

It would be reasonable to say that there is no widespread awareness and adoption of policies for child-friendly cities. However, there have been various initiatives that can serve as a lighthouse for coming

---

5   The URDPFI Guidelines [2014] were launched in January 2015 with amendments and comprise two volumes. These guidelines are focused on updating the process of planning and the implementation of plans in urban areas.

6   Healthcare centres for mothers and young children, set up under the Integrated Child Development Services (ICDS) by the Women and Child Development Ministry, Government of India.

decades. For instance, the 'Camino Imaginado (Imagined Path)' project conceived by Javier Duerto in Bogota City, Colombia, aims to improve social inclusion for the inhabitants of urban peripheries. Its objective is to promote safe access for students and teachers to schools and rehabilitate youth offenders by providing them jobs with the help of the Institute for the Protection of Children and Youth (IDIPRON). So far, some 40,000 sq m of public spaces and park areas have been recovered to provide access to nearly ninety public schools. The project has also created 1,300 jobs for local youth. In other parts of the world, some efforts are focused on safe transportation. Another such initiative is the United States' Department of Transportation's 'Safe routes to school' programme, which ensures safe passage for children to walk or cycle to school. It uses a range of measures such as enforcement, improving infrastructure, safety education, and incentives for non-motorized transport.

In the world after Covid-19, many cities will be moving towards becoming their own versions of the idea of a '15-minutes city'—a new concept that focuses on creating cities where 'daily urban necessities are within a 15-minute reach on foot or by bike' (Whittle, 2020). Led by Paris, this initiative has the potential to be replicated in other cities aspiring to be 'smart'. The proximity of daily urban necessities within walking distance will increase road safety for children, will encourage them to walk more, and will lead to more inclusive spaces for all, including children.

Some cities recognize that the best way to make changes in a city is at the planning level, and are leading the way. In India's immediate neighbourhood, Dhaka is setting the tone for participatory planning. City authorities, along with the Bangladesh Institute of Planners, are engaging children in promoting child-sensitive urban planning. Elsewhere, several municipalities in Latin America are planning child-friendly infrastructure and services by engaging with children through their mayor's office. In Boston, the mayor is engaging the youth (between the ages of twelve and twenty-five) through participatory budgeting. Indeed, it is the first US city in which the youth have been empowered to make decisions regarding the spending of a portion of their city's capital budget (Thakre and Ray, 2018).

There are also examples where an entire suburban area has been planned around the needs of children. The Dutch suburb of Houten in Utrecht has devised two transportation networks: the first is a network of paths for cyclists and pedestrians, which forms the core of the city and reaches important buildings and the town centre; and the second is a network for cars, which attempts to keep a distance from the first network. The city has delivered remarkable results on the safety, security, and health of its citizens. Children can travel to school or for leisure without being endangered by the possibility of a road accident. This, however, is less efficient in terms of GHG emissions as people have to drive longer if they are using cars (Montgomery, 2013, p. 359). The Dutch city of Rotterdam has also shown remarkable progress by spending resources on creating child-friendly cities. It converted an open space in a city park forest into a nature playground—Natuurspeeltuin de Speeldernis—which gives children a rare opportunity within a city to engage in unstructured play (Laker, 2018). The kids can access the biodiversity of a 'wild' space and take part in associated activities such as camping and rafting.

In India too there has been promising progress. There are ongoing initiatives in certain areas that focus, for example, on making police stations child-friendly. In Rajasthan's Dungarpur town, the child-friendly police station has a room that houses toys and books. It is designed to encourage police personnel to be sensitive to the child survivor's needs and put children at ease if they need to be in the presence of law enforcement agents. Kerala, too, has created its first child-friendly police station and is targeting to create one in each district (Save the Children, 2015).

In Bhubaneswar, officials have launched the 'Socially Smart Bhubaneswar' initiative, under which adolescent girls are being trained in self-defence techniques (NIUA, 2018b). The city has also joined the Urban95 initiative of the Bernard van Leer Foundation which aims to create cities that also meet the needs of a three-year-old, who on an average is 95 cm tall, hence the name Urban95 (Weedy, 2018). This initiative focuses on making changes at the urban planning level. The wider issue of pollution and road accident fatalities is now being addressed at the national level , which will lead to the creation of better, child-friendly cities.

Learning from the experience of other countries, some Indian cities have also started closing down roads for vehicles for certain times of the day or even for an entire day in the year (Garfield, 2017; Kumar, n.d.; Sultan, 2018). It would be encouraging if the city officials could engage schools and colleges nearby to come and spend their time on these streets—they could organize activities such as book fairs, cultural fairs, street art, and food carnivals. The idea is to get children to spend more time outside with other community members in a safe environment.

Amidst the Covid-19 pandemic, when children are having to deal with constraints on learning and playing, and thereby limiting the full use of their faculties, it would do well for India if the Union government, and state and city officials came together to find long-term solutions to the lack of child friendliness of India's cities. Child-friendly cities will bring gains not only for the children but for the cities too. This would bode well for India's initiatives in turning its urban regions into engines of economic growth (Dhar and Thakre, 2020).

ROAD TO SAFETY

Since the advent of cities, the roads and streets have been an integral part of the city's layout. The mobility of the workforce and transport of goods is a key function of cities and therefore, roads are a key part of cities. However, the advent of automobiles, technological progress and focus on expressways and wider streets had an unintended outcome of traffic deaths. Every year, more than 1.2 million people died in traffic accidents (Duduta et al., 2015). In 2015 alone, India recorded over 500,000 road accidents which led to the death of 146,133 people, which translates to fifty-seven road accidents and seventeen deaths every hour (UNESCAP, n.d.). Under major causes of road accidents, 78.4 per cent of accidents are the driver's fault, due to factors such as over-speeding, driving under the influence of alcohol or drugs, and hit and run cases (PRS India, 2017). Seventy per cent of the fatalities from road accidents occur among people in the age group of eighteen to forty-five, which highlights the huge economic cost of road accidents and deaths (Tewari, 2020). Thankfully, there has been a global agenda on reducing traffic deaths and as a signatory to the Brasilia declaration, India remains committed to reducing accidents by 50 per cent by 2022 under the UN Decade of Action of reducing road accidents (PIB, 2015). Although, this will be a long and ongoing battle for cities to ensure road safety, it is the fundamental issue to be solved if they are to be made safe and inclusive.

The Government of India has done a phenomenal job in legislating the very progressive Motor Vehicles (Amendment) Bill, 2019. This significantly changes the dynamics of road safety, given its focus on the range of road-safety related features. For instance, it has exponentially increased the fines for offenses such as juvenile driving, drunken driving, driving without licence, dangerous driving, and over-speeding, among others (PIB, 2019c). The increase in fines has already begun to influence the behaviour of drivers. For instance, the penalty for drunk driving has increased fivefold, from INR 2,000 to INR 10,000 (ibid.). Not wearing a seat belt invites a tenfold greater penalty (from INR 100 previously) to INR 1,000.

The Bill also introduces the constitution of the National Road Safety Board which will function as an advisory to the Central and state governments. A very important initiative of this legislation is to provide Good Samaritan guidelines, defining a 'Good Samaritan' as: 'a person who renders emergency medical or non-medical assistance to a victim at the scene of an accident, and provides rules to prevent harassment of such a person.' (ibid.)

All road users will be compulsorily insured through a Motor Vehicle Accident Fund. The Bill also has a provision for cashless treatment of road accident victims during the golden hour defined as, 'the time period lasting one hour following a traumatic injury during which there is highest likelihood of preventing death by providing prompt medical care *The Hindu* (2021).' The focus should be on implementation now given that the transport is a state subject.

India has the highest number of deaths due to road accidents (11 per cent) in the world, as per WHO (Athrady and Joy, 2020). We cannot just bank on one legislation, however comprehensive it might be. The states can play a constructive role in conducting a 'road safety cost curve' for cities, which compares different countermeasures according to the respective impact (Ghislanzoni et al., 2013). This analysis identifies the most cost-effective measures that can yield maximum impact per rupee spent. For instance, on-vehicle technologies such as seat-belt reminder, benefits outweigh their costs by eight times (ibid.). Moreover, measures such as road-building codes, the use of intelligent systems for traffic planning and movement, continued investments in upgrading roads, and further integration with urban planning and urban transport plans, will also make our cities' roads safe.

Smart Cities are undertaking many of these projects and it would be worthwhile to assess if these projects could bring down the numbers of road accidents and deaths. Behavioural changes at the city-level will result in a reduction in road accident fatalities. Cities will have to undertake sustained behaviour-change campaigns focusing on issues that reduce road accidents—adherence to rules, priority for movement of emergency vehicles, driving knowledge and skills, and others. When a behaviour-change campaign was driven by local authorities for the Swachh Bharat Mission, it made the maximum impact as it took into account the different sensitivities and sensibilities of different communities. The Zero Fatality Corridor Project (run by the Maharashtra government and SaveLIFE Foundation to reduce fatalities on the Mumbai–Pune Expressway) has been able to reduce fatalities by 43 per cent, using a mix of behaviour-change communication resolving issues in road engineering, ensuring higher enforcement, and optimizing trauma care (Tewari, 2020). Such cases are important to replicate since as per NCRB data, the national and state highways are most dangerous. They constitute only 5 per cent of the 58 lakh kilometres-long road network, but see more than half of all accidents (Athrady and Joy, 2020).

Lastly, Indian cities should expedite work on bus priority systems such as bus rapid transit (BRT). A study by World Resource Institute (WRI) highlights that apart from reducing congestion, pollution and increasing access to sustainable transport, bus priority systems are also known to be reducing severe and fatal injuries by 50 per cent (Duduta et al., 2015). Notorious for rash driving, bus drivers in Indian cities need to be continuously trained and monitored. Another report by WRI highlights the use of urban design to drastically increase road safety (Welle et al., 2015). The broad urban design takeaways suggested by WRI have also been discussed in various sections of the book *7 Proven Principles for Designing a Safer City* (Welle, 2015).

In the present book too I have discussed the promotion of compact and dense cities, as that reduces the need for cars for travel. A dedicated space for pedestrians and non-motorized transport on streets, and a connected cycling network, are keys to ensuring the safety of citizens. I have dedicated an entire section on promoting public transport, which can significantly bring down private vehicle usage.

The World Resources Institute also suggests ensuring lower automobile speeds (less than 40–50 kilometres per hour) to achieve 'area-wide traffic calming'. Some useful tools for this include speed humps, curves in the road, and raised pedestrian crossings. We see this missing around important places such as schools, hospitals, places of worship, and near major markets in Indian cities (Welle, 2015).

PRIORITIZING WOMEN'S SAFETY

We are at a landmark moment in our history. Fifty years later, we will recognize this time when the world's oldest form of violence was spoken of, fought fearlessly, and this fight gave us a better, braver world. Yes, this is the war against gender bias. No religion, era, community, or even profession can claim innocence on this issue. The new globalized world, categorized by cities that empower everyone, have brought gender-related issues to the forefront—violence, pay gap, harassment, deprivation, lack of opportunities and domestic abuse, among others. Gender-related issues need to be resolved at home, the workplace, during travel, and everywhere else in between.

Rural societies everywhere expected women to live, act and dress in a particular way. With the onset of cities, this distinction gets blurred as more women claim parity. Cities have always witnessed violence against women, and we are seeing extremely violent crimes against women in Indian cities that are not designed keeping their needs in mind. Like most things, cities are designed for men. Therefore, this is the right time for Indian cities to step up and correct the mistakes of the past. The issue that must be confronted head on is women's safety in cities. Gender-based violence is real and hurts cities as an ecosystem and space for people.

Globally, a staggering 30 per cent of women have experienced sexual or physical violence at the hands of an intimate partner in their lifetime (Fox and Goodfellow, 2016). Women are also willing to opt for a lower quality college or job, in return for lesser commute and greater safety (Rajagopalan, 2019). Imagine 50 per cent of the population willing to opt for suboptimal living just because they do not feel safe. It is the best example of safety tying into inclusivity. A study on the safety of women in five cities—Lima, Madrid, Kampala, Delhi and Sydney—presented results on locations where women felt unsafe (Plan International, 2018). In Delhi, women felt most unsafe on the streets and in public transport. This is corroborated by other evidence as well. A 2010 report highlighted that '51 per cent women in the capital faced harassment inside public transport, and another 42 per cent while waiting for public transport' (Adlakha, 2019). A 2019 survey by Ola revealed that merely 9 per cent of the women surveyed felt safe in public transport (ibid.). Another 2017 report by the Institute for Transportation and Development Policy (ITDP) highlighted that women may forgo better work opportunities when public transport is either not safe or not affordable or both, and will settle for low-paid jobs within walking distance (ibid.).

India's economic prosperity will depend on how women can leverage their capabilities as per their choice and the extent to which their workforce participation rate increases. As per World Bank, the Female Workforce Participation Rate in India has declined from 33.7 per cent in 1991 to 20.8 per cent in 2018 (Pyle, 2021). Thus, cities also must create safe living spaces for women. A combination of a variety of measures may produce the desired results—creating more and open public spaces; having street vendors play an important role in the city economy, which will make streets and markets safer for women; adopting mixed-use planning that will provide a sense of security round the clock; opening up night-time economy; and increasing access to public transport and micromobility.

Technology interventions can help us accelerate our progress on making cities safer for women. An app called SafetiPin allows its users to rate streets and areas on safety using the criteria of security, transportation, lighting, visibility and so on (Fleming, 2018). It has 51,000 data points in Delhi alone. The app identified 7,800 dark spots in the city and the government has addressed the lighting concern of 90 per cent of these spots. This Indian app is now being used in other world cities. While this app, allows us to see the city from the women's perspective, it is imperative that cities are planned around the needs of women. The best solution to this is to either have a female urban planner (which is going to be easier since we have discussed how India needs to exponentially increase the number of urban planners in coming decades) or have the plans vetted by an advisory of female planners. The latter solution is feasible in the near term since we do not have as many planners, let alone women planners.

Small planning initiatives can go a long way. For instance, in Barcelona, the Collective Point 6 group is ensuring such changes—limiting the height of streetside vegetation, mandating that the entry of homes face streets, and name streets or display murals focusing on women and their achievements (ibid.). Kigali in Rwanda has created sixteen mini markets for women street vendors, with all the necessary infrastructure (ibid.). When we think safety of women, we have to think of all women coming from different backgrounds, as the solutions might differ based on the background—women as a group do not form a single homogenous demographic.

The other important aspect is to collect and publish gender-segregated data at the city level, particularly on urban mobility. This will allow cities to study the patterns of issues faced by women and to take measures to increase safety. Mumbai has taken a significant step to reserve spaces inwards to build multipurpose women's hostels in dense and commercial areas of the city (Ratho, 2020b).

To address the gaps in mobility, the Canadian cities of Montreal and Toronto initiated a programme called 'Between the Stops', wherein during night hours women can get down from buses at any point between stops, to ensure that they have to walk less (O' Leary and Viswanath, 2011). Small measures such as street lighting are important for moving around cities. After 2008, many US cities saw a surge in crimes against women, when cities decided to cut down on street lighting to save costs (Panda, 2019). The CCTV craze is an added advantage, but like with most things urban, it can only complement other efforts. Audits worldwide have confirmed that women prefer broader footpaths and separate toilet facilities at transportation nodes and markets (ibid.). The Delhi Metro has reserved the first coach for women and has a female force at all stations.

India may have to undertake a gender-focused campaign, as the onus of women's safety doesn't and shouldn't lie with women, but should be the responsibility of all. The heinous sexual violence and crimes against women indicate that there is something fundamentally wrong with how Indian men perceive women. Men need to get used to seeing more women on the streets. They should mind their own business and act as a Good Samaritan if they see a woman at risk. Men need to also know that their crimes will not go unpunished. Such a campaign should also engage different stakeholders such as rickshaw drivers, bus and metro transport, and street vendors.

An important aspect is the role of the police force. As per a survey, the absence of police/security has been cited as an equally important reason for the need for well-lit streets and good quality roads when it comes to women's perception of their safety (Pyle, 2021). The same survey suggests that women are less likely to approach/call the police than men (ibid.). Clearly, there is a trust deficit between women and the police force. Gender-sensitive policing is the need of the hour. Kerala has constituted Pink Police Control Room and Patrol to address complaints by women and prevent any untoward incident, particularly in areas where reported cases of harassment are high (Bhowmick, 2019). This is a well-thought-out initiative, barring the gender stereotyping using the colour 'pink'. The presence of policewomen should be done at the broader level and not in silos. For instance, the Central government's 2009 advisory to have 33 per cent reservation for women in the police force has only been met by a handful of states, though their presence in the force has increased from 1.18 per cent in 1991 to 8.98 per cent in 2019 (Pyle. 2021). We have a long way to go but it's a start. It is also suggested by experts that more women should occupy senior ranks, as currently, only 1 per cent of policewomen hold senior police ranks (ibid.).

Tricky and unfortunate as this might be, there is also an opportunity for massive improvement for gender parity in India. If this battle has to be fought in cities, so be it. We should step up to the challenge. With the opportunities that cities have to offer, the fight for gender parity stands a better chance in cities.

AIR POLLUTION: TIME TO TACKLE IT

Almost all city dwellers across India are aware that we are in midst of an air pollution pandemic. As per WHO, in 2016, fourteen out of the world's most polluted twenty cities were in India (Jha, 2019). Around three-fourth of India's population is breathing polluted air (Harish, 2020). As per a 2013 World Bank study, air pollution led to the loss of welfare and labour income loss to the tune of 8.5 per cent of our GDP (Tharoor, 2020). Premature deaths further cost the country USD 500 billion (ibid.). There are many such statistics, but even in their absence we know we are in a state of emergency. The National Capital Region goes into a headspin every time the winter arrives. The smog of October/November, when vehicular pollution mixes with the pollution caused by stubble (paddy straw) being burnt on the farms of Haryana and Punjab, the construction dust and crackers burnt around Diwali, creates a toxic mix. The particulate matter (PM) 2.5 levels breach the 1,000 mark. It is a common sight to see people wearing masks, their eyes red and teary and their conversations punctuated with coughs. This phenomenon engulfs cities in north India impacting their liveability severely. In years when it is really bad, the authorities declare a public health emergency and schools are closed, flights are cancelled and public gatherings decline.

The pollution is leading to brain drain, because highly skilled people, worried about their own health and that of their families, are shifting from NCR to cities in south India or going abroad. If this goes unchecked, the economic potential of these north Indian cities will be curbed and we will be able to do little to turn this around when firms, skills, wages and innovation flee our cities. When the Covid-19 lockdown was imposed, people in north India could actually see blue skies because industrial activity, vehicular movement, and construction activity came to a halt—these activities constitute 75 per cent of the PM 2.5 emission (Tharoor, 2020).

In January 2019, the Union Government launched the National Clean Air Programme (NCAP) which has set the target for reducing the PM 2.5 and PM 10 concentrations by 20–30 per cent by 2024 with 2017 as the base year (MoEFCC, 2019a). The good thing about NCAP is that it has defined targets and will be focused on 102 cities. Another important aspect is that it is taking a cross-sector view to solve this menace. Under NCAP, the cities will prepare their plans, followed by extensive project monitoring at the state and local levels, capacity building, use of technology and focus on enforcement. The programme will take the intent and resources on fighting air pollution, to new heights. This initiative will complement existing efforts such as the India Cooling Action Plan, which aims to reduce the cooling and refrigerant demand by 25–30 per cent by 2038 (PIB, 2019d). However, the NCAP targets are not very ambitious—even with a 30 per cent decline, the PM 2.5 levels will still be at a hazardous level.

There has also been reasonable criticism of NCAP. The most direct one comes from Shashi Tharoor, who maintains that there was little consultation on this matter and that the NACP only covers 102 cities (Tharoor, 2020). Greenpeace's 'Airpocalypse' survey of 313 Indian cities, found that 241 cities suffered from poor air quality. Funding under the NACP is hardly commensurate with the problem at hand, nor does NACP have the legal power to impose implementation and seek accountability in case of non-compliance (ibid.). With NCAP punching below its weight, it is useful to know what the other strategies to fight the menace of air pollution could be. Apart from the stubble-burning issue which happens for a few months in a year, it is important to note what drives the pollution throughout the year.

SAFAR-India (System of Air Quality and Weather Forecasting and Research) of the Indian Institute of Tropical Meteorology in Pune found in a study of Delhi in 2018–19, that 40 per cent of the PM 2.5 pollution was caused by the transport sector (41 per cent), followed by re-suspended dust (21.5 per cent), industry (18.6 per cent), power sector emissions (4.9 per cent), and bio fuel (3 per cent). The remaining 11 per cent was found to come from solid waste disposal, crematoriums, aviation, and brick kilns, among others. As per Delhi's *Economic Survey 2018-19*, the city had more than 10 million vehicles, out of which around

70 per cent were two-wheelers (PTI, 2019d). The possible strategies here would be to use two-wheeler electric vehicles, greater penetration of public transport, shared micro-mobility, and more mixed-use and transit-oriented development. These strategies have been advocated throughout the book.

In an interview with *HuffPost*, Siddharth Singh, author of *The Great Smog of India*, distils the problem to identify prevalence of dust as the significant cause of pollution in India (Chatterji, 2018). In fact, a visit to cities like Singapore, Washington, El Paso, Kuala Lumpur, Tokyo, Sao Paulo, Duluth, London, Amsterdam, and so on, reveals they have good air and liveability because they have been able to tame the trouble of dust. Singh lists the sources—'the manufacturing industry, such as brick kilns … improper construction activities … poorly constructed roads and footpaths, and, importantly … agricultural activities such as extensive ploughing that leaves the topsoil to become loose' (ibid.). The solutions he offers include better dust-management at the industry level, enveloping construction sites, clean-up after construction is complete, proper construction of our roads and footpaths, paving or management of empty tracts of land and parking spaces (ibid.). Such solutions are much needed. Construction and demolition waste receive little attention in the dialogue on air pollution and the rules are not effectively followed.

Indian cities could do a lot more by studying what has worked in the developing countries. The cities of developed countries have had more time to clean up good. However, since the technology has really changed, we can catch up fast. Cities in Mexico and China (and even Delhi since the early 1990s) have been able to reduce air pollution drastically (Kanti, 2017). The availability of real-time data created a sense of urgency in these cities. Besides, the national and local governments provided funds to scrap older vehicles, retrofit and shut down power plants, relocate polluting industries, and create new standards for vehicles that reduced pollution. In the 1990s, aided by the Delhi government, the city converted 10,000 buses, 20,000 taxis, and 50,000 three-wheelers to compressed natural gas (CNG) (Kemper and Wahba, 2020).

Mexico and Beijing brought in multiple authorities to act in a time-bound manner. In the US, clear legislation resolved the issue. The

US's Clean Air Act, 1970, created monitoring and oversight, and as a consequence, the national emissions of six common pollutants (particles, ozone, lead, carbon monoxide, nitrogen dioxide and sulfur dioxide) declined by 73 per cent from 1970 to 2017 (EPA n.d.). During this time, the GDP grew by 324 per cent. There are two lessons for India here. First, the legislation helped the US to put in place regulations to make cars less polluting. Second, the amendments in 1990 to the US's Clean Air Act have led to immense economic benefits, a 2011 study stating that the benefits to costs were 30 to 1 (ibid.). The US has also benefited greatly from the pollution control technologies in power plants and factories. It seems like the recipe is known, now all we need is to recreate the magic.

URBAN HEALTH: A BLIND SPOT?

The health of its citizens is a priority for all levels of governments but, given the nature of schemes in India, it has largely been the domain of the Central and state governments. The ULBs, with their poor capabilities, finances, and empowerment, have had little role to play in India's health sector so far. When countries urbanize—i.e., when the creation of housing accessibility is outpaced by natural growth, accelerated migration, congestion, growth of new industries, lack of adequate infrastructure, and redefining of rural areas into urban areas—people are clustered into poor housing, with little ventilation, privacy and access to in-house infrastructure. Many are forced to live in unhygienic conditions with poor access to basic urban services such as water, sanitation and faecal sludge management. The air and sound pollution is a burden. Poor solid waste and water management makes them prone to vector-borne diseases such as malaria, dengue and encephalitis, among others. This is one part of the bigger problem.

Another side of the problem shows that due to changing dietary habits, higher purchasing power and sedentary lifestyle, people suffer from non-communicable (lifestyle) diseases such as diabetes, hypertension and obesity, among others. And, lastly, there is always a risk of epidemic contagion. There are also some health-related advantages that urban areas have over rural areas—lower infant and child mortality rates, lower burden of infectious diseases, and higher access to better healthcare and to institutional deliveries (Mullen et al., 2016). Given the rewarding income standards of urban areas, 60 per cent of all Indian hospitals and 80 per cent doctors are to be found in urban areas (PTI, 2016).

It's another issue that the ratio of doctors and beds in India per lakh population is so poor that cornering a large share of these numbers still doesn't bode well for urban areas. Under the National Health Mission, only 3 per cent of the funding is for the urban areas, the remaining 97 per cent is for rural areas (Khan, 2020). Although, the private sector is the biggest provider of healthcare services in the urban areas, the NHM funding does not have anything to do with the private sector's presence in urban areas. As the quality of healthcare in urban areas is better, the rural population travels (when possible) to urban areas to access quality services (Rajagopalan and Choutagunta, 2020).

The first aspect of poor access to infrastructure and basic services has been addressed in the section on urban infrastructure. The fight for urban housing will never cease to exist, but we have enough policy options to ensure that people have access to basic, at least minimum, and decent living space. Thus the issue of sanitation, solid waste management, and faecal sludge has been well addressed by the Swachh Bharat Mission which has transformed the state of sanitation in India. The missing link is water management and access to piped water supply. There is some movement at the city level to provide universal access to piped water supply, but urban health outcomes will significantly improve as and when the majority of the urban population gets plugged into piped water with quality assurance. Air pollution is another pressing issue that brings down our immunity and causes acute respiratory issues in people living in urban areas. The strategy for this too has been outlined in the previous sections.

As for lifestyle diseases, we can look at global cities such as Singapore, Washington, London, Tokyo and New York where mixed-use planning, provision of sufficient open public places, infrastructure for non-motorized transport and incentives to walk and exercise have had a tangible impact on limiting sedentary life. The incidence of non-communicable diseases also declines with a more active urban lifestyle—within the house and outside. A vibrant street-vendor culture and local markets could also act as an incentive to promote everyday walking. It is also worth emulating the success of Mohalla Clinics in Delhi and the Basthi Dawakhanas in Hyderabad (both, neighbourhood clinics) both of which are revamping urban healthcare (Lahiri, 2019). These community clinics are having a tangible impact in terms of improved access to healthcare, giving the marginalized population increased access to health services, free medicines and diagnostics tests (ibid.). All of this reduces the expenditure incurred by patients. These clinics also offer access to counselling services which are critical in reducing the burden of lifestyle diseases, and cost effectiveness in terms of low expenditure incurred in the setting up and operation of these clinics (ibid.).

As per NITI Aayog, preventable risk factors contributed the highest to the disease burden in 2016 (NITI Aayog, 2018). The top five risks were malnutrition, air pollution, dietary risks, high blood pressure and diabetes. The other factors were water and sanitation, use of tobacco, cholesterol, high body-mass index, and alcohol and drug use. Most of them can be addressed through better urban planning and behaviour-change campaigns. Experts point towards creating city-level health plans, on the lines of other sectoral plans such as city mobility plan and city sanitation plan (Udas-Mankikar and Girgaonkar, 2020). They point out that basic guidelines for urban health infrastructure exist, but cities have not been able to make noticeable progress on creating such spatial health plans (ibid.). Singapore, Sri Lanka, Nigeria and Afghanistan, all use some form of targeting to create a healthcare masterplan to align with their national priorities (ibid.).

The shortage of hospital beds, doctors and nurses has been a perennial curse of the Indian healthcare sector, in both urban and rural areas. As per a recent estimate, India has 131 beds per 100,000 persons (Rajagopalan and Choutagunta, 2020). As per the same study, India has 86.3 doctors per 100,000 persons in 2018. The same number in other countries stands at 214.9 in Brazil, 178.5 in China, 127.5 in the Philippines, against the world average of 150.5. These numbers correspond to different years, and the world average is for 2015 (ibid.). Population pressure combined with limited health expenditure has resulted in this paucity. The same paper notes that the government healthcare facilities in urban areas are largely non-existent. For instance, the number of government health workers in urban areas are not even 10 per cent of the number of government health workers present in rural areas (ibid.). India has already come up with an innovative solution. So far, India has 500-odd medical colleges that produce 100–150 students per year. However, we also have 700 district hospitals. India aims to convert these district hospitals into medical colleges, thereby increasing the availability of healthcare professionals twofold with limited new expenditure.

Out-of-pocket expenditure on healthcare in India is among the highest in the world, and constitutes around two-thirds of household medical expenditure (Rukmini, 2019). Worse still, the burden is highest for the urban poor (ibid). Primary healthcare in urban areas is quite weak, especially due to lower fund allocation for health infrastructure. As per an analysis, the NCT-Delhi has only eight primary health centres, no community health centres, but 134 tertiary care centres (Kumar and Saiyed, 2019). There is a proposal for private hospitals to bid for part of district hospitals to treat people for non-communicable diseases (Sethi and Rao, 2018). This is a win-win solution because non-communicable diseases are a silent pandemic that needs to be addressed.

As per NFHS-4, two-fifths of urban poor children are stunted and the health and nutrition status of the urban poor is worse than their rural counterparts (Kumar and Saiyad, 2019). Besides, as high as 36 per cent of urban children miss full immunization, and this ratio is as high as 58 per cent for the urban poor (ibid.). This could be attributed to fewer government health facilities and lesser investments in the urban areas, as compared to rural areas and the tendency of urban dwellers to go to private healthcare service providers. However, Mumbai, Surat and Ahmedabad show good examples of local governments/ULBs focusing on health and nutrition outcomes of the local population (ibid.).

The most important aspect of resolving the urban health system is to empower the city governments with the functions mentioned in the Twelfth Schedule of the Constitution. Out of these eighteen functions, one is public health. This combined with a mayor system will lead to empowerment and political accountability. Just as it does at the Centre and state levels, political economy at the city level is capable of driving people towards demanding better public-health services. NITI Aayog has advocated a public health system that can holistically address the issues in the urban healthcare system.

It advocates a preventive healthcare system, which was missing from the agenda previously. The government has launched an initiative to create 150,000 health and wellness centres (HWCs), all over India. This conversion of PHCs into HWCs will go a long way in reducing the burden of communicable and non-communicable diseases in both, urban and rural areas. It needs to be seen that cities again do not lose out on this allocation. The Mohalla Clinics in Delhi, which started in 2015 and Basthi Dawakhana that started in Telangana in 2018 are examples of fairly successful models of community clinics run by urban local bodies (Lahariya, 2020). The primary healthcare system defines the health outcomes of a country, lowers inequality and reduces the burden on the urban poor. One of the few good things to have come out of Covid-19 is the people's proclivity to stay healthy as comorbidities heighten the risk of Covid-19-related mortality. The move towards healthy eating and lifestyle should not be allowed to go waste. The referral system in district hospitals needs to be strengthened while ensuring that Indian cities move towards preventive healthcare than just curative healthcare. A separate focus on urban health is required, since urban health has been missing on the national agenda, and from city-level schemes too.

As per a recent analysis, the annual government healthcare spending per capita was only INR 1,657 in 2017–18, comparable to Sierra Leone and Nigeria (Rajagopalan and Choutagunta, 2020). Government expenditure on health (both Centre and state) currently stands at a mere 1.13 per cent of GDP, but that still has to be increased to 2.5 per cent of GDP (as per the National Health Policy, 2017) (Kant, 2020; Kumar and Prasad, 2020). Since, states constitute 65 per cent of this expenditure, their role will be much more pronounced (Kumar and Prasad, 2020). As per one analysis, only 1 per cent of the cost of the Smart City Mission (i.e., sixty-nine projects out of over 5,000 projects) focuses on health infrastructure (Idiculla, 2020). States may be partially relieved of this burden if they empower the urban local governments to raise resources and manage public health for their city.

This will allow India to create the right infrastructure, train a sufficient number of doctors, nurses and frontline workers; and importantly, pay a decent salary to frontline workers. Launched in 2013, the National Urban Health Mission was allocated a paltry INR 950 crore in the 2020 budget, which amounts to INR 2 per urban person per month (Shukla, 2020). Clearly, this needs to increase exponentially. The enthusiasm of the National Rural Health Mission in creating a line-up of formidable frontline workers (accredited social health activists or ASHAs and auxiliary nurse and midwives or ANMs), and the proliferation of primary and community health centres, needs to be replicated in urban areas. The gains will be easier to achieve, given that the urban population exists in proximity so the efficacy of such infrastructure and workforce would be higher.

As for epidemics and pandemics, we cannot know for sure what will be the next crisis. However, we can imbibe the lessons from the Covid-19 crisis. One of the important lessons is to create a public health cadre. A dedicated cadre is our only hope to track, trace and treat the next contagion. Experts indicate that the public health cadre should have trained personnel in epidemiology, biostatistics, demography and behavioural sciences, among others (Kumar and Prasad, 2020).

As per the Global Burden of Disease (GBD) initiative, in India in 2017, three out of the top five causes of mortality were infectious diseases. However, given how infectious Covid-19 is and how it has disrupted daily life, there are bound to be long-term changes in cities towards resilience focusing on pandemics. Such resilience could be developed by focusing on fine-tuning the emergency protocols developed during Covid-19 at the city level. States and cities are going to be better equipped in terms of financial and human resources. The role of control and command centres under the Smart Cities Mission also proved critical during Covid-19. This tech infrastructure should also map every physical health infrastructure—clinics, doctors, hospitals, possible isolation centres and manufacturing facilities for health-related equipment.

India should develop its own local governance health readiness framework based on which different cities of all sizes can be ranked and assessed. Telemedicine and the use of data in tracing and tracking proved extremely useful during Covid-19. These channels, systems and protocols should be further developed and can serve as a possible model for healthcare delivery in case the next pandemic strikes. India has launched the National Digital Health Mission; patient records can be accessed by certified practitioners following patient consent. This switch to digital healthcare access can prove a potent tool in fighting pandemics.

CITIES' INEVITABLE COLLISION WITH TERRORISM

I still remember reaching home from school in 2001 on a hot September afternoon to find my grandfather and uncles glued to the television. Disturbing visuals and commentary continued throughout the day; al Qaeda terrorists had used airplanes to demolish the World Trade Centre (WTC). They had come for the best of America—New York City—by air. Our distant relatives have been in and out of the US, and WTC was a known term, much like the Statue of Liberty.

A decade earlier in 1993, Indian-born leader of organized crime syndicate D-Company, Dawood Ibrahim, had planned and ruthlessly executed a series of thirteen bomb attacks across Mumbai. The sites of bomb blasts included, among others, the Bombay Stock Exchange, some of the city's most dense markets and the building that housed Air India's offices. Mumbai had been attacked from within. Fifteen years later, and seven years after the 9/11 attack in the US, Mumbai was once again under attack on 26 November 2008 by ten terrorists from the Lashkar-e-Taiba (a Pakistan-based terrorist organization). All ten carried satellite phones and Kalashnikovs. A sixty-hour siege of India's financial capital saw particular targets in luxury hotels (Taj and Oberoi), Leopold Cafe, Chhatrapati Shivaji railway station and a Jewish cultural centre (at Nariman House). This time terrorists had entered Mumbai by sea.

Cities reflect the best a country has to offer. They exemplify the success of a nation. Its businesses, innovation, infrastructure, vibrant society, public spaces, and everyday transactions. Cities are the modes through which countries project power. This makes them a unique and tempting target for terrorists worldwide. As more cities of India go on to become growth engines and house millions of people, the more will they become a target for terrorist attacks. Cities must adopt a culture of vigilant civic life.

The whole idea of terrorism is to instil fear and inertia in people and what better spectacle than to attack a country's symbol of prosperity, growth and global status. Urban warfare makes this very difficult. In the absence of any realistic Avengers options, we need to redefine our tools and tactics to prepare our cities. Terrorists till they enter the border are border management issue. Once they are in cities, it becomes a city issue too. We have only begun to see the city-based attacks and our approach should realign at a faster rate.

New forms of terror threats such as drone attacks, the vulnerability of city's infrastructure such as power plants, metro rail networks and water supply systems to cyber-attacks and bio-attacks among others are not outside the realm of realistic security assessment. Our only option is to calculate and mitigate risks by preparing city administrations and citizens for such eventualities. The city-level risk assessment, preparedness and response should align with national security enterprise.

9

Urban Resilience: Preparing for the Worst, Hoping for the Best

yūnān o misr o ruumā sab mitgaejahāñ se,
ab tak magar hai baaqī nām-o-nishāñ hamārā
kuchh baat hai ki hastī mittī nahīñ hamārī,
sadiyoñ rahā hai dushman daur-e-zamāñ hamārā

THESE lines are part of the longer poem 'Sare Jahan Se Achha', written by Allama Iqbal in 1904 (Rekhta, n.d.). It went onto become one of the anthems of India's freedom movement. In the above stanza, Iqbal says that ancient Greece, Egypt and Rome vanished, but our identity—the Indian civilization—survived. There must be something in us that we continue to survive adversities. A policy analyst doesn't sit easy with poetry, romanticized claims still need evidence. I see Iqbal's point; it seems to me that these civilizations vanished and their cities lost their glory for a variety of reasons. However, it is not like Indian cities have not seen a rise and fall.

The survival of cities is called urban resilience. Cities that did not survive can be termed not resilient and the ones that did, resilient. Before we move into the technicalities of urban resilience, I want to highlight that resilience is a very human trait. In fact, it is one of the basic human traits. Resilience in humans is the ability to take shocks but still bounce back, the knack and art of survival. Going back to Iqbal, I believe the essence of his couplet portrays resilience.

In the context of cities, the Harappan civilization declined due to a prolonged drought that impacted the seasonality of rivers. According to the paper 'Fluvial Landscapes of the Harappan Civilization: Hydroclimatic stress increased the vulnerability of agricultural production supporting Harappan urbanism, leading to settlement downsizing, diversification of crops and a drastic increase in settlements in the moister monsoon regions of the upper Punjab, Haryana and Uttar Pradesh' (Joseph, 2021). Harappan cities may have lacked resilience and that brought a once-flourishing and indomitable civilization to a knee-jerk halt. However, the civilization gave us cities in the Gangetic plain which ushered a new era of urbanization. Perhaps, the decline of the Indus Valley was the first reflection of the Anthropocene—the current and ongoing epoch marked by human activity influencing the natural ecosystems and the climate of Earth (Admiraal and Cornaro, 2020).

Many states in India are witnessing immense pressure from climate change and natural hazards. The former director-general, National Disaster Response Force, R.K. Pachnanda, wrote in 2020 in the *Tribune*: 'Over 58.6 per cent of the landmass is prone to earthquakes; over 12 per cent of the land is prone to floods; nearly 5,700 km of the 7,516-km-long coastline is prone to cyclones and tsunamis and 68 per cent of the cultivable area is vulnerable to droughts' (Pachnanda, 2020). When the eastern state of Odisha was hit by Cyclone Fani in 2019, the state government moved over a million people and contained the fatalities to less than ninety. Fifty-two towns in the state were impacted by the cyclone, and the state set up 880 disaster relief centres (Subudhi and Bilgrami, 2019). Compare this to the 1999 Super Cyclone that resulted in over 10,000 deaths in the same state.

The Kerala floods of August 2018 were another devastating natural calamity. Homes were destroyed, over 400 people lost their lives, the shock to livelihood and access to basic services such as clean water and hygiene was crippled, and the infrastructure collapsed. Major infrastructure projects such as airports had been built close to rivers and in the process, the natural water systems were damaged (Misra, 2018). In Kerala, Palakkad, Chengannur and Angamaly were built over flood plains (ibid.). Another reason was Kerala's hydropower dams, marked red in a government audit which stressed that they lacked emergency protocols, warning systems and plans in case of overflowing reservoirs. These reservoirs were already brimming with water before the monsoon of 2018 (ibid.).

The Gujarat earthquake of 2001, the Mumbai floods of 2005, the Chennai floods of 2015 and its water crisis of 2019, the Shimla water crisis of 2018, the ongoing urban heat-island effect in north Indian cities, and so on, are instances where cities witnessed shocks that caused massive devastation. Had these shocks occurred in the pre-industrial era, entire cities might not have survived. Modern economy, infrastructure, technology and connectivity helped these cities survive. In many ways, the title of this chapter encapsulates the best- and worst-case scenarios for our cities. Despite being relatively new, urban resilience has been able to firmly establish itself in the global development agenda. For instance, the Sustainable Development Goals (SDGs) advocate resilient cities. The Sendai Framework for Disaster Risk Reduction (2015–30) also considers the role of urbanization and the built environment in reducing the risk. We have already discussed the recognition of urban resilience by UN-Habitat III.

Sustainable cities have entered into our lexicon for good. Not surprisingly, the world is now operating on the pivot of the global development agendas—the SDGs. The term 'sustainable development' was first used by scientists at the Massachusetts Institute of Technology (MIT) in a 1972 report titled *The Limits to Growth*. However, the term gained currency after the report *Our Common Future* was released in 1987 by the World Commission on Environment and Development. The term continues to hold the same meaning as defined in that report: 'Development that meets the needs of the present, without compromising the ability of the future generations to meet their own needs' (Fox and Goodfellow, 2016). Within this comes the specific goal of 'sustainable urbanism' which filters the broader vision onto the canvas of sustainable cities.

The SDG on cities states, 'Make cities and human settlements inclusive, safe, resilient and sustainable.' Sustainability is an underlying goal of the recommendations made in this book too. How we achieve growth, how efficiently we use urban land, how to modify our planning processes and systems, how to create the right city infrastructure, what sort of transport is good for cities, how to achieve resource efficiency and how to make cities safe and inclusive for all, are efforts directed towards the lofty vision of sustainable cities.

By virtue of their economic dominance by contributing 80 per cent of the world's GDP, cities also contribute two-thirds of greenhouse gas emissions. As of date CO_2 emissions in Asian cities is as high as in developed countries (ADB, 2016). This problem will be exacerbated by the rapid rise in Asia's urban population. Major Asian cities are along coastlines and that makes them even more susceptible to climate change and urban disasters.

The risk cities face is different and greater than that faced by rural areas due to a variety of reasons: 1) cities agglomerate people and economic activity; 2) presence of urban poor, migrants and other vulnerable groups; 3) the contribution of urban areas to the environmental burden; 4) higher share of physical infrastructure per household as compared to rural counterparts; and 5) continued urban growth further intensifies the risk of urban areas (IIHS, 2015b). In India, 76 per cent of the population is exposed to high-to-medium hazard risk, out of which 30 per cent live in 468 one lakh-plus cities (ibid.).

Against this gloomy foresight, we have opportunities for cities to prepare themselves for this impending calamity. For instance, as per some estimates, 60–70 per cent of the built environment that will be required to house the urban population by 2050 in India and worldwide is yet to be built (World Bank, 2016). Plus, the agglomeration of people, the use of technology and right financing can help us deal with a major part of this issue. We can adapt our infrastructure to reduce risks, thus creating urban resilience. World Bank offers a simple and relatable definition of urban resilience: 'the ability of a system, entity, community, or person to adapt to a variety of changing conditions and to withstand shocks while still maintaining its essential functions' (ibid.).

As compared to other urban paradigms, urban resilience is a new phenomenon and Indian cities are in a unique position to leverage the benefits by imbibing this in the early stages of urbanization. The costs of such early correction, particularly in smaller cities, will be much lower whilst giving long-term benefits. Resilience is not a standalone issue and we have been suggesting strategies under urban housing, transport, planning, and governance that also positively impact the urban resilience of Indian cities.

In this section, we examine natural hazards and climate change as a risk to urban resilience. The role of climate change is pertinent because cities are the leading contributors to climate change action and also because climate change is likely to increase the intensity and frequency of such urban hazards. Resilience is key also because the urban poor bear disproportionate risk of such hazards. There are natural, technological and socio-economic hazards than can befall a city. In this section, we are looking at natural risks.

Policies focusing on urban resilience can be classified in two forms: 1) mitigation—reducing risks by working on the causes of risks and climate change; 2) adaptation—containing the impact of higher risks and climate change. For instance, creating resilient infrastructure and providing access to quality public transport, both help in reducing GHG emissions and, therefore, would come under mitigation measures. Whereas preparing populations to cope with higher risks of floods and sea-level rise is part of adaptation efforts. More importantly, adaption efforts have yielded massive impacts. After the 1991 Super Cyclone that hit India's eastern coastline as well as Bangladesh, the latter invested in an early warning system and public shelters. The 2007 cyclone that hit the region was of almost the same intensity as the 1991 Super Cyclone, but there was a thirty-twofold decline in the death toll (Fox and Goodfellow, 2016). Adaptation pays for itself but so does mitigation. It depends upon the city and what sort of approach it wants to use.

PLANNING OUR WAY OUT OF THE MESS: MAINSTREAMING RESILIENCE

The floods in Chennai and Mumbai and water and air pollution in Bengaluru and Delhi and even smaller cities are the obvious examples that highlight how lack of proper urban planning has led to a decline in urban resilience. It is important that the states, in the process of overhauling the urban governance and planning processes, lay importance on urban resilience as a key attribute. Given the infrastructure deficit, development plans mostly focus on the issues of water, sanitation, roads and others, while little attention is paid to urban shocks to local ecologies by flooding, earthquake and pollution among others. Indian cities, after proper devolution as envisaged under 74th Amendment, should voluntarily and strictly abide by urban resilience norms in urban planning. Given the unique local risks and hazards, there is no way that the Central and state governments in India can make cities resilient on their own; only cities will have to take the lead in preparing themselves to become truly resilient.

Cities worldwide are now making resilience an underlying paradigm of their urban planning exercise; Resilient Cities Network (formerly 100RC) is working with the cities of Pune, Surat and Chennai to make them resilient. The appointment of Chief Resilient Officer (currently supported by 100RC) is a lighthouse for other cities to ensure resilience doesn't stay out of the agenda and for coordination among different departments. The larger Indian cities are already warmed up to the idea, but we really need to take this to the last town possible.

Planning may have many shortfalls, but the inability to mainstream agendas is not one of them. Urban planning remains our most potent tool to plan for urban resilience and mainstream the agenda. The Central government has already launched the Climate Smart Cities Assessment Framework (CSCAF) 2.0, which will handhold cities to combat climate change. It provides a way ahead through twenty-eight indicators across five categories—energy and green buildings, urban planning, green cover and biodiversity, mobility and air quality, water management and waste management (Khanna, 2020). Small initiatives such as spending as little as USD 10 million to improve building regulation compliance in cities in Ethiopia can generate as much as USD 600 million worth of benefits by 2050 (World Bank, 2016). Clearly, the task is worth pursuing. India is urbanizing at a dizzying pace; rather incredible numbers are put out on how much commercial and residential space are we going to build every year for the next two decades. Major parts of many cities need to be redeveloped and more rural areas will be absorbed into urban areas.

This *is* the time to plug resilience, as refurbishment is always costlier than construction.

The critical and cost-effective way for planning to pursue resilience is to use the urban eco-system approach (Jha et al., 2013). It advocates that cities can use existing natural resources to reduce their vulnerability. This approach needs to be part of the city planning to reduce risks and increase resilience. This approach—referred to as using 'nature-based solutions' (NBS), which are the cheapest and surest way to achieve resilience—is defined as: 'actions taken to restore, protect and manage natural ecosystems, as well as to imitate the work of nature for social benefit' (ICLEI, 2019). Some important steps that increase urban resilience to disasters include tree planting, permeable pavements, vegetation planting for landslides, green roofs, mangroves and watersheds among others. Conserving and restoring existing natural resources is another low-cost measure that reduces risks and policymakers should consider it as a viable tool for urban resilience.

Pakistan planted 1 billion trees under the programme the Billion Tree Tsunami, to reduce the risk of flooding by increasing forest cover (Hutt, 2018). This will benefit its cities as much as its villages. In the process, it has also created local jobs such as the creation of private tree nurseries. London is another good example of using this approach for various benefits such as reducing flood risk, urban heat, pollution, energy demand along with increasing biodiversity and recreation, under its Green Grid programme. As part of Green Grid, London used the tools of green roof/walls, street trees, wetlands, river corridors, woodlands, and grasslands to achieve various benefits (Jha et al., 2013).

URBAN RESILIENCE POLICY: AT THE NEXUS OF LAND, MOBILITY, HOUSING, AND ENERGY

Local climatic conditions are extracting a toll on Indian cities, in terms of economic, social and physical infrastructure costs. Though making cities the engines of economic growth, and providing citizens with essential basic quality of life, the immediate priorities, the Central and state governments should also give shape to India's urban resilience policy. This policy will also spell out India's climate resilience orientation for Indian cities. Globally, cities have taken concrete initiatives on these lines. London has its Climate Adaptation Strategy 2007, New York its sustainability plan called PlaNYC 2007, and Cape Town its Framework for Adaptation to Climate Change in the City of Cape Town 2006 (TERI, 2014). In 2022, Mumbai also came out with the Mumbai Climate Action Plan which aims to make the city climate-resilient and achieve net-zero emissions by 2050 (Firstpost, 2022).

Challenges from natural hazards and the benefits of resilience are both large enough for us to focus on creating a separate policy on urban resilience. Cities and states have poor capacity, so a national agenda that highlights the issues, stakeholders, pathways, policy reforms and governance structures around an urban resilience policy would go far in shaping the narrative on urban resilience. Importantly, this policy would be designed according to the city's risk assessment. For instance, coastal cities and cities in the Himalayan region would require a different set of policies than would cities in the plains.

We have to learn from Japan, which has learned to live with the natural hazards that come with its geography. It doesn't have a separate urban resilience policy but its way of living and history has an influence on resilience. Tokyo has survived to date due to its innovative thinking on resilience. Since the start of the twentieth century, Tokyo city drew a large amount from its groundwater reserves; the extraction peaking in 1970 (Sato et al., 2006). The occurrence of land subsidence (which takes place due to excessive withdrawal of groundwater) was first discovered in 1910; it peaked in 1968 at 24 cm (Ruggeri, 2017). Tokyo city government passed tough laws to clamp down on pumping water. Almost immediately, the pace of land subsidence slowed down. By the early 2000s, it was as slow as 1 cm (ibid). The city's disaster preparedness has been accepted worldwide for its efficacy—early warning systems, capacity buildings and sensitization, and skilled ability to create disaster-resilient infrastructure.

Bloomberg covered how Japan, despite being so prone to natural hazards, is creating skyscrapers (Bloomberg Quicktake, 2021). Tokyo's tallest structure, the Tokyo Skytree, is 634 metres high, is close to the sea, and has to withstand the risks of cyclones and earthquakes. Its build is based on ancient Japanese architecture of a strong but flexible central pillar, the *shinbashira* (found in Japanese temples), the structure allows the wind to pass through and has a support structure that reduces the vibration. The core pillar sits on seismic isolators—rubber and steel structures that support heavy structures. Though traditionally Japan has extensively used wood for reducing the impact of natural hazards, it is now working on using wood and steel together in buildings in place of concrete and glass.

The *Financial Times* has done a deep dive on how the city has managed to live with the menace of flooding (JapanGov, n.d.). The city has the 6.3-kilometre-long Tokyo Flood Control Channel, which is the longest underground river, and protects the city from flooding. The channel has five shafts that collect runoff from five rivers and pump it to sea (ibid.). It cost USD 3 billion and took thirteen years to build. Each shaft is huge enough to accommodate a space shuttle. The channel was deliberately built underground to save costs. In 1991, with 19 cm of rain, 31,000 houses faced floods. In 2017, when the same amount of rain fell in the same timeframe, only forty-three houses were flooded. The disaster reducing infrastructure is paying for itself by limiting the damage. In the first ten years, it saved USD 930 million worth of property damage (ibid.).

Learning from Japan, such a resilience policy in the Indian context would sit at the confluence of land, mobility, housing and energy. In the previous sections of the book, we have discussed the issues faced in these four areas. Efficient use of land for compact and vertical growth, pollution reduction through urban mobility policies, proper housing for all to limit slum growth and efficient energy demand management can all ensure that we minimize the risks of urban hazards as we know them (for instance we know that buildings and mobility use the maximum amount of energy and produce the highest share of CO_2). How efficiently we use our land for economic and environmental purposes will go a long way.

Nagar Van is a Central government initiative announced in 2020, to create 200 urban forests over the next five years (PIB, 2020d). Many cities are independently pursuing this goal. Chennai has turned a garbage dump into an urban forest. After its success in increasing biodiversity, many more such urban forests are coming up in the city.

The city is trying to earmark land for creating such forests in every zone (TNN, 2020b). In Pune, 16.8 hectares of barren land has been converted into an urban forest with vibrant biodiversity (PIB, 2020d). The fight over the Aarey Milk Colony in Mumbai shows that even the most widely recognized 'lungs' of major cities cannot be taken for granted. Another option is to convert derelict urban land lying with public sector enterprises, defence, railways, ports and development authorities into green cover till they are not used for any other purpose.

The increase in private transport and stagnancy in the use of public transport is a major cause of local air pollution and urban heat effect. Many cities such as Paris, Bogota, Milan, Barcelona and London have allocated resources to create more walkable and cyclable streets, and worldwide cities are focusing on green mobility in the wake of Covid-19. The role of non-motorized transport, electric mobility, shared transport, and pedestrianization will determine how we can make cities resilient from the inside. A lot remains to be done on this. Delhi has seventeen buses for every 100,000 people, Beijing has 107 buses for every 100,000 people. As per a 2018 study, Delhi has only 5,200 buses against the demand of 11,500 buses (Halder and Gandhiok, 2019).

Likewise in the battle against climate change, the new frontier technologies are proving to be of tremendous aid. Big Data is being used by Google to assess GHG emissions at the city level. To date, cities such as Buenos Aires, Pittsburgh and Mountain View (California) have benefited from this tool (Kabbara, 2019). It also tells cities how much carbon emission they could have saved by reducing the number of car trips by a certain level. Artificial Intelligence and the Internet of Things is helping cities become energy efficient by monitoring use and cutting consumption wherever possible.

With more than a quarter of its urban population living in the slums, India has an enormous amount of unmet demand for residential housing. How these houses are built, how they are brought into the rental market, what material and technology are used, and where these houses are located—could all go a long way in ensuring the resilience of a city. Throughout the book, we have made the case for renewable energy and most importantly, for energy efficiency. Today, most of the globally produced energy is consumed by cities. However, as the density increases in urban areas, the per capita energy demand decreases and this points to great potential for energy savings through urbanization.

KEY IMPACT AREAS OF RESILIENCE: RIP (RISK, INVESTMENTS AND PREPAREDNESS)

I hope resilience doesn't RIP. We need to get our hands dirty to figure out the last details of what makes a city resilient. The generic words—risk, investment and preparedness—need to be understood by all of us.

Indian cities should undertake a thorough risk analysis. This broadly entails studying the probability and consequences of disaster and climate change events. Whatever framework cities might pick, their risk analysis should contain three critical components: 1) hazards—possible events or disturbances that may adversely impact life and property in cities; 2) exposure—those assets within a certain proximity to the hazardous event that may sustain damage/loss during the disaster; and 3) vulnerability—susceptibility of population and assets to different levels of risks (Jha et al., 2013).

Such an analysis would help Indian cities to identify the key risks they face, their chances of occurrence, key segments that may be exposed to risk-events, and how susceptible the population and assets are to these events. In light of this information, many resilience mitigation and adaptation efforts can be launched, which we discuss in this section. For instance, the urban poor and migrants may likely be most exposed to disaster events and we would need to find solutions in housing, economic integration, skill training. Another example is risk-based land use planning which encourages investment in the safest areas for urban development (ibid). No Indian city presently can claim of having conducted such detailed risk analysis. But it is just such a risk analysis that will decide the appropriate response, planning and financing. Risk mapping could be made a prerequisite to urban planning. Risk analysis for urban resilience is also getting mainstreamed by multilateral agencies such as World Bank, Asian Development Bank and others. Globally, the few cities that are creating their resilience plans will act as a lighthouse for other cities, if they can successfully manage their risks.

As per a World Bank estimate, the urban infrastructure investment need globally stands at USD 4.5–5.4 trillion; however, a premium of 9–27 per cent is needed to make such infrastructure climate-resilient and low emission (World Bank, 2016). Given the lifecycle benefits of such projects, the government should use innovative practices to attract such investment. Infrastructure investment for building urban resilience cannot follow traditional investment rationale. We have seen how Tokyo's Channel is practically paying for itself. Thus filtered investments into projects that will boost the resilience of cities and minimize economic loss over the long term should remain our priority. This move will also fund innovations and technologies that multiply the resilience of cities. Moreover, such a move will have a tangible impact on the quality of life of the local population, by providing more sustainable lifestyles. The body of literature advocating project-level resilience is constantly growing. For instance, a recent paper shows that a certain set of indicators can be incorporated to assess the resilience of road transport projects (Marcelo et al., 2018).

Part of such investments which focus on creating resilience to climate change are also called Climate Finance. Ballaney and Patel define it as: 'local, national and transnational financing—drawn from public, private and alternative sources—that seeks to support mitigation and adaption actions designed to address climate change' (Ballaney and Patel, 2009). Globally, while climate financing has gone up, it still falls short of the IPCC target of USD 1.6–3.8 trillion annual investments through 2016–50 (Buchner et al., 2019). The majority of the funds are directed towards mitigation projects of renewable energy. India alone requires around USD 3 trillion worth of investments up to 2030, with green buildings needing the highest funding (1.4 trillion), followed by electric vehicles (667 billion), renewable energy (404 billion), transport (250 billion), agriculture (194 billion), urban water (128 billion) and waste (11 billion) (IFC, 2017). In India too the majority of the investments are going to the renewable energy sector. Such allocation of funds confirms what we discussed in the previous section.

Another instrument for such financing is the green bond. A green bond is a debt security issued to raise capital specifically in support of climate-related or environmental projects (World Bank, 2018).

Those projects typically include renewable energies, energy efficiency, sustainable waste management, clean transportation, biodiversity, sustainable land-use, or climate change mitigation and adaptation. The green bond market has grown exponentially in recent years. The World Bank and its private-sector lending arm, the International Finance Corporation (IFC), are active issuers in the market. As of June 2021, the World Bank had issued USD 10.5 billion through more than 178 green bond transactions in twenty currencies (IFC, n.d.). As per the *Emerging Markets Green Bonds Report 2019*, China issued the majority of green bonds during 2012–19 (to the tune of USD 142 billion), whereas India only issued USD 11 billion worth (Amundi and IFC, 2020). However, such bonds are issued by public and private entities, and not ULBs. While India is increasing its focus on financing through bonds, it would be better to do so with green bonds (Sarma, 2020). Instruments aside, as per IFC, cities in developing countries can attract as much as USD 29 trillion in climate-related investments with a focus on six sectors (green buildings, public transport, electric vehicles, waste management, water treatment and renewable energy). Of this, the majority will go into green buildings (USD 24.7 trillion), public transport (USD 1 trillion), electric vehicles (USD 1.6 trillion), clean energy (USD 842 billion), water (USD 1 trillion), and waste management (USD 200 billion) (Taylor, 2018).

The last part of this value chain in disaster preparedness—how prepared are we to mitigate the risk of natural and manmade crisis when it hits us, how soon can we bounce back, using what measures. This will help cities prepare for disaster management too, depending upon the risk profile and kind of investments it is able to attract. For instance, in the Philippines, 5 per cent of the local budget is earmarked for a calamity relief fund, of which 70 per cent can be spent on relief and rescue equipment (Subudhi and Bilgrami, 2019). One Indian case study that is time tested is Odisha's response to cyclones. As discussed in the previous chapters, in 1999 a Super Cyclone hit India's eastern coast. Over 10,000 people died in Odisha and the property damage was very high. In 2019, when Cyclone Fani struck Odisha, the damage was very well contained. The state's chief minister pointed out that 1.2 million people had been evacuated, of whom 3.2 lakh were from Ganjam and

1.2 lakh from Puri; 45,000 volunteers had helped set up 9,000 shelters and 7,000 kitchens.

A 'zero casualty' approach was adopted and detailed instructions were issued on what to do before, during, and after the cyclone. The government sent out detailed instructions before the cyclone hit, what to do during the cyclone and after the cyclone. The high accuracy of predictions from the India Meteorological Department was key in focusing the efforts. The preparedness of Odisha highlights that it is possible to do this at the state and even city level (ibid.). Cities need to map out the critical infrastructure that can help them bounce back—transportation, drinking water, rail, road and air connectivity, and others. Early warning technologies and regular drills are our best safeguards to ensure that citizens are prepared. The city's fire, health and water departments need to be fully equipped and professionalized to deal with any mishaps. For instance, when the Kutch area of Gujarat suffered a massive earthquake and the ancient city of Bhuj was devastated, 20,000 people lost their lives and over a million structures were destroyed (Pachnanda, 2020). Since, then the state has done a good job in creating disaster management authorities—Gujarat State Disaster Management Authority (GSDMA), the Institute of Seismological Research and the Gujarat Institute of Disaster Management (ibid.). It has also published a hazard risk and vulnerability atlas. Such risk assessment reduces the risk exposure of investments.

The National Disaster Management Act, 2005, created the National Disaster Management Authority (NDMA) and constituted the National Disaster Response Force (NDRF) in 2006. Risk assessment and disaster management has been done by these agencies. The Indian government has also led the creation of the 'Coalition on Disaster-Resilient Infrastructure' (CDRI), adding institutional heft to this noble idea. Between the Sendai Framework for Disaster Risk Reduction and the CDRI, we have the guiding principles for disaster preparedness, but the cities cannot wait for national agencies to work for them. It's neither feasible nor desirable. They must internalize these principles in all aspects of urban services and infrastructure. It must also be noted that resilience is a way of life and the sooner cities make it part of everyday functioning, the better it is for them.

FLOODED WITH RISK

According to a global risk analysis of 616 major metropolitan areas, home to 1.7 billion people, constituting half of the global GDP, more people are at risk from floods than from any other natural hazard (World Bank, 2016). Migration into flood-prone urban areas, increases both the number of people at risk and the pressure on civic authorities to provide for them. In China alone, 20 million people per year move into urban areas. This is dangerous in the case of regions such as the flood-prone Pearl River Delta, which is the world's largest contiguous urbanized area (Anderson, 2016). As per an WEF report, 641 out of 654 largest cities of China face regular flooding (Muggah, 2019). Globally, 1.1 billion people are locationally at risk of facing floods (Fox and Goodfellow, 2016). Global Mean Sea levels have risen at the rate of 3.6 millimetres a year during 2006–15, and if things do not drastically improve, will have risen by 0.3-2.5 meters by 2100, ranging from best to worst case scenarios (Lindsey, 2020). As per the Centre for Research on the Epidemiology of Disasters at the University of Louvain, and the NGO SEEDS, more than 55 per cent of India's smart cities are likely to flood (*The Indian Express*, 2020). There is no singular definitive estimate of the risk of flooding in Indian cities, but going by history, the risk is immense.

The most notable instances of flooding in the previous two decades include Hyderabad (in 2000, 2016 and 2020), Ahmedabad (2001 and 2017), Delhi (2002, 2003, 2009 and 2010), Chennai (2004 and 2015), Mumbai (2005), Surat (2006), Kolkata (2007), Jamshedpur (2008), Guwahati (2010 and 2014), and in 2018 in Srinagar (2018) and in multiple cities in Kerala (Gupta 2020c). Experts attribute such flooding to illegal encroachments (especially on flood plains), lack of adequate stormwater drainage, reduction of urban water bodies and the urban heat islands effect (ibid.).

Preparing for flooding is a mix of mitigation and adaptation measures. How can we reduce the risk of flooding and if it does happen, how do we better prepare for it? There are confirmed reports that Indian cities are receiving a higher share of rainfall for fewer days, in other words, more rain in a shorter span of time (Udas-Mankikar, 2020a). This is when the role of stormwater drains, the least mentioned urban infrastructure, becomes pertinent. Its importance can be gauged from the fact that cities of the Indus Valley civilization had stormwater drains. Current Indian stormwater drains are designed to handle rainfall to the tune of 12–20 mm/hour, but with climate change-induced increases in the intensity of rainfall, we need to revamp the capacity of this vital piece of infrastructure. The Government of India has provided guidelines to upgrade these stormwater drains, but the implementation of these guidelines remains the key.

Observer Research Foundation has highlighted other issues related to stormwater drains (ibid.). First, cities do not even know how many they have and where each is located. Many of these drains are over a century old and need proper upgradation. This will not happen till we map all the drains. Second, their maintenance is key and, importantly, not a one-time affair. The guidelines state that every year, before the monsoon strikes, they need to be desilted and cleared of garbage. This is hardly complied with. Third, informal settlements don't have access to such drains and sewers. In case of heavy rains, the stormwater gets mixed with sewerage and solid waste. Stormwater coverage thus needs to be increased and also connected to reservoirs.

Flooding is going to be a risk for cities and we should look at avenues for adapting to it. Some adaption solutions involve new interventions such as rainfall monitoring stations, city-level risk analysis and the creation of detention basins. However, not much success has been achieved at the national level for India's cities (Gupta, 2020c). Till cities don't get to plan for themselves and have the resources to execute such plans, little progress should be expected. Empowered cities offer hope. For instance, one such exciting use of urban infrastructure was undertaken by Rotterdam in 2013 when it opened its water plaza, the Benthemplein, for community use such as skating and theatre (Ratho and John [eds], 2020). It is used for community purposes when there is no risk of flooding. When there is a risk of flooding, the city water square can retain the rainfall from adjacent areas to the tune of 1.7 million litres (ibid.). The infrastructure that can double up as storage reservoirs is a feasible idea going ahead. Another, but highly expensive project, has been executed by Kuala Lumpur—a massive stormwater drain and road tunnel, costing half a billion dollars. It is estimated that the tunnel has saved the city from seven flash floods over the last three years. This tunnel carries a large amount of water from the city to a storage reservoir (Subudhi and Bilgrami, 2019).

Another measure is China's rather appropriately named 'sponge city' initiative. Under this, by 2030, chosen districts should be able to capture, reuse and absorb 80 per cent of their stormwater run-off. As of now, thirty cities are part of this initiative and China aims to add another 600 cities (Muggah, 2019). 'Using techniques that mimic nature, sponge cities can catch, clean and store rain, which reduces the risk of flooding and keeps local drainage and water treatment systems from being overwhelmed (Jenkins, 2020). Sponge cities create permeable pavements, retention ponds, rejuvenate wetlands, expand green cover thus making streets green, and other green and blue infrastructure of the city. A city sinking due to land subsidence is a real threat worldwide. With excessive aquifer drainage, cities start to sink—it was Tokyo in the 1960s–70s, and Jakarta now. Tokyo has almost stopped sinking by banning groundwater pumping. At a certain point in time, Indian cities, with Central and state government inputs, will have to think about grand adaptation projects when the need arises.

Much of the Netherlands lies within the delta formed by its major rivers—the Rhine, the Meuse, the Scheldt—all of which together spill into the ocean. Besides, the majority of the Netherlands once lay below sea level. After facing repeated, severe flooding, the Dutch decided to do something about it and came up with the 'Delta Works'—a term given to the large number of its civil engineering projects (such as dams, locks, dykes, and others) aimed at reducing the risk of flooding by preventing water from breaching boundaries. Within Delta Works, the Dutch also launched a project called 'Room for the River', which aims to allow water to flow into the rivers without any obstacle as the water travels through the floodplain. This project has a range of activities including increasing the depth of rivers, storing more water, relocating dykes, creating high water channels and lowering floodplains, among others (AWPS, 2015).

In India, the density and overall chaos, coupled with the onset of flooding risk before we have become sufficiently prosperous, poses a grand challenge. In this regard, India will have to carefully choose its options on how it wants to manage the risk of urban floods.

URBAN WATER BODIES CAN ACT AS A FIRST LINE OF DEFENCE

As per the WWF Water Risk Filter (an online tool to assess water risk), as many as thirty Indian cities are prone to water risk from drought to outright flooding (Koshy, 2020). The filter has identified 100 cities, one-third of which are in India. China accounted for half of all such cities and the other global cities included Jakarta, Johannesburg, Istanbul, Hong Kong, Mecca and Rio de Janeiro (ibid.). Among natural disasters, floods are the most common and can cause great destruction to city infrastructure (UN-Habitat, 2015d). Indian cities must prepare themselves for such events. Open spaces have been ruthlessly taken over by concrete buildings, with little regard to treating cities as part of a larger ecosystem. Indian roads are hardly equipped to absorb rainwater or provide adequate stormwater drainage flow. This concern is further exacerbated by the massive amount of uncollected solid waste, improper faecal management and, of course, an ill-equipped drainage system.

Therefore, for creating truly resilient cities, Indian cities should give as much importance to water issues as they to land issues. The encroachment of water bodies in Indian cities is a sad but actual development. Among these, urban lakes in India especially face an abysmal situation. Ideally, lakes perform multiple functions including providing drinking water, supporting biodiversity, recharging groundwater, acting as sponges to control flooding, and providing livelihoods. In Krupa Ge's book *Rivers Remember: The Shocking Truth of a Manmade Flood*, she highlights how the 2015 Chennai floods were a compound outcome of a slew of bad decisions—building societies over what was once a lake, delay in releasing dam water, and useless disaster management plans (Bahuguna, 2019). We have seen umpteen times that when cities were built alongside water bodies (rivers, lakes, and oceans) but failed to exist in harmony with them, the fate of such cities was threatened. Water bodies in cities in India are coming down at an alarming rate and whatever is left is being fast encroached upon, built over, or polluted.

As per a survey by the Lucknow Municipal Corporation, the city had 964 ponds in 1952 but only 494 remained in 2006 (IANS, 2019a). As per the CPCB, in 2008 India had 150 polluted river stretches. This figure more than doubled, to 302, by 2015 (Jadhav, 2019). We have already discussed the horrendous treatment of the Najafgarh Jheel (lake). Najafgarh Jheel once spread over 220 sq km, is now reduced to 7 sq km (Rao, 2020). Bengaluru had 260 lakes in the 1960s, of which only 80 remained in 2019, and most of these have become dumping grounds for industrial waste (Kubernein Initiative, 2020). A survey of 105 wetlands showed that around 98 per cent of Bengaluru's lakes had been encroached upon by different forms of buildings and around 90 per cent were filled with sewage (Rao, 2018).

In Chennai, the area of water bodies declined from 12.6 sq km in 1893 to 3.2 sq km in 2017. During the same period, the surface water storage capacity declined from 37.8 billion litres to 9.5 billion litres (Kubernein Initiative, 2020). Wetlands are lands that have water for some part of the year or the entire year. As per a report, Indian cities lost 25 hectares of wetland for every 1 sq km of increase in built-up area over the last four decades (Khandekar, 2020). This is not uncommon as the world itself has lost 87 per cent of its wetlands since 1700, making this concurrent with the rise in urbanization (Davidson, 2016). The upside is that the Central government issued the Wetlands (Conservation and Management) Rules, 2017. But unless cities get to govern themselves, they will not be able to hold someone accountable and ensure corrective measures.

As per ADB experts, 'Between 1970 and 2014, Mumbai lost 71 per cent of its wetlands, Ahmedabad 57 per cent, Greater Bengaluru 56 per cent, Hyderabad 55 per cent and the NCR 38 per cent' (Kumar, 2020). This means that we are seriously losing out on the natural water regulation and flow. Wetlands are also an important source of biodiversity. The rejuvenation of water bodies is going to provide the cheapest way to create city-level resilience—urban water bodies recharge the groundwater aquifers and their catchment area provides ample space to absorb rainwater to prevent flooding. High penalty over encroachment, urban schemes for the rejuvenation of water bodies, an urban NREGA to create more such bodies, and entrusting local communities to develop and maintain such spaces, will go a long way. Lastly, cities should learn from the restoration of 48-acre Kaikondrahalli Lake in Bengaluru, the Hauz Khas Lake in Delhi and 400-acre Man Sagar Lake in Jaipur (NITI Aayog, 2015a).

TOO HOT TO NOT BE ADDRESSED

The onset of climate change, rampant economic activity, layering of built area and GHG emissions have all led to the rise of the phenomena of heatwaves, which refers to consecutive days when the temperature is higher than the expected normal temperature. As per the IMD, this period is categorized by temperatures reaching at least 40°C (104°F) in the plains and at least 30°C (86°F) in the hilly regions and reflect an increase of at least 5°C–6°C or 9°F–10.8°F above the normal temperature, it qualifies as a heatwave (Jha, 2021b). In the urban context, the heatwaves translate into creating 'urban heat island' effect—this happens when the difference between city and its surrounding rural area is 1°F-7°F higher in the daytime and about 2°F-5°F during night time (ibid.). As per a study that assessed the difference between rural and urban land surface temperature in forty-four major cities for 2001–17, there was significant difference in temperature between the city and its surrounding rural areas (Ghosh, 2020; Raj et al., 2020).

The occurrence of the urban heat island effect is problematic for a variety of reasons. As per ADB, urban heat is a leading cause of cloudbursts—a high amount of rainfall in short spells. Indian stormwater drainage lacks the capacity to carry the regular amount of rainwater, and such cloudbursts make the problem of flooding even worse (Kumar, 2020). Experts point that for every degree centigrade rise in temperature, clouds are able to hold 7 per cent more moisture (ibid.). As per a study by the IMD and IIT Madras, the heat index (a measure of how hot it feels when relative humidity is factored into the air temperature) of Delhi alone, is in the danger zone during the summer and monsoon seasons (Somvanshi, 2019). As per the Centre for Science and Environment, the average heat index during these two seasons has been rising, which also increases the risk of heatstroke.

The urban heat island effect also significantly brings down the productivity of people, as they find it difficult undertake physical work and tend to stay indoors. Lives can be lost due to heat-related issues. Studies show that such a rise in temperature, especially in the central business district, can be attributed to human activities, changes in land-use patterns, and vegetation density (ibid.). Such variation in heat also increases the electricity demand and CO_2 emissions.

The good news about mitigating the urban heat island effect is that solutions listed previously in this section—rejuvenating and creating water bodies, creating sponge cities, providing more green streets and green cover, urban forests, creating cool roofs, better urban planning and reducing the energy demand and carbon emission—can all be effectively used. Cities such as Paris and Medellin have undertaken initiatives to contain the urban heat island effect. Paris has replaced asphalt with porous materials and has created a green cover in 700 schools to reduce surface temperature and daytime air temperatures. Medellin has focused on greening thirty roads and waterways under its Green Corridor Project (Ratho and John [eds], 2020). India made a progressive move on this front by launching the India Cooling Action Plan, which has a direct bearing on the urban heat island effect, as recognized in the Plan too. The Plan's focus on thermal comfort for all, sustainable cooling, reduction of cooling demand across sectors, and reduction in cooling energy requirements, all mitigate the urban heat island effect (PIB, 2019d; MoEFCC, 2019a). It would be best if the heat island effect were declared a disaster; currently under National Disaster Management Act, it is not considered a disaster.

Ahmedabad is the first Indian city to come out with a Heat Action Plan (HAP) that has been widely recognized for its success. After witnessing more than 4,000 deaths due to heatwaves, the city came out with HAP in 2013 (Langa, 2017). The HAP has led to the creation of a collaborative project that includes a seven-day early warning system about impending heatwaves, community outreach activities, capacity building of healthcare professionals, changing school and college timings, providing excess water supply in slums, using sprinklers at crossroads and creating new centres to provide drinking water (ibid.). This is an adaptation measure, but its success has convinced thirty other Indian cities across eleven states to create their own HAP (MoEFCC, 2019a).

LESS IS MORE: CREATING AN INDIAN MODEL OF URBANIZATION

We started the book with the argument that the cities are the world's longest-running experiment. If India doesn't create its own model of cities, this experiment might blow up in our faces. We are in the midst of the Anthropocene epoch and scholar Elizabeth Kolbert writes that we are in midst of the sixth extinction (Kolbert, 2015). She also states, however, 'human ingenuity will outrun any disaster human ingenuity sets in motion' (ibid.). Indians have mastered the art of getting more with less. Our resource-efficient cities could show others the path ahead. We are showing tremendous promise on how we can consume less and also handle our waste better. Edward Glaeser remarked that if the per capita levels of both China and India were to rise to the level in the US, global carbon emissions would rise by 139 per cent; as against the 30 per cent rise if India and China's emissions followed the levels achieved by the French (Gleaser, 2012).

I think we can go the French way and beyond in being resource-efficient. One can naturally infer that efficient utilization of resources leads to higher quality of life and more resilience in cities. Resource efficiency can be described as, 'the sustainable management and use of resources throughout their life cycle, from extraction, transport, transformation, consumption to the disposal of waste, in order to avoid scarcity and harmful environmental impacts' (UN-Habitat, 2015c). As suggested in previous sections on urban infrastructure and urban land, it is critical that Indian cities adopt planning and governance that strongly encourage compact cities and at every step question whether the actions are increasing or decreasing resource efficiency. This not only makes economic sense but also ensures that cities are prepared to better respond to man-made or natural hazards. The better management of urban lakes, urban lands, energy, transport costs and time, housing and solid waste management can all together prove very critical in times of crisis such as flooding or earthquakes.

The good thing is that India has very early recognized the problem. This becomes important against the backdrop of sixfold growth in India's material consumption, from 1.18 billion tonnes in 1970 to 7 billion tonnes in 2015 (MoEFCC, 2019b). As per the draft National Resource Efficiency Policy, 2019, India's resource extraction stands at 1,580 tonnes/acre, considerably higher than the world average of 450 tonnes/acre (ibid.). The material productivity remains low. As we move ahead with increasing material consumption, the rate of recycling needs to go up. Presently, it stands at merely 20–25 per cent, as compared to 70 per cent in Europe. The draft policy to set up the National Resource Efficiency Authority is a step in the right direction. It will set sectoral targets, create standards and guidelines, monitor progress and provide capacity building (ibid.). It also lists some interesting policy initiatives at all life-cycle stages such as extraction (tax on virgin materials), design (standards for longevity and durability), production (emission standards), consumption (labelling and certification, behaviour-change campaigns and green public procurement), recycling (tax benefits and standards on recycled materials) and waste disposal (landfill taxes, promotion of waste disposal facilities) (ibid.). Since cities are centres of production and consumption, this would hold maximum value to the cities and how they get to implement it. China adopted a national energy and resource-saving policy in 2006 which led to the city-level focus on using incentives and punishments to encourage water saving (Fox and Goodfellow, 2016).

India is one of the only G20 countries, which is on course to meet its target to reduce emission intensity under UNFCCC (Climate Transparency, 2020). Our progress on renewable energy, solar mission, reducing emissions under the Perform, Achieve & Trade Scheme, use of energy-efficient LED bulbs, drastic reduction of solid biomass cooking and progress on the city gas-distribution network offer reason for hope. Our relatively low private vehicle ownership offers us a chance to mass-adopt public transport. The fact that we have to still build the majority of urban India and that buildings constitute 25 per cent of energy demand in India, gives us a chance to make both commercial and residential buildings energy-efficient as per the Bureau of Energy Efficiency's Energy Conservation Building Code (ECBC). Each ECBC-compliant commercial building delivers minimum energy savings of 25 per cent. The code for residential buildings is expected to lead to an energy saving of about 100 million tonnes of CO_2 emission (PIB, 2018c). With this broad approach to resource efficiency Indian cities can create their own path of urbanization that builds in resilience as a mitigation strategy.

10
Urban Governance: The Fountainhead of All Maladies

Sir Humphrey Appleby: 'Bernard, if the right people don't have the power, you know what happens? The wrong people get it! Politicians, councillors, ordinary voters.'
Sir Bernard Woolley: 'But, aren't they supposed to in a democracy?'
Sir Humphrey Appleby: 'This is a BRITISH Democracy, Bernard!'
Sir Bernard Woolley: 'How do you mean?'
Sir Humphrey Appleby: 'British democracy recognizes that you need a system to protect important things of life and keep them out of the hands of the Barbarians. Things like the Opera. Radio 3. The countryside. The law. The universities. Both of them. And we are that system.'

—*Yes, Prime Minister.*

BRITISH political satire—*Yes, Minister* (1980–84) and *Yes, Prime Minister* (1986–88) produced by BBC2—provides a masterclass on how the government functions, how it wants others to know about its functioning, and what it doesn't want others to know about its functioning. The exchange above is between two fictional bureaucrats about the repercussions of granting democratic powers to local governments and how that would affect their work.

The apparent sophisticated understanding among bureaucrats and politicians—that some matters should stay out of the reach of the masses just so that they (the bureaucrats and politicians) can continue to hold power—is the essence of vested interest and sums up the malady that ails urban governance in India. While we are at it, let's deep-dive into why cities in India do not offer governance that can play an effective role in the lives of their citizens. Through the entire book, I have shared solutions—mine and that of many global and Indian experts—for the many issues that plague urban life in India. It all seems so logical and easy and natural. But it isn't, because in resolving issues using these suggested solutions, we take away part of the power of those with vested interests. This is not acceptable to them.

Every story on Indian urbanization stops and starts with the discussion on issues with governance.

Since Independence, India has had two levels of government as defined in the Constitution—Central and state. Given their constitutional backing, both forms of government are highly sophisticated, though one can argue that the issues with national- and state-level governance make this a wobbly assumption. The failure of governance, of service-delivery and other such maladies can be attributed to how our political system views the pecking order of political and economic priorities, wherein city-level issues are at the bottom and not at par with national- and state-level issues. If anything, vested interests are really good at manipulating constitutionally-mandated political structures to systematically keep local self-government—the third and most nascent form of governance in India—underdeveloped and stunted.

It also suits the states to extract resources through their cities, which is easier when you directly control them. Cities are centres of economic growth and, therefore, contribute more to the Central and state revenues. They also house more taxpayers as compared to rural areas and further contribute to the exchequer through taxes such as property taxes. Due to the concentration of firms, economic activity and skilled workforce, the value of assets such as land is significantly higher in cities.

A report by WWF, *The Alternative Urban Futures Report*, summarizes the evolution of urban governance in India. The first municipal corporation was set up in India in Madras in 1687, followed by Calcutta and then Bombay (Sanyal et al., 2010). In the nineteenth century, urban governance in India witnessed some key changes as the British consolidated their control over India. This included the Improvements of Towns Act, 1850, which provided administrative powers to the newly-established system of councillors. In 1870, Lord Mayo institutionalized the system of municipalities and in 1882, Lord Rippon created a two-tier structure and created a system of municipal governance (ibid.). In 1920, the District Municipalities Act made municipal councils into elected bodies. However, it was the Government of India Act, 1935, that brought cities under the control of states/provinces (ibid.). Post-1947, newly independent India continued this structure and institutionalized it in its Constitution.

It was only more than four decades later that India made a move to correct the issue of the overwhelming control of the states over cities, by introducing a third tier of urban governance through the 74th Constitutional Amendment Act (CAA), of 1992. Until then the topic of local self-government remained under the State List—a matter assigned to the states by the Constitution. Prior to this (and the 73rd Amendment, which provided Constitutional backing to village-level governance), urban self-government institutions had lacked protection. Elected municipalities had been suspended and superseded, in many cases for over ten years in cities such as Chennai, Hyderabad, Kanpur and Lucknow (Mohanty, 2014). The 74th Amendment mandated that the state governments hand over eighteen functions under the Twelfth Schedule to ULBs. Some of these functions were town planning, regulation of land use, the construction of buildings, roads and bridges, provision of water, public health, sanitation and solid waste management (Ahluwalia, 2019b). As the 74th CAA came into force, the states—owing to intervention by the vested interests referred to above—circumvented local self-government institutions, using instead the development authorities and parastatal agencies at their disposal.

Cities generate the resources and no politician wants to give away that, especially when it comes in handy in financing election campaigns. Before we go into understanding the problems that plague urban governance, let us look at the list of institutions mandated by the 74th CAA. This will help to lay the groundwork for subsequent analysis and recommendations. The 74th CAA mandates following institutions (Mohanty, 2014):

1. State Election Commission: superintendence, direction, and control of the preparation of electoral rolls for and conduct of elections to rural and urban local bodies.
2. Municipalities: Article 243Q provides for three categories for municipalities—Nagar Panchayats (for areas transitioning from the rural to urban category); municipal councils (for smaller urban areas); and municipal corporations (for large cities). These are elected bodies at the ULB level.
3. Wards Committees: The 74th Amendment mandates the formation of ward committees in municipalities with a population of 300,000 or more.
4. State Finance Commission: State governments have to constitute an SFC every five years, which will review the financial health of ULB and rural local bodies.
5. Central Finance Commission: A CFC is appointed every five years and ensures devolution and linkage between Central, state, and local body finances.
6. District Planning Committee: Every district has to have a DPC, which consolidates the plan prepared by panchayats and municipalities in the district.
7. Metropolitan Planning Committee: The MPC has to work towards creating a draft metropolitan development plan for each metropolitan area.

Janaagraha's *Annual Survey of India's City-Systems* (a survey of the quality of urban governance in twenty-one Indian cities) uses the 'city-systems' framework which has four dimensions—1) urban planning and design; 2) urban capacities and resources; 3) empowered and legitimate political representation; and, 4) transparency, accountability and participation. The benchmark cities for this survey, London and New York, scored as high as 9.3 and 9.8 respectively, whereas Indian cities scored an average of 3.5 (Ganesh, n.d.). The report's key insights exhibit the state of poor urban governance in India: 1) larger cities with higher financial resources had relatively weak mayors and levels of devolution; 2) salary as a proportion of own revenues, in eleven out of the twenty-one city systems surveyed by Janaagraha, increased from 108 per cent in 2013 to 129 per cent in 2015, implying that revenues were not sufficient to cover staff salaries; and 3) smaller Indian cities spent considerably less on urban infrastructure and services (Nair et al., 2016). A more recent Janaagraha city-systems survey shows that a third of positions remain vacant; the average tenure of a commissioner is ten months; only two out of twenty-three surveyed cities had ward committees and area sabhas; and only nine out of twenty-three cities had a citizens' charter (Sreevatsan, 2018).

As per a study on urban governance by Praja Foundation in Delhi and forty other cities across twenty-eight states, found that cities in only five states had a directly elected mayor. None of the states had devolved all eighteen functions (Praja, 2020a). In another study of twenty-one cities, Praja Foundation found multiple agencies were involved in at least in seven out of the eighteen functions, and in nine cities, multiple agencies were involved in ten functions (Praja, 2020b). Not a single city had control over all eighteen functions, for instance Mumbai had control over nine functions and Lucknow had control over just one function (ibid.).

States rarely set up DPCs and MPCs, and wherever these do exist, not much has happened. The SFCs too have not performed a role that the Central Finance Commission expected of them (Ahluwalia, 2019b). Indian ULBs are considered to be the weakest in the world in terms of financial autonomy and capacity to raise resources (MoUD, 2011). The ratio of municipal revenues to GDP in India for 2012–13 is estimated at 1.03 per cent, as compared to 6 per cent in South Africa and 7.4 per cent in Brazil (Mohanty, 2016). Some of the key reasons behind the poor state of India's municipal revenues include a narrow, inflexible and non-buoyant tax base, the lack of capacity to borrow, and the inability of municipalities to levy and recover user charges. Though property tax rates and exemptions are ruled by state governments, ULBs are not allowed to undertake town planning for themselves; this further prevents them from using their land effectively to fund their plan (Ahluwalia, 2019b).

There also exists a gap between census towns (recognized as urban by the Census of India) and statutory towns (recognized as urban by the states), and their impact in holding back our cities. Between 2001 and 2011, 2,500 census towns remained unacknowledged by states, which did not give them urban governance structures (ibid.). The reason why state governments are reluctant to classify census towns as statutory towns is because they have to provide urban-level services and governance to statutory towns. Interestingly, even rural areas prefer not to be defined as urban because that would stop the enormous amount of money coming their way through rural development schemes (ibid.). Such categorization would also change the regulations that would govern them, for instance, they would have to pay property tax (ibid.).

Mayors in India—though at the head of city governance—are hardly empowered, and remain obscure in urban governance structures. As per the Praja Foundation's study only Chhattisgarh, Haryana, Jharkhand, Uttar Pradesh and Uttarakhand have directly elected mayors. When mayors are directly elected it increases their accountability and public pressure to perform. The best interests of a city's residents are taken care of, when they choose who will fight for them and will be answerable for providing them the right urban amenities. The world's major cities have directly elected mayors, which is a critical fact behind their success and continued prosperity.

States that do not follow this practice are seeing a stunting in the capacity of ULBs. We do not have professional municipal cadres and the recruitment rules are archaic. Multiple institutions like parastatals, development authorities, public works departments and ULBs report to different heads and have been entrusted with different responsibilities. In such states the ULBs struggle (or fail) to perform even the most basic functions such as bookkeeping and ensuring compliance, let alone setting up functions needed to create tech-savvy cities.

Compare these to the tasks that face cities—to function as economic engines of growth and provide better jobs, productivity and wages to the people leaving the agricultural sector. There is also immense ground to be covered on urban infrastructure by way of work on municipal solid waste, housing for migrants and marginalized sections, access to piped drinking water, toilet and faecal management. City governments need to have dynamic urban plans that could utilize urban land efficiently to provide for economic growth and provide high liveability in the urban areas. They need to rejuvenate public spaces and water bodies in urban areas and create inclusive cities for the specially abled, and for women, children and the elderly. They need to provide public transport and sufficient roads and streets, ensure safe public environments and make the city resilient when faced with natural calamities and disasters.

To solve the issues of urban governance, we suggest the following strategies.

APPROPRIATELY DEFINE URBAN AREAS

There are two main ways—statutory and census—to define urban areas in India. The statutory town includes all places with a municipality, corporation, cantonment board or notified town area committee. These towns are defined by state governments and place India's urbanization rate at 26.7 per cent. The census, however, adopts a triple criterion to define what is urban: 1) a minimum population of 5,000; 2) at least 75 per cent of the male working population engaged in non-agricultural pursuits; and 3) minimum population density of 400 persons per sq km. This pegs India's urbanization rate at 31 per cent. The total number of census towns stand at 7,933 and their cumulative population is 377 million. If we take India's population as 1.36 billion, the difference of 5 per cent between the cumulative population of the census towns and India's total population amounts to close to the population of France or to twelve Singapores.

This definition skews the policymaker's attention and budgetary allocation in a manner that is not in tandem with ground realities. There is growing evidence, mostly from satellite imagery, that India is way more urban than the 2011 census estimates. Scholars at IDFC Institute (now Artha Global) have been at the forefront of researching and advocating that India is more urban than we imagined. This is quite plausible because, as mentioned above, there is a large sum of money allocated for rural development and it is in the interest of state governments to under-represent the urbanization ratio. If classified as urban, villages will lose the money they receive under rural development schemes and will become subject to regulations and taxes such as property tax and building by-laws. Besides, the stringent definition of a census town was carved out by then Census Commissioner Asok Mitra, in 1961. It does not reflect the realities and requirements of twenty-first century India.

The IDFC points out that though there is no single global criterion of what constitutes 'urban', India has the rare distinction of using the combination of population, density, occupation and administrative status to define 'urban' (IDFC, 2019). Nevertheless, the think tank calculates the share of urban population in India using the criterion used in other countries. For instance, when measured by the population threshold of 5,000 (as in Ghana and Qatar), India is 47 per cent urban; a population threshold of 2,500 (as in Mexico and Venezuela), makes India 65 per cent urban. As per IDFC:

> An urban area governed by a ULB rather than an RLB could potentially benefit from a 147 per cent increase in road length per sq. km, a 128 per cent increase in water storage capacity in kilolitres per capita, a 25 per cent increase in the probability of establishing a higher education institution, and an 11 per cent increase in hospital beds per capita (Shah et al., 2020).

As per Janaagraha's annual city-systems survey, states also have varying definitions for statutory towns. As many as eight factors (including area, population size, density and occupation among others) are used in six varying ways to define a city. Moreover, the thresholds even within these factors also differ (Nair et al., 2016). Kerala, as per its own statutory definition, is 16 per cent urban; whereas if we use the population threshold of 5,000, it is 99 per cent urban (ibid.). This could be defined as the Great Indian Anomaly.

You cannot improve upon something that you have not measured properly. Urban infrastructure, services and governance are vital for geographical entities to work as efficient engines of growth, creating jobs for all and providing a better standard of living. If we continue to govern these as rural areas, we may not get a chance to correct things in time. It is best to do so now, as later it will be costlier to retrofit. The state and the Central governments need to balance the scales between rural and urban areas. The perverse incentives for continuing to be defined rural have to go before it is too late. This problem has now been recognized by the Central government, and it has directed state governments to convert census towns to ULBs (Tandel and Hiranandani, 2016). Many states, including Bihar and Maharashtra, are now converting such rural areas into urban areas.

Appropriately defining urban areas can have an impact that can go beyond generations. The IDFC mentions the most high-profile example of how planning paved the way for growth. Though New York was a small town in 1811, the Commissioners' Plan laid out a notional grid to be followed when the city expanded. When the grid was built, people were compensated. The grid, as IDFC puts it, remains 'sacrosanct' and has been key in creating infrastructure and roads (IDFC, 2019). We have already discussed how Ahmedabad is undertaking a similar exercise in India.

On a separate but related note there is also a case for revisiting delimitation (the process of redrawing the boundaries of Lok Sabha and assembly seats according to changing population sizes (Chopra, 2019). Article 81 of the Constitution mandates the same population-to-seat ratio for all states and so the number of Lok Sabha (Lower House) seats increased with every census till 1971. In 1976, when the number of seats touched 550, a delimitation freeze was imposed till 2001, as states in south India worried that their seats might be reduced. In the 2000s, another amendment froze the delimitation exercise till 2026.

The nation's population in 1971 was 548 million, less than half its present population. As a consequence, some seats today represent more people than the size of the populations of a lot of countries. The next revision will not happen before 2026. This is a rare opportunity to rectify this problem and increase the number of representatives so that urban voices are better heard in Parliament. As matters stand, the increasing population in urban areas means that the value of such votes is declining since the allotted seats remain the same. However, once delimitation happens it means for a while again all votes will amount to equal importance.

FULFIL THE PROMISE OF THE 74TH CONSTITUTIONAL AMENDMENT ACT

The 74th Constitutional Amendment Act (the 74th CAA) gave municipal bodies a constitutional status by recognizing them as the third tier of governance. It devolved eighteen functions mentioned in Schedule 12, to municipalities (NITI Aayog, n.d.). However as per Janaagraha's annual city-systems survey, on average, only three out of ten critical functions have been devolved to the cities. After close to three decades, the question that still remains is how can India make meaningful progress on decentralization through the 74th CAA? There are two strategies that can provide a solution. First, the 74th CAA needs to be further amended to include present-day city realities. This means that the list of eighteen functions mentioned in Schedule 12, needs to be expanded to include subjects such as urban transport, power of mayor and council, urban citizenship and migrants' issues, matters about urban safety, inclusiveness and resilience. The second strategy includes finding ways to encourage states to devolve the Schedule 12 functions to the cities. The Constitution will have to be amended to lend stronger purpose and intent to certain critical provisions that need to be devolved.

Research shows that Central and state governments are more adept at delivering on redistributive policies (healthcare, pension, insurance, even Universal Basic Income if it comes to that), and the local government should focus on developmental policies (transportation, sanitation, fire and so on) driven by political and economic interests (Peterson, 1995). In India, a considerable number of developmental policies, such as Swachh Bharat Mission, are delivered by the Central and state governments. It's time city governments provided these services. Covid-19 saw cities scampering for the single chain of command and political accountability, while facing dearth of resources. Why should a state chief minister or a bureaucrat without real local accountability, brief us about what is happening in our cities? If cities had mayors empowered under an amended 74th CAA, we would have known whom to ask questions of and where the buck would stop.

Redressing lacunae in the 74th CAA is as important—if not more important than—the reform of land, labour and capital that everyone keeps discussing. Who will take charge of amending the 74th CAA and bite the bullet? Only a constitutional amendment or a united demand from citizens can make states deliver on the 74th Amendment as it stands. No amount of reform-linked resources will persuade states to devolve. Think tanks like IDFC Institute, Janaagraha and Praja Foundation are doing a formidable job in making people aware of the 74th CAA and the principle of subsidiarity.

A 2020 study ('Urban Governance Index'), by the Praja Foundation, ranked states on four pillars: 1) empowered, local elected representatives and legislative structure; 2) empowered city administration; 3) empowered citizens; and, 4) fiscal empowerment (*Firstpost*, 2020). Each pillar was measured through further sub-indicators. None of the states scored above sixty (out of the total 100). The top five (relatively) better performing states were Odisha (56.86 per cent), Maharashtra (55.15 per cent), Chhattisgarh (49.68 per cent), Kerala (48.77 per cent) and Madhya Pradesh (45.94 per cent) (ibid.).

Villages are relatively more empowered through local self-governance thanks to the Panchayati Raj institutions and we see how far they have come in terms of taking big and small decisions—where to build their roads, how to increase immunization, improve health and education outcomes, where to build community toilets and what behaviour-change campaigns to pursue. The improvement of villages is explained by their ability to make decisions for themselves. The emancipation of Indian cities lies in constitutional reforms that make devolution of powers mandatory in a time-bound manner. The principle of subsidiarity should be the governing principle of urban governance and only functions that cannot be performed by local governments should be performed by higher authorities—whether state or Central.

EMPOWER CITIES WITH EMPOWERED MAYORS

Indian cities mostly follow the commissioner system, wherein states appoint a bureaucrat as a municipal commissioner who acts as the executive head of the municipal corporation. The mayor merely acts as a ceremonial head. This arrangement belies the true spirit of the 74th

CAA, which sadly does not define the tenure, power and manner of election of mayors/chairpersons of ULBs. And that lack of clarity has been tapped by the states to use commissioners to run cities (NITI Aayog, n.d). Many cities do not even have a mayor. Where the mayoral position exists, the incumbent is selected by the municipal corporation's councillors, who are directly elected but report to the municipal commissioner, a bureaucrat (Alexander, 2019). It is imperative that a mayor is directly elected and is accountable to the citizens of the city.

One possible strategy for states is to mandate what has been recently proposed in a Private Bill introduced in Parliament by Shashi Tharoor in 2016. As per the Bill, the mayor should be directly elected and should be accountable for citywide decisions. The mayor's term in office should be coterminous with that of the municipality. In other words, mayors should be given a full term of five years (Idiculla, 2016). However, the present situation is considerably different. As per Janaagraha's annual city-systems survey, larger cities have weaker mayors and lower levels of power are devolved down to them, than to mayor's in smaller cities. Moreover, of the 80 million residents across the twenty-one cities surveyed by Janaagraha for the survey, 46 million are governed by an indirectly elected mayor who had an average tenure of 2.5 years or less (Dash, 2017).

If India needs to prepare its cities for the challenges they face, the mayor should not only be directly elected but all civic agencies should report to him/her, who must also be vested with the veto power on matters of importance to cities. Vesting such powers would be validated because: 1) directly elected mayors enjoy the popular vote; 2) it would give them enough power to sway or execute decisions, even when these are contrary to the decisions of state-appointed parastatal agencies and commissioners; 3) it would redress an existing imbalance—the fact that councillors are more invested in hyperlocal issues and may not have the citywide perspective to execute decisions, while a directly elected mayor would think of the city as a whole; and, 4) an empowered elected mayor and elected councillors would (ideally) create a mechanism of mutual checks and balances (Alexander, 2019; IDFC, 2019).

Experts argue that the mayor should have a representation in key city-level programmes such as the Smart Cities Mission, and should have a say in the appointment of the municipal commissioner. The mayor must also have a fixed tenure that cannot be changed at a whim. These are critical reforms that Indian cities, particularly metropolitan areas, desperately need. Consider this, New York's mayor has a four-year term as does the mayor of London. Cities such as Tokyo and Johannesburg have elected mayors with fixed tenures (Mohanty, 2014). The tenure of Mumbai's mayor is 2.5 years, and in Delhi and Bengaluru the tenure is just a year (Vachana, 2020). Only after we fix the executive powers and the length of the tenure of an elected mayor, will we be able to solve the twin issues of accountability and responsibility when it comes to city issues. Parastatal authorities also must be brought under the mayor.

Some may wonder how yet another empowered top city post could alter urban governance in India, especially when roles for councillors and commissioners are carved out in detail. Imagine a state government run by a single bureaucrat (not elected) and hundreds of elected members of the legislative assembly (MLAs). Like the country and states, cities do need a captain who can look at city-level issues while working in tandem and cooperation with councillors and commissioners. Also, it is not a newly created position, the mayoral position has existed in cities for centuries but has remained largely absent in modern Indian cities. A mayor elected by popular vote is accountable, will face consequences, hold the fort against random actions by the state government, can act in the city's interest and innovate city-level governance. Elected mayors will be the guide and glue that bring together different agencies and stakeholders to change how Indian cities are presently governed.

Mayors worldwide have had a lasting impact and changed how we view and manage our cities. Consider the example of Curitiba in Brazil. Its three-time mayor, Jaime Lerner, started the first Bus Rapid Transit System which is now implemented in 300 cities worldwide (Adler, 2016). He started a programme on creating more public spaces and the city now has 50 sq m of green space per person as compared to 2 sq m in neighbouring Buenos Aires. Presently, 90 per cent of the city's population participates in the Green Exchange Programme—as per which four pounds of trash will get you one pound of produce.

Let us look at Istanbul. In the 1980s it was suffering from pollution, a proliferation of slums (*gecekondu*, which means 'built overnight'), poor public transport and other issues that are now a common sight in Indian cities (*The Economist*, 2016). But a slew of measures changed the picture. It sourced natural gas from Russia for heating purposes, granted legal title to *gecekondus* and got itself elected mayors (ibid.). These mayors became a conduit for national leaders, which led to constructive competition and as an offshoot benefited Istanbul and other Turkish cities.

Elected mayors of note include New York's Michael Bloomberg, the changes he made have been appreciated worldwide; London's Sadiq Khan brought about major infrastructure and greening changes which got him recognition the world over; in Paris, Anne Hidalgo championed the fifteen-minute-city concept in the aftermath of Covid-19 and many cities are warming up to this idea. In India, when Covid-19 cases (the majority in metropolitan areas) were at their peak, no metropolitan area with a population of more than 10 million had a directly elected mayor (Vachana, 2020).

An important legacy of empowered mayors is that they create a cadre of second-generation national leaders. Jawaharlal Nehru, Vallabhbhai Patel and Subhas Chandra Bose were all mayors—Nehru of Allahabad, Patel of Ahmadabad and Bose of Calcutta (Livemint, 2017). In China too, taking the mayoral route is the key to rise through the leadership ranks (Rohra, 2016). The mayoral system hones local leadership and the individual, in many cases, goes on to assume regional and national political leadership. India's development needs not just one prime minister and twenty-nine chief ministers; it also needs thousands of mayors who will innovate in the governance space. Maybe then the PM and CMs will not have to inaugurate city projects, and the mayors can assume the mantle for local governance as it should be.

In this aspect, rural India is considerably better off. You walk into a village and everyone knows who the sarpanch is, how to reach her or him, and how she/he can get things done. You go to a city and no one knows who the mayor is and how to reach her/him. Often people are not sure if the city has a mayor or not!

INDIA: RICH NATION, POOR CITIES

The National Urban Policy Framework (NUPF) provides an interesting history of municipal finance in India. Starting with British India in the nineteenth century, wherein the local governments were given more powers, the inadequacy of municipal finance has been a thorny issue since then. The NUPF quotes Gopal Krishna Gokhale's resolution in the Indian Legislative Council in 1912:

> That this Council recommends to the Governor General in Council that a Committee of officials and non-officials may be appointed to enquire into the adequacy or otherwise of the resources at the disposal of local bodies in the different provinces for the efficient performance of the duties, which have been entrusted to them and to suggest, if necessary, how the financial position of these bodies may be improved (MoHUA, 2018a).

The same still holds good for the present situation of municipal finance too. In 1919 the British demarcated powers to local governments and provided the mandate to raise finances through tax on a range of activities (ibid.). In 1935, the Government of India Act changed the administrative structure and drastically reduced the power to tax of local bodies, and entrusted them with states. The Constitution of free India inherited this structure, wherein the states could decide on the functions and financial powers of local governments. The NUPF says there was no provision of 'Municipal Finance List' in the 74th CAA and thus states should decide what financial powers they want to devolve (ibid.). The 74th CAA provided for a State Finance Commission to ensure that local governments received funds clearly and regularly. It is now established that SFCs have not lived up to this promise (ibid.).

Urban scholars and the NUPF classify municipal finance in the following categories: tax revenue (such as property tax); non-tax revenues (rent, user charges, parking fees); devolution of funds from the state government, grants from Central and state governments; and borrowings (ibid.). In 2011, the High Powered Expert Committee (HPEC) appointed by the Union Ministry of Urban Development projected urban infrastructure investment requirements of INR 39.2 lakh crore at 2009–10 prices from 2012–13 to 2031–32. Around 44 per cent of this investment is required to construct urban roads alone. The HPEC pointed out that 68 per cent of this total demand for finance needs to be realized by the ULB finances alone (Shenvi and Slangen, 2018). Municipal revenue in India as a share of GDP was close to 1 per cent for the period from 2007–08 to 2017–18; in 2010 municipal revenues stood at 13.9 per cent in the UK, 7.4 per cent in Brazil, 6 per cent in South Africa and 4.5 per cent in Poland (Rajagopalan, 2020).

A report by think-tank ICRIER for the Fifteenth Finance Commission noted that for thirty-seven municipal corporations, the total municipal revenue as a share of GDP declined from 0.49 per cent in 2012–13 to 0.45 per cent in 2017–18 (ICRIER Team, 2019). The report highlighted that the ability of these corporations to raise their sources of money also declined. Their own revenues (revenue raised using tax and non-tax measures; this is part of their municipal revenue apart from transfers from central and state government) as a share of GDP declined from 0.33 per cent in 2012–13 to 0.23 per cent in 2017–18 (ibid.).

Some solutions would need reform and action from all three levels of government. For instance, when the landmark Goods and Services Tax came into force in 2017, many celebrated the efficiency it might usher in, and many cried on the implementation. Not a tear was shed on how local body taxes were subsumed under GST, though there is no revenue sharing with the third tier of governance. This tier of governance should ideally be providing the basic services to the people of India and playing a critical role in making our cities competitive and engines of growth. This one step (addressing the fact that local body taxes have been subsumed under GST) will go a long way in setting right the affairs of our cities. Only the GST Council can take this decision, but for this the Centre and the states would have to understand that cities are at the forefront of governance and provision of services and infrastructure. Injustice has been meted out to local governments.

The other action that the Central government can undertake is to increase the ceiling on professional tax from INR 2,500 (current) to INR 10,000 (MoHUA, 2018a). It is now widely accepted that property tax is one of the most feasible ways to increase the revenue of local governments. As per the ICRIER study of thirty-seven municipal corporations, property tax revenue—taken as a share of their combined revenue—was 36.5 per cent, making it an important source of revenue (ICRIER Team, 2019). As per a World Bank report, as compared to OECD countries where property tax collection constitutes 1.1 per cent of national GDP, in India it only constitutes 0.2 per cent of national GDP (World Bank, 2020). In countries like South Africa, the property tax collection rates are as high as 90 per cent, whereas in India's thirty-six biggest municipal corporations property tax collection rates were at 37 per cent (Udas-Mankikar, 2019).

From NUPF to the *Economic Surveys*, it is understood that property tax collection in India suffers from a range of issues. The *Economic Survey 2016–17* points out that property tax faces 'problems of low coverage, low rates, low collection efficiency and lack of indexation of property values, making it a non-buoyant source of revenue' (MoF, 2017). It states that cities such as Bengaluru and Jaipur collect only 5–20 per cent of their prospective tax revenues.

We have discussed earlier what the major issues with property tax are—states still control the mandate on property-tax imposition; the tax is calculated based on the annual rental value, which leads to lower buoyancy; states prevent the increase in rental value; a large share of properties are outside the periphery of municipalities and are with development authorities; the collection process is complex; and there are many exemptions for a range of properties, from properties owned by charities to those owned by the Central and state governments. Municipal-level reforms, as discussed in a previous chapter ('Urban Land: Next Frontier for Urban Growth') can be summarized as follows: mapping properties using GIS, moving towards evaluation using unit area value and the capital value method, allowing self-assessment, regular revaluation, facilitating better payment processes and gateways, and stricter enforcement.

Pune and Bengaluru have achieved great success in increasing their tax revenues. The user charges are also a sustainable source of income for cities, if they can increase the quality of services. Central government programmes such as the Jawaharlal Nehru National Urban Renewal

Mission (JNNURM, which ran from 2005 to 2014), and now the Atal Mission for Rejuvenation and Urban Transformation (AMRUT, launched in 2015) are focused on creating key city infrastructure in the cities. These initiatives may break the cycle of poor quality of urban infrastructure and services, which make urban dwellers reluctant to pay for these services. Increasingly, the dialogue is shifting towards making user charges commensurate with capital and operations expenditure. In the case of solid-waste management, people have shown willingness to pay for services as they have seen improvement in the quality of services. This has to be achieved for water and sewerage services, which have been discussed in the chapter on urban infrastructure. Similarly, as also advocated by the NUPF, we have discussed that parking charges should reflect the actual price of land and should not be excessively subsidized (MoHUA, 2018a).

The most recent and biggest municipal financing opportunity to open for cities is in the space of municipal bonds. The municipal bond is an important source of raising capital, as the market forces compel cities and states to clean up their act—maintain accounts, show cash flow, increase user charges, reduce non-revenue heads and build local capacity. Under the Smart Cities Mission, credit rating was undertaken for 469 cities and 163 were found to be of Investible Grade (PIB, 2020e). The market forces have started to act and this will clean up the act of bigger cities, which should percolate down to the smaller cities too.

Municipal bonds were first issued by Bengaluru in the early 1990s (MoHUA, 2018a). In 1995, the Ahmedabad Municipal Corporation took the ground-breaking step of requesting a credit rating from one of India's leading credit rating agencies for a domestic municipal bond (World Bank, 2018). Ahmedabad's first credit rating was A+, indicating adequate security for investors. The city issued bonds worth INR 1 billion in 1998. In 1996, the Tamil Nadu Urban Development Fund (TNUDF) was set up as a public-private partnership to fund infrastructure creation (ibid.). The government of Tamil Nadu owns 72 per cent of the capital in Tamil Nadu Urban Infrastructure Financial Services Limited (TNUIFSL), the asset management company that manages TNUDF, and the remaining 28 per cent is owned by three

Indian private financial institutions. To fund projects of weaker ULBs, the TNUDF and the state government created the pooled fund called the Water and Sanitation Pooled Fund (WSPF). It brought together the financing needs of water and sanitation projects of thirteen cities to raise INR 304.1 million (ibid.).

In 2019–20 alone, eight Indian cities raised INR 3,390 through municipal bonds (PIB, 2020e). The latest to do is the capital of Uttar Pradesh, Lucknow. It plans to spend the amount raised (INR 200 crore) on housing and water supply projects. This shows how municipal finance has come a long way in cross-subsidizing; earlier, Lucknow used money that was earned in the cities of Kanpur and Noida. Other cities in UP launching municipal bonds include Ghaziabad, while a pooled bond will be accessed by Kanpur, Varanasi, and Agra (Mishra, 2020).

There is one other source for raising municipal finance and the NUPF defines it as: 'Value capture [that] is based on the principle that private land and buildings benefit from public investments in infrastructure and policy decisions of governments (e.g. change of land use)' (MoHUA 2018b). The NUPF recognizes it to be a better tool than the direct sale of urban land—which remains highly fragmented, and for which data is not available, and which is encroached upon by all types of stakeholders. The common tools of the value capture fund (VCF), as noted by NUPF are conversion charges, betterment charges, impact fees, and development charges. The Government of India has created a framework for VCF, and it has to be seen how this pans out in Indian cities. However, an ICRIER report notes that share of benefit charges such as betterment charges, impact fees, and other instruments of unlocking land value in municipal revenue declined for twenty nine-corporations from 11.7 per cent in 2012–13 to 10.3 per cent in 2017–18 (ICRIER Team, 2019).

There are of course, other instruments such as Transferable Development Rights (TDRs), sale of FSI, and vacant land tax, among others. For this, I'd recommend the books of Prasanna Mohanty who has done a comparative analysis of many land-based instruments, of which TDRs have begun to scale in India. Under TDR:

> The government acquires land from the landowner in exchange for development rights that are transferred to the landowner.

Such 'development rights,' issued as Development Rights Certificate (DRC), empowers the owner to go for extra floor area ratio (FAR), which shall be fixed by the government (Mahesh, 2015).

These TDRs can be used in the area left after land acquisition or can be used for any other property. It can also be traded with other parties. The TDR not only eases the land acquisition process but also earns revenue for ULBs. Mumbai was the first city to replicate TDRs in 1991 to emulate the success of New York's model (ibid.). The lesson of Chinese cities monetizing land assets discussed in the land section is an important one for Indian cities. But, we have to remember that in China local governments are highly empowered and the mayoral role in key cities grooms leaders for senior roles on the regional and national theatre.

GOVERNANCE IN A METRO

The 74th CAA's Article 243P(c) defines the formation of metropolitan areas whereas Article 243-ZE mandates the creation of a metropolitan planning committee. It notes that metropolitan areas go beyond cities and may include more than one district and municipality. The MPC has to prepare a plan for the metropolitan areas. However, as the late Isher Ahluwalia noted, 'MPCs remained a non-starter as states showed little interest in their establishment. There are no examples of any MPC carrying through a Draft Development Plan via a state government approval, financing and mechanism' (Ahluwalia and Khare, 2019c).

As per Janaagraha's annual city-systems survey in 2018, only half of the eighteen cities required to form an MPC did so (Vachana, 2019). Moreover, where MPCs do exist, there is little democratic representation. This needs to change since some of the pressing issues that Indian cities are facing—such as climate change, pandemic containment, transport woes, labour issues and economic growth—go beyond the city limits. As per Janaagraha, many countries are fast moving towards metropolitan governance structures (ibid.). China is planning nineteen super-city clusters. Likewise, Australia has also moved towards regional governance and created four such structures to date. The UK has created 'City Deals', where the national government and city economic region sign an agreement to create a 'combined authority'—which brings together two or more councils to work on four common issues. The UK has rolled out nine such 'City Deals'. In India, this role is instead played by metropolitan development authorities or MDAs which are not accountable to the local population.

There are three issues to be solved for streamlining metropolitan administration. The first issue is to resolve overlaps in jurisdiction between regional and city agencies, such as municipal authorities, parastatals, urban development agencies and urban utility organizations. Such streamlining will have to be spearheaded by states, starting with their million-plus cities. This reform that has already been suggested and the Central government will have to find constitutional means to bring states to undertake this streamlining.

The second issue is to find dispute resolution mechanisms between regional and city agencies. A separate dispute resolution mechanism will not only reduce long-drawn-out cases, but will also make the city agile enough to adapt to changing conditions. Third, the responsibility of raising revenue and accountability on this matter has to be clearly divided between the agencies. Dovetailing city governance under regional authorities with adequate representation from relevant quarters, will resolve the anomalies in the economic, geographical, political, and administrative boundaries.

WHO WILL GET THEIR HANDS DIRTY? THE CASE OF UNDERSTAFFED, UNDEREQUIPPED MUNICIPALITIES

If you go to a city government office, you are likely to struggle to find a single point of contact in charge of affairs. We all feel like the protagonist of the political satire *Office-Office* in which the legendary Pankaj Kapur played the role of Mussadi Lal, a harassed and hassled citizen trying to get work done in a government office. The ubiquitous Ushaji, Bhatiaji, Shuklaji and Pandeyji acted as difficult government officials to work with. In many ways, this is the image of local governments. More often than not, this is just half the picture. The reality is that the municipal staff in Indian cities is highly understaffed and underequipped to attend to the changing reality.

In a study of twenty-one cities, Praja Foundation found that none of the cities had a ratio of over eight municipal employees per 1,000 people (Praja, 2020b).[7] Mumbai and Kolkata had eight employees per 1,000 people, Gurugram had one employee and Patna had even less (0.3) per 1,000 people. There is a tremendous shortfall of municipal employees, as high as 81 per cent in Gurugram to 33 per cent in Mumbai. Not a single city had control over the recruitment process (ibid.). As per Janaagraha's city-systems survey, Mumbai had 1,300 staff for every 1,00,000 citizens, whereas New York had 5,000 employees for every 1,00,000 citizens (IDFC, 2019). As per Janaagraha's 2017 survey, average vacancy in the surveyed cities stood at 35 per cent (Nair et al., 2016). The survey also noted that seventeen out of twenty-three surveyed cities had access to a municipal cadre, but not in terms of hiring them through a job description which meets the requirement of twenty-first century cities (ibid.).

The solution first lies in changing the perception around vacancies in city governments. The perception that city staff is not useful for the city's growth, the state's prospects, and nation-building has to go lock, stock and barrel; it is an important lever of sustaining the Indian story. The myth that Indian bureaucracy is overburdened has to go as it is not true. The first principle for providing the right services and governance is to have adequate staff. The solution exists in building the narrative that there are millions of jobs waiting to be tapped. These, in turn, could create many more indirect jobs as well. The second issue is about the job description and capacity building. The AMRUT Scheme envisages the creation of a municipal cadre at the state level and as a key reform. It says that states should bear the cost of such a cadre, which should be transferrable among ULBs. It indicates three types of services: 1) administrative (executive, social development, staff); 2) technical (urban

---

[7] The ratio of municipal employees is significant here, in that this ratio reveals if the bureaucracy is well staffed or not. Worldwide, all categories of government staff are measured in terms of the number of employees per 1,000/10,000/100,000 population.

planning, engineering, transportation, e-governance); and 3) finance (accounts, revenue, financial, and audit) (MoHUA, 2016c).

States like Tamil Nadu have already created state-level recruitment rules but many states are yet to do so. Even where they exist, they are not on par with contemporary domain expertise and human resource (HR) practices. The fact that cities cannot hire by themselves is a major roadblock under the current archaic HR systems. Centre and state governments must start training courses on municipal roles mentioned above. Just as with management and engineering, if hundreds of institutes provide courses relevant to the needs of cities, only then will the quality of skills go up. However, the prerequisite for institutes to start teaching would be to tap an unmet need, and for that cities need to be empowered to fill vacancies and also map sanctioned posts as per global standards. Cities are currently making do with a chief resilience officer, a chief data officer and so on, like appendages. Instead, we need a system where such new positions get created within the system, and resources are part of the broader HR structure, else there is little utility and will not lead to a lasting impact.

The third issue is about quality. It is often reported that when it comes to executing projects that demand contemporary skills, or even awarding contracts, the city lacks quality skills and capabilities. This is an issue that can be resolved by creating a municipal staff labour market wherein people can freely move within and, possibly, among states. This will force them to upgrade and hone their skills, cities will compete to hire the best talent and the job market will be lucrative for people to consider municipal roles. It should be for states to mandate a minimum ratio between deputed and permanent staff and between in-house and outsourced contractors. In the end, the services and governance will be as good as the foot soldiers. Currently, we have a depleted rank and file, inadequately trained, overstretched and tired. Organizations like Janaagraha are doing a commendable job in advocating for the need to create a municipal cadre suited for 21st-century Indian cities.

Another avenue for talent acquisition is to hire Urban Fellows—a skilled workforce working in the city government across functions—to lend their expertise to different functions for a period of two to three years. A concept fast gaining traction in India at the CM level, the ULBs should hire Urban Fellows with a time-bound contract to help them on a range of issues. Given the embedded exit clause and talent brought by these Fellows, states and ULBs have much to gain by hiring Urban Fellows.

DATA, TECH AND CITY: THE TRIFECTA FOR LEAPFROGGING

All the talk these days is around Smart Cities, not only in India and but worldwide. When China launched sponge cities, it was the same. Before that, the buzzword was 'sustainable' cities and then 'liveable' cities and so on. This is the age of cities, of frontier tech, of 5G, data colonization and sovereignty, and e-governance; hence the world's focus on 'smart' cities. In the Indian context, smart cities are not just about high-tech interventions. However, data, technology and urban governance—together can help Indian cities leapfrog in more ways than one.

A city conducts hundreds of millions of transactions and interactions in a year—people to people, people to business, people to government, government to government, business to business and business to government. All this data, across departments, is stored but not made accessible. When cities put out such data in a consumable format, the researchers, academia, private sector, citizens and the government itself can study the nature of such interactions—time taken, number of interactions, major obstacles, efficiency and costs incurred, and so on. In studying this data, we can find the bottlenecks of governance.

It is highly pertinent to note that one doesn't go to a Central or state ministry for day-to-day transactions such as licence renewal, building permits, water connection, registering property, complaining about garbage or overflowing sewer, or paying property taxes. They go to local offices. So far as these transactions are made online, in a time-bound and cost-effective manner and have clear yet crisp instructions, hundreds of millions of Indians will save billions of hours every year that can be used in better living and economic activities. In resolving the local governance, India's growth story emerges. There is merit in following an Open Data policy—at the city level.

Open Data gained traction when Barack Obama passed an executive order in 2013, which made open and machine-readable data a default for government information (obamawhitehouse.archives.gov/open). Since then, worldwide and in India, it has been increasingly used at national and state levels, though much remains to be done at the city-level. India's Smart Cities Mission is using the Data Maturity Assessment Framework (DMAF) that evaluates the data readiness of smart cities. The DataSmart Cities Strategy has appointed chief data officers in smart cities to prepare the institutional and technical infrastructure for decisions to be made based on data (Chakraborty, 2019). Together they will help India move towards an open data policy.

There are two important areas where such an open data policy could help—the first is the workload around the Right to Information (RTI), a noble initiative that has solved many problems but has burdened the already overstretched bureaucracy (Raja, 2016). Putting data in public could reduce the number of RTI requests. Second is the unavailability of shape-files for drawing digital maps (ibid.). These files are sold at a high price, which excludes individual developers and researchers. More importantly, it might not earn as much revenue as it holds back the private sector solutions to public issues. Providing such maps for cities with a population of more than a lakh people could unlock a lot of economic value. Some cities are already leveraging open data for better governance.

Boston CityScore was launched in January 2015. It is an online tool that combines scores from twenty-three metrics, including library users, crime rates, and potholes repaired, among others (World Bank, 2018; CityScore, n.d.). A score over 1 means that Boston is outperforming the target and a score less than 1 implies under-performance. This has helped attract resources and attention towards city services that had been under-performing. For instance, the data helped the mayor to increase financial resources to improve emergency response times, commensurate with the increase in city population. This change is part of the overall trend in the US cities which gather data from wide-ranging sources to improve governance and services. Other cities with similar initiatives include Log Angeles, New York, Houston among others. In London too, Transport for London has 8,500 registered developers that have built over 500 apps, used by 42 per cent of Londoners (Raja, 2016). One app is Citymapper, which plans the route for travellers; another is the Colour Blind Tube Map, which helps colour-blind people understand the colour-coded London tube (ibid.). As mobile penetration and cheap mobile data continues to rise in India, the moment Indian cities apply an open data policy, the feedback and grievance redressal loop will be closed on major indicators in no time.

A fraction of Indians now use more data than many countries put together and data consumption in India is set to breach the data consumption levels of the US and China. There is no reason why this data consumption and technology penetration should not be leveraged for urban governance. The above discussed open-cities framework is one such reform. The other strategies include hiring chief data officers and chief technology officer cadre at the ULB level on a contractual basis, since the nature of data and tech-based governance is such that the talent hired should be updated with the latest developments and should be continuously sourced from outside the government. Moreover, the metropolitan cities should also be given the mandate eventually to design regulatory frameworks for emerging technologies. This will allow the cities to compete to provide a conducive regulatory environment to attract the best talent, new technologies and investments.

In the twenty-first century, the local governance devolution cannot overlook regulatory management at the ULB level of the data and technology environment. India would need to improve access to the internet. As per the Inclusive Internet Index 2019, India ranks forty-seventh, despite scoring high on affordability and readiness (EIU, 2019b). The arrival of the Jio Network and the consequent competition in the market, apart from policy and literacy readiness, are factors that work in India's favour. The low rank on the Inclusive Internet Index 2019 is largely a function of relevance—local and relevant content availability—poor usage and network quality. If technology has to become a defining feature of urban governance, internet access, quality and affordability would remain key.

India launched the Smart Cities Mission in 2015. It was one of the key planks of the development narrative painted by Narendra Modi during his 2013–14 election campaign. Indians heard about it for the first time and to date are coming in terms of the definition. The book *Smart Cities Unbundled,* by Sameer Sharma, the first mission director of Smart Cities Mission in India says:

> The Indian Smart Cities Mission adapted and redefined the global discourse around 'Smart Cities' to create its own unique take on a 'Smart City', one that features but is not centred exclusively on technology and includes a strong emphasis on area-based development, citizen preferences and basic infrastructure and services (Sharma, 2018).

The Mission includes projects on city improvement (retrofitting), city renewal (redevelopment), city extension (greenfield development) and pan-city initiatives. India shortlisted 100 cities for smart city projects and they are executed through a 50:50 Special Purpose Vehicle (SPV) between the state and the Central government. Unlike in many other countries, Indian smart cities do not only focus on the use of technology but also on change in urban governance, planning, financing and infrastructure changes that improve the ease of living. Some of these projects are smart roads, smart solar, smart wastewater, public private partnerships (PPP), and smart water projects. Since we have already discussed such moves in the book, we are more concerned about the use of technology. We are very far from the dystopian future of science fiction novels, but the change is still a sharp departure from what our cities used to be.

First, with the use of information and communication technology (ICT) and tech-enabled solutions cities can create insights that can resolve major issues in the city such as infrastructure creation, crime rates, road safety, improvement in governance and ease of doing business. These are bound to support the growth potential of our cities. The ongoing initiatives of Data Maturity Assessment Framework, City Investments to Innovate, Integrate and Sustain (CITIIS) Challenge, CimateSmart Cities Assessment Framework and India Urban Observatory will yield long-term benefits. The frontier technologies of artificial intelligence, 3-D printing, machine learning, Internet of Things and blockchain together form a set of powerful new technologies that can help solve issues that India has struggled with for decades.

Second, such projects in smart cities give an option to urban ecology in India to experiment that it wouldn't have otherwise had (due to the absence of agenda-setting or separate resources). Such experiments are important for innovation in an urban context. These projects could act as a lighthouse for other cities to emulate, with ready standard operating procedures to follow. Third, the recognition of the importance of data in cities has gained traction due to such a dedicated mission. It is a matter of time before a large amount of such data is put in the public for all stakeholders to study and analyse. There have been instances where cities have been transformed as they made their data available.

In 2009 Michael Bloomberg launched a competition called BigApps in which he offered a prize to people who could come up with a software to 'help people "use" New York better' (Hollis, 2013). He opened up the city's online data resource, the NYC Data Mine. Within three months, eighty apps were launched. Some of them helped people find cabs, some helped in locating subway stations and some even to find public libraries. The following year, a second competition was launched with higher prize money. This led to the generation of a new set of apps, one focused on finding a parking spot and one helped in telling the real-time info on public transit and road conditions (ibid.). Some Indian smart cities are already working towards this. For instance, Surat's SURATiLAB and Bhopal's B-Nest Foundation are providing platforms to support start-ups working on city issues (Chakraborty, 2019). The civic-tech is soon going to reach a tipping point in India. Smart cities can serve as laboratories to innovate and scale such solutions. The Indian government is already trying to match cities with start-ups to do the same (ibid.).

Fourth, the introduction of the word 'smart' has influenced the narrative in favour of ease of living in cities. This adds an extra element of quality, affordability, financial sustenance, lower transaction costs, and experiential value to day-to-day activities and interactions within the city. Fifth, the smart cities could lead to transforming governance as the digital interaction between people, government, private sector and infrastructure could instantly close the feedback loop through triangulation. It would be easier, faster and cheaper to respond to citizen's issues.

Sixth, and perhaps most important in the aftermath of the Covid-19 crisis, is the role of smart cities in integrated and emergency response to citywide calamities and contagions. Forty-seven operational Integrated Command and Control Centres (ICCCs), created under SCM, acted as 'war rooms' to monitor citywide efforts (PIB, 2020e). Cities like Bengaluru, Surat and Pune (for the Pimpri-Chinchwad area) got city staff, volunteers and health workers to operate these centres (Kumar et al., 2020). As per a WEF report, some of the key activities executed by these ICCCs during Covid-19 included tracking and providing healthcare to infected people, ensuring the doorstep supply of essential goods, supplying food to vulnerable sections of the city, information dissemination and setting up healthcare and quarantine facilities.

The advent of smart cities comes with its own set of risks and concerns. One of the risks a tech-driven citizen faces is that of digital resilience. As more people, businesses, infrastructure, services and data are connected digitally, the risk of cyber blackouts, either due to natural hazards, terrorist attacks, technical issues, or even poor administration, increases. Worse still, the awareness of cyber security issues is lower in residents of smaller cities as compared to people in larger cities; thereby, making them more vulnerable to cyber attacks (*HinduBL*, 2019). The concern around managing India's digital resilience will grow with the rising uptake of SCM; but, as the world move towards such adoption of ICT and frontier technology, it is worth the risk.

A city's resilience strategy should allocate at least the minimum resources needed to create a plan to pre-empt and resolve such a crisis. Second is the ongoing issue of parallel administrative capacities functioning separately from the local government. Councillors and mayors do not hold leadership positions under the SCM, instead, these are headed by state government officials (Praja, 2020b). Separate administrative structures would not help in building local capacities and, hence, there must be an expiry date by when such projects would be converged with the local government. Capacity building to handle such projects is key. Municipal staff, in Tier 2 and Tier 3 cities, fail to deliver on even the most basic things on time, such as issuing contracts. Therefore, to leverage such technologies, they would need people from the outside—lateral hires.

Third, the issue of digital divide needs to be addressed to ensure that there is universal digital literacy and access, to ensure marginalized sections are not further marginalized. Fourth, Indian cities would have to create the right governance structures. The twenty-first century new technologies are operating in the realm that cannot be governed by twentieth-century laws and institutions (India still manages with nineteenth-century laws). Will the Twelfth Schedule need amendment to help cities execute the functions related to smart cities? The issues of digital literacy, safety, security, data localization, cyber warfare, hacking, privacy and surveillance are some of the dangers of these technologies and unprotected data.

The function of cities has been to push up and forward the limits of human civilization's capabilities. The prosperity, jobs, innovation, human resource, connectivity, efficiency and governance are all part of this broader goal. 'Smart cities' is just a new term to accommodate the new developments in the world. There were many such terms before smart cities and there will be many more after this. However, like all those maxims of sustainability, liveability, safety, inclusivity, equity and economic efficiency, smart cities also need to be capitalized till we move on to the new global development in the world. For cities are nothing but humankind's longest-running experiment.

Epilogue

Few non-urban planning scholars have attempted such a comprehensive academic exercise and fewer still from the younger generation. So it's a special occasion indeed when I write the epilogue to my former colleague Devashish's first book.

The topic of urbanisation attracts mostly the senior citizens like me. In that sense, Devashish's work is a brave endeavour. In post-independence India, cities were largely considered a hangover from the days of the centralized planned economy. Devashish's work reinforces the growing trend of (finally, at least in India) recognizing that cities are primarily economic entities – often the principle drivers of growth and employment in emerging economies – whose success underpins the progress of the nation.

A study of urbanization is largely the study of the entire economy and major political-economic trends. A brief but fascinating tour of global and Indian history through the lens of cities and urbanization would be a delight for political economy enthusiasts. As he did in NITI Aayog, Devashish has brought his piercing insights, intellectual honesty and bucketful of facts to establish that the relevance and importance of Indian cities will only grow exponentially in the coming decades. The world is already taking notice, and our cities will become a major draw for global investors and entrepreneurs.

This book cogently deals with multiple dimensions of urbanization and lucidly unpacks all major issues thwarting the rapid growth of our cities. While several specific issues are dealt with in relevant sections, the constant themes in the book are economics, history, international relations and governance.

Devashish's academic training and strong interdisciplinary knowledge and experience gives this text a lucidity and wholesomeness that's accessible to lay readers as well. I hope this starts conversations on many under-explored issues and reinvigorates debates that have lost the desired sharpness and focus. The book will be of interest to a wide readership, including policymakers, global corporate managers, investors, and all those in India and abroad who are curious to understand India's past performance and likely future trajectories.

It is important to approach this volume keeping in mind the flux around us, India's rise in the global theatre, and the vagaries of the post-Covid-19 world. It is indeed a fortuitous coincidence that Devashish was working on this volume when it seemed fashionable to write off cities.

This is a remarkable debut, which should not be ignored. Over the coming years, I see it emerging as an essential reference on Indian cities and India's political economy. I hope readers enjoy the book as much as I did!

Dr Rajiv Kumar
Chairman, Pehle India Foundation
Former Vice-Chairman, NITI Aayog

Acknowledgements

At NITI Aayog, when I started working on urbanization in 2016, I only knew the basics about urbanization, and I looked for a one-stop book to ramp up myself. Since I could not find any, in 2019, I decided to write one. To write about urbanization and Indian cities is to write about the entire Indian political economy.

NITI Aayog gave me that opportunity. I want to thank Dr Rajiv Kumar, Amitabh Kant and Dr Arvind Panagariya for giving me an opportunity to work on India's defining national policy documents— Three Year Action Agenda and Strategy for New India@75. For throwing the 'VC-team' in the deep end on new sectors and believing that we will not disappoint. For giving incredible opportunities to be in the same room that hosted labour and farmer representatives, India's most powerful corporate leaders, leading economists and maverick thought leaders, young innovators and veteran think tanks and enthusiastic NGOs. For anchoring Prime Minister and Cabinet Minister-level stakeholder consultations and giving a chance to write speeches for the Prime Minister and the President of India. Five Years at NITI Aayog were a masterclass in policymaking. Without such holistic knowledge of Indian political economy this book would not have been possible. I specially convey my gratitude to Dr Rajiv Kumar and Amitabh Kant for encouraging the 'VC team' to write and write—

and creating a NITI-Aayog-wide culture of young laterals and seasoned bureaucrats writing on policy issues. This had a wider impact of many young people contributing to the national discourse on policy.

At NITI Aayog, I learned about specific topics and policymaking from senior bureaucrats—urbanization from Sunita Sanghi, Parag Gupta, Jeetendra Singh; energy and power from Anil Jain and Rajnath Ram; water resources from Avinash Mishra and Jeetendra Kumar; education from Dr Prem Singh; science and technology from Dr Neeraj Sinha; health from Alok Kumar; and many other senior civil servants working on range of issues.

The other part of learning came from a young workforce of lateral entrants of which I was a part as well. These young people, trained in specific areas, from world's best universities, decided to deep-dive into the rumble tumble of policymaking in India. Out of few hundred lateral entrants that I worked and interacted with, I should mention Dhiraj Nayyar, Rahul Ahluwalia, Urvashi Prasad, Atisha Kumar and Chinmay Goyal, who along with Vaibhav Kapoor, Ranveer Nagaich and I comprised a team that worked with the two vice-chairmen and the CEO of NITI Aayog. We undertook several challenging assignments, and I came out a stronger and better professional as they strove for the best. Vaibhav and Ranveer as friends, peers and brothers believed in the book—constantly reading the drafts, brainstorming and providing an escape to think big. Above all—in the long corridors, massive conference rooms and not-so-well-lit rooms of NITI Aayog—I had a chance to hear and speak to countless stakeholders across all walks of professions about ideas and policies for India to meet its promised destiny. In doing so, urban policy and cities came up again and again and I am deeply indebted to those conversations. There are many conversations that I will never be able to fully acknowledge but have left an indelible impact on my policy career and intellectual curiosity. Such exposure of working with senior civil servants and young laterals allowed me to truly take a multidisciplinary approach to writing this book.

As urbanization covers a whole range of topics, I turned towards stalwarts and sector specialists to build upon their work and learn the basics. Dr Romila Thapar on history of Indian civilization, Tony Joseph for tracing early urbanization and migration, Late Dr Isher Judge Ahluwalia for championing urbanization when it wasn't fashionable to do so, Dr Prasanna Mohanty for writing the most elaborate and accessible books on Indian cities and how to leverage them, Sanjeev Sanyal for his deep understanding of Indian cities and urbanization, Dr Partha Mukhopadhyay for keeping alive the debate on cities and its merits outside of the government, Indu Banga for her work on history of Indian cities, Dr Bimal Patel for his practitioner's perspective, Dr Chinmay Tumbe for his dedicated work on migration, Jane Jacobs for her activism in twentieth-century America and detailed works of Lewis Mumford among others. I also received incredible learnings from the works of Prof. Edward Glaeser of Harvard University—all his books and papers have waged a worthy battle in defense of cities. The book by Prof. Sean Fox and Prof. Tom Goodfellow on urbanization was a steady guiding light in navigating topics of urban political economy. Prof. Enrico Moretti's book, *The New Geography of Jobs*, refreshed my understanding of urban economics and jobs.

In the context of urban policy in India, there are few organizations that are doing outstanding work for advancing the cause of cities in India. These include Centre for Policy Research, Indian Council for Research on International Economic Relations, World Resources Institute, IDFC Institute (now Artha Global), ORF and Janaagraha. I want to specially thank Srikanth Viswanathan of Janaagraha and Dr Samir Saran and his team at ORF working on urban policy, including Rumi Aijaz, Aditi Ratho and Sayli Udas Mankikar. They have together stepped up the conversation around Indian cities. IDFC Institute is doing a formidable job in advancing the role of cities in the Indian growth story and I have relied on the works of their scholars including—Dr Reuben Abraham, Pritika Hingorani, Dr Vaidehi Tandel, Patrick Lamson-Hall and Kadambari Shah. The work of all these organizations was critical in shaping my thought process and providing evidence for my recommendations. These organizations together are filing a lacuna in our national understanding of cities, and we should be thankful for their work. The above-mentioned experts, organizations and NITI Aayog assignments and colleagues are the building blocks of my book.

I have built over their work. I have tried to the best of my abilities to attribute relevant references and any omission to due reference is purely inadvertent and regretted.

There are different people who have at different stages supported my journey in public service career and writing. They all believed in me and played a critical role in shaping my thought process, work ethics, professional journey and risk-taking appetite. I want to thank my friends Varun Madan, Sidharth Dhawan, Satyam Arora, Vishal Saxena, Kushal Sinha, Manish Thakre (he also provided feedback on drafts and trusted the project a little more than I did), Sandeep Ghosh, Pramod Bhat, Varun Reddy, Ruchi Gupta and Ravi Pokharna. A special thanks to Dr Vinay Sahasrabuddhe, Dr Shashi Tharoor, Dr Rajiv Kumar and Amitabh Kant for giving me an opportunity to contribute to nation-building, while I continued to invest in my career. Some teachers indulged my passion for public service and my professional pursuits—the kind that leaves little room for pauses as you talk about what you want to do in life. These professors are Shalini Prakash, Dr Razeen Sally, Dr Arun Thiruvengadam, Dr Yuen Foong Khong, Dr Namrata Chindarkar and Dr Karen Dynan.

I cannot thank Prema Govindan of HarperCollins India enough for accepting the idea of this book in its raw form, patiently working with me and keeping me on track to finish this huge project. I thank the HarperCollins team—Antony Thomas for proofreading, Saurav Das for designing the cover and Sashi Aiyer for copy-editing. Their effort and insight have carried this project to fruition.

The first seeds of pursuing a career in public service were sown when I grew up in a large joint family in Lucknow. Some family members conscientiously fueled the habits of thinking big, reading, writing and following my interests. My grandparents on both sides believed in simple and principled living and they inculcated the sense of 'us' with the family and larger community. I think that was the first spark of contributing to public service. And this book is continuation of my public service work.

My parents—Neelam and Ashok—have done a rare job in creating a safe space for me to switch careers multiple times, take massive pay cuts, not pursue money alone and aspire way beyond the means of a typical middle-class family of Lucknow. I will never know the source of such indefatigable optimism and support; but I hope to inherit part of it as I do want to inherit their spiritual pursuits. This sense of love and undying support has been extended to me by my family—Ankit, Saumya and Anshul. If it were not for Ankit and Anshul, I would have to be more 'practical' in my professional pursuits.

I would like to thank the work and words of Pandit Nehru and Theodore Roosevelt—great men with faults of their own. But they are my intellectual north stars and their work has taught me a lot about compassion, public service, curiosity, power of writing and the outcome of boundless optimism and energy.

All this inspiration and motivation would have mattered less to nothing, if it wasn't for my partner and friend, Shruti. I lucked out with her believing in my ridiculous projects, unrealistic goals and believing in lifelong learning—this book lies at the intersection of these pursuits. It doesn't seem as unrealistic as she has pursued a similar life trajectory. She supported this project in countless ways—everyday feedback, pulling me back when I digressed, holding me accountable and honest, and most importantly, being a huge cushion between this project and more practical and wiser worldly pursuits.

Thinking of and thanking one and all.

Bibliography

Abbas, G. (2019). '65% of India's Reservoirs Running Dry, Maharashtra Worst Affected, Shows Water Panel's Report'. *News18.com*, 25 June. https://www.news18.com/news/india/water-crisis-two-third-of-indias-reservoirs-have-below-normal-storage-maximum-are-dry-in-maha-2202279.html

Abbas, M. (2018). 'India has 22 cars per 1,000 individuals: Amitabh Kant'. *ETAuto*, 12 December. https://auto.economictimes.indiatimes.com/news/passenger-vehicle/cars/india-has-22-cars-per-1000-individuals-amitabh-kant/67059021

Abraham, R., Batra, K., and Gandhi, S. (2017). 'Dismantling the permit raj in housing.' *Mint*, 28 March. https://www.livemint.com/Opinion/cdZVqLFVQrDeDP3FyzP2SK/Dismantling-the-permit-raj-in-housing.html

Abraham, R. and Tandel, V. (2020), 'Don't blame dense cities. They have been resilient.' *Hindustan Times*, 15 July. https://www.hindustantimes.com/analysis/don-t-blame-dense-cities-they-have-been-resilient/story-4HJrLnUyT0N3UdzI6y4mWI.html

Acuto, M. (2020). 'Covid-19: Lessons for an Urban(izing) World.' *One Earth* 2, (4): 317–19. https://www.ncbi.nlm.nih.gov/pmc/articles/PMC7159854/

ADB (2015). *Women in the Workforce: An Unmet Potential in Asia and the Pacific.* Manila: Asian Development Bank. https://www.adb.org/sites/default/files/publication/158480/women-workforce-unmet-potential.pdf

———(2016). *Promoting Sustainable Urbanization in Asia and the Pacific.* Proceedings of the ADB–Asian Think Tank Development Forum, 27–28 October. Manila: Asian Development Bank. http://dx.doi.org/10.22617/TCS178713-2

Adlakha, N. (2019). 'Taken for a ride: On India's gender-blind transport system.' *The Hindu,* 19 August. https://www.thehindu.com/society/why-indias-gender-blind-transport-system-needs-an-overhaul/article28935125.ece

———(2020). 'Urban planning for the post-pandemic world.' *The Hindu,* 30 April. https://www.thehindu.com/real-estate/urban-planning-for-the-post-pandemic-world/article31473376.ece

Adler, D. (2016). 'Stories of cities #37: How radical ideas turned Curitiba into Brazil's "green capital".' *The Guardian,* 6 May, https://www.theguardian.com/cities/2016/may/06/story-of-cities-37-mayor-jaime-lerner-curitiba-brazil-green-capital-global-icon

Admiraal, H. and Cornaro, A. (2020). 'Future cities, resilient cities: The role of underground space in achieving urban resilience.' *Underground Space* 5, (3): 223–28. https://doi.org/10.1016/j.undsp.2019.02.001

Agrawal, A. (2017). 'When Bombay overtook Calcutta: A history of India's financial geography.' *Mint,* 24 June. https://www.livemint.com/Sundayapp/Z8DStEXICwm3MFvlE7PFXI/When-Bombay-overtook-Calcutta-A-history-of-Indias-financia.html

Ahluwalia, I.J., and Patel, U. (2018). 'Solid Waste Management in India: An Assessment of Resource Recovery and Environmental Impact.' Working Paper No. 356. New Delhi: Indian Council for Research on International Economic Relations (ICRIER). https://icrier.org/pdf/Working_Paper_356.pdf.

Ahluwalia, I.J. and Patel, A. (2019a). 'How Tamil Nadu got waste management right.' *Financial Express,* 24 April. https://www.financialexpress.com/opinion/how-tamil-nadu-got-waste-management-right/1557142/

———(2019b). 'On waste management, small towns drive big change.' *Financial Express*, 27 February. https://www.financialexpress.com/opinion/on-waste-management-small-towns-drive-big-change/1499461/

Ahluwalia, I.J., and Khare, A. (2019c). 'Cities at Crossroads: A better blueprint for the city.' *The Indian Express*, 31 July. https://indianexpress.com/article/opinion/columns/urban-planning-infrastructure-metropolitan-city-gdp-development-5864860/

Ahluwalia, I.J. (2019a). 'Indian cities need a new planning template'. *Financial Express*, 31 July. https://www.financialexpress.com/opinion/indian-cities-need-a-new-planning-template-heres-why/1661159/

———(2019b). 'Urban governance in India.' *Journal of Urban Affairs* 41, (1): 1–20. https://smartnet.niua.org/sites/default/files/resources/urban_governance_in_india.pdf

AISHE (n.d.). *All-India Survey of Higher Education*. http://aishe.nic.in/aishe/home

Alexander, S. (2019). 'Why Indian cities need directly elected mayors.' *Mint*, 26 November. https://www.livemint.com/politics/news/why-indian-cities-need-directly-elected-mayors-11574751482335.html

Amundi and IFC (2020). *Emerging Market Green Bonds Report 2019: Momentum Builds as Nascent Markets Grow*. Paris: Amundi Asset Management; Washington DC: International Finance Corporation. https://www.ifc.org/wps/wcm/connect/a64560ef-b074-4a53-8173-f678ccb4f9cd/202005-EM-Green-Bonds-Report-2019.pdf?MOD=AJPERES&CVID=n7Gtahg

Ambedkar, B.R. (1936). *Annihilation of Caste*. New Delhi: POD Only Publishing.

Anderson, D. (2016). 'Stories of cities #future: what will our growing megacities really look like?' *The Guardian*, 26 May. https://www.theguardian.com/cities/2016/may/26/story-cities-future-growing-megacities-waste-floating-smart

Annapurani, V. (2019). 'Interactive: India's new mobility story.' *The Hindu BusinessLine*, 15 July https://www.thehindubusinessline.com/economy/interactive-indias-new-mobility-story/article28444434.ece

Aruni, S.K. (2013). 'Made for all communities.' *The Hindu*, 13 March. https://www.thehindu.com/news/cities/bangalore/made-for-all-communities/article4481321.ece

Ashar, S. and Shukla, S. (2014). 'It's no solution to Mumbai's slum problem.' *The Indian Express*, 12 March. https://indianexpress.com/article/cities/mumbai/its-no-solution-to-mumbais-slum-problem/

Athrady, A., and Joy, S. (2020). 'Keeping people safe on India's killer roads.' *Deccan Herald*, 13 September. https://www.deccanherald.com/specials/insight/keeping-people-safe-on-india-s-killer-roads-886704.html

Awasthi, R. and Nagarajan, M. (2020). 'Property Taxation in India: Issues Impacting Revenue Performance and Suggestions for Reform.' Governance Discussion Paper No. 5. Washington, DC: World Bank. https://openknowledge.worldbank.org/bitstream/handle/10986/33655/Property-Taxation-in-India-Issues-Impacting-Revenue-Performance-and-Suggestions-for-Reform.pdf?sequence=1&isAllowed=y

AWPS (2015). 'How Water is Governed: What is Room for the River?' Calgary: Alberta Water Portal Society. https://albertawater.com/how-is-water-governed/what-is-room-for-the-river

Bahuguna, U. (2019). 'When a City Sinks: Chronicling Chennai's flood and the many failures of multiple stakeholders to mitigate and respond to the disaster.' *Open*, 26 August. https://openthemagazine.com/special/when-a-city-sinks/

Bairoch, P. and Goertz, G. (1986). 'Factors of Urbanisation in the Nineteenth Century Developed Countries: A Descriptive and Econometric Analysis.' *Urban Studies* (23): 285–305. https://deepblue.lib.umich.edu/bitstream/handle/2027.42/68656/10.1080_00420988620080351.pdf

Balachandran, P.K. (2019). 'Dimensions of India's water crisis and ways to meet it.' NewsIn Asia, 1 October. https://newsin.asia/dimensions-of-indias-water-crisis-and-ways-to-meet-it/

Balantrapu M. (2017). 'Uber launches Movement, boon for urban planners.' *The Hindu*, 9 January. https://www.thehindu.com/sci-tech/technology/uber-launches-movement-boon-for-urban-planners/article17013513.ece

Ballaney, S. and Patel, B. (2009). 'Using the "Development Plan—Town Planning Scheme" Mechanism to Appropriate Land and Build Urban Infrastructure.' In *India Infrastructure Report*. New Delhi: Oxford University Press.

Ballaney, S., Bertaud, M.A., Clarke Annez, P., Koshy, C.K., Nair, B., Patel, B., Phatak, V., and Thawakar, V. (2013). 'Inventory of Public Land in Ahmedabad, Gujarat, India.' Policy Research Working Paper No. 6664. Washington, DC: World Bank. https://openknowledge.worldbank.org/handle/10986/16878

Banchariya, S. (2019). 'India needs 3 lakh town planners by 2031. Know how you can be one.' *The Times of India*, 8 January. https://timesofindia.indiatimes.com/home/education/news/india-needs-3-lakh-town-planners-by-2031-know-how-you-can-be-one/articleshow/67431428.cms

Banga, I. (ed.). (1991). *The City in Indian History: Urban Demography, Society and Politics*. New Delhi: South Asia Publications.

Bansal, S. (2020). 'Swachh Survekshan 2020: Indore tops in cleanest city category.' India Water Portal, 25 August. https://www.indiawaterportal.org/articles/swachh-survekshan-2020-indore-tops-cleanest-city-category

Barnagarwala, T. (2019). 'Inside India's cleanest city, Indore.' *The Indian Express*, 7 April. https://indianexpress.com/article/india/indore-indias-cleanest-city-swachh-bharat-mission-5662774/

Bathla, N. (2020). 'Housing the migrant worker.' *The Indian Express*, 16 May. https://indianexpress.com/article/opinion/housing-the-migrant-worker/lite/?__twitter_impression=true

Batra, L. (2009). 'A Review of Urbanisation and Urban Policy in Post-Independent India.' Working Paper Series CSLG/WP/12. Centre for the Study of Law and Governance. New Delhi: Jawaharlal Nehru University. https://www.jnu.ac.in/sites/default/files/u63/12-A%20Review%20of%20Urban%20%28Lalit%20Batra%29.pdf

Bertaud, A. (2o02). 'The economic impact of land and urban planning regulations in India.' Memorandum on 'India – Urban Land Reform', April 11. https://alainbertaud.com/wp-content/uploads/2013/06/AB_-India_-Urban_Land_Reform.pdf

———(2018). *Order Without Design: How Markets Shape Cities.* Cambridge, MA: MIT Press.

Bhagat, R.B. (2011). 'Emerging Pattern of Urbanisation in India.' *Economic and Political Weekly* 46, (34): 10–12.

Bharti, A. and Bindushree, D. (2020). 'An unlikely common strand of 2020: land and property rights.' *Hindustan Times*, 24 December. https://www.hindustantimes.com/analysis/an-unlikely-common-strand-of-2020-land-and-property-rights/story-U9WkOuxxzlOW7CCb844GnI.html

Bharathi, N., Malghan, D.V., and Rahman, A. (2018). 'Isolated by Caste: Neighbourhood-Scale Residential Segregation in Indian Metros.' Working Paper, 2018–08. Ithaca, NY: Dyson School Applied Economics and Management, Cornell University.

———(2019). *The Hindu* on Twitter, 20 January. https://www.thehindu.com/news/cities/bangalore/study-reveals-caste-based-segregation-in-bengaluru/article26039905.ece/amp/?__twitter_impression=true

Bharathi, N. and Ul-Huda, K. (2020). 'Why Lucknow, Jaipur don't see communal riots but Delhi and Ahmedabad do.' The Print, 13 March. https://theprint.in/opinion/why-lucknow-jaipur-dont-see-communal-riots-but-delhi-and-ahmedabad-do/380171/

Bhowmick, N. (2019). 'How women in India demanded—and are getting—safer streets.' *National Geographic*, 15 October. https://www.nationalgeographic.com/culture/article/how-women-in-india-demanded-and-are-getting-safer-streets-feature

Blattman, C., Green, D., Ortega, D., and Tobon, S. (2017). 'Place Based Interventions at Scale: The Direct and Spillover Effects of Policing and City Services on Crime.' Last revised 2 December 2021. Abdul Latif Jameel Poverty Action Lab (J-PAL) http://dx.doi.org/10.2139/ssrn.3050823

Bloomberg Quicktake (2021). 'How Japan Is Building Disaster-Proof Skyscrapers.' YouTube video, 13:02, 15 January. https://www.youtube.com/watch?v=c5X8OK1V2_c&t=23s

Brown, C., de Lannoy, A., McCracken, D., Gill, T., Grant, M., Wright, H., and Williams, S. (2019). 'Leading Editorial, Special issue: child-friendly cities.' *Cities & Health* 3, (1-2): 1–7. DOI: 10.1080/23748834.2019.1682836

Buchner, B., Clark, A., Falconer, A., Macquarie, R., Meattle, C., Tolentino, R. and Wetherbee, C. (2019). 'Global Landscape of Climate Finance 2019.' Climate Policy Initiative. https://www.climatepolicyinitiative.org/publication/global-landscape-of-climate-finance-2019/

Business Today (2020). 'India surpasses France, UK to become world's 5th largest economy: IMF'. *BusinessToday.in*, 23 February. https://www.businesstoday.in/current/economy-politics/india-surpasses-france-uk-to-become-world-5th-largest-economy-imf/story/396717.html

——— (2021). 'India adds 28 unicorns in 2021 to take total to 66; over 3.3 lakh people employed: Nasscom'. *BusinessToday.in*, 5 December. https://www.businesstoday.in/entrepreneurship/news/story/india-adds-28-unicorns-in-2021-to-take-total-to-66-over-33-lakh-people-employed-nasscom-307845-2021-09-28

Carr, C. (2015). 'The best idea to redevelop Dharavi slum? Scrap the plans and start again.' *The Guardian*, 15 February. https://www.theguardian.com/cities/2015/feb/18/best-ideas-redevelop-dharavi-slum-developers-india

Chakrabarty, A. (2020a). 'COVID-19, JAGA Mission and the value of already existing solutions.' Guest Blog, 4 June. London: International Institute for Environment and Development. https://www.iied.org/covid-19-jaga-mission-value-already-existing-solutions

Chakraborty, N. (2020b). 'Demand for retail units may go up but supply may not match up.' *Mint*, 4 June. https://www.livemint.com/money/personal-finance/demand-for-rental-units-may-go-up-but-supply-may-not-match-up-11591291508285.html

Chakraborty, P. (2019). 'Game-Changing the Smart City Mission.' BW SmartCities, 9 December. http://bwsmartcities.businessworld.in/article/-Game-Changing-the-Smart-City-Mission/09-12-2019-180075/

Chandra, J. (2020). 'Only 7 in 100 anganwadi beneficiaries are in cities.' *The Hindu*, 5 February. https://www.thehindu.com/news/national/only-7-in-100-anganwadi-beneficiaries-are-in-cities/article30736445.ece

Chandra, S. (2020). *History of Medieval India.* Hyderabad: Orient BlackSwan.

Chandrasekhar, C.P. and Ghosh, J. (2018). 'Rise of Contract Workers in Manufacturing.' *The Hindu,* 12 March. https://www.thehindubusinessline.com/opinion/columns/c-p-chandrasekhar/rise-of-contract-workers-in-manufacturing/article20761216.ece1

Chandrashekhar, S. and Naik, M. (2020). 'Giving migrant workers a better deal: Centre, states must ensure migrant workers are not left in the lurch.' *Financial Express,* 8 May. https://www.financialexpress.com/opinion/giving-migrant-workers-a-better-deal-centre-states-must-ensure-migrant-workers-are-not-left-in-the-lurch/1951684/

Chatterji, R. (2018). 'India's Pollution Problem Can't Be Solved By State Governments In Isolation, Says Writer Siddharth Singh.' *HuffPost,* 3 December. https://www.huffpost.com/archive/in/entry/indias-pollution-problem-cant-be-solved-by-state-governments-in-isolation-says-writer-siddharth-singh_a_23601785?ncid=other_huffpostre_pqylmel2bk8&utm_campaign=related_articles

Chaturvedi, A. (2017). *Police Reforms in India.* New Delhi: PRS Legislative Research. https://prsindia.org/files/policy/policy_analytical_reports/Police%20Reforms%20in%20India.pdf

Chaudhury, K.S. (2020). 'India emerges as the second-largest mobile phone manufacturer: Ravi Shankar Prasad.' Times Now, 2 June. https://www.timesnownews.com/technology-science/article/india-emerges-as-the-second-largest-mobile-phone-manufacturer-in-the-world-ravi-shankar-prasad/600184

Chen, M.A. and Raveendran, G. (2014). 'Urban Employment in India: Recent Trends and Patterns.' WIEGO Working Papers. Manchester: Women in Informal Employment Globalizing and Organizing.

Chitlangia, R. (2019). 'Five Delhi Metro stations shortlisted for transit-oriented development.' *Hindustan Times,* 14 March. https://www.hindustantimes.com/delhi-news/five-delhi-metro-stations-shortlisted-for-transit-oriented-development/story-f4yCuzweZXK0h71kcS7ZYP.html

Chopra, R. (2019). 'Explained: Why Lok Sabha is still 543.' *The Indian Express,* 14 October. https://indianexpress.com/article/explained/article-81-constitution-explained-why-lok-sabha-is-still-543-6067542/

Churchill, W. (1946). 'Cold War.' Transcript of excerpts from former British Prime Minister Winston Churchill's Speech (5 March) at the Potsdam Conference. https://www.nationalarchives.gov.uk/education/coldwar/G3/cs2/s1_t.htm

CII (n.d.). 'Urban Development.' New Delhi: Confederation of Indian Industry. http://www.cii.in/sectors.aspx?enc=prvePUj2bdMtgTmvPwvisYH+5EnGjyGXO9hLECvTuNtoz3TzLW8nZchXA7a5U/wJ

CityScore (n.d.). 'Health scores for the City of Boston.' https://www.boston.gov/innovation-and-technology/cityscore

Clarke Annez, P. and Gangopadhyay, S. (n.d.). 'India's Public Lands: Responsive, Transparent, and Fiscally Responsible Asset Management.' Gurugram IDF. https://www.idfresearch.org/uploads/R_a_c_e/1547204311_92201612234653.pdf

Clark, G. (2016). *Global Cities: A Short History*. Washington DC: Brookings Institution Press.

Climate Transparency (2020). *Climate Transparency Report: Comparing G20 Climate Action and Responses to the Covid-19 Crisis*. https://www.climate-transparency.org/wp-content/uploads/2020/11/Climate-Transparency-Report-2020.pdf

Dalal, M. (2019). 'IITs in Delhi, Mumbai churn out most tech entrepreneurs.' *Mint*, 16 September. https://www.livemint.com/companies/news/iits-in-delhi-mumbai-churn-out-most-tech-entrepreneurs-1568652902193.html

Das, R. Krishna (2017). 'Thanks to women, Ambikapur becomes first waste-free town in Chhattisgarh.' *Business Standard*, 16 May. https://www.business-standard.com/article/current-affairs/thanks-to-women-ambikapur-becomes-first-waste-free-town-in-chhattisgarh-117051600735_1.html

Dash, D.K. (2017). 'Centre asks states to professionalise municipal cadres.' *The Times of India*, 28 February. https://timesofindia.indiatimes.com/india/centre-asks-states-to-professionalise-municipal-cadres/articleshow/57397822.cms

Dasra India (2017). 'India's First Faecal Sludge Treatment Plant.' YouTube video, 7:56. 19 May. https://www.youtube.com/watch?v=WZgT2Vwfvwc

Davidson N.C. (2016). 'Wetland Losses and the Status of Wetland-Dependent Species.' In *The Wetland Book*, edited by C. Finlayson, G. Milton, R. Prentice and N. Davidson. Dordrecht: Springer. https://doi.org/10.1007/978-94-007-6173-5_197-1

Davies, S. (2018), Cities go wild with child-friendly design'. Thomson Reuters Foundation, 30 May. https://news.trust.org/item/20180530070028-5aplu/

Deb, S. (1996). *The India Infrastructure Report: Policy Imperatives for Growth and Welfare.* Report of the Expert Group on the Commercialisation of Infrastructure Projects. New Delhi: National Council of Applied Economic Research; Ministry of Finance, Government of India.

Desilver, D. (2016). 'The growing Democratic domination of nation's largest counties.' Washington, DC: Pew Research Centre, 21 July. https://www.pewresearch.org/fact-tank/2016/07/21/the-growing-democratic-domination-of-nations-largest-counties/

De Soto, H. (2000). *The Mystery of Capital: Why Capital Triumphs in the West and Fails Everywhere Else.* London: Bantam Press.

Dhar, D. and Kapoor, V. (2018). 'Indian cities as investment destinations.' *Financial Express*, 19 July. https://www.financialexpress.com/opinion/indian-cities-as-investment-destinations/1250003/

Dhar, D. (2018a). 'Power sector: India's new found tool for strategic posturing.' *The Times of India*, 20 October. https://timesofindia.indiatimes.com/blogs/palimpsest/power-sector-indias-new-found-tool-for-strategic-posturing/

———(2018b). 'Why there should be more pedestrians.' *Mint*, 25 October. https://www.livemint.com/Opinion/Y4PVDCDQUYuk0iXlWKjXcK/Opinion--Why-there-should-be-more-pedestrians.html

———(2018c). 'Realistic policies to revive public spaces.' *Mint*, 3 April. https://www.livemint.com/Opinion/pFzFKRAIo1FQ4FMrpbjADP/Realistic-policies-to-revive-public-spaces.html

Dhar, D and Thakre, M. (2020). 'No Child's Play: The Enduring Challenge of Creating Child-Friendly Cities.' *ORF Issue Brief No. 415*. New Delhi: Observer Research Foundation.

Divya, A. (2020). 'Explained: Who is a 'street vendor' in India? What is the Street Vendors Act?' *The Indian Express*, 6 November. https://indianexpress.com/article/explained/street-vendor-act-pm-svanidhi-scheme-explained-6911120/

DNA (2019). 'Higher FSI to make homes cheaper: Gujarat CM Vijay Rupani.' *DNA*, 24 September. https://www.dnaindia.com/ahmedabad/report-higher-fsi-to-make-homes-cheaper-gujarat-cm-vijay-rupani-2791973

Dobbs, R., Remes, J., Manyika, J., Roxburgh, C., Smit, S. and Schaer, F. (2012). *Urban world: Cities and the rise of the consuming class.* Washington DC: McKinsey Global Institute. https://lobbyfacts.eu/representative/80577823dc594bd6b065c9bb8667a3ae/mckinsey-global-institute

Duduta, N., Adriazola-Steil, C., Hidalgo, D., John, V. and Wass, C. (2015). 'Traffic Safety on Bus Priority Systems.' Washington DC: World Resources Institute. https://www.wri.org/research/traffic-safety-bus-priority-systems

EIU (2019a). *Safe Cities Index 2019: Urban security and resilience in an interconnected world.* London: The Economist Intelligence Unit Ltd. https://safecities.economist.com/wp-content/uploads/2019/08/Aug-5-ENG-NEC-Safe-Cities-2019-270x210-19-screen.pdf

———(2019b). 'The Inclusive Internet Index 2019.' https://theinclusiveinternet.eiu.com/explore/countries/IN/?year=2019

Elgin, C. and Oyvat, C. (2013). 'Lurking in the Cities: Urbanization and the Informal Economy.' *Structural Change and Economic Dynamics* 27, (C): 36–47.

ENS (2020). 'Eastern waterfront: "Redevelopment will lead to 62% of open space".' *The Indian Express*, 29 February. https://indianexpress.com/article/cities/mumbai/eastern-waterfront-redevelopment-will-lead-to-62-per-cent-of-open-space-6292007/

EPA (n.d.). 'Clean Air Act Overview: Progress Cleaning the Air and Improving People's Health.' United States Environmental Protection Agency. https://www.epa.gov/clean-air-act-overview/progress-cleaning-air-and-improving-peoples-health

ET Bureau. (2018). 'ET View: Policy focus needed for sewage treatment plants.' *The Economic Times*, 2 October. https://economictimes.

indiatimes.com/opinion/et-view/et-view-policy-focus-needed-for-sewage-treatment-plants/articleshow/66041958.cms

Fan, P. (2018). 'Catching Up In Economic Transition: Innovation in the People's Republic of China, and India.' ADBI Working Paper 809. Manila: Asian Development Bank Institute.

Firstpost (2020). 'Decentralised urban governance a far cry in most Indian cities, shows NGO Praja Foundation's urban governance index.' 9 December. https://www.firstpost.com/india/decentralised-urban-governance-a-far-cry-in-most-indian-cities-shows-ngo-praja-foundations-urban-governance-index-9093451.html

Firstpost (2022). 'Mumbai Climate Action Plan: BMC's plan to build climate-resilient city, achieve net-zero carbon emissions by 2050.' 14 March. https://www.firstpost.com/india/mumbai-climate-action-plan-bmcs-plan-to-build-climate-resilient-city-achieve-net-zero-carbon-emissions-by-2050-10458531.html#:~:text=Brihanmumbai%20Municipal%20Corporation%20(BMC)%20on,zero%20carbon%20emissions%20by%202050.

Fitjar, R. and Rodriguez-Pose, A. (2016). 'Purpose-built versus serendipitous innovation links: New survey evidence.' *Vox-EU CEPR,* 11 April. https://voxeu.org/article/marshall-was-wrong-nothing-air

Fleming, A. (2018). 'What would a city that is safe for woman look like?' *The Guardian*, 13 December. https://www.theguardian.com/cities/2018/dec/13/what-would-a-city-that-is-safe-for-women-look-like

Florida, R. (2019). 'How Some Shrinking Cities Are Still Prospering.' Bloomberg CityLab, June 14. https://www.bloomberg.com/news/articles/2019-06-13/some-cities-are-getting-smaller-richer-and-elite

Fox, S. and Goodfellow, T. (2016). *Cities and Development.* Second edition. Routledge Perspective on Development series. New York, NY: Routledge.

Frangoul, A. (2020). 'India has some huge renewable energy goals. But can they be achieved?' *CNBC,* 3 March. Sustainable Energy series. https://www.cnbc.com/2020/03/03/india-has-some-huge-renewable-energy-goals-but-can-they-be-achieved.html

Frankopan, P. (2015). *The Silk Roads: A New History of the World.* London: Bloomsbury.

Ganesh, V. (n.d.). 'Revitalising urban governance in India: What does it really take?' Urban Canvas series. Bengaluru: Janaagraha. http://www.janaagraha.org/revitalising-urban-governance-in-india-what-does-it-really-take

Garfield, L. (2017). '13 cities that are starting to ban cars.' *Business Insider*, 5 August. https://www.businessinsider.in/tech/13-cities-that-are-starting-to-ban-cars/articleshow/59932753.cms

Garg. A. (2020). 'Average Bengaluru Driver Waste 243 Hours in Traffic Every Year, Worst Congestion in the World.' News 18, 3 February. https://www.news18.com/news/auto/average-bengaluru-driver-waste-243-hours-in-traffic-every-year-worst-congestion-in-the-world-2477621.html

Gaur, P. (2013). 'Ahmedabad: The perfect metropolis.' *Mint*, 23 January. https://www.livemint.com/Politics/fQ5eWMXxCfAYXU4V527vfN/Ahmedabad-The-perfect-metropolis.html

Ghani, E., Grover Goswami, A. and Kerr, W.R. (2012). 'Is India's Manufacturing Sector Moving Away from Cities?' Working Paper 17992, NBER Working Paper Series. Cambridge, MA: National Bureau of Economic Research. https://www.nber.org/system/files/working_papers/w17992/w17992.pdf

Ghislanzoni, G., Myerson, G. and Faure Ragani, A. (2013). 'A cost-effective path to road safety.' McKinsey on Society. https://www.mckinsey.com/~/media/mckinsey/industries/public%20and%20social%20sector/our%20insights/a%20cost%20curve%20to%20improve%20road%20safety/a%20cost%20effective%20path%20to%20road%20safety.pdf

Ghosh, S. (2020). 'Why are Indian cities taking longer to cool down than their surrounding areas?' Scroll.in, 16 February. https://scroll.in/article/952007/why-are-indian-cities-taking-longer-to-cool-down-than-their-surrounding-areas

Ghurye, G.S. (1953). 'Cities of India.' *Sociological Bulletin* 2, (1): 47–80.

Glaeser, E.L., Kallal, H.D., Scheinkman, J.A. and Shleifer, A. (1992). 'Growth in Cities.' *Journal of Political Economy* 100, (6). https://scholar.harvard.edu/files/shleifer/files/growthincities.pdf

Glaeser, E.L., Gyourko, J., and Saks, R. (2003). 'Why is Manhattan so Expensive? Regulation and the Rise in Housing Prices.' Working Paper 10124, NBER. Cambridge, MA: National Bureau of Economic Research. https://www.nber.org/system/files/working_papers/w10124/w10124.pdf

Glaeser, E.L. (2010). *Making Sense of Bangalore.* London: Legatum Institute.

——(2012). *Triumph of the City; How Urban Spaces Make us Human.* New York: Penguin Books.

——(2020). 'Cities and Pandemics have a Long History.' *City Journal,* Spring. https://www.city-journal.org/cities-and-pandemics-have-long-history

GoI (2015). *Report of the Fourteenth Finance Commission (2015–2020).* New Delhi: Government of India.

Goldin, C. and Katz, L.F. (2008). *The Race between Education and Technology.* Cambridge MA: Harvard University Press.

Greentechlead (2017). 'India Launches new Energy Conservation Building Code.' 20 June. https://greentechlead.com/green-building/india-launches-new-energy-conservation-building-code-32803

Gupta, S. (2020a). 'India may have 800 million internet users by 2023 if it can get this factor right.' *Financial Express,* 8 January. https://www.financialexpress.com/industry/technology/india-may-have-800-million-internet-users-by-2023-if-it-can-get-this-factor-right/1816771/

Gupta, N. (2020b). 'India: New Bus Rapid Transit System makes travel faster, safer and more convenient in Hubballi-Dharwad.' World Bank Blogs, 27 February. https://blogs.worldbank.org/endpovertyinsouthasia/india-new-bus-rapid-transit-system-makes-travel-faster-safer-and-more

Gupta, K. (2020c). 'Challenges in developing urban flood resilience in India.' *Philosophical Transactions of the Royal Society*, Series A, Mathematical, Physical, and Engineering Sciences (378): 20190211. http://dx.doi.org/10.1098/rsta.2019.0211

Gupta, P. and Dhar, D. (2020). 'Learn from Singapore: Key take away from the island nation's turnaround story.' *Financial Express*, 7 April. https://www.financialexpress.com/opinion/learn-from-singapore-

key-take-away-from-the-island-nations-water-turnaround-story/1920804/
Guruswamy, M. (2017). 'India at 70: The good and bad of India's growth story'. *Hindustan Times,* 15 August. https://www.hindustantimes.com/opinion/india-at-70-the-good-and-bad-of-india-s-growth-story/story-Y2aLsMN1nbQVr8mmI4kPON.html
Guturu, K. (2015). 'Is FSI Dependent on Land Availability and Densities? A Comparative Review of FSI in Indian Cities.' *European Journal of Sustainable Development* 4, (2): 27–34. 10.14207/ejsd.2015.v4n2p27
Halder, R. and Gandhiok, J. (2019). 'Delhi has 17 buses for every lakh people to Beijing's 107.' *The Times of India,* 9 July. https://timesofindia.indiatimes.com/city/delhi/delhi-has-17-buses-for-every-lakh-people-to-beijings-107/articleshow/70136383.cms?utm_source=twitter.com&utm_medium=social&utm_campaign=TOIDesktop
Harish, S. (2020). 'Confronting everyday sources of pollution across the country.' *Hindustan Times,* 10 December. https://www.hindustantimes.com/analysis/confronting-everyday-sources-of-pollution-across-the-country/story-tXXS7tRxrNRzKfjB4WF1aJ.html
HinduBL (2019). 'Cybersecurity awareness level low among users in smaller cities.' *Hindu BusinessLine,* 23 December. https://www.thehindubusinessline.com/info-tech/cybersecurity-awareness-level-low-among-users-in-smaller-cities/article30380978.ece
Hindustan Times (2019a). 'Padma awardee Bimal Patel to guide Pune civic body for town planning scheme.' 30 January. https://www.hindustantimes.com/pune-news/padma-awardee-bimal-patel-to-guide-pune-civic-body-for-town-planning-scheme/story-5gBN49WqcpVl6djYj4rm6N.html
———(2019b). 'Town planning scheme: Pune municipal corporation takes city back to the future.' 31 January. https://www.hindustantimes.com/pune-news/town-planning-scheme-pune-municipal-corporation-takes-city-back-to-the-future/story-iq7ehz4zQECTtYDHfvRcVM.html

———(2020). 'Khoj.City: Revolutionising the lives of artisans across India.' 26 February. https://www.hindustantimes.com/brand-post/khoj-city-revolutionising-the-lives-of-artisans-across-india/story-Zim31eQOTPqsFgPwyIhX1M.html

Hollis, L. (2013). *Cities Are Good for You: The Genius of the Metropolis*. London: Bloomsbury.

Hutt, R. (2018). *Pakistan has planted over a billion trees*. WEF, 2 July. Geneva: World Economic Forum. https://www.weforum.org/agenda/2018/07/pakistan-s-billion-tree-tsunami-is-astonishing/

IANS (2019a). 'Lucknow loses almost half its water bodies to builders.' India TV, July 8. https://www.indiatvnews.com/news/india-water-pollution-water-bodies-in-lucknow-land-grabbing-construction-533597

———(2019b). 'Tap water undrinkable in Delhi, 13 state capitals: Union Minister Ram Vilas Paswan.' *The New Indian Express*, 16 November. https://www.newindianexpress.com/cities/delhi/2019/nov/16/tap-water-undrinkable-in-delhi-13-state-capitals-union-minister-ram-vilas-paswan-2062711.html

ICLEI (2019). *Resilient cities, thriving cities: The evolution of urban resilience*. Bonn: ICLEI – Local Governments for Sustainability e.V. https://e-lib.iclei.org/publications/Resilient-Cities-Thriving-Cities_The-Evolution-of-Urban-Resilience.pdf

ICRIER Team (2019). *Finances of Municipal Corporations in Metropolitan Cities of India: A Study Prepared for the Fifteenth Finance Commission*. New Delhi: Indian Council for Research on International Economic Relations. https://fincomindia.nic.in/writereaddata/html_en_files/fincom15/StudyReports/Finances%20of%20Municipal%20Corporations%20in%20Metropolitan%20cities%20of%20India.pdf

IDFC (2019). *Reforming Urban India*. Mumbai: IDFC Institute. https://www.idfcinstitute.org/site/assets/files/15116/reforming_urban_india_idfc_institute.pdf

Idiculla, M. (2016). 'Should mayors be directly elected?' *The Hindu*, 23 August. https://www.thehindu.com/opinion/columns/Should-mayors-be-directly-elected/article14583765.ece

———(2020). 'Hardly smart about urban health care.' *The Hindu*, 13 July. https://www.thehindu.com/opinion/lead/hardly-smart-about-urban-health-care/article32060296.ece

IFC (n.d.). 'Green Bonds'. IFC.org. https://www.ifc.org/wps/wcm/connect/corp_ext_content/ifc_external_corporate_site/about+ifc_new/investor+relations/ir-products/grnbond-overvw

———(2017). *Climate Investment Opportunities in South Asia: An IFC Analysis*. Washington, DC: International Finance Corporation, World Bank Group. https://www.ifc.org/wps/wcm/connect/fa3bea68-20f1-4cb4-90b9-3e812d38067f/Climate+Investment+Opportunities+in+South+Asia+-+An+IFC+Analysis.pdf?MOD=AJPERES&CVID=l.raVua

IIHS (2015a). 'Instituting Rental Housing.' Policy Brief # 5. Bengaluru: Indian Institute for Human Settlements. http://iihs.co.in/knowledge-gateway/wp-content/uploads/2015/07/5_Rental_Housing.pdf

———(2015b).'Indian cities are at high risk.' Policy Brief #8. Bengaluru: Indian Institute for Human Settlements. https://iihs.co.in/knowledge-gateway/wp-content/uploads/2015/08/8_Risk_and_Resilience.pdf

Ikenberry, G.J. (2005). 'Power and liberal order: America's postwar world order in transition.' *International Relations of the Asia-Pacific* (5): 133–52. https://scholar.princeton.edu/sites/default/files/gji3/files/power_and_liberal_order.pdf

Infrastructure Channel. (n.d.) 'Interview with Kishore Mahbubani: Meritocracy and Pragmatism Keys to Singapore's Success.' https://www.infrastructure-channel.com/article/-/content/meritocracy-and-pragmatism-keys-to-singapore-s-success

Invest India. (n.d.). 'Sectors in India'. New Delhi: Invest India: National Investment Promotion & Facilitation Agency, Government of India. https://www.investindia.gov.in/sectors

Isaacson, W. (2017). *Leonardo da Vinci*. New York: Simon & Schuster.

ITDP India (n.d.). 'Growth of Bus Rapid Transit in India.' Chennai: Institute for Transportation and Development Policy-India. https://www.itdp.in/growth-of-bus-rapid-transit-in-india/

Iyer, N. (2020). 'Rental housing scheme must avoid predictable pitfalls.' ORF, 7 September. New Delhi: Observer Research Foundation. https://www.orfonline.org/expert-speak/rental-housing-scheme-must-avoid-predictable-pitfalls/

Jacobs, J. (1992). *The Death and Life of Great American Cities*. New York: Vintage Books.

Jadhav, R. (2019). 'Maximum cities being pushed to the limits.' *Hindu BusinessLine*, 27 January. https://www.thehindubusinessline.com/specials/businessline-25/maximum-cities-are-being-pushed-to-the-limits/article26105074.ece

Jain, V. (2019). 'Examining the Town Planning Scheme of India and Lessons from Land Readjustment in Japan.' ADBI Working Paper Series, No. 1037. Tokyo: Asian Development Bank Institute. https://www.adb.org/sites/default/files/publication/539736/adbi-wp1037.pdf

JapanGov (n.d.). 'Japan: Pillars of Resilience.' *Financial Times*. https://www-ft-com.ezp-prod1.hul.harvard.edu/brandsuite/cabinet-office-japan/japan-pillars-of-resilience.html

Jebaraj, P. (2018). 'Proposal for city-level GDP under study'. *The Hindu*, 18 August. Retrieved 10 September 2018. https://www.pressreader.com/india/the-hindu/20180818/281938838759295.

Jenkins, M. (2020). 'Sponge City: Shenzen Explores the Benefits of Designing with Nature.' Cambridge, MA: Lincoln Institute of Land Policy. https://www.lincolninst.edu/publications/articles/sponge-city-shenzhen-explores-benefits-designing-with-nature

Jha, A.K., Miner, T.W., and Stanton-Geddes, Z. (2013). *Building Urban Resilience: Principles, Tools, and Practice*. Directions in Development series: Environment and Sustainable Development. Washington, DC: World Bank. https://openknowledge.worldbank.org/handle/10986/13109

Jha, R. (2019). 'Indian cities and air pollution.' Urban Futures series. New Delhi: Observer Research Foundation. https://www.orfonline.org/expert-speak/indian-cities-and-air-pollution-51628/

——— (2020). 'The impact of Gandhi on post-Independence treatment of cities.' Urban Futures series. Mumbai: Observer Research

Foundation, 5 December. https://www.orfonline.org/expert-speak/the-impact-of-gandhi-on-post-independence-treatment-of-cities/

———(2021b). 'Extreme Heat Events in India's Cities: A Framework for Adaptive Action Plans.' https://www.orfonline.org/research/extreme-heat-events-in-indias-cities/

Jha, A. (2021a). 'Explaining the decline in women's role in workforce.' *Hindustan Times*, 13 December. https://www.hindustantimes.com/india-news/explaining-the-decline-in-women-s-role-in-workforce-101639333923098.html

JL LaSelle (2012). 'India – Affordable Housing – An Inclusive Approach To Sheltering The Bottom Of The Pyramid.' Gurugram: Jones Lang LaSalle India.

Joseph, T. (2021). *Early Indians: The Story of Our Ancestors and Where We Came From.* New Delhi: Juggernaut Books.

Joshi, H. (2020). 'Vanishing landscape of "smart city" Dehradun.' Mongabay, February 3. https://india.mongabay.com/2020/02/vanishing-landscape-of-smart-city-dehradun/

Kabbara, M. (2019). '5 ways cities can use emerging technologies to fight climate change.' WEF, 5 April. Geneva: World Economic Forum. https://www.weforum.org/agenda/2019/04/5-ways-cities-can-leverage-emerging-technologies-to-mitigate-climate-change/

Kaka N. and Madgavkar, A. (2016). 'India's Ascent: Five Opportunities for Growth and Transformation.' Report. McKinsey Global Institute, 11 August.

Kalaskar, U. (2019). 'Pune Municipal Corporation – Municipal Bonds'. https://www.thegpsc.org/sites/gpsc/files/session_b2_03_ms._ulka_pune_municipal_bonds.pdf

Kamdar, B. (2019). '25 Years After the Genocide – Quota, Power and Women in Rwanda.' The Wire, 12 April. https://thewire.in/world/25-years-genocide-quota-power-women-rwanda

Kant, A. (2018). *The Path Ahead: Transformative Ideas for India.* New Delhi: Rupa Publications.

———(2019). 'The challenge of water: India's ability to manage and govern water will determine its future.' *The Times of India*, 3 July. https://timesofindia.indiatimes.com/blogs/toi-edit-page/the-challenge-of-water-indias-ability-to-manage-and-govern-water-will-determine-its-future/

———(2020). 'Next driver of growth? Covid-19 pandemic offers unique opportunity for radically reforming India's healthcare system.' *The Times of India*, 10 September.

Kanti, A. (2017). '5 Global Success Stories On Battling Air Pollution: Can Delhi Learn From Them?' *Business World*, 17 November. http://www.businessworld.in/article/5-Global-Success-Stories-On-Battling-Air-Pollution-Can-Delhi-Learn-From-Them-/13-11-2017-131422/

Kapil, S. (2019). 'Nearly 80 per cent Indian households without piped water connection.' *Down to Earth*, 25 November. https://www.downtoearth.org.in/news/water/nearly-80-per-cent-indian-households-without-piped-water-connection-67928

———(2020). 'Link sanitation, solid waste to agriculture, Niti Aayog advises states.' *Down to Earth*, 17 January. https://www.downtoearth.org.in/news/agriculture/link-sanitation-solid-waste-to-agriculture-niti-aayog-advises-states-68839

Kapur, D., Somanathan, T.V., Subramanian, A. (2014). 'Land Shackled–I.' *Business Standard*, 21 July. https://www.business-standard.com/article/opinion/devesh-kapur-t-v-somanathan-arvind-subramanian-land-shackled-i-114072000708_1.html

Kaur, C. (2019). 'Chhattisgarh: How a small town scores big in waste management.' *The Times of India*, 7 December. https://timesofindia.indiatimes.com/city/raipur/how-a-small-town-scores-big-in-waste-mgmt/articleshow/72407952.cms

Kaveri, M. (2020). 'Why Chennai's dream of a single transport authority remains unfulfilled.' *The News Minute*, January 29. https://www.thenewsminute.com/article/why-chennai-s-dream-single-transport-authority-remains-unfulfilled-117073

Kaza, S., Yao, L.C., Bhada-Tata, P. and Van Woerden, F. (2018). *What a Waste 2.0: A Global Snapshot of Solid Waste Management to 2050*. Urban Development. Washington DC: World Bank. https://openknowledge.worldbank.org/handle/10986/30317

Kazmi, Z. (2018). 'Imperial Delhi: How the British built a "New Delhi" at the cost of the old.' *Hindustan Times*, 30 January. https://

www.hindustantimes.com/delhi-news/imperial-delhi-how-the-british-built-a-new-delhi-at-the-cost-of-the-old/story-0teV8d6fhcAb8IudCZtmMP.html

Kemper, K., and Wahba, S. (2020). 'Tackling poor air quality: Lessons from three cities.' World Bank Blogs, 2 November. https://blogs.worldbank.org/voices/tackling-poor-air-quality-lessons-three-cities

Ken, Wong Lin. (1978). 'Singapore: Its Growth as an Entrepot Port, 1819–1941.' *Journal of Southeast Asian Studies* 9, (1): 50–84.

Kennard, M., and Provost, C. (2016). 'Story of cities #25: Shannon – a tiny Irish town inspires China's economic boom.' *The Guardian*, 19 April. https://www.theguardian.com/cities/2016/apr/19/story-of-cities-25-shannon-ireland-china-economic-boom

Khan, S. (2020). 'Covid-19 crisis underlines false urban-rural binary, neglect of urban areas.' *The Indian Express*, 24 July. https://indianexpress.com/article/opinion/columns/coronavirus-covid-19-pandemic-india-urban-cities-6520574/

Khandekar, N. (2020). 'World Wetlands Day: What Is a Wetland, and Why Does India Need so Many?' *The Wire*, 2 February. https://thewire.in/environment/world-wetlands-day-ramsar-convention-catchment-water-pollution-urbanisation

Khanna, P. (2020). 'Centre launches initiative for cities to combat climate change'. *Mint*, 11 September. https://www.livemint.com/news/india/centre-launches-initiatives-for-cities-to-combat-climate-change-11599827808063.html

Kirpal, N. (2019). 'Indian Heritage Recovery and Google – A Project You Have Not Heard Of.' *India Currents*, 14 May. https://indiacurrents.com/indian-heritage-recovery-and-google-a-project-you-have-not-heard-of/

Kolbert, E. (2015). *The Sixth Extinction: An Unnatural History*. London: Bloomsbury Publishing.

Konda, G.R. (2020). 'Slum numbers show cities don't help Dalits shed caste.' *The Indian Express*, 29 November. https://indianexpress.com/article/opinion/columns/slum-numbers-show-cities-dont-help-dalits-shed-caste-7072206/

Koppikar, S. and Purohit, K., (2014). 'Mumbai gets second chance to transform.' *Hindustan Times*, July 17. https://www.hindustantimes.com/mumbai/mumbai-gets-second-chance-to-transform/story-8ZrorZvwfcZH2k6U6TqWCP.html

Koshy, J. (2019). 'Emission levels rising faster in Indian cities than in China.' *The Hindu*, 5 February. https://www.thehindu.com/sci-tech/energy-and-environment/emission-levels-rising-faster-in-indian-cities-than-in-china/article26178211.ece

Koshy, J. (2020). '30 Indian cities will face "water risk" by 2050: report.' *The Hindu*, 3 November. https://www.thehindu.com/news/national/30-indian-cities-will-face-water-risk-by-2050-report/article33007337.ece

Kron, J. (2012). 'Red State, Blue City: How the Urban-Rural Divide Is Splitting America.' *The Atlantic*, 30 November. https://www.theatlantic.com/politics/archive/2012/11/red-state-blue-city-how-the-urban-rural-divide-is-splitting-america/265686/

Kubernein Initiative (2020).'The Challenges of Urban water Security and Growth in India.' Working Paper 1. Mumbai: Kubernein Initiative. https://kuberneininitiative.com/wp-content/uploads/2020/12/KI-Working-Paper-1_Urban-Water-Security-and-Growth.pdf

Kumar, M. (n.d.). 'India Experiments with Car Free Sunday Streets and Bus Day to Popularize People Friendly Cities.' Smart Cities Dive. https://www.smartcitiesdive.com/ex/sustainablecitiescollective/india-experiments-car-free-sunday-streets-and-bus-day-popularize-people-friendly/211016/

Kumar, R.V. (2020). '"Urban heat island" phenomenon responsible for heavy rains in short spells.' *Hindu BusinessLine*, 23 October. https://www.thehindubusinessline.com/economy/agri-business/urban-heat-island-phenomenon-responsible-for-heavy-rains-in-short-spells/article32931016.ece

Kumar, K, Kalaskar, U., Mandwale, K., and Thakur, P. (2018). *Pune's Pathbreaking Success in the Municipal Bond Market: A Case Study*. Pune: Spectrum Offset Press.

Kumar, A. and Saiyed, K. (2019). 'Does India Need New Strategies For Improving Urban Health And Nutrition?' New Delhi: Niti Aayog,

Government of India. https://www.niti.gov.in/does-india-need-new-strategies-improving-urban-health-and-nutrition

Kumar, R., and Prasad, U. (2020). 'Towards a resilient public health system: India's response to the Covid-19 outbreak has been commendable'. *Financial Express*, 19 March.

Kumar, K., Guha, A., and Mallick, A. (2020). 'Indian smart cities offer a model for pandemic recovery.' WEF, 21 December. Geneva: World Economic Forum. https://www.weforum.org/agenda/2020/12/indian-smart-cities-offer-a-model-for-pandemic-recovery/

Kunzig, R. (2011). 'The City Solution.' *National Geographic*, December. https://www.nationalgeographic.com/magazine/article/city-solutions

Kushwah, V.K. (2018). 'Why India needs urgent police reforms.' New Delhi: Observer Research Foundation. https://www.orfonline.org/expert-speak/why-india-needs-urgent-police-reforms-46003/

Kwatra, N. (2019). 'Skills are concentrated in big cities, says study.' *Mint*, 28 March. https://www.livemint.com/industry/human-resource/skills-are-concentrated-in-big-cities-says-study-1553789555043.html

Lahariya C. (2019). '*Basthi Dawakhana* of Hyderabad: The first Urban Local Body led community clinics in India.' *Journal of Family Medicine and Primary Care* 8, (4): 1301–07. https://doi.org/10.4103/jfmpc.jfmpc_380_18

———(2020). 'Health & Wellness Centres to Strengthen Primary Health Care in India: Concept, Progress and Ways Forward.' *Indian Journal of Paediatrics*, 87 (11): 916–29. https://doi.org/10.1007/s12098-020-03359-z

Laker, L. (2018). 'What would the ultimate child-friendly city look like?' *The Guardian*, 28 February.

Lalwani, A. (2019). 'This is how India can become the next Silicon Valley.' WEF, 2 October. Geneva: World Economic Forum. https://www.weforum.org/agenda/2019/10/india-technology-development-silicon-valley/

Lamson-Hall, P., Agrawal, H., Pachisia, H.V., and Shah, K. (2020). 'Urban Growth in India: Horizontal, Chaotic, and Informal.' IDFC Institute Position Paper 01. Mumbai: IDFC Institute. https://www.

idfcinstitute.org/site/assets/files/16100/urban_growth_in_india_december_2020-1.pdf

Langa, M. (2017). 'How Ahmedabad beat the heat.' *The Hindu*, 2 April. https://www.thehindu.com/sci-tech/health/how-ahmedabad-beat-the-heat/article17759591.ece

Lindsey, R. (2020). 'Climate Change: Global Sea Level.' Climate.gov, 14 August. https://www.climate.gov/news-features/understanding-climate/climate-change-global-sea-level

Likhi, A. (2019). 'Water Use Efficiency Through Micro Irrigation In India: The Way Forward.' *Outlook*. 9 August. https://www.outlookindia.com/website/story/india-news-water-use-efficiency-through-micro-irrigation-in-india-the-way-forward/335886

Lim, H. (2008), 'Infrastructure Development in Singapore'. In *International Infrastructure Development in East Asia: Towards Balanced Regional Development and Integration*, edited by N. Kumar. ERIA Research Project Report 2007-02, Chiba: IDE-JETRO, 228–62. https://www.eria.org/uploads/media/Research-Project-Report/RPR_FY2007_2_Chapter_8.pdf

Litman, T. (2018). 'Generated Traffic and Induced Travel.' Victoria Travel Policy Institute, 14 April. http://www.vtpi.org/gentraf.pdf

Livemint (2017). 'India needs strong, directly elected mayors.' *Mint*, 12 July. https://www.livemint.com/Opinion/oTVlQ2WNVeISPprBH0NX7I/India-needs-strong-directly-elected-mayors.html

———(2018). 'Opinion: No time left to waste on waste.' *Mint*, 17 December. https://www.livemint.com/Opinion/YZdMHLT4eXYSZyVCYIK1KK/Opinion--No-time-left-to-waste-on-waste.html

Mahaprashasta, A.A. (2016). 'How the Once Flourishing Kanpur Textile Mills Decayed.' The Wire, 16 April. https://thewire.in/labour/faulty-govt-policies-corruption-and-exploitation-of-labour-how-the-once-flourishing-kanpur-textile-mills-decayed

Mahesh, M.L. (2015). 'TDR, a winning formula for all.' *The Hindu*, 22 May. https://www.thehindu.com/features/homes-and-gardens/tdr-a-winning-formula-for-all/article7235427.ece

Malka, R. (2019). 'Based on Israel's success story, we want to help India in its quest for water'. *Hindustan Times*, 24 November. https://www.hindustantimes.com/analysis/based-on-israel-s-success-story-we-want-to-help-india-in-its-quest-for-water-opinion/story-dG8BrpIBsYkH8hurynpyoK_amp.html?__twitter_impression=true

Marcelo, D., House, S., and Raina, A. (2018). 'Incorporating Resilience in Infrastructure Prioritization: Application to the Road Transport Sector.' Policy Research Working Paper, No. 8584. Washington DC: World Bank. https://openknowledge.worldbank.org/handle/10986/30429

Marshall, C. (2016) 'Story of Cities #27: Singapore – the most meticulously planned city in the world.' *The Guardian*, 21 April. https://www.theguardian.com/cities/2016/apr/21/story-cities-singapore-carefully-planned-lee-kuan-yew

Masani, Z. (2012). 'English or Hinglish: which will India choose?' BBC News, 27 November. https://www.bbc.com/news/magazine-20500312

Mascarenhas, A. (2020). '8.6 lakh kg Covid-19 biomedical waste generated, Pune hospitals protest "unfair" rate as they attract large disposal bills.' *Indian Express*, 22 December. https://indianexpress.com/article/cities/pune/pune-8-6-lakh-kg-Covid-19-biomedical-waste-generated-hospitals-protest-unfair-rate-as-they-attract-large-disposal-bills-7114103/

Matthan, R. (2017). 'The great manure crisis of 1894.' *Mint*, 20 April. https://www.livemint.com/Opinion/ENSPBlY7T8et98Go88DrVI/The-great-manure-crisis-of-1894.html

McCarthy, N. (2020). 'This chart shows where the world's highly-educated migrants come from.' Geneva: World Economic Forum, 2 December. https://www.weforum.org/agenda/2020/12/where-do-highly-educated-migrants-come-from?utm_source=twitter&utm_medium=social_scheduler&utm_term=economist.com/international/2015/05/30/rus-in-urbe-redux

McDonnell, T., and Kapur, M. (2020). 'India's megacities aren't prepared for a wave of climate migrants.' *Quartz*, 3 September. https://

qz.com/1895253/climate-change-in-india-is-fueling-unchecked-urbanization/

McCurry, J. (2016). 'Story of cities #24: how Hiroshima rose from the ashes of nuclear destruction.' *The Guardian*, 18 April. https://www.theguardian.com/cities/2016/apr/18/story-of-cities-hiroshima-japan-nuclear-destruction

Mehta, S. (2004). *Maximum City: Bombay Lost and Found*. New Delhi: Penguin Random House India.

Meng, X., Zhidian, J., Wang, X., and Long, Y. (2021). 'Shrinking Cities on the Globe: Evidence from LandScan 2000–2019.' *Environment and Planning A: Economy and Space* 53, (6): 1244–48. https://doi.org/10.1177/0308518X211006118

Mint (2018). 'Which way will the new urban Indian voter tilt?' 9 July. https://www.livemint.com/Opinion/IchdPnZwNHmvwAxMXqijmI/Which-way-will-the-new-urban-Indian-voter-tilt.html

Mishra, R.R. and Chary, S.V. (2020). 'Opinion: Beyond "flush and forget" approach, urban India must look for co-treatment of faecal sludge.' ET Government.com, 22 August. https://government.economictimes.indiatimes.com/news/smart-infra/opinion-beyond-flush-and-forget-approach-urban-india-must-look-for-co-treatment-of-faecal-sludge/77688234

Mishra, A., and Dhar, D. (2018). 'India needs to focus on water efficiency'. *Mint*, 12 July. https://www.livemint.com/Opinion/Cbw6kcycrx0QtCPLKneAHP/India-needs-to-focus-on-water-efficiency.html?facet=amp&__twitter_impression=true

Mishra, P., and Suhag, R. (2017). 'Land records and titles in India.' Ideas for India, 20 November. https://www.ideasforindia.in/topics/macroeconomics/land-records-and-titles-in-india.html

Mishra, D.S. (2020). '…[INR] 3,640 cr through Municipal Bond in last 3 years…' Twitter Post, 2 December. https://twitter.com/Secretary_MoHUA/status/1334124799342247941

Misra, T. (2018). 'The Kerala Floods: A Disastrous Consequence of Unchecked Urbanization.' Bloomberg CityLab, 31 August. https://www.citylab.com/environment/2018/08/the-kerala-floods-a-disastrous-consequence-of-unchecked-urbanization/569014/

MoEFCC (2019a). *India Cooling Action Plan.* Ozone Cell. New Delhi: Ministry of Environment, Forest and Climate Change. http://ozonecell.nic.in/wp-content/uploads/2019/03/INDIA-COOLING-ACTION-PLAN-e-circulation-version080319.pdf

MoEFCC (2019b). 'National Resource Efficiency Policy, 2019.' Draft. New Delhi: Ministry of Environment, Forest and Climate Change. http://moef.gov.in/wp-content/uploads/2019/07/Draft-National-Resourc.pdf

Mohan, S. (2018). 'What makes India's cleanest city tick?' *Hindu BusinessLine*, 20 November. https://www.thehindubusinessline.com/blink/cover/binless-in-indore/article25631563.ece

Mohanty, P.K. (2014). *Cities and Public Policy: An Urban Agenda for India.* New Delhi: Sage Publications.

———(2016). *Financing Cities in India: Municipal Reforms, Fiscal Accountability and Urban Infrastructure.* New Delhi: Sage Publications.

———(2019). *Planning and Economics of Cities: Shaping India's Form and Future.* New Delhi: Sage Publications.

MoF (2017). *Economic Survey 2016–17.* New Delhi: Ministry of Finance, Government of India. https://www.indiabudget.gov.in/budget2017-2018/es2016-17/echapter.pdf

MoHUA (2016a). 'India Habitat III: National Report 2016.' New Delhi: Ministry of Housing & Urban Affairs, Government of India.

———(2016b). *Handbook for Urban Development Statistics 2016.* New Delhi: Ministry of Housing & Urban Affairs, Government of India. https://mohua.gov.in/pdf/5853c4c9864675832b25ba492dhandbook%20of%20urban%20statistics.pdf

———(2016c). 'Reforms Incentive Claims Toolkit (F.Y. 2016-17).' AMRUT. New Delhi: Town & Country Planning Organisatioin, Ministry of Housing & Urban Affairs, Government of India. http://amrut.gov.in/upload/uploadfiles/files/Reforms_Incentive_Claims_Toolkit1.pdf

———(2018a). 'National Urban Policy Framework 2018'. New Delhi: Ministry of Housing & Urban Affairs, Government of India. https://smartnet.niua.org/sites/default/files/resources/nupf_final.pdf

———(2018b). 'Pilot on Formulation of Local Area Plan (LAP) & Town Planning Scheme (TPS) For Selected Cities.' New Delhi: Ministry of Housing & Urban Affairs, Government of India. News Release. http://amrut.gov.in/upload/newsrelease/5d6f8bda8c3fd7amrutbook.pdf

———(2019). *Handbook of Statistics 2019*. New Delhi: Ministry of Housing & Urban Affairs, Government of India. https://mohua.gov.in/pdf/5c80e2225a124Handbook%20of%20Urban%20Statistics%202019.pdf

———(2020). 'Now we have notified standards for MetroLite ... and MetroNeo ...' Tweet by Secretary MoHUA Durga Shanker Mishra on 7 December, 5.45 p.m. https://twitter.com/Secretary_MoHUA/status/1335920891507589122

MoJS (2020). Draft National Policy on Safe Reuse of Treated Water. New Delhi: Ministry of Jal Shakti, Government of India. https://kspcb.karnataka.gov.in/sites/default/files/inline-files/WATER%20REUSE%20POLICY.pdf

Montgomery, C. (2013). Happy City: Transforming Our Lives through Urban Design. Toronto: Doubleday.

Moretti, E. (2012). *The New Geography of Jobs*. New York: Mariner Books.

MoSPI (2020). *Periodic Labour Force Survey (July 1018–June 2019): Annual Report*. New Delhi: National Statistical Office, Ministry of Statistics and Programme Implementation, Government of India. https://cse.azimpremjiuniversity.edu.in/wp-content/uploads/2019/06/Annual_Report_PLFS_2018_19_HL.pdf

MoUD (n.d.). 'Primer on Faecal Sludge and Septage Management.' New Delhi: Ministry of Urban Development, Government of India. http://swachhbharaturban.gov.in/writereaddata/Primer%20on%20Faecal%20Sludge%20&%20Septage%20Management.pdf?id=cmwonoj5beqagmm2

———(2011). 'Report on Indian Urban Infrastructure and Services'. The High Powered Expert Committee for Estimating the Investment Requirements for Urban Infrastructure Services. New Delhi: Ministry of Urban Development, Government of India. http://icrier.org/pdf/FinalReport-hpec.pdf

———(2014). 'National Urban Transport Policy.' New Delhi: Ministry of Urban Development, Government of India.

———(2015). *Urban and Regional Development Plans Formulation and Implementation (URDPFI) Guidelines, Volume 1.* New Delhi: Town and Country Planning Organization, Ministry of Urban Development, Government of India.

Muggah, R. (2019). 'The world's coastal cities are going under. Here's how some are fighting back.' WEF, 16 January. Geneva: World Economic Forum. https://www.weforum.org/agenda/2019/01/the-world-s-coastal-cities-are-going-under-here-is-how-some-are-fighting-back

Mukhopadhyay, P. and Kunduri, E. (2019). 'To get more women in labour force, India must stop pushing industrial areas to city limits.' *The Print*, 8 July. https://theprint.in/opinion/to-get-more-women-in-labour-force-india-must-stop-pushing-industrial-areas-to-city-limits/260050/

Mukhopadhyay, P. and Naik, M. (2018). 'For equitable growth, India must unthink the urban.' *Hindustan Times*, 7 December. https://www.hindustantimes.com/analysis/for-equitable-growth-india-must-unthink-the-urban/story-7FvJDsWGVW0XedI5XJGyhJ.html

Mullen, P., Nair, D., Nigam, J., and Seth, K. (2016). 'Urban Health Advantages and Penalties in India Overview and Case Studies.' Discussion Paper. Report No: AUS7433. Health, Nutrition & Population Global Practice South Asia. Washington DC: World Bank Group. https://smartnet.niua.org/sites/default/files/resources/india-urban-health-p149479-24feb2016-final.pdf

Mumford, L. (1961). *The City in History: Its Origins, Its Transformations, and Its Prospects.* London: Martin Secker and Warburg Limited.

Nag, D. (2020). 'During lockdown over 1 crore migrants returned to home states on Indian Railways Shramik trains and on foot.' *Financial Express*, 23 September. https://www.financialexpress.com/infrastructure/railways/during-lockdown-over-1-crore-migrants-returned-to-home-states-on-indian-railways-shramik-trains-and-on-foot/2089914/

Naik, M. (2019). 'India must shun Nehruvian metropolis bias & turn to small cities for urban economic growth.' The Print, 7 June. https://theprint.in/opinion/india-needs-to-shun-nehruvian-megacity-bias-turn-to-small-cities-for-urban-economic-growth/246459/

Naik, M., Khan, S., and Roy, S.N. (2019). 'India's urbanisation isn't just happening in cities. Modi govt must tap these new areas.' The Print, 4 July. https://theprint.in/opinion/indias-urbanisation-isnt-just-happening-in-cities-modi-govt-must-tap-these-new-areas/257991/

Nair, A., Nair, V.A., Nair A.A., Vachana, V.R. (2016). 'Annual Survey of India's City-Systems 2016: Shaping India's Urban Agenda.' Bengaluru: Janaagraha. https://www.janaagraha.org/reports/ASICS-2016.pdf

Narayan, S. (2015). 'Gurgaon is an example of how not to urbanise India.' *Hindustan Times*, 10 August. https://www.hindustantimes.com/columns/gurgaon-is-an-example-of-how-not-to-urbanise-india/story-KqAcFBWI8jp62fCvKTEPwK.html

NCRB (2016–19). *Crime in India.* Various volumes. New Delhi: National Crime Records Bureau, Ministry of Home Affairs, Government if India. http://ncrb.gov.in/

NIUA (2018a). *Status of Children in Urban India, Baseline Study 2018.* Second Edition. New Delhi: National Institute of Urban Affairs.

———(2018b). *'Children' in the Urban Vision of India, 2019.* New Delhi: National Institute of Urban Affairs.

Nations Online Project (n.d.). 'A Brief History of Singapore.' nationsonline.org. Retrieved on 31 October 2021. https://www.guidemesingapore.com/business-guides/immigration/get-to-know-singapore/a-brief-history-of-singapore

NFHS-4 (2017). *National Family Health Survey 4: 2015–16.* Mumbai: International Institute for Population Sciences; New Delhi: Ministry of Health and Family Welfare, Government of India. http://rchiips.org/nfhs/nfhs-4Reports/India.pdf

NIPFP (1994). *The Implications of the Constitution Seventy-Fourth Amendment for the Finances of Municipalities: An Interim Assessment.* New Delhi: National Institute of Public Finance and Policy, Ministry of Finance, Government of India. https://www.nipfp.

org.in/media/medialibrary/2014/10/The_Implications_of_the_Constitution_Seventy_Fourth_Amendment_for_the_Finances_of_Municipalities.pdf

Niti Aayog (n.d). 'Report of the Working Group on Urban Governance.' New Delhi: Niti Aayog, Government of India.

———(2015a). 'Report of the Sub-Group of Chief Ministers on Swachh Bharat Abhiyaan.' New Delhi: Government of India.

———(2015b). '2.11 Lake Restoration: Two successful models of lake restoration in Rajasthan (Mansagar) and Karnataka (Kaikondrahalli).' In *Social Sector Service Delivery: Good Practices Resource Book 2015*. New Delhi: Government of India. https://www.niti.gov.in/writereaddata/files/bestpractices/Lake%20Restoration%20Two%20successful%20models%20of%20lake%20restoration%20in%20Rajasthan%20%28Mansagar%29%20and%20Karnataka%20%28Kaikondrahalli%29.pdf

———(2017). *India: Three Year Action Agenda, 2017–18 to 2019–20*. New Delhi: Government of India. https://www.niti.gov.in/sites/default/files/2018-12/India_ActionAgenda.pdf

———(2018). *Strategy for New India @ 75*. New Delhi: Government of India. https://www.niti.gov.in/sites/default/files/2019-01/Strategy_for_New_India_2.pdf

NITI Aayog and BCG (2018). 'Transforming India's Mobility: A Perspective.' New Delhi: Government of India; Gurugram: Boston Consulting Group. https://www.niti.gov.in/writereaddata/files/document_publication/BCG.pdf

Nitnaware, H. (2020). 'IAS Makes Indore India's First to Earn Rs 50 Lakh Through Carbon Credits'. *The Better India*, 24 November. https://www.thebetterindia.com/243019/ias-hero-carbon-credits-indore-smart-city-aditi-garg-first-carbon-credit-earn-mitigate-carbon-emissions-compost-unfccc-him16/?utm_source=Article&utm_medium=TwtShareButton&utm_campaign=April-20

OECD (2015). 'A short history of urbanisation.' In *The Metropolitan Century: Understanding Urbanisation and its Consequences*. Paris: Organization for Economic Co-operation and Development, OECD Publishing. https://doi.org/10.1787/9789264228733-en

———(2018). 'Rethinking Urban Sprawl: Moving Towards Sustainable Cities.' Paris: Organization for Economic Co-operation and Development, OECD Publishing. https://doi.org/10.1787/9789264189881-en

O'Leary, R., and Viswanath, K. (2011). *Building Safe and Inclusive Cities for Women: A Practical Guide.* New Delhi: Jagori. https://smartnet.niua.org/sites/default/files/resources/Building-Safe-Inclusive-Cities-for-Women_A-Practical-Guide_2011.pdf

Oxford Economics (2018). *Global Cities: The Future of the World's Leading Urban Economies to 2035.* Oxford: Oxford Economics.

Pachnanda, R.K. (2020). 'Preparing for a disaster-resilient nation.' *The Tribune*, 11 August. https://www.tribuneindia.com/news/comment/preparing-for-a-disaster-resilient-nation-124962

Pai, N. (2019a). 'Night-time commerce offers India a growth opportunity.' *Mint*, 18 March. https://www.livemint.com/opinion/columns/opinion-night-time-commerce-offers-india-a-growth-opportunity-1552835386085.html

———(2019b). 'Opinion: How military bases could seed new cities and create jobs.' *Mint*, 26 May. https://www.livemint.com/opinion/columns/opinion-how-new-military-bases-could-seed-new-cities-and-create-jobs-1558885126976.html

Panagariya, A., Chakraborty, P. and Govinda Rao, M. (2014). *State Level Reforms, Growth, and Development in Indian States.* Studies in Indian Economic Policies series. New Delhi: Oxford University Press.

Panda, S. (2019). 'How to Make Our Cities Safer for Women.' The Wire, 8 March. https://thewire.in/women/how-to-make-our-cities-safer-for-women

Patel, B. (2015). 'How to make urban planning work.' *Mint*, 14 January. https://www.livemint.com/Politics/NBu03YnZHcRSC8r47M1VPN/Bimal-Patel--How-to-make-urban-planning-work.html

Patel, U. (2019). 'Solid Waste Management in India'. Presentation, 4 January. New Delhi: Indian Council for Research on International Economic Relations (ICRIER).

Peterson, P. (1995). 'Who Should Do What? Divided Responsibility in the Federal System.' *The Brookings Review.* 13(2): 6–11.

Peterson G.E. (2014). 'Unlocking Land Values for Urban Infrastructure Finance: International Experience – Considerations for Indian Policy.' Policy Research Working Paper, No. 6683. Washington, DC: World Bank.

Pethe, A., Nallathiga, R., Gandhi, S. and Tandel, V. (2014). 'Re-thinking urban planning in India: Learning from the wedge between the de jure and de facto development in Mumbai.' *Cities* (39): 120–32.

Philip, C.M. (2020). 'Incentivise smart card use; allow top-up through UPI apps: Bengaluru Metro passengers tell BMRCL.' *The Times of India*, 2 September. https://timesofindia.indiatimes.com/city/bengaluru/remove-rs-50-min-balance-rule-demand-namma-metro-users/articleshow/77878735.cms?utm_source=contentofinterest&utm_medium=text&utm_campaign=cppst

PIB (2015). 'India is Committed to Improving Safety, Efficiency and Sustainability in the Transport Sector, Says Shri Nitin Gadkari at the Global Conference on Traffic Safety in Brazil'. Press Release, 19 November. New Delhi: Press Information Bureau. Ministry of Road Transport & Highways, Government of India. https://pib.gov.in/newsite/PrintRelease.aspx?relid=131677

———(2018a). 'Cabinet approves Action Plan for Champion Sectors in Services.' Press Release, 28 February. New Delhi: Press Information Bureau; Ministry of Commerce & Industry, Government of India. https://pib.gov.in/Pressreleaseshare.aspx?PRID=1522078

———(2018b). 'Realized Energy Saving of 8.67 MTOE under PAT Scheme exceeds Energy Saving Targets of 6.68 MTOE by about 30%: Shri R.K. Singh.' Press Release, 2 January. New Delhi: Press Information Bureau; Ministry of Commerce & Industry, Government of India. https://pib.gov.in/newsite/erelcontent.aspx?relid=175112

———(2018c). 'ECO Niwas Samhita 2018 - an Energy Conservation Building Code for Residential Buildings launched.' Press Release, 14 December. New Delhi: Press Information Bureau; Ministry of Power, Government of India. https://pib.gov.in/newsite/PrintRelease.aspx?relid=186406

———(2019a). 'UNESCO has designated Mumbai as a member of UNESCO Creative Cities Network (UCCN) in the field of FILM and Hyderabad in the field of GASTRONOMY'. Press Release, 1 November. New Delhi: Press Information Bureau; Ministry of Culture, Government of India. https://pib.gov.in/newsite/PrintRelease.aspx?relid=194177

———(2019b). 'National Common Mobility Card.' Press Release, 1 July. New Delhi: Press Information Bureau; Ministry of Finance, Government of India. https://pib.gov.in/Pressreleaseshare.aspx?PRID=1576492

———(2019c). 'Rajya Sabha passes Motor Vehicles (Amendment) Bill 2019, Shri Gadkari says the Bill will provide an Efficient, Safe and Corruption Free Transport System in the Country.' Press Release, 31 July. New Delhi: Press Information Bureau. Ministry of Road Transport & Highways, Government of India. https://pib.gov.in/newsite/PrintRelease.aspx?relid=192424

———(2019d). 'India Cooling Action Plan Launched.' Press Release, 8 March. New Delhi: Press Information Bureau. Ministry of Environment, Forest and Climate Change. https://pib.gov.in/PressReleaseIframePage.aspx?PRID=1568328

———(2020a). 'Cabinet Approves PLI Scheme to 1o Key Sectors for Enhancing India's Manufacturing Capabilities and Enhancing Exports – Atmanirbhar Bharat.' Press Release, 11 November. New Delhi: Press Information Bureau; Union Cabinet, Government of India. https://www.pib.gov.in/PressReleasePage.aspx?PRID=1671912

———(2020b). '6 cities rated 5 Star, 65 Cities rated 3 Star and 70 Cities rated 1 Star: MoHUA announces results of Star Rating of garbage free cities'. Press Release, 19 May. New Delhi: Press Information Bureau; Ministry of Housing and Urban Affairs, Government of India. https://pib.gov.in/PressReleasePage.aspx?PRID=1625076

———(2020c). 'Medical waste management during COVID-19 pandemic.' Press Release, 20 September. New Delhi: Press Information Bureau; Ministry of Health and Family Welfare, Government of India. https://pib.gov.in/PressReleseDetailm.aspx?PRID=1657061

———(2020d). 'Urban Forest scheme to develop 200 "Nagar Van" across the country in next five years. "Urban Forest will revive the age old tradition of village forest in cities": Shri Prakash Javadekar.' Press Release, 5 June. New Delhi: Press Information Bureau; Ministry of Environment, Forest and Climate Change, Government of India. https://pib.gov.in/PressReleasePage.aspx?PRID=1629563

——(2020e). '5th Anniversary of Urban Missions.' Press Release, 25 June. New Delhi: Press Information Bureau; Ministry of Housing and Urban Affairs, Government of India. https://pib.gov.in/PressReleaseIframePage.aspx?PRID=1634268

——(2021). 'India's Merchandise Trade: Preliminary Data July 2021.' Press Release, 02 August. New Delhi: Ministry of Commerce and Industry, Government of India. https://pib.gov.in/PressReleasePage.aspx?PRID=1741676

Pipa, A.F. (2018). 'Can US cities help the world achieve the Sustainable Development Goals?' Blog, 29 November. Future Development series. Brookings. https://www.brookings.edu/blog/future-development/2018/11/29/can-us-cities-help-the-world-achieve-the-sustainable-development-goals/

Pisa, K. and Fleming, K. (2014). 'This little card is why people in Hong Kong don't carry cash.' CNN. 9 July. https://edition.cnn.com/2014/06/12/business/hong-kong-octopus-card/index.html

Planning Commission (2011). 'Report of Panel of Experts on Reforms in Central Public Sector Enterprises (CPSEs)'. New Delhi: Planning Commission, Government of India.

Plan International (2018). *Unsafe in the City: The Everyday Experiences of Girls and Young Women. The State of the World's Girls, 2018*. Woking: Plan International. https://plan-uk.org/file/because-i-am-a-girl-2018-unsafe-in-the-citypdf/download?token=03CgPDjk

Poovanna, S. (2020). 'Bengaluru has the worst traffic in the world: Report.' *Mint*, 29 January. https://www.livemint.com/news/india/bengaluru-has-the-worst-traffic-in-the-world-report-11580278531554.html

Porter, M.E. (1990). *The Competitive Advantage of Nations*. New York: Free Press.

——(1998). 'Clusters and the New Economics of Competition. Government Policy and Regulation.' *Harvard Business Review* (November–December). https://hbr.org/1998/11/clusters-and-the-new-economics-of-competition

Potocnik, J. and Gawel, A. (2019). 'The World's economy is only 9% circular. We must be bolder about saving resources.' weforum.org, 11 November. Geneva: World Economic Forum. https://www.weforum.org/agenda/2019/11/economy-circular-recycling

Praja (2020a). 'Praja's Urban Governance Index 2020.' Mumbai: Praja Foundation. https://praja.org/praja_docs/praja_downloads/Highlights%20of%20UGI%202020.pdf

———(2020b). 'National Consultation on Urban Governance: Key Findings from 21 States.' Mumbai: Praja. https://praja.org/praja_docs/praja_downloads/National%20Consultation%20On%20Urban%20Governance-%20Key%20Finding%20From%2021%20States.pdf

Prasanna, A. (2020). Rethinking Urban Planning and Governance in Light of Covid-19'. Blog, 16 April. Vidhi: Centre for Legal Policy. https://vidhilegalpolicy.in/blog/rethinking-urban-planning-and-governance-in-light-of-covid-19/

PRS India (2017). 'Overview of Road Accidents in India.' New Delhi: New Delhi: PRS Legislative Research. https://prsindia.org/files/policy/policy_vital_state/Overview%20of%20Road%20Accidents.pdf

PTI (2016). '80 per cent of Indian doctors located in urban areas.' *The Economic Times*, 19 August. https://economictimes.indiatimes.com/industry/healthcare-biotech/80-per-cent-of-indian-doctors-located-in-urban-areas/articleshow/53774521.cms?from=mdr

———(2019a). 'India joins global alliance on responsible use of smart city technologies.' *The Economic Times*, 11 October. https://economictimes.indiatimes.com/news/economy/infrastructure/india-joins-global-alliance-on-responsible-use-of-smart-city-technologies/articleshow/71535525.cms?utm_source=contentofinterest&utm_medium=text&utm_campaign=cppst

———(2019b). 'Pollution worse in Indian cities as registered vehicles up by 700 times since 1951: Study.' *Financial Express*, 12 June. https://www.financialexpress.com/india-news/pollution-worse-in-indian-cities-as-registered-vehicles-up-by-700-times-since-1951-study/1605754/

———(2019c). '11 agencies accepting national common mobility card.' *Deccan Herald*, 5 December. https://www.deccanherald.com/national/11-agencies-accepting-national-common-mobility-card-783021.html

———(2019d). 'Number of vehicles on Delhi roads over 1 crore, with more than 70 lakh two wheelers: Economic Survey.' *ETAuto*, 23 February. https://auto.economictimes.indiatimes.com/news/industry/number-of-vehicles-on-delhi-roads-over-1-crore-with-more-than-70-lakh-two-wheelers-economic-survey/68128444

———(2020a). 'Remittances to India to fall by 9% to $76 billion in 2020 due to COVID-19: World Bank.' *BusinessToday.in*, 10 October. https://www.businesstoday.in/current/economy-politics/remittances-to-india-to-fall-by-9-to-76-billion-in-2020-due-to-covid-19-world-bank/story/420345.html

———(2020b). 'Niti Aayog releases draft model Act on land titles.' *The Economic Times*, 30 October. https://economictimes.indiatimes.com/news/economy/policy/niti-aayog-releases-draft-model-act-on-land-titles/articleshow/78955482.cms?from=mdr

Puliyel, Nia. (2020). 'Why Covid-19 can—and should—change how our cities are designed.' *The Caravan*, 4 May. https://caravanmagazine.in/health/why-covid-19-and-should-change-how-our-cities-are-designed

Puri, H.S. (2020). 'Towards "atma nirbhar" cities and building 70% of future India.' *The Free Press Journal*, 18 December. https://www.freepressjournal.in/analysis/towards-atma-nirbhar-cities-andbuilding-70-of-future-india-writes-hardeep-puri

Pyle, K. (2021). 'India needs senior female cops for safer cities, 90% women retire as police constables.' The Print, 13 January. https://theprint-in.cdn.ampproject.org/c/s/theprint.in/opinion/india-needs-senior-female-cops-for-safer-cities-90-women-retire-as-police-constables/584221/?amp

Raj, S., Paul, S.K., Chakraborty, A. and Kuttippurath, J. (2020). 'Anthropogenic forcing exacerbating the urban heat islands in India.' *Journal of Environmental Management* 257. https://www.sciencedirect.com/science/article/pii/S0301479719317244#

Raja, D.J.S., (2016). 'Better governance, citizen engagement via open data.' *Mint*, 2 August. https://www.livemint.com/Specials/Cf6r7xS9WYTHddIyXOXPhL/Better-governance-citizen-engagement-via-open-data.html

Rajagopalan, S. (2019). 'The single-word answer to what Indian women want.' *Mint*, 19 August. https://www.livemint.com/opinion/online-views/the-single-word-answer-to-what-indian-women-want/amp-1566236143934.html?__twitter_impression=true

———(2020). 'India's centripetal structure is impending governance.' *Mint*, 27 April. https://www.livemint.com/opinion/online-views/india-s-centripetal-structure-is-impeding-governance-11588003200529.html

Rajagopalan, S., and Choutagunta, A. (2020). 'Assessing Healthcare Capacity in India.' Mercatus Working Paper. Arlington, VA: Mercatus Center, George Mason University. https://www.mercatus.org/system/files/rajagopalan-india-healthcare-mercatus-v2.pdf

Randolph, G. and Gandhi, S. (2019). 'Migrants aren't streaming into cities, and what this means for urban India.' *Hindustan Times*, 22 July. https://www.hindustantimes.com/analysis/migrants-aren-t-streaming-into-cities-and-what-this-means-for-urban-india/story-FcyA2hJkzq4cpyf1T9Yz3L.html

Rao, R. (2018). 'Bengaluru lakes on the verge disappearing as urbanisation takes centre stage.' CNBCTV18, 26 July. https://www.cnbctv18.com/economy/bengaluru-lakes-on-the-verge-of-disappearing-as-urbanization-takes-centre-stage-381651.htm

———(2020). 'Najafgarh jheel to nala — How Delhi and Gurugram ruined their second-largest waterbody.' The Print, 6 September. https://theprint.in/opinion/najafgarh-jheel-to-nala-how-delhi-gurugram-ruined-second-largest-waterbody/496091/

Rath, M., Schellenberg, T., Rajan, P. and Singhal, G. (2020). 'Decentralized Wastewater and Fecal Sludge Management: Case Studies from India.' ADBI Development Case Study No. 2020-4 (September). Tokyo: Asian Development Bank Institute. https://www.adb.org/sites/default/files/publication/634586/adbi-cs2020-2.pdf

Ratho, A. (2019). 'Slum Tourism: Promoting participatory development or abusing poverty for profit?' ORF Issue Brief. New Delhi: Observer Research Foundation.

———(2020a). 'How urban planning can make Indian cities more inclusive for women.' The Print, 23 December. https://theprint.in/opinion/how-urban-planning-can-make-indian-cities-more-inclusive-for-women/572032/

———(2020b). 'Cities for Women: Taking stock of gender-sensitive urban planning and design.' Urban Futures series. New Delhi: Observer Research Foundation. https://www.orfonline.org/expert-speak/cities-women-taking-stock-gender-sensitive-urban-planning-design/

Ratho, A. and John, P.L. (Eds) (2020). *Rethinking Cities in a Post-COVID-19 World.* New Delhi: Observer Research Foundation and *Global Policy Journal.*

Reddy, G.V. (2018). 'The Big Urban Mobility Opportunity.' In Kant, *The Path Ahead: Transformative Ideas for India.* New Delhi: Rupa Publications. 268–83.

Rekhta (n.d.). 'Tarana-i-Hindi, Allama Iqbal'. Rekhta.org. https://www.rekhta.org/nazms/taraana-e-hindii-saare-jahaan-se-achchhaa-hindostaan-hamaaraa-allama-iqbal-nazms

Riis, J.A. (1890). *How the Other Half Lives: Studies among the Tenements of New York.* New York NY: Charles Scribner's Sons.

Rodríguez-Pose, A. and Tijmstra, S. (2007). 'Local Economic Development as an alternative approach to economic development in Sub-Saharan Africa.' *Environment and Planning C: Government and Policy* 25, (4): 516–36.

Rohra, S. (2016). 'Organizing for urban governance.' *Mint*, 12 July. https://www.livemint.com/Opinion/Hsm1BMPHSErv0mzaClZWFJ/Organizing-for-urban-governance.html

Rose, J.F.P. (2016). *The Well-Tempered City: What Modern Science, Ancient Civilizations, and Human Nature Teach Us About the Future of Urban Life.* New York: HarperCollins.

Roy, S.N. and Manish. (2020). 'Institutional challenges to migrants' welfare.' *Financial Express,* 27 April. https://www.

financialexpress.com/opinion/institutional-challenges-to-migrants-welfare/1940368/

Roy, D. and Meera, S.L. (2020). 'Housing for India's Low-Income Urban Households: A Demand Perspective.' Working Paper 402. New Delhi: Indian Council for Research on International Economic Relations (ICRIER). https://icrier.org/pdf/Working_Paper_402.pdf

Ruggeri, A. (2017). 'The ambitious plan to stop the ground from sinking.' BBC.com, 1 December. https://www.bbc.com/future/article/20171130-the-ambitious-plan-to-stop-the-ground-from-sinking

Rukmini, S. (2019). 'Why India needs more mohalla clinics.' *Mint*, 9 December. https://www.livemint.com/news/india/why-india-needs-more-mohalla-clinics-11575876056919.html

Rumi, A. (2020a). 'Water Supply in Delhi: Five Key Issues.' ORF Occasional Paper No. 252. New Delhi: Observer Research Foundation. https://www.orfonline.org/research/water-supply-in-delhi-five-key-issues-67477/

———(2020b). 'Rainwater harvesting strategy of Delhi government.' New Delhi: Observer Research Foundation, 31 July. https://www.orfonline.org/expert-speak/rainwater-harvesting-strategy-delhi-government/

———(2020c). 'Scaling-up urban rainwater harvesting.' New Delhi: Observer Research Foundation, 2 May. https://www.orfonline.org/expert-speak/scaling-up-urban-rainwater-harvesting-65535/

Sadik-Khan, J. and Solomonow, S. (2020). 'Janette Sadik-Khan: we must rethink our streets to create the six-foot city.' *The Guardian*, 4 September. https://www.theguardian.com/cities/2020/sep/04/janette-sadik-khan-we-must-rethink-our-streets-to-create-the-six-foot-city

Sai, M. (2016). 'Who will buy 4,000 acres of PSU land coming up for sale?' *Business Standard*, 11 October. http://www.business-standard.com/article/economy-policy/who-will-buy-4-000-acres-of-psu-land-coming-up-for-sale-116101100617_1.html

Sala, I.M. (2016). 'Story of cities #39: Shenzhen – from rural village to the world's largest megalopolis.' *The Guardian*, 10 May. https://

www.theguardian.com/cities/2016/may/10/story-of-cities-39-shenzhen-from-rural-village-to-the-worlds-largest-megalopolis

Salat, S. and Ollivier, G. (2017). *Transforming the Urban Space Through Transit-Oriented Development: The 3V Approach.* Washington DC: World Bank. https://openknowledge.worldbank.org/handle/10986/26405

Sanghi, S., and Dhar, S. (2018). 'A pressing need for a national urban policy.' *Mint*, February 12. https://www.livemint.com/Opinion/v7wDDjmE4jscMQpm5aYIfO/A-pressing-need-for-a-national-urban-policy.html

Sankhe, S., Vittal, I., Dobbs, R., Mohan, A., Gulati, A., Ablett, J., Gupta, S., Kim, A., Paul, S., Sanghvi, A. and Sethy, G. (2010). *India's Urban Awakening: Building inclusive cities, sustaining economic growth.* McKinsey Global Institute, 1 April.

Santdasani, D. (2020). 'Why every city should adopt the Indore model of waste management.' *DailyO*, 16 September. https://www.dailyo.in/politics/swachh-bharat-indore-clean-city-waste-management/story/1/33625.html

Sanyal, S. (2013a). *Land of the Seven Rivers: A Brief History of India's Geography.* Gurugram: Penguin India.

———(2013b). 'Sanjeev Sanyal: Reuilding Mumbai for the 21st Century.' *Business Standard*, 21 January. https://wap.business-standard.com/article-amp/opinion/sanjeev-sanyal-rebuilding-mumbai-for-the-21st-century-109111100032_1.html?__twitter_impression=true

———(2017). 'Why Indian cities need flexible plans.' *Mint*, 4 February. http://www.livemint.com/Politics/PPdBqRH7ysBTi07J7Adu1H/Why-Indian-cities-need-flexible-plans.html

———(2018). 'Design Indian Cities for People, Not Buildings.' In A. Kant, *The Path Ahead: Transformative Ideas for India.* New Delhi: Rupa Publications. 284–92.

Sanyal, S., Nagrath, S., and Singla, G. (2010). *The Alternative Urban Futures Report: Urbanisation & Sustainability In India: An Interdependent Agenda.* New Delhi: WWF-India. https://wwfin.awsassets.panda.org/downloads/urbanisation_report.pdf

Saran, S. (2019). 'India's Climate Change Policy: Towards a Better Future.' New Delhi: Ministry of External Affairs, Government of India.

https://www.mea.gov.in/articles-in-indian-media.htm?dtl/32018/Indias_Climate_Change_Policy_Towards_a_Better_Future

Sarma, N. (2020). 'Municipal bonds: A sustainable source of finance for Indian cities.' *Expert Speak* series, 10 June. New Delhi: Observer Research Foundation. https://www.orfonline.org/expert-speak/municipal-bonds-sustainable-source-finance-indian-cities-67646/#click=https://t.co/2Gqu1oNvSC

Sasi, A. (2016). 'Why Rajasthan's new titling law for property is great for faster development.' *Financial Express*, 7 May. https://www.financialexpress.com/economy/why-rajasthans-new-titling-law-for-property-is-great-for-faster-development/250186/

Sato, C., Haga, M. and Nishino, J. (2006). 'Land Subsidence and Groundwater Management in Tokyo.' *International Review for Environmental Strategies* 6, (2). https://www.iges.or.jp/en/pub/land-subsidence-and-groundwater-management/en

Save the Children (2015), 'How India's Police Stations can be made Child-Friendly.' Gurugram: Save the Children, India. https://www.savethechildren.in/news/how-india-s-police-stations-can-be-made-child-1/

———(2018). *WINGS 2018 World of India's Girls: A study on the perception of girls' safety in public spaces.* London: Save the Children International.

Searchinger, T., Hanson, C., Waite, R., Lipinski, B. and Leeson, G. (2013). *Achieving Replacement Level Fertility: Creating a Sustainable Food Future, Installment Three.* Washington DC: World Resources Institute, 7 August. https://www.wri.org/publication/achieving-replacement-level-fertility

Seetharaman, G. (2019). 'How India is reviving its heritage'. *The Economic Times*, 13 January. https://economictimes.indiatimes.com/news/politics-and-nation/how-india-is-reviving-its-heritage/articleshow/67503462.cms

Sen, R. (n.d.). 'The Fall of the Manchester of the East'. *WWF*. https://www.wwfindia.org/news_facts/feature_stories/the_fall_of_manchester_of_the_east/

Sen, S. (2018), 'If 80% water consumption in India is for agriculture, why is it unregulated and inefficient?' ORF, 3 May. New Delhi:

Observer Research Foundation. https://www.orfonline.org/expert-speak/if-80-water-consumption-in-india-is-for-agriculture-why-is-it-unregulated-and-inefficient/

Sengupta, S. (2018). *Down to Earth*, 20 November. 'Cities across India have started water rationing.' https://www.downtoearth.org.in/news/water/cities-across-india-have-started-water-rationing-62187#:~:text=Cities%20like%20Mumbai%2C%20Jaipur%2C%20Lucknow,many%20have%20started%20water%20rationing

Sethi, N. and Rao, M. (2018). 'Model contract for privatising urban health care.' *Business Standard*, 2 April. https://www.business-standard.com/article/current-affairs/model-contract-for-privatising-urban-health-care-117071900249_1.html

Shah, A. (2019), 'How the ride will replace the drive.' *Mint*, 15 March. https://www.livemint.com/technology/tech-news/how-the-ride-will-replace-the-drive-1552585130633.html

Shah, K., and Agrawal, H. (2019). 'Failing to acknowledge urbanisation undermines quality of life.' *Hindustan Times*, 16 April.' https://www.hindustantimes.com/analysis/failing-to-acknowledge-urbanisation-undermines-quality-of-life/story-ZqrYjOIEllIxqjQkYYYPF8O.html

Shah, K., Tandel, V., and Agrawal, H. (2020). 'Why India has the fastest-growing cities.' *Mint*, 20 January. https://www.livemint.com/news/india/why-india-has-the-fastest-growing-cities-11580053066942.html

Shah, S. (2020). 'Walk the chowk.' *India Today*, 31 August. https://www.indiatoday.in/magazine/leisure/story/20200907-walk-the-chowk-1716433-2020-08-31

Sharma, K. (2000). *Rediscovering Dharavi: Stories From Asia's Largest Slum*. New Delhi: Penguin Books India.

Sharma, S. (2018). *Smart Cities Unbundled: Ideas and Practice of Smart Cities in India*. New Delhi: Bloomsbury India.

Sharma, A.K. (2019). '11.09 mn homes lying vacant in India: Report.' *Mint*, 15 October. https://www.livemint.com/news/india/11-09-million-vacant-houses-in-india-says-report-11571053150289.html

Shaw, A. (1996). 'Urban Policy in Post-Independent India: An Appraisal.' *Economic and Political Weekly* 31, (4): 224–28. http://www.jstor.org/stable/4403721

———(2012). *Oxford India Short Introductions: Indian Cities.* New Delhi: Oxford University.

Sheehan, S. (2017). 'China's Houkou Reforms and the Urbanization Challenge.' *The Diplomat*, 22 February. https://thediplomat.com/2017/02/chinas-hukou-reforms-and-the-urbanization-challenge/

Shenvi, A., and Slangen, R.H. (2018). 'Enabling Smart Urban Development in India Through Floor Area Ratio Incentives.' No. 48. ADB South Asia Working Paper Series. Manila: Asian Development Bank. https://www.adb.org/sites/default/files/publication/435936/swp-058-smart-urban-redevelopment-india.pdf

Shukla, A. (2020). 'What lessons does the Covid-19 pandemic hold for India's health system?' Scroll.in, 29 May. https://scroll.in/article/962794/what-lessons-does-the-covid-19-pandemic-hold-for-indias-health-system

Siddhanta, P. (2015). 'Bypassing Land Acquisition Trouble: Govt may use surplus PSU land for new projects.' *The Indian Express*, 22 July. https://indianexpress.com/article/india/india-others/bypassing-land-acquisition-trouble-govt-may-use-surplus-psu-land-for-new-projects/

Singh, U. (2009a). *A History of Ancient and Early Medieval India: From the Stone Age to the 12th Century.* New Delhi: Pearson Education India.

———(2005). 'Review of Urban Transportation in India.' *Journal of Public Transportation* 8, (1): 79–97.

———(2020a). 'Solid Waste Management in Urban India: Imperatives for Improvement.' ORF Occasional Paper 283, 19 November. New Delhi: Observer Research Foundation.

Singh, M. (2020b). 'India's shift from mass transit to MaaS transit: Insights from Kochi.' *Transportation Research Part A: Policy and Practice* 131, (C): 219–27.

Singh, D. (2020c). 'Mumbai: Waterfront project is more for public.' *The Free Press Journal*, 29 February. https://www.freepressjournal.in/mumbai/mumbai-waterfront-project-is-more-for-public

Sivaramakrishnan, S. (2019). '120,000 tonnes of faecal sludge: why India needs a market for human waste.' weforum.org, 29 September. Geneva: World Economic Forum. https://www.weforum.org/agenda/2019/09/how-to-improve-sanitation-in-india/

Smith., T. (2019). 'A Brief History of Beijing's 798 Art District.' Culture Trip, 18 June. https://theculturetrip.com/asia/china/articles/a-brief-history-of-the-798-art-district-in-beijing/

Somvanshi, A. (2019). 'Indian cities are simmering in their own waste heat.' *Down To Earth*, 14 June, https://www.downtoearth.org.in/news/environment/indian-cities-are-simmering-in-their-own-waste-heat-65084

Sreevatsan, A. (2018). 'Pune tops urban governance survey of 23 major Indian cities.' *Mint*, 15 March. https://www.livemint.com/Politics/aPNlkAptjRXiDGJnvN4fJO/Pune-tops-urban-governance-survey-of-23-major-Indian-cities.html

Sridhar, K.S. (2010). 'Impact of Land Use Regulations: Evidence from India's Cities.' *Urban Studies* 47, (7): 1541–69. https://doi.org/10.1177/0042098009353813

———(2011). 'Addendum to Determinants of City Growth and Output in India.' *Review of Urban and Regional Development Studies* 23, (2–3): 162–65.

———(2016). 'Costs and Benefits of Urbanization: the Indian Case'. No. 607, ADI Working Paper Series. Tokyo: Asian Development Bank Institute. https://www.adb.org/sites/default/files/publication/204406/adbi-wp607.pdf

Sridharan, K. (2015). 'Opportunities for "planners" are immense.' *The Hindu*, 17 August. https://www.thehindu.com/features/education/careers/opportunities-for-planners-are-immense/article7549928.ece

Stromberg, J. (2015). 'The "fundamental rule" of traffic: building new roads just makes people drive more.' *Vox*, 18 May. https://www.vox.com/2014/10/23/6994159/traffic-roads-induced-demand

Subudhi, S., and Bilgrami, S. (2019). 'Urban planning: Building resilient cities for the future.' *Financial Express*, 12 August. https://www.financialexpress.com/opinion/urban-planning-building-resilient-cities-for-the-future/1672871/

Suhag, R. (2016). 'The status of groundwater: Extraction exceeds recharge.' The PRS Blog, 6 May. https://prsindia.org/theprsblog/the-status-of-ground-water-extraction-exceeds-recharge

Sultan, P. (2018). 'Dinpanah and Shergarh of Purana Qila: Why 2 rival kings chose the same site to raise cities'. *Hindustan Times*, 26 January. https://www.hindustantimes.com/delhi-news/dinpanah-and-shergarh-why-two-rival-kings-chose-the-same-site-to-raise-cities/story-nrx0p8i6WZcdo48INjiuOL.html

———(2018). 'Ban on motor vehicles in Delhi's Chandni Chowk; pedestrians, cycle and e-rickshaws to be allowed.' *Hindustan Times*, 28 August. https://www.hindustantimes.com/delhi-news/ban-on-motor-vehicles-in-delhi-s-chandni-chowk-pedestrians-cycle-and-e-rickshaws-to-be-allowed/story-e6ajVlGQ3sn95Y2A2HiRIM.html

Swiney, C. F., and Foster, S. (2019). 'Cities Are Rising in Influence and Power on the Global Stage.' Bloomberg CityLab, 15 April. https://www.citylab.com/perspective/2019/04/city-leadership-international-policy-mayors-u20-uclg-c40/587089

Tandel, V., Patel, S., Gandhi, S., Pethe, A. and Agarwal, K. (2016). 'Decline of rental housing in India: the case of Mumbai.' *Environment and Urbanization* 28, (1): 259–74.

Tandel, V. and Gandhi, S. (2019). 'Why is India's real estate market stagnating.' *Hindustan Times*, 10 April. https://www.hindustantimes.com/analysis/why-is-india-s-real-estate-market-stagnating/story-w4AdYUPoLAzUBlc5TsryFN_amp.html?__twitter_impression=true

Tandel, V., and Hiranandani, K. (2016). 'Recognizing urban India.' *Mint*, 6 July. http://www.livemint.com/Opinion/mjzfbOmd7uFCyJUWDRx5fO/Recognizing-urban-India.html

Taylor, M. (2018). 'Emerging cities could attract $29 trillion in climate-cash: World Bank.' Thomas Reuters Foundation, 29 November. https://news.trust.org/item/20181129085608-47aaj/

———(2020). 'Large areas of London to be made car-free as lockdown eased.' *The Guardian*, 15 May. https://www.theguardian.com/uk-news/2020/may/15/large-areas-of-london-to-be-made-car-free-as-lockdown-eased?fbclid=IwAR0iQNyvcwmbWeQXuAQ8AiaIFsdbPkbturDvyOUbKgPh8XcPwqCdWr5QZvM

TERI (2014). 'Climate Proofing Indian Cities: A Policy Perspective.' Policy Brief, March. New Delhi: The Energy and Resources Institute. https://www.teriin.org/policybrief/docs/Urban.pdf

Tewari, P. (2020). 'Road safety pays: If India cuts accidents by half, it could add 14% to GDP per capita by 2038.' Scroll.in, 30 September. https://scroll.in/article/973490/road-safety-pays-if-india-cuts-accidents-by-half-it-could-add-14-to-gdp-per-capita-by-2038

Thakre, M. and Ray, M. (2018). 'In Need for a National Urban Policy with Child-centered lens.' *The India Saga*, 26 April. https://theindiasaga.com/opinion/in-need-for-a-national-urban-policy-with-child-centered-lens/

Thapar, R. (2002). *The Penguin History of Early India: From the Origins to AD 1300*. Gurugram: Penguin Random House.

Tharoor, S. (2020). 'Locked under blue skies: Air quality and the pandemic.' Terra Nova series. New Delhi: Observer Research Foundation. https://www.orfonline.org/expert-speak/locked-under-blue-skies-air-quality-and-the-pandemic-65882/

The Economic Times (2019). 'PollPourri: 62% of Highly Urban Seats go to BJP.' *ET* on Twitter, 29 May. https://twitter.com/EconomicTimes/status/1133602618519969793

The Economist. (2013). 'The Urban Investment.' 21 May. https://www.economist.com/free-exchange/2013/03/21/the-urban-investment

———(2014a). 'Where China's future will happen.' 16 April. https://www.economist.com/leaders/2014/04/16/where-chinas-future-will-happen

———(2018). 'A tale of 19 mega-cities: China is trying to turn itself into a country of 19 super-regions.' 23 June. https://www.economist.com/china/2018/06/23/china-is-trying-to-turn-itself-into-a-country-of-19-super-regions

The Indian Express (2020). 'City and the deluge.' Editorial, 17 October. https://indianexpress.com/article/opinion/editorials/telangana-rains-city-floods-6758058/

The Hindu (2000). 'Rediscovering Dharavi'. Excerpt, 17 September. https://www.thehindu.com/todays-paper/tp-miscellaneous/tp-others/rediscovering-dharavi/article28043920.ece

The Hindu (2021). 'Govt. offers reward for rescuing road crash victims.' 5 October. https://www.thehindu.com/news/national/govt-offers-reward-for-rescuing-road-crash-victims/article36846292.ece

Thornton, A. (2019). 'These countries have the most women in parliament.' WEF, 12 February. Geneva: World Economic Forum. https://www.weforum.org/agenda/2019/02/chart-of-the-day-these-countries-have-the-most-women-in-parliament/

TNIE (2018). 'How India's Tier-3 and Tier-4 cities emerging as the next IT destinations.' *The New Indian Express*. 4 August. http://www.newindianexpress.com/business/2018/aug/04/how-indias-tier-3-and-tier-4-cities-emerging-as-the-next-it-destinations-1853220.html

TNN (2020a). 'In 30 yrs, India Tipped to Double the Waste it Generates.' *The Times of India*, 4 March.

———(2020b). 'Chennai: Urban forests spring up amid concrete jungle.' *The Times of India*, 11 November. https://timesofindia.indiatimes.com/city/chennai/chennai-urban-forests-spring-up-amid-concrete-jungle/articleshow/79163667.cms

Trivedy, S. (2019). 'Parliament to Kashi Vishwanath: Why Modi always hires architect Bimal Patel for pet projects.' The Print, 4 December. https://theprint.in/features/parliament-to-kashi-vishwanath-why-modi-always-hires-architect-bimal-patel-for-pet-projects/329968/

Tumbe, C. (2016). 'Urbanisation, demographic transition, and the growth of cities in India, 1870–2020'. Working Paper, C-35205-INC-1. New Delhi: International Growth Centre, IGC-India. https://www.theigc.org/wp-content/uploads/2016/11/Tumbe-2016-Working-paper.pdf

———(2018). *India Moving: A History of Migration*. Gurugram: Penguin Random House.

———(2019). 'A million migrations: Journeys in search of jobs'. *Mint*. 17 January. https://www.livemint.com/Politics/8WPPsZygqR7Mu6e3Fgy55N/A-million-migrations-Journeys-in-search-of-jobs.html

Udas-Mankikar, S. and Girgaonkar, P. (2020). 'Stepping towards a health masterplan.' Urban Futures series. Delhi: Observer Research Foundation, 1 October. https://www.orfonline.org/expert-speak/stepping-towards-health-masterplan/

Udas-Mankikar, S. (2019). 'Municipal finance reforms in South Africa and its applicability for India.' ORF, 27 May. New Delhi: Observer Research Foundation. https://www.orfonline.org/expert-speak/municipal-finance-reforms-in-south-africa-and-its-applicability-for-india-51313/?amp#_edn2

——(2020a), 'Inadequate storm water infrastructure biggest hurdle in urban flood resilience.' ORF, 13 August. New Delhi: Observer Research Foundation. https://www.orfonline.org/expert-speak/inadequate-storm-water-infrastructure-biggest-hurdle-in-urban-flood-resilience/

——(2020b), 'Property-tax reforms key for India's post-Covid-19 urban transformation.' ORF, 24 September. New Delhi: Observer Research Foundation. https://www.orfonline.org/expert-speak/property-tax-reforms-key-india-post-covid-urban-transformation/ [6]

UN-DESA (2018). '68% of the world population projected to live in urban areas by 2050, says UN.' New York: Department of Economic and Social Affairs. United Nations, 16 May. https://www.un.org/development/desa/en/news/population/2018-revision-of-world-urbanization-prospects.html

——(2015). *Habitat III Issue Papers – 19: Transport and Mobility*. New York: United Nations Department of Economic and Social Affairs, United Nations. https://uploads.habitat3.org/hb3/Habitat-III-Issue-Paper-19_Transport-and-Mobility-2.0.pdf

UNESCAP (n.d). 'Road Safety in India – Status and Challenges.' Bangkok: United Nations Economic and Social Commission for Asia and the Pacific. http://www.unescap.org/sites/default/files/17.%20%20Road%20Safety%20in%20India%20-%20Status%20and%20Challenges.pdf

UN-Habitat (2015a). *Habitat III Issue Papers – 3: Safer Cities*. New York & Kenya: United Nations Human Settlement Programme.

——(2015b). *Habitat III Issue Papers – 11: Public Space*. New York & Kenya: United Nations Human Settlement Programme.

———(2015c). *Habitat III Issue Papers – 16: Urban Ecosystems and Resource Management.* New York & Kenya: United Nations Human Settlement Programme.

———(2015d). *Habitat III Issue Papers – 15: Urban Resilience.* New York & Kenya: United Nations Human Settlement Programme.

———(2016). *World Cities Report 2016: Urbanization and Development – Emerging Futures.* Nairobi: United Nations Human Settlements Programme. https://unhabitat.org/sites/default/files/download-manager-files/WCR-2016-WEB.pdf

———(2017). *Habitat III Policy Papers – 10: Housing Policies.* United Nations Conference on Housing and Sustainable Urban Development. New York: United Nations. https://uploads.habitat3.org/hb3/Habitat%20III%20Policy%20Paper%2010.pdf

UNICEF (2009). 'Child Friendly Cities promoted by UNICEF National Committees and Country Offices – Fact sheet, September 2009.' New York: United Nations Children's Fund.

———(2012), *The State of the World's Children 2012: Children in an Urban World.* New York: United Nations Children's Fund. https://www.unicef.org/media/89226/file/The%20State%20of%20the%20World's%20Children%202012.pdf

Upadhyay, P.S. (2020). 'About 70% of the vaccines used around the world are made in India.' *DNA*, 11 April. https://www.dnaindia.com/world/report-about-70-of-vaccines-used-around-the-world-are-made-in-india-2820585

Vachana, V.R. (2019). 'Unleashing the potential of urban India.' *The Hindu*, 18 June. https://www.thehindu.com/opinion/op-ed/unleashing-the-potential-of-urban-india/article28022190.ece

———(2020). 'The COVID-19 crisis as a metropolitan battle.' *The Hindu*, 1 August. https://www.thehindu.com/opinion/op-ed/the-covid-19-crisis-as-a-metropolitan-battle/article32243597.ece

van der Zee, R. (2015). 'How Amsterdam became the bicycle capital of the world.' *The Guardian*, 5 May. https://www.theguardian.com/cities/2015/may/05/amsterdam-bicycle-capital-world-transport-cycling-kindermoord

Varma, N. (2019). 'Micromobility: A mode to combat traffic woes.' *Deccan Herald*, 2 June. https://www.deccanherald.com/business/

economy-business/micromobility-a-mode-to-combat-traffic-woes-737728.html

Venkataraman, M. (2014). 'What is Title Guarantee Worth in Land Markets? Evidence from Bengaluru, India.' Working Paper No. 473. Bengaluru: Indian Institute of Management Bangalore.

Venkatesh, M. (2017). 'India ranks 120th among 131 nations in women workforce, says World Bank Report.' *Hindustan Times*, 29 May. https://www.hindustantimes.com/india-news/india-ranks-120th-among-131-nations-in-women-workforce-says-world-bank-report/story-Q5AVD5aRlmLHA1RAFpnZuJ.html

Vishwanath, S. (2012). 'Managing the sludge'. *The Hindu*, 8 September. https://www.thehindu.com/todays-paper/tp-features/tp-propertyplus/managing-the-sludge/article3872615.ece

Vidal, J. (2006). 'Heart and soul of the city.' *The Guardian*, 1 November. https://www.theguardian.com/environment/2006/nov/01/society.travelsenvironmentalimpact

Voce, A. (2018). 'Cities Alive: Designing for Urban Childhoods.' *Children, Youth and Environments* 28, No. 2: 78–81. https://doi.org/10.7721/chilyoutenvi.28.2.0078

Wangchuk, R.N. (2021). 'How a Determined IAS Officer Transformed Surat Forever After a Deadly Plague'. *The Better India*, 26 February. https://www.thebetterindia.com/250052/surat-pneumonic-plague-1994-clean-city-india-ias-hero-sr-rao-inspiring-nor41/

WEF (2017). *Migration and Its Impact on Cities*. Geneva: World Economic Forum.

———(2019a). *Future of Consumption in Fast-Growth Markets: INDIA*. Geneva: World Economic Forum. http://www3.weforum.org/docs/WEF_Future_of_Consumption_Fast-Growth_Consumers_markets_India_report_2019.pdf

———(2019a). 'The Next Frontier: Natural Resource Targets.' White Paper. Geneva: World Economic Forum.

Weedy, S. (2018). 'Bhubaneswar joins Urban95 Child-Friendly City Movement.' Child in the City, 31 May. https://www.childinthecity.org/2018/05/31/bhubaneswar-joins-urban95-child-friendly-city-movement/#:~:text=%E2%80%9CThe%20Foundation%20has%20 been%20working,for%20the%20Foundation's%20Urban95%20initiative

Welle, B. (2015). '7 Proven Principles for Designing a Safer City.' Washington DC: World Resources Institute. https://www.wri.org/blog/2015/07/7-proven-principles-designing-safer-city

Welle, B., Li, W., Adriazola-Steil, C., King, R., Obelheiro, M., Sarmiento, C. and Liu, Q. (2015). 'Cities Safer by Design.' Washington DC: World Resources Institute. https://www.wri.org/research/cities-safer-design

Wheeling, K. (2019). 'Major cities in India are starting to run out of water.' *The Week*. 13 July.

Whiting, K. (2019). 'The world's 10 fastest growing cities are all in India.' *Insider*, 27 January. https://www.businessinsider.com/all-of-the-10-fastest-growing-cities-in-the-world-are-in-india-2019-1?IR=T

Whittle, N. (2020). 'Welcome to the 15-minute city.' *Financial Times*, 17 July. https://www.ft.com/content/c1a53744-90d5-4560-9e3f-17ce06aba69a

Willsher, K. (2016). 'Story of cities #12: Haussmann rips up Paris – and divides France to this day.' *The Guardian*, 31 March. https://www.theguardian.com/cities/2016/mar/31/story-cities-12-paris-baron-haussmann-france-urban-planner-napoleon

World Bank Data (n.d.). 'Intentional homicides (per 100,000 people) – Colombia.' UN Office on Drugs and Crime's International Homicide Statistics database. https://data.worldbank.org/indicator/VC.IHR.PSRC.P5?locations=CO

World Bank (2016). *Investing in Urban Resilience: Protecting and Promoting Development in a Changing World*. Washington, DC: World Bank. https://openknowledge.worldbank.org/handle/10986/25219

——— (2018). 'Urban Sustainability Framework.' First edition. Global Platform for Sustainable Cities. Washington, DC: World Bank. https://documents1.worldbank.org/curated/en/339851517836894370/pdf/123149-Urban-Sustainability-Framework.pdf

——— (2020). Property Taxation in India: Issues Impacting Revenue Performance and Suggestions for Reform. Washington DC: World Bank.

WRI India (2021). 'Urban Flooding: Insights from Hyderabad.' Based on WRI India's ongoing research. New Delhi: WRI India –Ross Center. https://www.wricitiesindia.org/content/urban-flooding

WRI India and MoHUA (n.d.). *Greening Indian Cities through Efficient Buildings: A Guidebook For Local Governments To Design And Implement Green Buildings Policies.* New Delhi: WRI India –Ross Center, and the Ministry of Housing & Urban Affairs, Government of India. https://smartnet.niua.org/csc/assets/pdf/RepositoryData/Energy_&_Green_Building/Greening_Indian_Cities_through_efficient_buildings.pdf

Wünsch, S. (2017). 'The museum that changed a whole city: Guggenheim Museum Bilbao turns 20.' *DW,* 19 October. https://www.dw.com/en/the-museum-that-changed-a-whole-city-guggenheim-museum-bilbao-turns-20/a-41013716

Yang, Y. (2019). 'Asian cities are competing to woo tech start-ups with incentives.' *South China Morning Post,* 6 February. https://www.scmp.com/tech/start-ups/article/2185092/asian-cities-are-competing-woo-tech-start-ups-incentives

Yengde, S. (2019). *Caste Matters.* Gurugram: Penguin Random House India.

Yeung, J., Gupta, S. and Guy, M. (2019). 'India has just five years to solve its water crisis, experts fear. Otherwise hundreds of millions of lives will be in danger.' CNN World, 4 July. https://edition.cnn.com/2019/06/27/india/india-water-crisis-intl-hnk/index.html

ZeeBiz (2019). 'Ambikapur launches India's first garbage cafe! Here is how this innovative idea is bringing change.' Zee Business, 18 July. https://www.zeebiz.com/india/news-ambikapur-launches-indias-first-garbage-cafe-here-is-how-this-innovative-idea-is-bringing-change-105961

Zevenbergen, C., Fu, D. and Pathirana, A. (2018). 'Transitioning to Sponge Cities: Challenges and Opportunities to Address Urban Water Problems in China.' *Water* 10, (9): 1230. https://www.mdpi.com/2073-4441/10/9/1230/htm

Index

Abdul Kalam, APJ, 66
Abraham, Reuben, 215
affordable housing, 90, 107, 138–145, 222, *see also* Housing for All; urban housing
Affordable Rental Housing Complex (ARHC), 70, 148
Afghanistan, 248
Africa, 22–23, 41–42, 44, 89, 171, 219, 224
ageing population, 43
agglomeration, 37, 58–65, 172, 196, 257
Agra, 9–10, 28, 68, 116, 206, 296; Taj Mahal in, 206
agriculture, 6, 29, 77, 265; water efficiency in, 112–113, *see also* groundwater, depletion
Ahluwalia, Isher J., 126, 297
Ahmedabad, 141, 151, 182, 189, 207, 211–212, 268, 272, 274, 286, 295; Sabarmati riverfront, 207, 226
Akbar, 10, 116
Allahabad, 68, 291
The Alternative Urban Futures Report, WWF, 280
Amazon, 91
Ambani, Dhirubhai, 66
Ambedkar, B.R., 37–39
Ambikapur, 128–130, 133
Amritsar, 95–96, 208; Golden Temple, 96, 208; Jallianwala Bagh, 97, 208
Andhra Pradesh, 195, 229; 'Maithri,' 229
Anganwadi centres, 233
Annihilation of Caste, Ambedkar, 38
anti-caste movement, 37, *see also* caste
Appleby, Humphrey, Sir, 278

Arrow, 58
artificial intelligence, 54, 263, 305
ASHAs (accredited social health activists), 251
Asian Infrastructure Investment Bank, 35
Assam, 'Meira Paibi,' 229
Atal Mission for Rejuvenation and Urban Transformation (AMRUT), 18, 111, 213, 295, 300
Australia, 21, 32, 51, 131, 162, 183, 191, 193, 222, 298; Sydney, MaaS, 166
Austria, Vienna, 12, 14, 219
Automatic Fare Collection Gate Standards, 157
Automobiles & Auto Components, 76
autonomous vehicles (AVs), 169–171
auxiliary nurse-midwives or ANMs, 251

Baker, Herbert, 14
Ballaney, Shirley, 182, 211, 265
Bangladesh, 30, 258
Bank of San Francisco, 73
Baron Georges-Eugène Haussman, 102–103
barter system, 6
Beijing Consensus, 35
Belgium, 12, 219
beneficiary-led construction (BLC), 144
Bengal Global Business Summit, 93

Bengaluru, 28, 60, 89, 109, 117, 119–120, 153, 164, 191, 193–194, 272–273, 294–295; as cantonment, 13; Malleswaram and Basavanagudi, 3; MICO (Bosch subsidiary), 62; population of, 61; talents in, 62; Tender S.U.R.E (Specifications for Urban Roads Execution) model in, 167; Transport Corporation's AC and feeder buses, 158
Bernard van Leer Foundation, 46, 235
Bertaud, Alain, 152, 175
Bharatiya Janata Party (BJP), 18, 34; NDA government, 121; Minimum Government Maximum Governance, 34
Bhopal, B-Nest Foundation, 305
BigApps, 305
Bihar, 57, 113, 158, 224, 286
Bill on Indian Easement 2018, 114
biodiversity, 47, 226, 235, 259, 266, 271
Bio-medical Waste Management (BMWM) Rule, 2016, 134
bio-methanation plant, 51
black death, 2
Bloomberg, Michael, 305
Bombay City Improvement Trust, 3
Bombay Stock Exchange (BSE), 63, 252
bore wells, 117, *see also* groundwater extraction; water bodies
Bose, Subhas Chandra, 291

Brazil, 19, 92, 119, 135, 150, 158, 168, 174, 282, 290, 293; Curitiba, 150–151, 158, 209, 290; Sao Paulo, 162, 245
Bretton Woods systems, 31, 35
Brexit, 44
Britain, 12
Buddhism, 7
Building and Other Construction Workers Act 1996, 70
infrastructure building, 108, 135; water and sanitation, 108–139
Bureau for Energy Efficiency (BEE), 51, 115, 277
Bureau for Water Efficiency (BWE), 115
Business and Knowledge Process Outsourcing (BPO), 99
Bus Rapid Transit System (BRTS), 151, 158, 181, 212, 238, 290

Calcutta. *See* Kolkata
Cambodia, Phnom Penh Water Supply Authority, 120
Canada, 51, 89, 162, 184, 191, 193, 222; Montreal, 241; Toronto, 12, 73, 221, 241; Toronto metro system, 155; urbanization rate, 12; Weather Protected Walkway System, 162
cantonments, 13–14
capitalism, 32
carbon: emissions, 48–49, 52, 170, 275; footprint, 50–51, 165, 189; neutral, 49, 51–52
Caribbean, 23

caste, 8; based segregation, 37–39; Brahmins, 38; Dalits, 38–39; ghettoization of, 38; occupation-based structure of, 8; oppression, 41
Caste Matters, Yengde, 38
Catherine of Braganza, 12
Census of India 1881, 15; of 2011, 19, 109, 180
Central Pollution Control Board (CPCB), 117, 125, 272
central public-sector entities (CPSEs), 182–184
Central Vista, 207
Central Water Commission (CWC), 116
Chadwick, Edwin, 135
champion sectors, 30–31
Chandigarh, 164, 201; creation of, 16
Charnock, Job, 12
Chen, M.A., 84
Chennai (formerly Madras), 13, 15, 280, 76, 83, 89, 109, 116–117, 119, 125, 149, 160, 258–259, 262, 268, 280; Masulipatnam became 11; as Detroit of Asia, 108; floods, 256, 271; Mass Rapid Transit System, 155; water bodies, 272
Chennai Metro Rail Limited, 155
Chennai Unified Metropolitan Transport Authority Act in 2011, 155
Chhattisgarh, 57, 128, 130, 195, 283, 288
Chief Data Officer, 300

Chief Resilience Officer, 300
Childe, Gordon, 8
Child-Friendly Cities, 230–236
Child-Friendly City Initiative, UN-Habitat II conference, 231
China, 29–30, 46, 48, 51, 88, 268, 270–271, 275–276, 297–298; Beijing, 29, 35, 53, 65, 76, 89, 149, 190, 208, 245, 263; Belt and Road Initiative, 7, 35; capitalism, 32; Dongguan, 22, 53, 89; Foshan, 22, 53; Guangdong province, 53; Guangzhou, 22, 53, 77, 89; Huizhou, 22, 53; Hukou system of household registration, 22–23, 44, 69; Jiangmen, 22, 53; losing legitimacy, 32; losing legitimacy, (*see also* Covid-19 pandemic); Nanjing, 89; Pearl River Delta, 22, 76; Shanghai, 12, 35, 53, 76–77, 89, 185, 187–188; Shenzhen, 22, 31, 53, 60, 76, 89; start-up Unicorns, 53–54, 83; urban population share, 22; urbanization, 22, 27; as world's factory, 31; Wuhan, 31, 89; Zhaoqing, 22, 53; Zhongguancun hub, 53; Zhonghan, 53; Zhuhai, 22, 53
cholera epidemic, 112; in London, 2
Churchill, W. on cities of Soviet Union, 14
cities, 2–4, 18–21, 32–36; Class I, 20, 90; 1-tier as nexus, 89; 2-tier as hubs, 89; 3-tier as nodes, 89; defining, 4–5; dwellers, 26; as evolving system, 1; function of, 2, 88, 236, 307; governance, 94, 283; growth of, 13; innovation in 52–53, 89; leverage, 88–89, 223; planning, 6, 9, 196–200, 214, 260, (*see also* Harappan civilization); smaller, 89–92; smart, 46, 86, 204, 223, 238, 268, 301–302, 304–307; sustainable, 20, 256–257, 301

Cities and Public Policy, Mohanty, 59, 209

Cities are Good for You, Hollis, 213

City Alliance, 46

City Economic Councils, 78

City Gas Distribution network, 51

City Investments to Innovate, Integrate and Sustain (CITIIS), 304

city life vs. rural, 3–4

City Master Plans, 181, 197

civilizations, 6, 41, 254; Harappan, 6, 255

Civil Lines, 13–14

civil society, 73, 98, 162, 190; Ajeevika Bureau, 74; Disha Foundation, 73; role in healthcare, 73

clean energy, 50, 266, *see also* energy

climate change, 45–52, 161, 255, 257–258, 261, 263, 265, 273–275, 298; mitigation, 266

Climate Mobilization Act, 49

climate-related investments, 49, 266

Climate Smart Cities Assessment Framework (CSCAF), 259

Climate Transparency Report, 50
Clinton, Hillary, 33
clusters, 1–2, 52–53, 60, 63, 74–80, 91, 134, 156, 233
CO2 emissions, 51, 115, 257, 274, 277
Coalition on Disaster-Resilient Infrastructure' (CDRI), 36, 50, 267
Colombia: Bogota, 163, 168–169, 210, 227, 234, 263; Bogota, Poverty Action Lab, 227; Bogota, Protection of Children and Youth, 234; Bogota, TransMilenio in, 210; Cali, 227; homicides in, 227
colonialism, 12, 14, 219–220
Columbus, Christopher, 9
commercial activity, 13, 31
Commissionerate system, 229
communal: pogroms, 223, (see also Sikhs, pogrom against); tension, 141
compressed natural gas (CNG), 245
Conference on Housing and Sustainable Urban Development, 20
Congress Party, 34
Constitutional Amendment Act (CAA), 74th, 17, 93–94, 280–281, 287–289, 292
constitutionalism, 37
consumers, 27–28, 55, 67, 86, 131–132, 174
consumption, 28–31, 47–48, 50–51, 112–114, 125, 130–132, 136, 158, 160, 164, 275–276; as city focused, 55
Covid-19 pandemic, 1–2, 29–31, 41, 71–72, 86, 91, 108, 112, 134, 139, 143, 147, 159, 163, 178, 215, 232, 234, 236, 250–251, 263, 287, 306; based migrant crisis, 70; and China, 30; government diktat, 67; and informal workers, 85; lockdown, 1, 70, 67, 148, 243; and migrants, 67; migrations exodus of 10 million, 67, 70; personal protective equipment (PPE), 31, 134; related biomedical waste, 134; social distancing in public transport, 159; vaccines, 2, 32
creative economies. *See under* economy/economies
credit, access to, 73
crude oil, 160, 170
cyclists, 210, 235
cyclones, 255, 258, 261, 267; Cyclone Fani, 255, 266; Odisha's response to, 266; Super Cyclone 1991, 255, 258, 266; of 2007, 258

da Gama, Vasco, 9
Dalrymple, William, 95
Damascus, 5
data consumption, 303
Data Maturity Assessment Framework (DMAF), 302, 304
DataSmart Cities Strategy, 302
da Vinci, Leonardo, 3

De Architectura, Vitruvius, 7
decentralization, 94, 287
Dehradun, 200
Delhi, 15–16, 60–61, 82, 89, 98, 109, 115–118, 151, 187–188, 203–204, 221, 223, 240, 244–245, 263, 273–274; capital of British India moving to, 14; Chandni Chowk, 216, 226; Connaught Place, 227; as Dinpanah or 'the Asylum of Faith,' 10; Eastern Peripheral Expressway, 153; master plans, 198; Mohalla Clinics, 248, 250; moving capital from Calcutta to, 14; RK Puram, 192; Vasant Kunj, 216
Delhi Consensus, 35–36
Delhi Development Authority (DDA), 16
Delhi–Gurgaon highway, 226
Delhi Metro, 151, 158, 242
Delhi-NCR, 28, 66, 83, 133
demand management, 163
democracy, 32, 37, 52, 105, 220, 224, 278
Denmark, Copenhagen, 168, 209, 221; 'the Finger Plan,' 209
De Soto, Hernando, 176
de-urbanization, 13, 69
Development Rights Certificate (DRC), 297
Dhaka Water Supply and Sewerage Authority (DWASA), 121
Dhar, Devashish, 230
Dharavi, 135, 137–139; as 'six great Koliwadas of Bombay,' 137

Dharavi Redevelopment Project, 138
Digital India, 54
disaster preparedness, 266–267
District Municipalities Act 1920, 280
diversity, 38–39, 59, 165, 216, 222
'dualistic city', 13
Duerto, Javier, 234
Durbar of 1911, and coronation of V, George King George coronation of, 14

Ease of Doing Business, 54, 66, 78, 94, 304
East Asia, 22–23, 31, 42, 202, 219
East India Company (EIC), 10–12, 104
Ebola crisis, 2
ECBC-compliant, 51, 277
economic: development, 18, 74; growth, 55–57, 74, 77, 87–88, 90, 150, 174–175, 197, 200, 223, 226, 279, 284; liberalism, 32–34
economically weaker sections (EWS), 128, 136, 139–140, 142–143, 175
economy/economies, 35–36, 43, 46–47, 59, 92, 100–101, 121, 124, 140, 142; creative, 97–98; informal, 137, 197, 203; of localization, 59; of Singapore, 105
education, 9, 14, 34, 38–39, 42, 61, 68, 81–82, 142, 147, 202–203, 225; public schools, 71, 234; Skilling programmes, 71

electricity-powered vehicles/electric vehicles (EVs), 19, 31, 50-1, 165, 169–171, 245, 265–266
Electronic/Technology Products, 76
Elgin, C., 84
Elwell, Cyrill, 80
empires, 14, 56, 116
energy, 47–52, 128, 131, 138, 259–260, 262–263, 276; Advanced Chemistry Cell (ACC) Battery, 76; conservation, 51; efficiency, 51, 115, 263, 266; fossil fuel, 169–170; global use of, 49; renewable, 50, 263, 265–266, 276
Energy Conservation Building Code (ECBC), 51, 277
Energy Saving Companies (ESCOs), 115
English language: in freedom movement, 43; speaking, 31, 99; speaking workforce, 35–36, 43, 62
environment, 47–52, *see also* climate change
Ethiopia, 259
Europe, 9, 12, 22–23, 42–43, 53, 65, 77, 96, 173, 222, 276; cities in, 9, 11, 98; population of, 12; Roman Empire in, 7
Europeans, 44
European-style architecture, 14
European Union's (EU's) debt crisis, 45
EWC households, 144
exports: product, 30; services, 30

faecal sludge treatment plants (FSTPs), 124, *see also* SWaCH (Solid Waste Collection and Handling)
Fairchild, Sherman, 80
Fair Price Shops (FPS), 72
fake news-driven, 223
Faridabad, 68
Fatehpur Sikhri, by Akbar, 10
Federal Telegraph Corporation (FTC), 80
female workforce participation rate (FWPR), 87–88, 240, *see also* women
15th Finance Commission, 293
First Urbanites, Joseph on, 6
Five Year Plans, 16–17
floods, 105, 117, 259–260, 262, 268–271, 273, 276; in Chennai, 258; cloudbursts and, 273; Kerala, 255; in Mumbai, 256, 258
floor area ratio (FAR), 147, 175, 181–182, 205, 212, 297
Floor Square Index (FSI), 140, 144, 185–189, 209, 213, 296
flying cars, 169
food products, 76
Ford, Henry, 64, 173
foreign direct investment (FDI), 18
foreign investment, 33
Fox, Sean, 5
France, 12, 36, 49, 193, 206, 219, 284; Paris, 12, 102–104, 119, 163, 167–168, 186, 234, 263, 274; Paris by Baron-Haussman, 103–108

Future of Consumption in Fast-Growth Consumer Markets, 29–30

G20, 46, 50, 276
Gandhi, Rajiv, 63
Gandhi, Sanjay, 204
GDP: of Ahmedabad, 74; of France 36; of Mumbai, 74
Gehry, Frank, 98
gender: based violence, 239; bias, 39, 239; oppression, 39, 41; sensitive policing, 242
Germany, 12, 35, 130–131, 134, 164, 219; Berlin, 12, 14, 35, 53, 169, 219
GHG emissions, 48–49, 130, 133, 235, 258, 263, 273
GIS, 195
Glaeser, Edward, 48–49, 52, 60–62, 64, 79–81, 89, 103, 136, 172–173, 275
Global Aqueduct Water Risk Atlas, 107
Global Burden of Disease (GBD) initiative, 251
Global Cities report, 28, 56
Global Compact on Migration, 49
Global Compact on Refugees, 49
global: carbon emissions, 48–49, 275; consumption, 29–30; governance, 9, 31, 36; labour movement, 41–44; politics, 35–36; value-chains, 27, 30–32, 47, 52
Global Innovation Index, 53
globalization, 25
Global Liveability Ranking, 222
Global Smart Cities Alliance on Technology Governance, 46
Goa, 206
Goh Keng Swee, 106
Gokhale, Gopal Krishna, 292
Goldin, C., 83
Goodfellow, Tom, 5
Good Samaritan guidelines, 237
Goods and Services Tax (GST), 193, 293
Google maps, 95; *see also* GIS
Government of India Act, 1935, 280, 292
Greater Bay Area, 53
Great Indian Migration Wave, 42
The Great Smog of India, Siddharth Singh, 245
green buildings, 50, 259, 265–266
Green Corridor Project, 274
greenery, 4, 222
green waste, 125
gross value added (GVA), 85
groundwater: depletion, 112–115, 261; extraction, 117; Japan and withdrawal of, 261; recharge, 114, 117; resources, 112–114, *see also* water
Gujarat, 57, 70, 74, 93, 106, 113, 137, 145, 189, 211, 223; earthquake, 256, 267
Gujarat State Disaster Management Authority (GSDMA), 267
Gulf countries, 44
Gully Boy, 138; *see also* Dharavi; Slumdog Millionaire

Gurugram (formerly Gurgaon), 76, 99, 117, 203–204, 225, 299
Guterres, Antonio, 41
Guwahati, 268

H1N1 influenza, 2
Hank Lim, 104
Happening Haryana, 93
Haryana, 57, 71, 106, 203–204, 243, 255, 283
Haussmann, Baron (Georges-Eugène Haussmann), 167
Health and Wellness Centres (HWCs), 250
healthcare, 73, 145, 231, 233, 247–248, 306; private service providers, 249
Heat Action Plan (HAP), 274–275
heatwaves, 95, 274–275; 'urban heat island,' 273
heavy industries, 16
Henry, Prince, 77
heritage sites, 98; *see also* tourism
Hewlett, William, 80
Hidalgo, Anne, 291
High Efficiency Solar photovoltaic (PV) Modules, 76
High Powered Expert Committee's (HPEC), 108, 293
Hinglish, 43; *see also* English language speaking workforce
Hollis, Leo, 10, 135, 172, 213, 215
Homo Sapiens, 47
Hong Kong, 12, 22, 53, 76, 155, 165, 188, 210–211, 215, 271, 274
Hong Kong Mass Transit Railway Corporation, 210

Hong Kong Metro Corporation, 158
housing, 16–18, 20, 42, 68–71, 174–175, 192, 194, 196, 209, 260, 262, 264 urban, 108, 135–142, 180, 247, 258; shortage, 135, 139–148
Housing and Urban Development Corporation (HUDCO), 17
Housing for All, 18, 136, 141, 143, 262
Hubballi-Dharwad, 151
human civilization, 4, 23, 41, 52, 174; ingenuity, 47, 275; life, 1
Humayun, 10
Hyderabad, 54, 60, 66, 97–98, 119, 123, 125, 194, 198, 268, 272; dial-a-desludger service, 123; as political centre, 13
hyper-connectivity with mass transit, 156–157, 163

Ibrahim, Dawood, 252
ICLEI-Local Governments for Sustainability network, 46
Ikenberry, John, 31
immunization, 233, 249, 288
Improvements of Towns Act, 1850, 280
independence, 15–16, 24, 37, 40, 61, 63, 105, 136, 279; war of, 13
India Cooling Action Plan, 244, 274
India Easement Act of 1882, 114
India Lost and Found Foundation, 95
India Moving, Tumbe, 42, 68

IIM: Lucknow, 82
Indian Institute of Technology (IITs), 16, 62, 64, 80–81, 118; Bombay, 81; Delhi, 81; Kanpur, 82; Kharagpur, 82
Indo-Gangetic plain, 7
Indonesia, 19, 106; Jakarta, 145, 270–271
Indore, 3, 51–52, 126–127, 129–130, 132–133, 151, 187
Industrial Model Township (IMT), Manesar, 71
informal: sector, 57, 68, 70, 84–88, 181; wage employment, 84; workers, 84–85, 138, 222
information and communication technology (ICT), 304
Infosys, 61–62
infrastructure, 18, 82–83, 91–92, 102–103, 105, 110–111, 138–139, 162–163, 212, 217, 246–247, 251–252, 255–257, 269, 306; development, 60, 149, 209–211; security, 221–223
innovation, 1, 11, 36, 53–54, 59, 66, 74–77, 88–81, 88–89, 172, 305, 307; in cities, 52–53, 89
Innovative City Index, 89
Integrated Child Development Services (ICDS), 233
Integrated Command and Control Centres (ICCCs), 306
Integrated Development of Small and Medium Towns (IDSMT), 17
Intelligent Transport Systems, 164

Intended Nationally Determined Commitments (INDC), 50
International Finance Corporation (IFC), 49, 265–266
International Labour Organization (ILO), 87
International Monetary Fund (IMF), 35
International Solar Alliance, 36, 50
Internet of Things, 54, 263, 305
intra-city travel networks, 70
Invest India, 30, 106
Invest Karnataka, 93
investment destinations, 92–101
investment promotion arms or agencies, 92–93
Iqbal, Allama, 254–255
Ireland, 22
Isaacson, W., 3
ISB Mohali, 82
Ismail, Mirza, 61
Israel, 6, 113, 193; Tel Aviv, 53
Italy, Milan, 3, 163, 263

Jacobs, Jane, 58, 60, 213–216, 218, 225
Jainism, 7
Jaipur, 97, 108, 125, 141, 187, 193, 273, 294
Jamshedpur, 16, 268
Janaagraha, 282, 285, 287–289, 297–299
Japan, 22–23, 32, 51, 65, 125, 130, 132, 134, 156, 193, 261–262; disaster reducing infrastructure, 262; Hiroshima, 95–96; Osaka, 221; Tokyo, 12, 188, 210, 219,

221, 245, 247, 261, 270, 290;
Tokyo, Shinjuku in, 210; Tokyo
Flood Control Channel, 262;
waste generation, 132
Jawaharlal Nehru National Urban
Renewal Mission (JNNURM),
18, 148, 199, 203, 295
Jharkhand, 57, 224, 283
Jio Network, 303
Jodhpur, 98
Joseph, Tony, 6, 8, 44

Kanpur/Cawnpore, 13, 60, 62–64,
79, 125, 192, 225, 280, 296; as
Manchester of the East, 64;
now as Detroit of East, 64
Kant, Amitabh, 112–113
Karnataka, 61, 90, 106, 123, 157
Katz, L.F., 83
Kee Yeon Hwang, 226
Kerala, 166, 206, 229, 235, 242,
256, 268, 285, 288; floods, 255;
Janamaithri Suraksha Project,
229
Khan, Sadiq, 101, 291
khap panchayat, 39
knowledge spillover, 58–59, 74–75,
81, 83
Kochi, 166
Kochi one, 166
Kolbert, Elizabeth, 47, 275
Kolkata (formerly Calcutta), 12–14,
20, 46, 89, 98, 109, 113, 135,
145, 149, 153, 280, 291; funding
of, 13; Sanyal on, 12
Korean War, 96, 226
Krugman, Paul, 59

Krupa Ge, 271
Kuala Lumpur, 245, 269
Kunduri, E., 85, 87
Kyoto climate summit, 49

labour, 4, 8, 37–39, 58, 67, 88, 94,
288; agricultural, 40
land, 17, 133, 141–148, 150,
174, 176–178, 185, 190, 192,
257, 263, 275–276, 294, 296;
artificial scarcity of, 179–182;
mismanagement, 20; prices,
139–140, 146, 175; recycling,
189–193
landfills, 133–134, 218
land titling, 176–179
Land Titling Act, 177
land use, 154–155, 181–182, 189–
190, 197–198, 200, 202, 205,
209, 264, 280, 296; Integrated
transport, 198; Shaw on state
and, 17; sustainable, 266
Lashkar-e-Taiba, 252
Latin America, 23, 42, 171, 219,
234
law and order in cities, 227–230
Le Corbusier, 16, 214
Lee Kuan Yew, 105–106
Lee Myung Bak, 226
Lerner, Jaimie, 150
Lewis, Arthur, 21
liberalism versus conservatism,
32–36
light-emitting diodes [LED], 76
local economy, 57, 77, 79, 81, 84,
100, 138, 190
Lodis, 9

Lübeck's Law, 77
Lucknow, 63, 97, 108, 111, 116, 141, 161, 187, 280, 282, 296; Charbagh Railway Station, 205; Hazratganj, 216
Ludhiana, 68
Lutyens, Edwin, 14

MaaS, 166
Macaulay, Thomas Babington, 43
machine learning, 54, 305
Madhya Pradesh, 57, 195, 288
Madras Metropolitan Development Authority, 16
Magnetic Maharashtra, 93
Maharashtra, 57, 100, 115, 130, 142, 180, 195, 229, 286, 288; 'Mohalla Committees', 229
Mahbubani, Kishore, 106
malaria, 2, 246
Malaysia, 102, 104–106
Manila, 145
mankind, 4, 173
man-made fibre (MMF), 76
marriage: inter-caste, 33; inter-religion, 33
Marshall, Alfred, 52
Marshall, C., 58
master plans, 16–17, 107, 152, 181, 189, 197–198, 200, 204
Masulipatnam. *See* Chennai (formerly Madras)
mayoral system, 291
mayors, elected, 93, 282–283, 288–292
McCarty, Francis, 80
McKinsey, 74

#MeToo movement, 39
medium and small-scale enterprises (MSMEs), 54
Meera, S.L., 142
megacities, 20
Mehta, Suketu, 138
Melbourne, 221
metro, governance in, 297–298
MetroLite, 157
MetroNeo, 157
metropolitan: areas, 29, 33, 57, 78–79, 88, 90, 203, 281, 290–291, 297; cities, 20, 74, 139, 160, 232, 303; integration, 77; towns, 28
Metropolitan Planning Committee, 200, 203, 281, 297
metro systems, 153, 157
Mexico, 19, 135, 245, 285
Microsoft, 91
middle-class, 28, 30, 188
migrants, 22, 26, 41–42, 66–74, 86, 90, 137–138, 215, 222, 257, 264, 284, 287; domestic, 66, 72; exodus, 67–68, 70, (*see also* Covid-19 crisis); to Gulf countries, 44; in Organization of Economic Co-operation and Development), (OECD), 44; studies on, 68–69
migration, 6, 36, 43–44, 46, 57, 66, 68, 72–73, 137, 268; global, 42–44; internal, 41, 68; international, 21, 41–42, 66; role in urbanization, 65–74
Migration and Its Impact on Cities, WEF report, 41
Mitra, Asok, 285

Model Police Bill, 228
Model Tenancy Act in 2019, 146, 180
modern cities, 8–14, 116, 157
modernization, 19, 203
Modi, Narendra, 18, 93, 304
Mohanty, Prasanna, 29, 56, 59, 174, 188, 197, 199, 209, 297
monorails pods, self-driving, 169
Moretti, Enrico, 59, 74, 76, 79–81, 83, 88, 91
Moses, Robert, 213–215
Motor Vehicle Accident Fund, 237
Motor Vehicles (Amendment) Bill, 2019, 237
MRT networks, 188
Mughal empire, 10
Mukhopadhyay, P., 88, 90
Mumbai (formerly Bombay), 15, 28–29, 60, 89, 97–100, 108–109, 119, 135, 138–139, 153, 180–181, 187–188, 192, 194, 207–208, 221, 280, 299; Aarey Milk Colony in, 263; beaches, 227; birth of, 12; bubonic plague in, 3; as dowry to Charles II, 12; entrepreneurs, 63; floods, 256; Master Plan of, 198; Port Trust Land of, 191; riots, 223; seven islets of, 12; terror attack 26/11, 252
Mumbai Municipal Act, 1888, 290
Mumbai Port Trust, 207
Mumford, Lewis, 4, 8, 214
municipal: bonds, 17, 111, 295–296; financing, 295; shortfall of employees, 299

municipalities, 99, 129, 134, 189, 193–195, 280–282, 284, 287, 289, 294, 297
Muzaffarpur riots, 223
Mysore, creation of, 13

Nadella, Satya, 36
Nagpur, 13, 28, 108, 187
Narayana Murthy, N.R., 62
National Aids Control Organization, 73–74
National Capital Region, 243
National Clean Air Programme (NCAP), 244
National Common Mobility Card (NCMC), 157, 165–166
National Crime Record Bureau (NCRB), 232
National Democratic Alliance (NDA), 18
National Digital Health Mission, 252
National Disaster Management Act, 2005, 274
National Disaster Management Authority (NDMA), 267
National Disaster Response Force (NDRF), 255, 267
National Health Mission, 247
National Heritage City Development and Augmentation Yojana (HRIDAY), 95
National Land Records Modernization Programme, 177
National Resource Efficiency Authority, 276

National Resource Efficiency
    Policy 2019, 276
National Road Safety Board, 237
National Rural Health Mission,
    251
National Solar Mission, 50
National Urban Faecal Sludge and
    Septage Management (FSSM)
    Policy, 122
National Urban Health Mission,
    251
National Urban Policy Framework
    (NUPF), 78, 82, 121, 182, 199,
    292, 294–296
National Urban Rental Housing
    policy, 146
National Urban Transport Policy,
    153
National Water Policy 2012, 114
nation states, 9
'nature-based solutions' (NBS), 260
Navi Mumbai, creation of, 66
NCT-Delhi, 249
Nehru, Jawaharlal, 16, 61, 291
Netherlands, 78, 270; Amsterdam,
    10–11, 77, 116, 149, 162, 221,
    245; bicycle use in, 162; Dutch,
    11; Dutch Flower Cluster,
    78; Room for the River, 270;
    Rotterdam, 235, 269
The New Geography of Jobs, 74, 91
new National Education Policy, 54
New Urban Agenda, 20
New Zealand, 51
NFHS-4, 40, 249
NGO, SEEDS, 268
Nigeria, 23, 248, 250

Night Economy, 99–101
rape case: Hathras, 39; Nirbhaya,
    39, 221, *see also* sexual violence
Nirbhaya Fund, 229
Nirmal Bharat Abhiyaan, 121
NITI Aayog, 45, 110, 167, 177,
    202, 248, 250
Non-banking finance companies
    (NBFCs), 73
Non-Cooperation Movement, 15
non-invasive technologies, 120
non-motorized transport (NMT),
    152–153, 161–165, 202, 211,
    217, 234, 239, 247, 263
Nooyi, Indira, 36
North America, 12, 22–23, 42

Obama, Barack, 34, 302
Odd-Even Scheme, 153
Odisha, Bhubaneswar, 'Socially
    Smart Bhubaneswar' initiative,
    235; JAGA mission, 145, 178
Odisha Land Rights to Slum
    Dwellers Act, 2017, 145, 178
Ogura, Keiko, 95
Ola, 81, 164, 171, 240
One Nation One Card (National
    Mobility Card), 72–73, 160,
    165
on-site sanitation (OSS), 122
Open Data, 302
Organization of Economic Co-
    operation and Development
    (OECD), 23, 44
Oyvat, C., 84

Pachnanda, R.K., 255

Pakistan, 260; Billion Tree Tsunami, 260
Panagariya, Arvind, 179
Panchayati Raj Institutions, 201, 288
Paris Agreement, 46, 49–50
parking facilities, 160–161
Partition, 43, 67, 223
Patel, Almitra, 126
Patel, Bimal, 192, 203, 207, 211, 265
Patel, Vallabhbhai, 291
Peace of Westphalia, 9
pedestrians, 162, 167–168, 235, 239
Peñalosa, Enrique, 227
People's Action Party (PAP), 104
per capita income, 29, 35, 56, 60
Per Drop, More Crop' scheme, 112
Perform, Achieve, and Trade (PAT) sceme, 50, 115, 276
Periodic Labour Force Survey (PLFS), 87
Peru, Lima, 240
Pethe, A., 200
Pharmaceutical drugs, 76
Philippines, 248, 266
Pichai, Sundar, 36
piped drinking water, 284
plague, 2, 102, 200, 279, 281; in Bengaluru, 3; in Surat, 3
Planning and Economics of Cities, Mohanty, 59
planning, reforming, 200–202
plastic carry bags, ban on, 130
PM Street Vendors AtmaNirbhar Nidhi' or SVANidhi, 86
police force, 227–229, 242

pollution, 4, 152, 154, 158, 160–161, 168, 170, 235, 238, 243–245, 259–260; air, 66, 207–208, 243–248, 258; in Bengaluru, 258; in Delhi, 258; vehicular, 141, 243
Pondicherry, 13
population, 5, 12, 14–15, 19–20, 22, 28–29, 35–36, 42, 64, 89–90, 124–126, 186, 219, 232–233, 264, 284–286, 291; in Chhattisgarh, 128; decline, 43; density, 26, 48, 186–188; of India, 26, 31; live in urban, 19; rising, 125; share of Class I towns, 17; share of smaller towns, 17; working, 284; of world, 4, 23, 110, 175, 221; of world in 1800 and 1900, 11
port cities, 13, 65
Porter, M.E., 75
Power and liberal order, 31
Pradhan Mantri Gram Sadak Yojana, 149
Praja Foundation, Delhi, 282–283, 288, 299
Primary and Community Health Centres, 251
private sector, 17, 38, 139, 168, 170, 180, 185, 202–205, 247, 301, 306
privatization, 17, 33
Production Linked Incentive (PLI), 76
productivity, 1–2, 19, 21, 59, 66, 75–76, 149, 152, 161, 164, 274
Progressive Punjab, 93

property taxes, 147, 193–195, 279, 283, 285, 292, 294
Public Distribution System (PDS), 72
public health: cadre, 2, 249–251, 280; services, 250, *see also* healthcare
Public Private Partnerships (PPP), 29, 296, 304
Public Sector Land Development Authority, 183
public spaces, 161–162, 182, 191–192, 199, 206–207, 213, 215–218, 221, 224–227, 234, 284, 290
public transport, 48, 50–51, 152–155, 157–160, 163–165, 188, 192, 211, 222, 239–240, 245, 263, 266
Pune, 46, 51, 89, 111, 125, 128–129, 133, 151, 153, 259, 263
Punjab, 10, 57, 113, 243

Al-Qaeda terrorists, 252
Quad,' (Quadrilateral Security Dialogue), 32

Railway Land Development Authority (RLDA), 184
rainwater, 117, 271, 273; flooding and, 273; harvesting (RWH), 106, 118–119
Raisina Dialogue, 36
Rajaratnam, 106
Rajasthan, 57, 71, 74, 91, 146, 157, 206; Dungarpur town, child-friendly police station, 235; 'Joint Patrolling Committees,' 229
Rajasthan Urban Land (Certification of Titles) Act, 2016, 178
Rajiv Awas Yojana, 148
Rajkot, 28, 151, 189
Raveendran, G., 84
real estate market, 146, *see also* urban land
Real Estate Regulatory Authority, 142
recycling, 105–106, 138; *see also under* land; water
Rediscovering Dharavi, Sharma, 137
redistributive policies, 287
reforms 2.0, 46, *see also* planning, reforming
refugees, 16, 49
Registration Act 1908, 176–177
regulatory environment, 144, 146, 165, 175
religions, 7–8, 27, 39, 222, 231, 239; in state policy, 33
Rent Control Acts, 146, 180
replacement-level fertility (RLF), 43
Reserve Bank of India (RBI), 63, 139
Resilient Cities Network, 259
Resurgent Rajasthan, 93
Right to Education, 83
Right to Information (RTI), 233, 302
RIICO Bhiwadi, 71
Riis, Jacob, 135
Rio+20 climate summit, 49

Rio De Janeiro, 138, 271
risk assessment, 267
Rivers Remember, Kurupa, 271
roads, 239; in Indian cities, 167, 231; pedestrianize, 168–169; safety, 236–239
Rockefeller Foundation's 100 Resilient Cities, 45
Romer, 58
Roongta, S.K., 183
Roosevelt, Eleanor, 214
Rose, Jonathan, 77, 131, 226–227
Rowlatt Satyagraha, 15
Roy, D., 142
Roy, Ram Mohan, 13
rural vs. urban, 3–4
Russia: Moscow, 12, 14, 219; St. Petersburg, 12, 219
Rwanda, Kigali, 29, 223–224, 241

safety, 220
Sally, Razeen, 35
Samjhauta bomb blast, 223
sanitation, 18, 21, 61, 66, 68, 107–109, 121–134, 138–139, 145, 246–248, 280, 287
Sanjay Reddy, G.V., 170
Sanyal, Sanjiv, 12, 82, 192, 225
Saudi Arabia, Mecca, 271
Save the Children's World of India's Girls (WINGS) 2018 report, 232
self-help groups, 124
Sendai Framework for Disaster Risk Reduction, 256, 267
Sensor-based technologies, 120
Sepoy mutiny 1857, 15

74th Constitutional Amendment Act (CAA), 17, 94, 201, 259, 280–281, 287–288, 292, 297
Seshadri Iyer, K., 61
settlements, 5, 5–8, 255; agricultural, 6
severe acute respiratory syndrome (SARS), 2
sewage treatment plants (STPs), 122–123, 192
sewerage systems, 107–112, 118, 122, 167, 212, 269
sexual violence, 40, 242
Shah Jahan, 10
Shahjahanabad, by Shah Jahan, 10
shared mobility, 165, 171
Sharma, Kalpana, 137–138
Sharma, Sameer, 304
Shimla water crisis, 256
Shockley, William, 80
shreni (guilds), 8
Siddiqui, Nawazuddin, 66
Sikhs, pogrom against, 223
Silicon Valley, 53, 60, 62, 80–81; USA, 53
Silk Road network, China's, 7
Singapore, 82, 102, 104–107, 111, 113, 160, 169, 188–189, 201, 245, 247–248; congestion pricing in, 164; EDB offices, 106; Hawker Centres, 227; hawker centres in, 86; Infrastructure Development in, 105; MRT in, 210; public transport system in, 155; sheltered walkways in, 162
Singh, Manmohan, 18

Singh, Siddharth, 245
Singh, Upinder, 6
The Sixth Extinction, Kolbert, 47
Skytrain service, 169
slum, 38–39, 66–67, 70–71, 73, 82, 103–104, 135–139, 142, 144–145, 147, 178, 181, 232–233; Chadwick study on, 135; dwellers, 147, 178; Gujarat model of redevelopment, 145; names of, 135; reduction, 45; redevelopment, 135, 144–148; resettlement, 145; tourism, 138, *see also* Dharavi
Slum Areas (Improvement and Clearance) Act, 16
Slumdog Millionaire, 138
Smart Cities Mission (SCM), 18, 153, 164, 251, 289, 295, 302, 304, 306
Smart Cities Unbundled, Sharma, 304
Smart City Mission, 213, 250
Smith, Stephen, 3
Snow, Jon, 2
social cohesion, 42, 68, 218, 221, 224–225
Solid Liquid Resource Management (SLRM), 128
Solid Waste Collection and Handling (SWaCH), 128
solid-waste management, 107–108, 118, 121–122, 124–127, 134, 247, 276, 280, 295; in Tamil Nadu, 126
South Africa, 157, 185, 194, 282, 293–294; Cape Town, 12, 138;

Cape Town, Adaptation to Climate Change, 261; cities in, 224; Johannesburg, 271, 290
South Korea, 23, 226; Seoul, 188, 190, 209, 221, 226
Spain: Barcelona, 135, 241, 263; Guggenheim Effect/ Bilbao Effect, 99; Madrid, 168, 240
Spanish flu, 2–3
Special Economic Zone (SEZ), 22, 76
Speciality Steel, 76
Special Purpose Vehicle (SPV), 138, 208, 304
Sreedharan, E., 151
Sridhar, Kala, 56
Sri Lanka, 248
Srinagar, 268
Stanford, Leland, 80
start-ups, 53, 81, 91, 171, 305; ecosystem, 54; Khoj.city, 98
State Finance Commission, 281, 292
state policies, 33, 143
state-to-state relations, 9
stormwater drainage, 6, 107–108, 111, 121, 167, 268–269
street vendors, 84–87, 161, 240, 242
The Street Vendors (Protection of Livelihood and Regulation of Street Vending) Act 2014, 85–86
Surat, 28, 60, 68, 70, 83, 109, 125, 151, 249, 259, 268; European factories in, 11; plague and clean-up, 3; SURATiLAB, 305

Suri, Sher Shah, 10; Shergarh by, 10
Survey of Villages and Mapping with Improvised Technology in Village Areas (SVAMITVA), 178
Sustainable Development Goals, (SDGs), 20–21, 44–46, 217, 256
Sustainable Development Summit in September 2015, 20
Swachh Bharat Mission, 7, 18, 121, 126–127, 238, 247, 287; Urban, 134
Sweden, 130, 155
Sydney, 12, 221, 240

Tamil Nadu, 90, 106, 124, 126–130, 138, 195, 206, 229, 296; 'Friends of Police,' 229; taking staff issues, 300; urbanization rate of, 57
Tamil Nadu Urban Development Fund (TNUDF), 296
Tamil Nadu Urban Infrastructure Financial Services Limited (TNUIFSL), 296
Tandel, Vaidehi, 215
Technical Urban Group on Urban Housing Shortage, 135
Telangana, 92, 250; Tier-II cities, 92
Telecom & Networking Products, 76
Terman, Fredrick, 80
terrorism, 221, 252–258, 306
Textile Products, 76

Thackeray, Aditya, 100
Thakre, Manish, 230
Thapar, Romila, 6
Tharoor, Shashi, 244, 289
Total Fertility Rate (TFR), 23, 40, 43
tourism, 94–99, 106, 168, 206, 218; economy, 96; infrastructure, 206
towns: of India 28; planners, 202; planning, aesthetics of, 205–206, *see also* cities
trade, 6–9, 11, 13, 28, 52, 55, 87, 92
Traffic Signal Synchronization in Mumbai, 153
Transferable Development Rights (TDRs), 198, 296–297
Transfer of Property Act 1882, 176
transit-oriented development (TOD), 155, 158, 189, 209–211, 245
Triumph of the City, Glaeser, 48
Trump, Donald, 33, 44
Tumbe, Chinmay, 42, 68–70
Turkey, Istanbul, 135, 271, 291
Twelfth Schedule, 249, 280, 307
Tyabji, Laila, 95
typhoid, 2

Uber, 164, 171, 204–205
Ujjwala scheme, 50
UNESCO Creative Cities Network (UCCN), 97
UN Framework Convention on Climate Change (UNFCCC), 50, 52, 276
UN-Habitat II, 231
UN-Habitat III, 256

UN-Habitat World City's 2016 Report, 19
Unified Metropolitan Transport Authority, 155
United Kingdom (UK), 193; City Deals, 298; London, 11, 35, 51, 53, 111, 135, 163, 245, 247, 290; footprint, 48; Green Grid programme, 260; London based Arup, 231; London Climate Adaptation Strategy 2007, 261; congestion pricing, 164; London, Jubilee Line Extension in, 210; Town and Country Planning Act of 1947, 197; Transport for London, 155
United Nation's Urban Habitat III policy paper, 141
universities, 74, 79–82, 92, 268, 278; foreign campuses of, 82
unmanned aerial vehicles (UAVs, also called drones), 169–170
UN Population Fund (UNFPA), 38
UN's Urban Habitat, 221
urban: areas defining, 284–287; centres, 3, 5–6, 10, 12–13, 15, 17–18, 21, 37, 56, 72, 94; cluster deficit, 78–84; development, 8, 17–18, 102, 175, 182, 194, 205, 264, 293; eco-system approach, 260; elite, 15, 26; expansion, 5; governance, 15, 18, 66, 93, 278, 280, 282, 284, 288, 290, 304; heat island effect, 268, 273–274; health, 246–252; informal employment, 84; innovation, 52–54, 172; poor, 107, 121, 128, 137, 147, 188, 233, 249–250, 257–258, 264, 274; population, 5, 11, 15–16, 19–20, 22, 29, 34, 110–111, 114, 230, 247, 251, 257; renewal, 7; resilience policy, 260–264; scholars, 225, 292; services, 22, 69–70, 267; transport, 19, 100, 149, 151–152, 154, 156, 161, 164, 166, 205, 209; voters, 34; water bodies, 271–273; workforce, 31, 66, 69, 85, 301
Urban and Regional Development Plans Formulation and Implementation (URDPFI), 200, 233
Urban Development Fund, 18
Urban Development Investment Companies (UDICs), 184
urban forests, 262, 274; in Chennai, 262; Nagar Van, 262; in Pune, 263
Urban Habitat III, 20, 141, 221
urban housing, 108, 135–142, 180, 247, 258; shortage, 135, 139–148
urbanization, 5–7, 18–26, 37–38, 42, 44, 46–49, 56–66, 142, 144, 196, 212–213, 220, 222, 255–256, 275–277; boom, 26; and climate change, 47–49, 130; defining, 5; economies, 59; level of, 13, 18–19, 57, 84; and migration, 42; policies, 21; population, 89; rates of, 5, 12, 19, 29, 219, 284; role of Manmohan Singh in, 18;

sustainable, 20, 50, 256; wave, 23, 53
urban land, 17, 133, 139–148, 150, 174, 176–179, 182, 185, 190, 192, 257, 263, 275–276, 294, 296, *see also* land; land use
Urban Land Ceiling and Regulation Act (ULCRA 1976), 17–18, 179–180
Urban Land Title Certification Authority, 178
urban local bodies (ULBs), 17–18, 70, 118, 147, 191, 194–195, 201–203, 246, 249–250, 280–281, 283, 285–286, 289, 297, 300–301
urban planning, 140–142, 155, 159, 197, 200, 202–203, 214, 216, 259, 264, 274, 281; aesthetics in 205; gender-blind, 199; guidelines of 2014, 189
United States of America (US/USA), 35, 60; Apple, 81; Austin, 53; Boston, 12, 53, 175, 234, 302; Boston CityScore, 302; Chicago, 12, 49, 173, 188, 217, 219; cities, 42, , 79, 234, 241, 303; Clean Air Act, 1970, 246; Democrats in, 33–34; Duluth, 245; eBay, 81; El Paso, 245; Fair Housing Act of 1968, 141; Federal Fair Housing Act Amendments Act of 1988, 141; Federal Telegraph Corporation (FTC), 80; Google, 81, 169, 263; Hewlett and Packard, 81; Manhattan, 175, 188; markets, 31; MassMEDIC cluster, 78; National Bureau of Economic Research (NBER), 92; New York, 12, 53, 77–78, 167–168, 186, 188–189, 215, 217, 219, 252, 297, 299, 303, 305; New York, car in, 48; New York, Metropolitan Health Board, by Smith, 3; New York, NYC Data Mine, 305; New York, Oculus Station, 210; New York, sustainability plan as PlaNYC 2007, 261; 'New York better,' 305; New York Metropolitan Transportation Authority, 155; Philadelphia, 12, 219; San Francisco, 73, 149, 175, 182; Seattle, 53, 91; sun-belt region of, 33; urbanization rates, 219; Venture Capital Kleiner Perkins, 80; Washington, 35, 96, 175, 221, 245, 247; Washington's Mall, 227; Yahoo, 81
US-China trade war, 30, 45
Uttarakhand, 200, 283
Uttar Pradesh (UP), 15, 57, 116, 138, 206, 223–224, 255, 283, 296; Investors Summit, 93; launching municipal bonds, 296

Vajpayee, Atal Bihari, 149
value capture fund (VCF), 296
Varanasi, 60, 95, 97, 116, 207, 296; Kashi Vishwanath corridor in, 207
Vellore, 13; as entrepot, 13

Verified Carbon Standard programme of the UNFCCC, 52
Vibrant Gujarat, 93
Vickrey, William, 163
Vietnam, 30, 74, 96, 119
villages, 7–8, 23, 26, 37–42, 46–47, 97, 99, 149–150, 201, 285, 288, 291
violence, 40, 96–97, 223–224, 227, 229, 231, 239; against women, 240, *see also* violence
Visvesvaraya, Mokshagundam (Sir MV), 61
voters, 34

Washington Consensus, 35
waste generation, 21, 125, 129–130; Global, 124; Japan and, 132
waste management, 50, 121, 128, 130, 259, 266; biomedical waste, 134; biomining, 129, 133; bioremediation, 129, 133; composting, 128, 133–134; disposal technologies, 127; door-to-door collection, 126, 194; incineration, 128, 133–134; recycling, 21, 105-6, 113, 115, 128–130, 132–133, 151, 190–192, 276; segregation, 126–128, 130; sustainable, 266; treatment, 128–132
water, for drinking, 104–105, 109–110, 113, 138, 145, 204, 267, 275 efficiency in urban area, 115–121; piped, 109–110, 247; purifier systems, 115–116; supply, 6, 94, 106, 108, 110, 113, 116, 119, 212; and sanitation, 21, 48, 52, 61, 66, 108–134, 196, 248, 296; treatment, 50, 266
Water and Sanitation Pooled Fund (WSPF), 296
water bodies, 99, 116–118, 122, 185, 218, 271–273, 284; loss of, 116; baolis (step-wells), 116; Hauz Khas Lake in Delhi, 116, 273; Kaikondrahalli Lake in Bengaluru, 273; Najafgarh Jheel, Delhi-Gurugram border, 117, 272; rejuvenation, 116
water-drainage system, 118–119, 271
Water Saving Companies (WSCOs), 115
West Africa, Sierra Leone, 250
West Bengal, 'Community Policing Project', 229
wetlands, 10–11, 260, 272
White Goods (air conditioners [ACs] , 76
Whyte, William H., 214
Wipro, 61–62
Wirth, Louis, 4
women, 33, 37, 39–41, 43, 66, 68, 70–71, 74, 87–88, 128, 159, 224–225, 239–243; hygienic methods and, 40; SafetiPin (safety app), 240; safety of, 100, 239–243; Trump and, 33
workforce: BPO/KPO, 99; English-speaking, 35–36, 43, 62; female, 87–88; global, 36, 44; skilled urban 301

World Economic Forum, 68
World Resource Institute (WRI), 107, 238–239
World Trade Organization (WTO), 31
World Urbanization Prospects report, 23

WWF Water Risk Filter, 271

Yengde, Suraj, 38

Zero Fatality Corridor Project, 238
Zika outbreak, 2

About the Author

Devashish Dhar is a former Public Policy Specialist at NITI Aayog. He is a Mason Fellow from the Harvard Kennedy School and Li Ka Shing Scholar from the Lee Kuan Yew School of Public Policy, Singapore. He is also a Raisina Fellow, an IVLP Fellow, and has authored several articles for national publications.

30 Years *of* HarperCollins *Publishers* India

At HarperCollins, we believe in telling the best stories and finding the widest possible readership for our books in every format possible. We started publishing 30 years ago; a great deal has changed since then, but what has remained constant is the passion with which our authors write their books, the love with which readers receive them, and the sheer joy and excitement that we as publishers feel in being a part of the publishing process.

Over the years, we've had the pleasure of publishing some of the finest writing from the subcontinent and around the world, and some of the biggest bestsellers in India's publishing history. Our books and authors have won a phenomenal range of awards, and we ourselves have been named Publisher of the Year the greatest number of times. But nothing has meant more to us than the fact that millions of people have read the books we published, and somewhere, a book of ours might have made a difference.

As we step into our fourth decade, we go back to that one word – a word which has been a driving force for us all these years.

Read.

     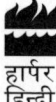